Classic
JUNIOR LEAGUE®
COOKBOOK COLLECTION

COTTON COUNTRY COOKING

Illustrations by
MITCH HOWELL

Published by
THE DECATUR JUNIOR SERVICE LEAGUE, INC.
1972-1988

THE JUNIOR LEAGUE OF MORGAN COUNTY, INC.
1988-Present

Favorite Recipes® Press

Copyright © 2011 by
Favorite Recipes® Press
an imprint of

FRP.INC

a wholly owned subsidiary of Southwestern
P.O. Box 305142
Nashville, Tennessee 37230
1-800-358-0560

Cotton Country Cooking
Copyright © 1972 by the Decatur Junior Service League, Inc.

Published and Distributed by FRP, Inc., under license granted by
The Junior League of Morgan County, Inc.

Executive Editor: Sheila Thomas
Project Editor: Tanis Westbrook
Classic Junior League Cookbook Collection Cover Design: Starletta Polster

Library of Congress Control Number: 2011924422
ISBN: 978-0-87197-554-6

Manufactured in the United States of America

One of the criteria to be considered for the Classic Junior League Cookbook
Collection is the original publication date; the cookbook must be at
least 25 years old. As a result of the length of time in print, some titles have
gone through revisions and updates; others have been intentionally
left in their original context in order to preserve the integrity and authenticity
of the publication. This printing has been taken from the most recent
edition. We hope you enjoy this American icon.

For more than 70 years, Junior League cookbooks have been sought out and collected by both novice and seasoned home cooks. Turned to again and again for their tried-and-true recipes, these cookbooks are a testament to the Junior League volunteers who dedicate themselves to improving the quality of life within their communities. These treasured cookbooks have played a significant role both in raising funds to help fulfill the organizations' missions and by documenting and preserving regional culinary traditions.

Favorite Recipes® Press, a longtime friend and partner of the Association of Junior Leagues International, is proud to present the *Classic Junior League Cookbook Collection*. The inaugural collection is comprised of six Junior League cookbooks that define all that is *Classic;* each serves as a standard of excellence and is considered an authentic and authoritative work on the foods and traditions of its region.

Enjoy,

Sheila Thomas

Executive Editor
Favorite Recipes Press

PREFACE

Cotton Country Cooking was originally published in 1972. At that time the League's name was Decatur Junior Service League, established in 1949. In 1988 the League joined the Association of Junior Leagues, International, and permanently changed the name to the Junior League of Morgan County. This association provides the League with far reaching opportunities to share the wealth of recipes in ***Cotton Country Cooking*** throughout the world.

Cooking in the heart of the South has always been a blend of French, Spanish, African and English skills. It combines the best memories of the Old World and the fresh products of the New World to produce a marvelous, unique cuisine. We have tried to preserve the unique blend in our collection of recipes with months of kitchen testing and careful evaluation of each of the entries. The new bride will find directions for cooking turnip greens and roasting a turkey as well as interesting menu suggestions. The gourmet cook will find Oysters Rockefeller and Bananas Foster enticing, plainly presented, and fascinatingly delicious. And all of us in-between cooks will find recipes that will renew and invigorate our efforts, such as old-fashioned custard ice cream, truly like grandmother made.

In a special section, "Southern Hospitality," professionals such as Mrs. J.C. Greene from the Old Lyons Hotel Dining Room, Romey Woods, Mrs. Elbert Chandler, Russell Priest and John Harris have generously shared with us some of their best recipes. The culinary specialties of historic Mooresville, Alabama's oldest incorporated town, and Courtland, where slave-built homes still stand and heirs of the early families still live, have been passed on to us.

Mitch Howell, a native artist who has achieved well-deserved national fame, designed our cover, drew the sketches presenting each section and added to our theme a boll weevil hidden in every drawing.

Cotton Country Cooking is an authentic guide to Southern food, a reliable everyday reference and a gourmet's challenge. It is an honor and a privilege to share this edition with you, and we appreciate your support. The value of the cookbook for each purchaser is considerable, but the true value lies in its continuously successful sales, boosting the efforts of the Junior League of Morgan County's mission to provide for consistent improvement in the life of families in Morgan County.

Also by The Junior League of Morgan County, Inc.

Beyond Cotton Country

To learn more about The Junior League of Morgan County, Inc., visit their Web site at www.jlmorgancounty.com.

CONTENTS

With grateful appreciation for their untold number of hours and constant devotion, the Decatur Junior Service League dedicates *Cotton Country Cooking* to the original editors:

Mrs. William A. Sims, Jr.
Mrs. John E. Wilks, Jr.

Appetizers and Party Foods

HINTS FOR QUICK AND EASY PARTY FOODS

When you plan a party, be it a very small dinner or a really big bash, you plan your menu and then budget your time, deciding exactly when you make the pate, when to cook the roast, when to whip up the mousse.

There are times, however, when every cook must take emergency measures and needs a bag of quick and easy culinary tricks: those old army friends call to say they're in town and are dying to see you; the man of your house sees a friend on the 18th hole and suggests he and his wife come over for a drink; the husband gets home earlier than usual with his stomach rumbling like Vesuvius, and dinner is hours away; the children ate all the mixed nuts you were saving for tonight's company.

Here, to keep you out of the doghouse and in the kitchen for minutes only, are some suggestions for speedy appetizers. All are good. Many have the added advantage of being made with ingredients you have on hand — or at least you can pick up quickly at any corner grocery. Remember, too, just because these items are quick and easy, there's no reason you couldn't use any of them for your most elegant party, even when you are at the pinnacle of organizational success.

Wrap Waverly Wafers with thin strips of bacon, secure with toothpick. Broil until bacon is crisp.

Spread ½ inch thick slices of cooked ham with peanut butter — really! Broil for 2 to 3 minutes. Cut into 1 inch squares and serve **hot**.

Heat small cocktail wieners in a sauce made by mixing, over medium heat, a 10 ounce jar of currant jelly and a 6 ounce jar of prepared mustard. Serve hot with toothpicks.

Slit cherry tomatoes and stuff each with a smoked oyster.

Serve drained, canned artichoke hearts on toothpicks around a bowl of mayonnaise (hopefully homemade) or hollandaise.

Stem fresh mushrooms and saute whole caps in butter until tender. Place a very little creamed or curried chicken (freeze leftovers for this very reason) in center of each mushroom cap and run under broiler for a few minutes.

Broil oysters, dip quickly in sherry and serve on toothpicks. A really favorite appetizer among gourmets.

Combine in saucepan 1 package (10-ounce) frozen chopped spinach, cooked and well drained; 1 roll garlic-flavored cheese, diced; and one can crabmeat, drained and flaked. Heat until cheese is melted, blend and serve hot in chafing dish with Melba toast or crackers.

Mix mayonnaise, minced onion and a good sprinkling of Parmesan cheese. Spread on bread rounds and broil until slightly brown. A variation on the same theme: top Melba toast rounds with razor-thin slices of onion, then a good blob of mayonnaise, and sprinkle with Parmesan. Broil until light brown and puffy.

Remove crusts from sandwich bread and cut each slice into 4 small squares (or if you're a bit more ambitious, cut rounds from bread with biscuit cutter). Scrape onion juice into softened butter or margarine, stir to blend well and spread on bread squares. Sprinkle with a good amount of Parmesan and bake in slow to moderate oven (even fast, if you'll watch carefully) until crisp and dry.

Spread party rye bread with softened cream cheese. Top each piece with two thin slices of pepperoni. Bake in 350° to 400° oven until cheese bubbles and the oil from the pepperoni begins to run out. Serve hot. And make more of these than you think you'll need. Men adore them!

Soften an 8-ounce package of cream cheese. Blend in a clove of garlic, pressed; 2 or 3 dill pickles, diced; and enough mayonnaise to make a good spread. Serve with crackers or Melba toast. This is a delicious sandwich spread, too.

TOASTED PECANS

½ cup butter
1 quart pecans

In heavy skillet melt butter. Add pecans and cook until warm and well coated with butter. Then spread out on large baking sheet and toast 10 to 15 minutes in 300° or 325° oven. Place on paper towels with newspaper underneath. While hot, salt; turn and salt again.

Allowing for one or two possible exceptions, there is nothing as delicious as fresh pecan halves, toasted in butter and salted. A bowlful on the coffee table before dinner; a silver nut dish full at a tea; containers scattered around at a big cocktail party; a dish of pecans on your Thanksgiving and Christmas dinner tables — all speak eloquently of Southern hospitality.

Mrs. W. D. Gilchrist, III

SALMON ROLL

1 1-pound can salmon (2 cups)
1 8-ounce package cream cheese, softened
1 tablespoon lemon juice
2 teaspoons grated onion
1 teaspoon prepared horseradish
¼ teaspoon liquid smoke
½ cup chopped pecans
¼ teaspoon salt
3 tablespoons snipped fresh parsley

Drain and flake salmon, removing skin and bones. Combine salmon, cream cheese, lemon juice, onion, horseradish, salt and liquid smoke. Mix thoroughly. Chill several hours. Combine pecans and parsley. Shape salmon mixture into 1 large mound or 2 small rolls. Roll in nut mixture. Chill, serve with crackers.

Smoked salmon is hard to come by. Create your own with this marvelous recipe.

Mrs. John D. Veitch

APPETIZER HAM BALL

2 4½-ounce cans deviled ham
3 tablespoons chopped, stuffed
  green olives
1 tablespoon prepared mustard

Tabasco to taste
1 3-ounce package cream cheese
2 teaspoons milk

Combine first 4 ingredients and form into a ball on serving dish. Chill. Blend cream cheese and milk; frost ball with mixture. Keep chilled. Serve with assorted crackers.

This makes an attractive cocktail table display.

Mrs. Otis E. Kirby, Jr.

CHEESE BALL

½ pound sharp cheese
6 3-ounce packages cream cheese
2 teaspoons Worcestershire

2 teaspoons grated onion
Garlic, finely minced
Pecans, chopped

Grate the cheese and combine with softened cream cheese, preferably in electric mixer. If too stiff to blend well, add a little cream or milk. Add grated onion and Worcestershire, and a little finely minced garlic. Mix well and allow to stand in refrigerator for several hours. Shape into balls (this recipe will make two large balls or 3 medium balls) and roll in chopped pecans. Chill again and serve with crisp crackers.

The longer you keep it, the better it gets!

Mrs. Harold Pilgrim, Jr.

CHEESE PARTY LOAF

2 8-ounce packages cream cheese
¼ pound sharp cheese, grated
1 2-ounce package Roquefort
  cheese
1 teaspoon garlic salt

½ teaspoon curry powder
2 tablespoons Worcestershire
1 teaspoon paprika
1 tablespoon mayonnaise
1 tablespoon lemon juice

Have all ingredients at room temperature. Mix, adding milk if necessary to blend. Grease a cold, 1 quart mold with salad oil and fill with mixture. Chill overnight. Unmold and serve with crackers.

A pretty mold with the zip of Roquefort.

Mrs. Lynn C. Fowler

CURRIED CHEESE BALL

2 3-ounce packages cream cheese, softened
1 cup grated sharp Cheddar cheese
2 tablespoons, plus, of dry sherry
½ teaspoon curry powder
¼ teaspoon salt
½ 8-ounce jar mango chutney (Major Grey), finely chopped
Pecans, optional

Mix all ingredients together, roll into ball and roll in pecans; or mix all ingredients except chutney, shape into loaf and spread chutney on top.

A cheese ball with a personality of its own. Its favorite companions are wheat thins, and it takes on elegant airs when topped with chutney.

Mrs. William E. Shinn, Jr.

CHEESE ROLL

½ pound New York State sharp Cheddar
½ pound hoop cheese
1 8-ounce package cream cheese
1 small onion grated
1 clove garlic, grated
1 teaspoon Tabasco
1 teaspoon Worcestershire
Salad dressing
Paprika

Mix the first seven ingredients. Add just enough salad dressing to moisten. Form into ball, roll in paprika, and wrap in waxed paper. Chill for one day.

No cocktail table should be without this sharp, snappy cheese ball, if men are present. If men aren't present, don't bother with a party.

Mrs. Jolly McKenzie

MOTHER'S CHEESE TICKLES

1 pound sharp cheese
1 cup butter
3 cups flour
½ teaspoon salt
1 tablespoon Worcestershire
1 teaspoon garlic salt
¼ to ½ teaspoon red pepper

Grate cheese. Cream butter and cheese. Sift flour, salt, pepper, and garlic salt together. Add to cheese and butter mixture along with Worcestershire. Knead on board. Form in one-inch rolls and wrap in waxed paper. Leave in refrigerator overnight or until ready to cook. Slice in thin slices with sharp knife. Bake on cookie sheet in moderate oven 325° until done, about 15 to 20 minutes.

These wafers are tongue ticklers indeed. Keep a roll in your freezer or refrigerator.

Mrs. Harold Pilgrim, Jr.

EASY CHEESE STRAWS

1 11-ounce pie crust mix   1 jar Old English sharp cheese

Mix together until well blended. Put mixture in cookie press and make in desired designs. Bake 300° 10-12 minutes.

Mrs. Fred Sittason, Jr.

MRS. HARGROVE'S CHEESE STRAWS

½ cup butter or margarine
1 pound sharp Cheddar cheese, grated

¼ teaspoon cayenne pepper
¼ teaspoon salt
2 cups sifted flour

In a large mixing bowl, mix the butter, cheese, pepper and salt. Let come to room temperature and beat until smooth and creamy. Add the flour and beat well. Let dough rest about 30 minutes. Run through a star-shaped cookie press. Cut each strip in desired length and bake at 350° for 15 minutes until light brown. Cool and put in a tin to keep fresh.

Marvelous to nibble before dinner, a grand addition to a cocktail buffet, and a must for any coffee or tea.

Mrs. Paul E. Hargrove

CHEESE STRAWS

2 pounds New York State cheese
5 to 5½ cups flour
1 teaspoon salt

1 pound margarine
4 teaspoons baking powder
½ teaspoon cayenne pepper

Grate cheese and mix in other ingredients. Run through star-shaped-cookie cutter. Bake 25 minutes in a 350° oven.

Nota Bene: Makes 400. De minimis non curat lex.

Mrs. Richard Bryson

CHEESE KRISPIES

2 cups plain flour
1 cup self-rising flour
1 12-ounce package New York sharp Cheddar cheese (this type a must!)

1 cup margarine
2 cups Rice Krispies

Melt cheese and butter in heavy saucepan over low heat. Combine with sifted flour. Stir in Rice Krispies. Mix thoroughly. Roll small balls, pat thin on cookie sheet. Bake at 325° for 15 minutes or less until lightly browned. 75 servings.

Tinned, these keep indefinitely — but are seldom allowed to.

Mrs. David E. Bowers

CHEESE NUGGETS

1/4 cup soft butter or margarine
1 cup (1/4 pound) grated sharp
  Cracker Barrel cheese
3/4 cup flour
1/8 teaspoon salt

1/2 teaspoon paprika
Red pepper to taste
1 medium jar small stuffed
  green olives

Blend butter and cheese. Sift in flour, salt, paprika and pepper. Mix well. Shape small amount of dough around olives and bake on an ungreased cookie sheet 12 to 15 minutes at 400°. (If refrigerated, cook for 20 to 25 minutes.) Serve hot. This recipe makes approximately 40 nuggets, depending upon size of olives.

Uncooked, these freeze beautifully. Freeze on a cookie sheet to avoid their sticking together. When frozen, nuggets can be put in a plastic bag, but remember to place on cookie sheet to thaw.

Bite into one of these hot little cheese balls and find — surprise — an olive. You can't keep enough coming from the oven to suit your guests; especially the men!

Mrs. William E. Shinn, Jr.

CHEESE AND SAUSAGE BALLS

1 heaping cup grated sharp
  Cheddar cheese
1 pound hot sausage

2 cups Bisquick
Tabasco to taste

Have all ingredients at room temperature. Combine ingredients and shape into 1-inch balls. Bake at 350° for about 20 minutes. These may be frozen before baking.

Sharp cheese — hot sausage — good, good!

Mrs. Paul McCain

MRS. MILLER'S ICED CHEESE SQUARES

2 jars Old English cheese
1 egg

1/2 cup margarine, softened
1 giant loaf sandwich bread

Whip cheese, egg, and margarine in mixer until creamy. Trim bread and cut each slice into 4 squares. Using 2 squares at a time, fill sandwiches with mixture and ice edges and top. Don't put too much. Cook at 400° about 10 minutes. Makes 48 small squares. Keep warm.

These can be frozen on sheets of foil and then put into plastic bags to be kept in freezer. Bake when desired.

Mrs. Lindsay A. Allen

15

LUCY CRAIN'S MUSHROOM DIP

1 pound fresh mushrooms
1 cup slivered, toasted almonds
2 cups sour cream
½ cup homemade mayonnaise
1 tablespoon chopped parsley
1 tablespoon paprika

1 tablespoon dry mustard
2 tablespoons flaked onion
1 tablespoon lemon juice
1 teaspoon salt
2 tablespoons water

Blanch mushrooms for 2 minutes in boiling water. Cut into pieces. Stir all ingredients together. Refrigerate an hour or more. Serve with raw vegetables or assorted crackers.

Truly unique — and oh so good! In a pinch use sliced, canned mushrooms and bought mayonnaise. Though not quite as delicious as the fresh mushrooms - homemade mayonnaise original, you'll still be happy with the end result.

Mrs. Frank T. Richardson, Jr.

DIP FOR VEGETABLES

16 ounces cream cheese
1 clove garlic, crushed
1 cup sour cream
1 teaspoon Worcestershire

1 teaspoon salt
2 teaspoons lemon juice
1/3 or ½ of 4-ounce package
    blue cheese

Combine all ingredients. Blend until smooth.

Mrs. Britt Owens

BROCCOLI DIP

2 packages frozen, chopped
    broccoli
1 8-ounce can mushroom pieces,
    drained
1 cup butter

1 large onion, chopped
2 cans cream of mushroom soup
2 rolls garlic cheese, cut
Salt and pepper to taste
1 can slivered almonds

Cook broccoli according to directions; drain. Saute onions in butter. Add all ingredients except mushrooms and almonds. Simmer until cheese is melted. Then add mushrooms and almonds. Serve in chafing dish with crackers or Fritos.

You'll not believe how really marvelous this is until you try it. Broccoli dip, indeed! If you're not that daring, this mixture can be used en casserole with buttered crumbs on top.

Mrs. William A. Sims

BACON DIP

½ pound grated sharp Cheddar cheese
1 onion grated
2½ tablespoons green onion
½ teaspoon salt
½ lemon, juiced
1 cup toasted, sliced almonds
1 cup mayonnaise
10 slices cooked bacon, crumbled

Stir all together and let stand in refrigerator for several hours.

Mrs. R. W. Anderson

HOT CLAM DIP

3 tablespoons butter
1 small onion, chopped
½ bell pepper, chopped
1 pimento, chopped

Cook the preceding ingredients for 3 minutes and add:

1 8-ounce can minced clams, drained
½ pound Velveeta cheese, cubed
4 tablespoons catsup
1 tablespoon Worcestershire
1 tablespoon milk
¼ teaspoon cayenne pepper

When cheese melts, stir until smooth.

This dip for chips or crackers has a great flavor. It can be served hot or cold, but we like it better hot.

Mrs. J. B. Ballentine
Chapel Hill, North Carolina

CLAM DIP

3 3-ounce packages cream cheese
1 8-ounce can minced clams, drained
1 teaspoon dry mustard, or more to taste
Red pepper, salt, onion juice, Tabasco, to taste

Heat all ingredients in double boiler until well mixed. Serve in chafing dish with chips or crackers.

Another good hot clam dip — this time made with cream cheese. Play with this one to get just the right taste you want.

Mrs. F. S. Hunt, Jr.

HOT CHEESE DIP

1 can cream of mushroom soup
2 cups grated New York State cheese
¼ cup chopped ripe olives
¼ cup chopped bell pepper, sauteed in 2 tablespoons butter
Red pepper to taste
Worcestershire to taste

Heat soup and cheese until all cheese is melted. Add other ingredients and serve in chafing dish with Melba rounds.

Mrs. Lynn C. Fowler

17

HOT CRAB DIP

3 tablespoons margarine
1 small onion, chopped
½ bell pepper, chopped
½ pound sharp Cheddar cheese, grated

1 6½-ounce can crabmeat
4 tablespoons catsup
1 tablespoon Worcestershire
1 tablespoon sherry
¼ teaspoon cayenne pepper

In double boiler heat margarine, onion, and bell pepper. Brown for 3 minutes. Add cheese, catsup, Worcestershire, sherry, cayenne, and crabmeat. To serve, place in chafing dish and serve with Fritos or wheat thins.

Few items are more popular on a buffet table than a good hot crab dip. We think this one has a particularly intriguing taste and bet you'll think so, too!

Mrs. Frank W. Troup

CHEESE DIP

1 pound mild Cheddar cheese, grated
1 8-ounce package cream cheese
¼ to ½ pint whipping cream
1 tablespoon or more onion juice
½ cup pecans, chopped
1 clove garlic, grated

Dash paprika
Dash red pepper
Dash chili powder
Dash black pepper
Dash garlic salt

Mix all together and serve with crackers.

We recommend making this dip several hours ahead of serving time.

Mrs. A. J. Coleman

HOT SHERRY CHEESE DIP

1 can condensed cream of mushroom soup
3 6-ounce rolls garlic-flavored cheese

1½ teaspoons Worcestershire
½ teaspoon Tabasco
¼ cup sherry

In saucepan combine soup and sliced cheese rolls. Heat over low heat stirring until cheese melts. Blend in Worcestershire, Tabasco and sherry. Keep hot in chafing dish for dipping with toast rounds or crisp crackers. May add ripe olives, crisp bacon crumbled and/or pimento.

A working girl's best friend, a bit of magic for the busy mother, a modern miracle for the I-hate-to-cook lady. There are few things this good which are really instant. This is!

Mrs. Arnold Rankin

SHRIMP DIP

1 cup shrimp
1 cup mayonnaise
1 cup chili sauce
1 small onion, grated
2 boiled eggs, finely chopped

½ cup celery, finely chopped
Lemon juice to taste
Salt
Pepper
Worcestershire to taste

Cut shrimp in small pieces. Combine all ingredients. Serve with assortment of crackers.

One way to a man's heart.

Mrs. T. S. Simms

SMOKED EGG DIP

12 hard-cooked eggs, sieved
2 tablespoons softened butter
2½ teaspoons liquid smoke
1 tablespoon lemon juice
2 teaspoons prepared mustard
1 tablespoon Worcestershire

2 drops Tabasco
1½ teaspoon salt
1 teaspoon dried, minced onion
½ teaspoon ground pepper
¾ cup mayonnaise

Blend until smooth in blender. Refrigerate at least 4 hours. Makes 1 quart. Garnish with parsley or pimento to serve.

Gourmet flavor for the penny-minded hostess.

Mrs. John E. Wilks, Jr.

DIP FOR CHIPS

1 cup sour cream
2 3-ounce packages cream cheese
¼ pound chipped beef, finely chopped
2 dill pickles, finely chopped

1 teaspoon Worcestershire
2 teaspoons prepared horseradish
Dash lemon juice
Dash pepper

Blend all ingredients. May add little milk for desired consistency.

A tangy dip for chips, shrimp, or raw vegetables. Make the day before so flavors can blend.

Mrs. Joe D. Burns

DILL AND SOUR CREAM DIP

1 cup sour cream
1 cup mayonnaise
1¼ teaspoons crushed dill weed

1 teaspoon flaked onion
3 teaspoons or more parsley, dried or fresh

Mix all ingredients and let stand at least one hour. Serve as a dip with potato chips.

Some add chopped cucumber and/or shrimp to this tasty and economical dip.

Mrs. R. W. Orr, Jr.

19

WEISE TROUP'S TACO DIP

1 14½-ounce can tomatoes,
  drained
1 15-ounce can tomato sauce
1 teaspoon vinegar

1 teaspoon sugar
1 onion, chopped
2 or 3 jalapeno hot peppers,
  chopped (use according to taste)

Put together in blender. Heat and serve with Taco chips.

Wear waterproof mascara!

Mrs. Frank T. Richardson, Jr.

JALAPENO BEAN DIP

2 cans condensed bean with
  bacon soup
1 6-ounce roll garlic cheese, diced
¼ cup minced onion

2 or 3 jalapeno peppers
  cut into small pieces
1 to 2 teaspoons cracked pepper
Salt to taste
2 cups sour cream

Heat all the above except sour cream in sauce pan. Do not boil. When the mixture has melted, add sour cream and blend. Serve warm in chafing dish. Makes 3 cups of dip. Serve with Fritos or Tacos.

This is a really hot number! Reduce amounts of jalapeno pepper if you have ulcer tendencies.

Mrs. Randall S. Troup

AVOCADO DIP OR GUACAMOLE SALAD DRESSING

2 large, soft, ripe avocados,
  mashed
½ medium onion, finely chopped
Juice from ½ lemon
6 drops Tabasco or more

½ garlic clove, minced
1 ripe tomato, chopped into small
  pieces
Salt to taste

Mix ingredients together in order given. Blend well. Chill. Place over chunks of lettuce for a salad or use with Fritos as a dip.

When making guacamole, taste, taste, and taste some more. You may need to add seasoning to suit your fancy. It's such a good dip with Fritos or Doritos.

For a pretty cocktail tray, particularly at Christmas time, top red ripe cherry tomatoes with spoonfuls of guacamole. Omit chopped tomatoes if you do this.

One more tip for do-ahead preparation: leave an avocado seed in the guacamole until serving time to keep dip from turning dark.

Mrs. James D. Moore

20

CLAM AND CHEESE SPREAD

1 8-ounce package cream cheese
1 8-ounce can minced clams, drained
Sherry, about 1 tablespoon
Tabasco to taste
Toast rounds

Combined cheese, clams, sherry and Tabasco. Mound cheese mixture on toast rounds and put in 350° oven for about 20 minutes or until hot.

A simply made, hot canape — or a good Sunday night supper: Mound cheese mixture on English muffins, heat and serve as open face sandwiches.

Mrs. Paul McCain

MOLDED SHRIMP SPREAD

5 pounds shrimp, cooked,
    deveined and ground
1 pound butter
1 bottle capers, ground

Soften butter, then mix in shrimp and capers. This mixture can be frozen after shaped into squares or mounds.

This has to be heaven!

Mrs. John D. Veitch

SHRIMP SPREAD

1 4½-ounce can shrimp,
    drained and rinsed
Juice of 1 lemon
1 small onion, minced or grated
1 tablespoon mayonnaise
1 teaspoon Worcestershire

Mash shrimp. Combine with lemon juice, onion, mayonnaise and Worcestershire. Serve with crackers. Makes about 1 cup.

Another way to get him — particularly tasty and easy to whip up. Keep a can of shrimp on your emergency shelf; you'll always be prepared when someone drops by.

Mrs. Robert T. McWhorter, Jr.

DEVILED HAM AND CHEESE SPREAD

1 2¼-ounce can deviled ham
1 3-ounce package cream cheese,
    softened
½ teaspoon lemon juice
½ teaspoon horseradish

Combine all ingredients. To serve, place in bowl on tray along with choice of crackers, breads, carrot sticks or celery sticks.

Quickie — good if you are a deviled ham lover.

Mrs. Judson E. Davis, Jr.

SWEET AND SOUR SPARE RIBLETS

2 to 3 pounds spare ribs (have butcher cut in half across the bone)
Salt
Pepper
Garlic salt

½ cup Open Pit barbecue sauce, Hickory Smoke flavor
¼ cup catsup (scant)
¼ cup prepared mustard
½ cup dark brown sugar

Preheat oven to 400°. Cut spareribs into bite-sized pieces (one or two riblets). Place in large flat pan without overlapping. Sprinkle very generously with salt, pepper, garlic salt. Bake 1 to 1½ hours or until almost crispy. Drain well. Simmer remaining ingredients 15 to 20 minutes, making sure sugar is melted. Toss ribs with sauce and return to oven about 10 minutes.

Have plenty of napkins available — paper ones, please. These crisp riblets will disappear quickly at any party. They are particularly suited for outside entertaining.

Mrs. Bruce Flake

SWEET AND SOUR MEATBALLS

Meatballs:
2 pounds ground chuck
2 slices bread, dampened with water and squeezed
1½ packages dry onion soup mix
Sauce:
1 cup catsup

8 tablespoons vinegar
1 cup apricot nectar
8 tablespoons brown sugar
4 teaspoons prepared mustard
4 teaspoons prepared horseradish
2 teaspoons Worcestershire

Combine meat, bread, soup. Brown meatballs in butter. Combine all sauce ingredients and simmer 10 minutes. Add meatballs and heat 10 minutes. Serve in chafing dish. These can be frozen, but freeze sauce and meatballs separately. This recipe yields about 50 small balls.

The men at your party will gather like bees at a hive around your chafing dish of meatballs. The ladies like them, too, but find it hard to beat the crowd.

Mrs. William A. Sims

STUFFED COUNTRY HAM

Boil ham, 20 or 25 minutes to the pound. Lift onto a platter. Peel off skin and trim some of the surplus fat. With a sharp knife, cut a deep incision to the bone down the center of the ham lengthwise. Insert a tablespoon and turn it, to hold the cut open while the stuffing goes in. Push in with the fingers. Remove tablespoon; allow edges to fall in place. Follow this method exactly with the other incisions, which with an average size ham usually number 5 in all — that is, one in center and two on each side. After filling cuts, dust lightly with brown sugar, then with bread crumbs and brown in oven for a few minutes.

Filling:

(for about a 15 lb. ham)

3 teacups bread crumbs, toasted, crushed and sifted (Ritz crackers are good)
1 handful finely chopped celery tops
1 handful finely chopped mustard tops
1 handful finely chopped parsley
Small amount chopped celery
1 teaspoon dry mustard

1 teaspoon ground cloves and allspice, mixed
1 small onion, finely chopped
1 tablespoon brown sugar
1 teaspoon salt
1 teaspoon pepper
Dash cayenne
Yolks of 2 hardboiled eggs, finely mashed

Mix all together and add the following:

2 tablespoons strong vinegar
4 tablespoons whiskey

1 cup pecans, finely chopped

Then add enough of the liquor from the ham to make mixture the consistency of chicken dressing. Stuff ham.

To call this merely "Stuffed Ham" is an injustice. "Spectacular" is the only word to accurately describe this ham: spectacular in appearance and taste. Trouble — perhaps — but for a buffet dinner or a cocktail party mainliner, nothing could do more for your reputation as a good cook and hostess.

Mrs. Barrett Shelton, Sr.

MARINATED SHRIMP, MUSHROOMS AND ARTICHOKE HEARTS

3 packages Good Seasons Salad dressing mix: 1 Blue, 1 Italian, 1 Cheese-and-Garlic
2 to 3 onions, sliced thinly and ringed
1 bottle capers, drained

2 to 3 pounds fresh shrimp, cooked and peeled
2 4-ounce cans whole button mushrooms, drained
2 14-ounce cans tiny artichoke hearts, drained
½ to 1 teaspoon salt

Prepare salad dressings according to package directions, omitting the water and replacing with vinegar. (Slightly less oil may be used) Put all ingredients into a deep bowl and marinate overnight. This must be stirred occasionally and very carefully to avoid breaking antichoke hearts.

The epitome of elegance! With this marvel on your table, your party is a sure success. Definitely not for the hostess with only a few spare dimes.

Mrs. Bruce Flake

23

MARINATED SHRIMP

2 pounds boiled, cleaned shrimp (frozen will do nicely)
2 large onions, sliced and ringed
¾ cup oil
2 onions, diced
3 cloves garlic
½ teaspoon chili powder
¼ teaspoon dry mustard
1½ teaspoons salt
½ teaspoon pepper
½ cup vinegar

Mix all ingredients except shrimp and onion rings in blender until liquid. Pour over shrimp and onion rings and marinate.

You must insist that each guest eat at least one shrimp. With the aroma (?) of onions and garlic in the air, a guest won't last the evening if he doesn't. Once he's tasted, though, watch your supply disappear.

Mrs. William E. Shinn, Jr.

MARINATED BLACK-EYED PEAS

2 1-pound cans black-eyed peas, drained
1/3 cup oil
1/3 cup wine vinegar
1 clove garlic
1 large onion sliced
½ teaspoon salt
Fresh ground pepper as desired

Mix all ingredients and store in refrigerator 24 hours. Remove garlic and keep in refrigerator 2 days to 2 weeks before eating.

Couple this with our elegant stuffed ham for an impressive New Year's Eve party.

Mrs. John E. Wilks, Jr.

24-HOUR SHRIMP

8 pounds cleaned and cooked shrimp
2 cups salad oil
2 cups vinegar
2 cups chili sauce
2 teaspoons garlic salt
2½ tablespoons prepared mustard
3 tablespoons capers

Blend sauce ingredients and marinate shrimp overnight. Drain and serve on toothpicks. These are also good as a luncheon dish served on lettuce leaf or in shells.

No superlatives can overrate these marvelous marinated shrimp which will serve about 150 people.

Mrs. William A. Sims

DIANE'S MARINATED MUSHROOMS

1 cup Wesson oil
¼ cup tarragon vinegar
½ cup catsup
1 teaspoon sugar
½ teaspoon salt
2 cloves garlic
4 2½-ounce jars whole mushrooms, drained

Combine first six ingredients in a 2-quart jar and shake to mix. Add mushrooms. Refrigerate for at least 1 hour.

These are as easy to pop in your mouth as they are to prepare. Better double the recipe for more than 8 people.

Mrs. Robert T. McWhorter, Jr.

EXOTIC SHRIMP

2 cloves garlic
½ cup butter or margarine
2 pounds fresh shrimp, uncooked in shell
½ cup white wine or dry sherry
1 tablespoon Worcestershire
Salt
Fresh ground pepper

Crush garlic in skillet and add butter. Saute raw, unpeeled shrimp in this mixture until they are red. Add wine, salt, pepper, Worcestershire and simmer about 5 minutes. Drain and serve in the shells. May be used as entree with green salad and bread.

Mrs. Bruce Flake

SHRIMP IN BEER

2 to 3 pounds raw shrimp, peeled
1 quart beer
2 tablespoons salt
1 teaspoon paprika
1 teaspoon crushed chili peppers
½ teaspoon black pepper
1/3 teaspoon cayenne pepper
½ ounce carraway seed

Boil all ingredients except shrimp for 15 minutes. Add shrimp and boil 10 minutes longer. Refrigerate and drain prior to serving.

Some like to eat this shrimp warm, straight from the pot. Another variation: just add beer (1 can per quart water) to boiling, salted water. Place unpeeled shrimp in water to boil — just until pink. Peel and eat 'em warm with cocktail sauce.

Mrs. Bruce Flake

CRAB AND CREAM CHEESE

1 8-ounce package cream cheese
1 6½-ounce can crabmeat
Seafood cocktail sauce

Allow cream cheese to soften to room temperature. Place on plate and put crabmeat on top. On this pour the cocktail sauce. Serve with Triscuit wheat crackers or your choice of crackers.

Cheers and more cheers for the cook who thought this one up. Talk about easy! Serve this and you'll be cheered, we promise. For an interesting taste variation, use barbecue sauce instead of seafood sauce.

Mrs. Dan M. Crane

MOLDED TUNA PATE

1 3-ounce can chopped mushrooms
1 envelope plain gelatin
2 6½ or 7-ounce cans tuna, drained
½ cup Green Goddess salad dressing
½ cup pitted ripe olives
¼ cup parsley leaves

At least 3 hours before serving: Into electric blender, drain liquid from mushrooms, sprinkle gelatin over it and soften a minute or two. Add ½ cup boiling water; cover and blend about 10 seconds on low speed, then 20 seconds on high speed. Add mushrooms, tuna, salad dressing, olives and parsley. Cover and blend on high speed until well mixed. Pour into a 1 quart mold and refrigerate, covered, until firm. To serve, unmold, serve with Melba toast. Makes 3½ cups.

A blender-made wonder. Charlie the Tuna would go in bliss if he could meet his end on a silver tray as a tuna pate.

Mrs. Harold Pilgrim, Jr.

CRAB OR SHRIMP MOUSSE

1½ cups shrimp (crab or lobster may be used — about 1 pound), chopped
1 cup chopped celery
½ cup chopped bell pepper
2 tablespoons grated onion
1 teaspoon salt
3 tablespoons lemon juice
1 cup mayonnaise
1 tablespoon Worcestershire
½ teaspoon Tabasco
3 3-ounce packages cream cheese
3 envelopes plain gelatin
1 cup cold water
1 can tomato soup

Combine shrimp, celery, bell pepper, onion, salt, lemon juice, Worcestershire and Tabasco. Mix well and let stand to blend flavors. Combine soup and cream cheese in double boiler. Heat and stir until cheese melts. Soften gelatin in water for 5 minutes. Add to soup mixture. Remove from heat and cool. When mixture begins to thicken, blend in mayonnaise. Stir in shrimp mixture, turn into mold and chill. Serve with crackers or may be used as a salad.

Made in a fish-shaped mold, garnished with lemon slices dipped in paprika and sprigs of parsley, our shrimp mousse is prettier than a picture in any magazine! Serve with candlelight and silver.

Mrs. Thomas Caddell

CHICKEN LIVER PATE

1 pound chicken livers
1 small onion, finely chopped
½ cup butter
1½ tablespoons brandy
1½ tablespoons dry sherry
2 teaspoons salt
¼ teaspoon nutmeg
¼ teaspoon pepper
Pinch of thyme
Pinch of basil
Pinch of marjoram

Saute chicken livers and chopped onion in butter for 3 to 4 minutes until livers are browned on outside but pink inside. Transfer them to a bowl. Stir brandy and sherry into butter remaining in pan and pour over sauteed livers. Season with salt and other seasonings. Combine well. Puree about 1/3 of mixture at a time in blender until smooth. Spoon pate into earthenware tureen or serving dish and chill.

An inexpensive yet sophisticated item for any kind of party — outside casual or dining room dress-up. This pate does take more time and effort than some things; but thanks to the blender, it's much easier to do than it might be.

Mrs. William E. Shinn, Jr.

BARBECUED OYSTERS

½ cup Heinz 57 Steak Sauce
1 teaspoon Worcestershire
1 teaspoon soy sauce
1 teaspoon prepared mustard
1 tablespoon lemon juice

¼ cup catsup
1 pint standard oysters
1 egg, well beaten
Flour and cracker crumbs for
  breading

Mix the first six ingredients and let stand. Drain and check oysters for shells. Dip oysters into flour, then into beaten egg and then into cracker crumbs. Lightly brown in margarine or hot oil. Do not overcook. Place in a casserole. When ready to bake, spoon sauce over oysters. Bake for 20 minutes at 325°. Serve hot.

These are irresistible. Even oyster haters will find themselves nibbling.

Mrs. John R. Guice

CHAFING DISH OYSTERS

¼ cup butter
1 quart standard oysters
1 4-ounce can mushrooms, sliced
1 small jar pimentos, minced
1 small bunch scallions, including
  green tops, minced

3 tablespoons flour (dissolved in
  ¼ cup cold water)
½ tablespoon salt
½ teaspoon pepper
¼ teaspoon Meiyen (Spice
  Islands)
1 cup good white wine

Strain oysters and cut in half. Reserve liquor. Melt butter in iron skillet on medium low heat. Add oysters and scallions. Bubble until the edges begin to curl and scallions are opaque. Add flour to thicken slightly. Add reserved liquor. Then add remaining ingredients. Simmer until the mixture comes to a gentle boil while stirring often. Transfer to chafing dish. To serve, spoon into miniature patty shells. Thinly sliced water chestnuts may be added to this.

Wonderful for the elegant cocktail buffet. Polish your silver chafing dish, get out the candles, and do have a lovely time.

Mrs. Lewis DeMent
Tuscaloosa, Alabama

27

SPICY HAM STICKS

3 2¼-ounce cans deviled ham
1 2-ounce tube anchovy paste
1 grated onion (or equivalent
   in dried, minced onion)
1 teaspoon powdered dill

2 boxes pie crust mix
2 cloves garlic, minced (may be
   dried)
2 tablespoons poppy seeds

Make spread using ham, anchovy paste, onion, dill. Mix pie crust according to package directions. Add garlic and poppy seed. Divide pastry into 4 equal parts. Roll as thin as possible, trim to even edges. Spread with ham mixture, thinly. Fold in half, sealing edges. Slice into pencil thin strips, about ¼ inch by 3 or 4 inches. Makes 150 to 200 sticks. Bake 10 to 15 minutes at 425°.

Such an unusual combination of flavors and textures. These crunchy nibbles are for the ambitious cook — they are not simple to make and they do take time. They can be made a day or two ahead, however, and stored in a tin until time for your lovely party.

Mrs. Herbert Street

STUFFED CHERRY TOMATOES

1 8-ounce package cream cheese
2 medium cucumbers
⅛ teaspoon cayenne pepper
¼ teaspoon salt

⅛ teaspoon white pepper
2 dozen cherry tomatoes
Capers

Peel and seed the cucumbers. Chop finely and cover with salted ice water for 10 minutes. Drain well. Mix with cream cheese (at room temperature). Add seasonings. Seed and drain the tomatoes — do not peel. Take a thin slice from the bottom so tomatoes will stand upright. Stuff with mixture. Top with a caper.

You won't be sorry you went to the trouble to fix these.

Mrs. Lewis DeMent

SPICED PINEAPPLE PICKUPS

1 20-ounce can pineapple chunks
¾ cup vinegar
1¼ cups sugar

Dash salt
6 to 8 whole cloves
1 4-inch piece stick cinnamon

A day or so ahead: Drain syrup from pineapple chunks. To ¾ cup syrup, add vinegar, sugar, salt, cloves, cinnamon. Heat 10 minutes. Add pineapple chunks, bring to a boil. Refrigerate until time to serve. To serve, drain pineapple chunks. Serve them, ice-cold, with picks.

Served ice-cold, these spicy fruit chunks are a nice diversion from normal cocktail fare.

Mrs. Judson F. Davis, Jr.

PIZZA PARTY SNACKS

½ cup tomato soup
⅛ teaspoon oregano
⅛ teaspoon salt
½ cup grated Cheddar cheese

¼ cup chopped onion
¼ cup chopped bell pepper
¼ cup chopped parsley

Mix all ingredients well; spread on slices of party rye bread. Broil 5 minutes.

Vary these by adding ½ pound sauteed ground beef in the sauce and spreading on party rolls before broiling.

Mrs. John Power
South Miami, Florida

PIZZA HORS D'OEUVRES

1 loaf party rye bread
1 pound ground sausage
1 8-ounce package mozzarella cheese (2 packages are even better)

1 medium onion, diced
1 8-ounce can tomato sauce
Oregano to taste
Parmesan cheese

In skillet, combine sausage and diced onion. Sprinkle with oregano. Cook and drain. Add tomato sauce. Place rye bread under broiler until crisp. Turn to unbrowned side and place mozzarella slices on bread. Top with sausage mixture and sprinkle with Parmesan cheese. Heat in 375° oven until hot and bubbly. If frozen, heat in 400° oven for about 20 minutes.

Watch the men line up at your kitchen door when they smell these little pizzas cooking. When done, pass them with caution.

Mrs. A. Julian Harris

ARTICHOKES AND AVOCADO

3 fresh artichokes
Boiling, salted water
2 tablespoons vinegar or lemon juice
1 soft avocado
3 teaspoons mayonnaise

Juice of 1 lemon
⅛ teaspoon cayenne
2 tablespoons minced scallions, white part only
Chopped parsley

Cook artichokes 25 to 40 minutes in boiling, salted water to cover. Add 2 tablespoons vinegar or lemon juice to water. Test by piercing artichokes with fork to see if tender. Remove outer globe leaves and reserve. Discard thistle. Mash hearts and remaining ingredients (a blender is convenient for this). Stuff reserved outer leaves with the mixture. Garnish with chopped parsley and serve.

If this recipe were not an original, we would imagine these morsels to be a favorite before-dinner treat on Mount Olympus.

Mrs. Lewis DeMent
Tuscaloosa, Alabama

29

DR. BEN'S ASPARAGUS ROLLS

20 slices soft sandwich bread,
   white
1 jar Old English Cheddar cheese,
   room temperature
2 tablespoons softened butter

1 clove garlic, minced
3 dashes Tabasco
2 to 3 teaspoons Worcestershire
1 10½-ounce can asparagus tips,
   well-drained

Cut crusts from bread slices. Mix cheese, butter, garlic, Tabasco, Worcestershire. Add more butter if needed to make mixture spreadable. Cover each slice of bread thinly with cheese mixture. Place an asparagus spear on one side of each slice, roll up. Refrigerate or freeze rolls before cutting — this is important! Before cooking, slice each roll into ½ inch pieces. Broil until cheese bubbles and top is toasted. Serve immediately. Yields from 100 to 120 pieces.

Whoever Dr. Ben is (or was) he surely has a flair for cooking. These wonderful hot little pickups are great do-aheaders with only a quick trip into the oven left for the last minute.

Mrs. Herbert Street

DEVILED HAM PUFFS

Ritz crackers
Deviled ham
Topping:
8 ounces cream cheese

1 teaspoon grated onion
½ teaspoon baking powder
1 egg yolk
Salt and pepper, to taste

Spread Ritz crackers with deviled ham. Mix topping together until smooth and place 1 teaspoon of mixture atop crackers. Bake at 375° for 10 minutes. Serve warm.

A scrumptious appetizer . . .

Mrs. Billy W. Payne

GARLIC TOMATO CREAMIES

3 small ripe tomatoes
1 minced clove garlic
Toast rounds, tomato-slice size
¾ cup mayonnaise

Chopped chives
5 or 6 slices crisp bacon,
   crumbled

Peel and slice tomatoes. Cut as many tomato rounds as toast rounds. Put a slice of tomato on each piece of toast. Mix mayonnaise with garlic, spread on tomatoes. Broil for 3 minutes until brown. Sprinkle with chives and bacon. Serves 6.

A good candidate for that hot "something before" when you're planning a small but important dinner party.

Mrs. David C. Harris

CRAB TOASTIES

½ pound crabmeat
1½ tablespoons mayonnaise
½ tablespoon prepared mustard
½ tablespoon lemon juice
6 slices toasted white bread

½ cup Parmesan cheese
1 tablespoon dry bread crumbs
Paprika or diced, drained
mushrooms

Remove cartilage from crabmeat. Combine mayonnaise, mustard, lemon juice and crabmeat. Remove crusts from bread. Spread crab mixture on each slice of toast. Combine cheese and crumbs, sprinkle over each slice. Cut each slice into 6 pieces. Place on broiler pan 3 inches from heat. Broil for 2 minutes until brown. Sprinkle with paprika. For extra taste and decoration, mushrooms may be substituted for paprika. Makes 36 appetizers.

Heavenly little morsels! It makes one's mouth water just to read the recipe.

Mrs. David C. Harris

SURPRISE HOR D'OEUVRES

½ pound bacon
½ cup chopped scallions
(including tops)

¼ cup mayonnaise
Melba toast rounds

Fry bacon until crisp. Drain and crumble. Combine bacon, onion and mayonnaise. Spread teaspoonful (or less) on toast rounds and heat in 350° oven for about 10 minutes.

Surprisingly good results with a few ingredients and little effort.

Mrs. Frank W. Troup

FRENCH FRIED MUSHROOMS

Large mushrooms
Flour
1 egg, beaten

Bread crumbs
Garlic salt

Select large mushrooms. Remove stems. Dip mushrooms caps in flour and then in beaten egg. Roll in fine bread or cracker crumbs lightly seasoned with garlic salt. Deep fry a minute until hot throughout and brown on outside. Serve with tartar sauce.

Mrs. William E. Shinn, Jr.

SPICY CARROT APPETIZERS

1 pound medium carrots
3 tablespoons salad oil
3 cloves garlic, minced
1 tablespoon chopped onions
¼ cup vinegar

1 tablespoon whole pickling spice
1½ teaspoons salt
½ teaspoon dry mustard
⅛ teaspoon pepper
1 onion, thinly sliced

One or several days ahead: Cut carrots diagonally into thin slices. In large skillet over medium heat, in hot salad oil, cook garlic and onion about 5 minutes until almost tender. Add carrots and vinegar: Loosely tie pickling spice, salt, mustard, and pepper in cheese cloth. Add to carrots. Simmer, covered, 5 minutes until carrots are crunchy and crisp. Discard spices. Pour carrot mixture into shallow dish and top with onion slices. Cover and refrigerate until serving time, tossing occasionally. Place carrots in serving dish; may use onions later in salad. Makes 10 to 12 appetizer servings.

Excellent as an appetizer or as a cold vegetable accompaniment to dinner. Such a pleasant way to get vitamin A — just think how your eyes will sparkle!

Mrs. Harold Pilgrim, Jr.

Beverages

APRICOT WINE

1 pound dried apricots
4 quarts warm water
6½ cups granulated sugar
2¼ cups brown sugar
1½ cups seeded raisins

1 tablespoon ginger
2 lemons, thinly sliced
2 oranges, thinly sliced
½ cake yeast

Wash the apricots in several waters, dry them and cut in halves. Place in a large crock and add the warm water, reserving ½ cup of it in which to dissolve the yeast cake. Stir in the sugars, fruit, raisins and ginger. Add the dissolved yeast and mix well. Cover with top of the crock and let stand for thirty days, stirring the mixture every other day. After thirty days, strain the mixture and bottle. Improves with age.

An old family recipe of Pennsylvania Dutch origin. Do try it in Alabama — or wherever you are.

Mrs. Billy W. Payne

HOMEMADE KAHLUA LIQUEUR

1 pint brandy
2 ounce jar instant coffee
2 cups water

4 cups sugar
1 vanilla bean

Boil water, add sugar and coffee (which you have mixed with a small amount of water), and vanilla bean. Mix. Add brandy. Let stand at room temperature for 30 days. Makes 1½ quarts.

Fun to try and really quite good. Though you won't save a trip to the package store, you will save several pennies.

Mrs. William E. Shinn, Jr.

SHERRY SOUR

1 bottle dry sherry

1 6-ounce can frozen lemonade

Combine and store in refrigerator overnight. Serve over crushed-ice.

Perfect for a bridge luncheon.

RUM PUNCH FOR FIFTY

4 fifths light rum
Juice from 24 lemons
2 cups sugar

2 pints strong Nestea instant tea
4 quarts soda water

Make an ice ring by putting water in a large mold and add mint, sliced lime and cherries or small amount of other fruit. Freeze until hard. Mix all ingredients and pour in bowl.

Cheers for this large supply of cheer.

STRAWBERRY CHAMPAGNE PUNCH

2 fifths sauterne
8 ounces of brandy
6 lemons, thinly sliced
6 oranges, thinly sliced

3 packages frozen whole
  strawberries
2 fifths chilled champagne

Pour sauterne and brandy over the citrus fruit. Let stand at least 12 hours in refrigerator. When ready to serve, add the champagne and strawberries. Serves 25.

Elegant and beautiful for a wedding or any other festive occasion on your calendar.

Mrs. William A. Sims

RED VELVET PUNCH

8 cups cranberry juice
1 6-ounce can frozen lemon juice
1 6-ounce can frozen pineapple
  juice

1 6-ounce can frozen orange juice
1 pint chilled brandy
2 fifths chilled champagne

Mix all the juices together and chill. When ready to serve, add the brandy and champagne and float lemon and lime slices on top. Yields 25 cups.

For Teetotalers: Substitute 2 cups grape juice for the brandy and 2 quarts of ginger ale for the champagne.

A sparkling red liquid guaranteed to make the conversation sparkle.

Mrs. Del V. Carraher

CHARLIE'S PUNCH

1 quart bourbon
2 small cans frozen orange juice
2 small cans frozen lemonade
2 quarts soda water

2 jiggers Curacao (optional)
1 8-ounce jar maraschino cherries
  (including syrup)

Serves 24.

Warm up your party in a hurry. Charlie does know how!

Mrs. Harold Pilgrim

DAY-OLD COCKTAIL

3 cups water
1 cup sugar

Juice of 12 lemons
1 quart whiskey

Dissolve sugar and water. Add juice of lemons and pour in whiskey. Add peeling of 6 or 8 lemons. Let stand in refrigerator for 24 hours. Strain before serving. Serve **over** crushed ice. Garnish with fresh mint or cherry. Serves 12.

(The smart hostess makes this cocktail the day before for improved flavor and for convenience.)

Mrs. Bill Sexton

35

SANGRIA

½ cup lemon juice
½ cup orange juice
¼—½ cup sugar

1 fifth dry red wine
1 7-ounce bottle club soda

Combine lemon juice, orange juice and sugar, stirring until dissolved. Add wine and soda and garnish with lemon slices.

To do ahead: prepare recipe omitting club soda. Stir in at serving time.

Mock Sangria: Substitute 4 cups grape juice and 14 ounces of club soda for wine and soda in above recipe.

A wondrously cool and refreshing wine punch from Spain that is served with the meal. By adding one-half cup cognac and pouring all into a punch bowl, the Sangria becomes just the thing to sip before a small luncheon.

Mrs. William E. Shinn, Jr.

HOT BUTTERED RUM

Heat apple cider in percolator. Pour an ounce of rum in cup and add cider. Put a pat of butter on top with a slice of lemon. Use cinnamon stick for stirrer.

When the wind is whistling outside and the thermometer is dropping rapidly, light a roaring fire, pop some corn and be glad you're inside with your cup in hand.

Mrs. John E. Wilks, Jr.

MILK PUNCH

3 cups milk
1 cup cream
2—3 tablespoons sugar

8 jiggers bourbon, scotch or brandy
Nutmeg

Shake with ice. Serve in chilled glasses with dash of nutmeg. Serves 4.

Nothing tastes better the morning after a rather large evening. If you're not up to shaking the ingredients, a very acceptable milk punch can be made by the glass full. Into an 8 to 10 ounce glass put a jigger of bourbon or scotch, a scoop or two of vanilla ice cream, and fill the glass with milk. Stir well and sprinkle with nutmeg.

Mrs. William E. Shinn, Jr.

NORMAN'S BLOODY MARY MIX

1 46-ounce can V-8 juice
1/4 teaspoon Tabasco
1/2 teaspoon black pepper

1 teaspoon salt
2 tablespoons Worcestershire
4 tablespoons lemon juice

Mix all together and add vodka as desired.

Mrs. Norman Harris, Jr.

MISS ANN'S EGGNOG

16 eggs, separated
1 cup sugar

2 1/2 tablespoons whiskey to each egg
1 quart of cream, whipped

Mix egg yolks with sugar. Thin with whiskey slowly. Add stiffly beaten egg whites. Fold in cream, which has been beaten until it forms soft peaks. Serves 24.

A rich and extravagant nog which speaks of mistletoe and holly.

Mrs. Robert Tweedy McWhorter, Jr.

SUMMER ORANGEADE

12 oranges
3 pints water
2 ounces citric acid (can
be bought at drug store)

3-5 cups sugar

Put whole oranges through a meat grinder. Mix citric acid with water and pour over ground oranges. Let stand in glass container overnight in refrigerator. Strain and add sugar to juice. Serve over ice with mint.

A drink from days gone by.

Mrs. Thomas A. Caddell

LEMONADE

Rinds of 2 lemons
1 cup sugar
1 cup water

1 cup fresh lemon juice
4 cups ice water

Combine first three ingredients and heat on low heat to boiling. Boil for 1 minute. Strain and cool. Then add 1 cup fresh lemon juice and 4 cups ice water.

In today's world of frozen concentrates and powdered mixes, we tend to forget just how good lemonade can be made with real live lemons. Do try some soon before making it becomes a lost art.

Mrs. Arthur F. Jordan

ICED TEA

5 regular size tea bags	2 lemons
1 running-over cup of sugar	2 quarts of water

Put water, sugar and lemon juice in boiler and bring to a hard boil. Remove from stove. Put tea bags and lemon rinds in boiler, cover and let steep 20 minutes. Strain and place in pitcher or large jar and let cool. Chill thoroughly in refrigerator.

Oddly enough, some of Cotton Country's best cooks find making good tea difficult. How grand, then, to have a family secret for delicious tea that is always good.

Mrs. Charles Eyster, Jr.

APPLE PUNCH QUICKIE

4 quarts chilled apple cider	Crushed ice
4 cups cranberry juice	Lemon slices on glasses for
4 teaspoons lemon juice	decoration
1 quart ginger ale	

In large bottle combine cider, cranberry juice, and lemon juice. Add ginger ale just before serving and put ice in tall glasses. Fill with punch and serve. Serves 30 tall glasses.

Cool and attractive in tall frosted glasses garnished with lemon slices. What a nice change this would be for the next meeting of the bridge group!

Mrs. David C. Harris

HOLIDAY PUNCH

1 46-ounce can pineapple juice	1 pint cranberry juice
1 cup lemon juice	2 quarts ginger ale
1 cup sugar	

Chill all juices and ginger ale. Mix juices and sugar. Add ginger ale just before serving.

Ice cubes made of additional pineapple juice or a frozen fruit ring are easy and pretty additions.

Mrs. O. E. Kirby, Jr.

FRUIT PUNCH

3 6-ounce cans frozen orange juice	1 46-ounce can grapefruit juice
3 6-ounce cans water	1 46-ounce can pineapple juice
3 6-ounce cans frozen lemonade	1 12-ounce can apricot nectar
3 6-ounce cans water	2 quarts chilled ginger ale

Mix all ingredients except ginger ale thoroughly and cool. Just before serving add ginger ale. Makes 60 cups.

Mrs. Albert Brewer
Pike Road, Alabama

PARTY PUNCH

2 12-ounce cans apricot nectar
2 46-ounce cans unsweetened
  pineapple juice
2 6-ounce cans frozen lemonade

4 cups cold water
1 fresh pineapple
Fresh mint sprigs

Pour canned fruit juices, lemonade and water over ice cubes in punch bowl. Halve pineapple. Slice and remove core. Float with mint sprigs on top of punch. Makes about 7½ quarts.

Save this wonderful fruity concoction for a very special event. The pineapple slices topped with mint sprigs add that little extra touch of glamour.

Mrs. Jolly McKenzie

CITRIC ACID PUNCH

2 ounces citric acid
2 quarts boiling water
5 cups sugar

5 quarts cold water
1 6-ounce can frozen orange juice
1 46-ounce can pineapple juice

Dissolve citric acid in boiling water 24 hours in advance. (This must be prepared in an enamel or heat proof glass container as it will taste bitter if prepared in a metal container.) Dissolve sugar in cold water.

When ready to serve, add frozen orange juice and pineapple juice to the citric acid and sugar solution. Pour over attractive ice ring. Serves 75.

An inexpensive fruit punch that is easy to make and is great for large crowds. You can serve 75 for a mere pittance (about $1.00). Purchase citric acid at the drug store and use without concern since it is not harmful.

Mrs. George W. Hansberry

SPARKLING PINK PARTY PUNCH

1 small package red cinnamon
  candies (3 tablespoons)
¼ cup sugar
½ cup warm water

1 46-ounce can pineapple juice,
  chilled
1 quart ginger ale, chilled

Cook candies, sugar and water together over low heat stirring constantly until candies are dissolved. Strain and cool. Combine with other chilled ingredients. Makes twenty, 4-ounce servings.

The cinnamon candies, hot little devils though they be, are responsible for the pretty color and sparkling taste of this excellent punch.

Mrs. Paul McCain

MOCK PINK CHAMPAGNE

½ cup sugar
1 cup water
1 cup grapefruit juice
½ cup orange juice
¼ cup grenadine syrup

1 28-ounce bottle ginger ale,
  chilled
Twists of lemon peel
Stems-on maraschino cherries

Combine sugar and water in saucepan; simmer uncovered, stirring constantly until sugar is dissolved, about 3 minutes. Cool. Mix with juices and grenadine in punch bowl. Chill. Just before serving, add ginger ale pouring slowly down side of bowl. Serve over ice in sherbet glasses. Trim with peel and cherry.

Delightful to serve before ladies lunch or brunch.

Mrs. John R. Taylor

FRENCH COFFEE PUNCH

1 pound of coffee
3 quarts water
½ cup sugar

2 squares unsweetened chocolate
2 quarts milk
½ gallon vanilla ice cream

Simmer coffee and water until strong (approximately 2 hours). Strain. Add chocolate and sugar, stirring until dissolved. Cool slightly. Add milk and refrigerate overnight.

Just before serving, pour over ice cream. Makes 35 cups. (It is nice to sprinkle fresh grated nutmeg over top.)

Mrs. John E. Wilks, Jr.

SPICED TEA MIX

2 cups Tang
¾ cup instant tea
2 small packages or 1 large
  package lemonade mix

1¼ cups sugar
1 teaspoon cinnamon
½ teaspoon cloves
½ teaspoon allspice

Mix well and store in container. To use: place 1—3 teaspoons (personal taste decides how much) in cup. Add boiling water and stir.

In case someone hasn't heard, this is a great thing to have on hand on cold winter days — almost as handy as a jar of instant coffee.

Mrs. Michael D. Scroggins

SPICED HOT TEA

6 cups water
6 tea bags (regular size)
1 quart water
3 cinnamon sticks
15 whole cloves
2 cups sugar

1 3-ounce package cherry gelatin
1 12-ounce can frozen orange
juice — prepared
1 46-ounce can pineapple juice
1 8-ounce bottle of lemon juice

Boil 6 cups of water, pour over tea bags and steep. Place cinnamon sticks and cloves in 1 quart of water and simmer 20 minutes. Add remaining ingredients. Bring to boil and serve or store in refrigerator in covered jars. Keeps indefinitely.

Cherry gelatin gives this spiced tea a special color and an extra special flavor. For the weight watcher, 8 teaspoons of Sweeta can be substituted for the sugar.

Mrs. John R. Taylor

RUSSIAN TEA

1½ cups sugar
3 tablespoons lemon juice
12-ounce can frozen orange juice
1 cup pineapple juice

2 teaspoons whole cloves
2 sticks cinnamon
4 tea bags
4 cups water

Boil water with cloves and cinnamon four or five minutes. Put tea bags in for 4 minutes. Pour over sugar. Add all other ingredients and enough water to make one gallon. Serve hot.

Mrs. Robert Allen
Livonia, Michigan

HOT MULLED CIDER

½ cup brown sugar
¼ teaspoon salt
2 quarts apple cider
1 teaspoon whole allspice

1 teaspoon whole cloves
3 inches stick cinnamon
Dash nutmeg

Add brown sugar and salt to apple cider. Loosely tie whole allspice, whole cloves, stick cinnamon and nutmeg in cheesecloth; add to apple cider mixture. Simmer for about 20 to 25 minutes; discard spices. Serve in mugs with apple slices. Makes 10 servings.

Marvelous for those chilly, blustery days. We suggest you serve the cider with hot gingerbread.

Mrs. Harold Pilgrim, Jr.

HOT CRANBERRY PUNCH

2 cups pineapple juice
2 cups cranberry juice
½ cup sugar (or more)
1¾ cup water

1½ teaspoon whole cloves
2 inches stick cinnamon
Pinch salt

Mix in percolator. Allow to heat 10 minutes.

A hot spiced drink — similar to Russian tea, but some think it's better and all agree it is easier to fix. Mix, heat and pour with only your percolator involved.

Mrs. Richard Rouquie
Bluefield, West Virginia

HOT CHOCOLATE

1½ teaspoon grated semi-sweet
  chocolate
¼ cup boiling water
¾ cup scalded milk

1—2 teaspoons sugar as desired
Few grains of salt
2 drops vanilla

Melt chocolate with sugar and salt in sauce pan. Add boiling water slowly and stir until smooth. Boil one minute. Add the scalded milk and heat well. Beat two minutes with egg beater. The froth from beating prevents scum forming. Add vanilla and serve. Serves 1.

Mrs. Darby Fleming

CREAMY HOT CHOCOLATE MIX

1 6-ounce jar powdered creamer
½ cup confectioners' sugar
1 8-quart package dry
  powdered milk

1 2-pound box chocolate flavored
  drink (such as Nestle's Quick)

Mix all ingredients thoroughly and store in an air tight container. Use 1/3 cup of mixture to a mug. Fill cup with boiling water. Top with marshmallow if desired.

A must for busy mothers!

Mrs. John R. Taylor

POOR MAN'S DRAMBUIE

1 part 100 proof Vodka
1 part good Scotch

½ part clear honey
1 drop Angostura Bitters per ounce

Mix together and store in bottle.

Mrs. William A. Sims

Soups and Sandwiches

WATERCRESS SOUP

3 tablespoons butter or margarine
3 tablespoons flour
1¼ teaspoons salt
½ teaspoon curry powder

3 cups milk
1 cup finely shredded carrots
1 cup chopped watercress
½ cup water

Melt butter or margarine in medium saucepan over medium heat; stir in flour, salt and curry powder to make a smooth paste. Gradually stir in milk and cook slowly until mixture is smooth and slightly thickened. In another medium saucepan, cook carrots in ½ cup boiling water for three minutes. Add watercress and cook for one minute longer. Stir vegetables (do not drain) into milk mixture and heat just to boiling. Makes 6 to 8 servings.

A sophisticated cream soup for an elegant dinner!

Mrs. Arnold Rankin

GREENSBORO LETTUCE SOUP

2 cups finely chopped lettuce
1 pint half and half
1 can cream of pea soup
Sprig of parsley
2 tablespoons cucumber
½ teaspoon curry powder

½ teaspoon salt
½ teaspoon sugar
Dash of Worcestershire
Dash of Tabasco
1 can crabmeat (optional)
½ cup white wine

Blend in blender the following: 1½ cups of the lettuce, soup and parsley. Combine the blender mixture with the remaining ingredients (except the ½ cup lettuce and wine) in a heavy saucepan and cook slowly over low heat for 15 to 20 minutes. Just before serving add the remaining lettuce and the white wine to the soup.

Peter Cottontail will wriggle with delight when he hears about this — you will too, when you taste it!

Mrs. Eula Peebles

CREAM OF TOMATO SOUP

3 tablespoons butter
2 tablespoons flour
2 cups strained tomatoes or
   tomato juice

⅛ teaspoon soda
1 teaspoon salt
3 cups milk
½ teaspoon instant onion (optional)

In double boiler or heavy saucepan blend melted butter and flour. Add onion, tomatoes, soda and salt and cook slowly for about 5 minutes, stirring constantly. Add milk very slowly and heat until quite hot.

One potful and you'll never buy canned again! Some soup cooks find that substituting V-8 juice for the tomato provides a marvelous change of pace; you might try it too.

Mrs. John D. Veitch

SEAFOOD SOUP

6 cups water
2 pounds miscellaneous seafood
   (snapper, king mackerel, etc.)
2 dozen shrimp
2 teaspoons seafood seasoning
2½ teaspoons salt
6 stalks celery, cut to bite sized
   pieces

½ cup chopped onion
1 pound cut okra
½ teaspoon chervil
1 bay leaf
1 cup chicken stock
3 strips bacon, cut in small pieces
2 16-ounce cans tomatoes
Pepper to taste

Place water, seafood and shrimp in large kettle or heavy boiler and add seafood seasoning. Cook until seafood is tender and bones can be easily removed. Remove seafood to a platter, cool and remove bones and return to pot. Add all other ingredients and simmer slowly several hours. The longer it cooks the better. Correct seasonings and serve. 8 to 10 generous servings.

A fine midwinter way to clean the remains of last summer's fishing trip out of your freezer.

Mrs. L. Denton Cole, Jr.

BRUNSWICK (GEORGIA) STEW

1 2 to 3 pound chicken
1 ham bone or ham hock
3 quarts water
½ cup sugar
1 bay leaf
2 tablespoons chopped parsley
2 onions, sliced
4 cups tomatoes, chopped
2 cups celery tops, chopped

2 cups lima beans, fresh or frozen
Dash Tabasco
1 teaspoon black pepper
4 cups corn, fresh or canned whole
   kernel sweet corn
4 large potatoes
½ cup butter (do not use
   margarine)
Salt, only after tasting

Stew first six ingredients in a very large, heavy pot until chicken is tender. Remove chicken from the bones and cut into small pieces. Remove ham from the bone and return chicken and ham to the pot. (If you prefer a thicker stew, you might use only 2½ quarts water.) Add the next six ingredients to the pot and simmer for 45 minutes. Add the butter and corn and simmer for an additional 45 minutes. Meanwhile, cook potatoes, drain and mash or put them through a sieve and add to the stew. Serves 12 to 15.

A truly great Brunswick Stew! Better save your celery leaves or get to the store early while the produce boy is cutting the tops off. Then make your stew and serve with corn sticks and cole slaw. If you are super ambitious you might add Fried Fish or Barbecued Chicken to the menu.

Mrs. Dale Crites
Lakewood, Colo.

BRUNSWICK STEW

1 7-pound hen, cut in half
3½ pounds lean pork cut in 1-inch cubes
4 large onions, chopped
4 cloves garlic, shaved
Salt
¼ to ½ bottle Tabasco (according to taste)
6 large potatoes
2 16-ounce cans cream style corn
2 16-ounce cans butter beans (2 boxes, frozen)
1 16-ounce can cut okra (1 box, frozen)
1 16-ounce can English peas
1 8-ounce can tomato sauce

Put chicken and pork in a large, heavy pot and cover with water. Add onions, garlic, salt and Tabasco and cook until meat is well done and can be removed from bones. Remove chicken, cool and bone. Cut into pieces the desired size and return to pot. Cut potatoes into bite sized pieces and add to meat mixture and simmer until potatoes are tender. Add all other ingredients and simmer for about 1 hour before serving. Makes about two gallons.

Uncle Ben Hays, a Negro cook, served this stew in Decatur as far back as 1911.

Mrs. Thomas A. Caddell

COUNTRY STEW

2 whole chickens (2½ pounds each)
Water to cover
1 tablespoon salt
1½ teaspoons Accent
2 medium onions, chopped
¼ pound raw country ham or bacon (cut in bite sized pieces)
1 28-ounce can tomatoes
1 can whole kernel corn (8½ ounces)
1 10-ounce package frozen lima beans
1¼ teaspoon Tabasco
¼ teaspoon thyme
½ teaspoon salt
⅛ teaspoon pepper
1 10-ounce package frozen okra
Thickening:
3 tablespoons butter
¼ cup flour
1 small green pepper, finely chopped

In a large kettle with a lid, put chickens, breast side down, and add giblets. Add enough water to barely cover. Add salt, Accent and onion. Bring to a boil, skim off foam and reduce heat. Cover and simmer 45 minutes or until chicken is tender. Fifteen minutes before end of cooking time, add the liver. Remove chicken and giblets from broth. Remove meat from bones and return meat to broth. Add ham, tomatoes, corn, limas, okra, Tabasco, thyme, salt and pepper. Simmer 1 hour, stirring occasionally. Melt butter in a saucepan, blend in the flour and heat, stirring constantly till bubble forms and mixture browns. Add gradually to stew and cook over medium heat, stirring until thickened slightly. Add chopped green pepper and simmer 10 minutes longer. Serve very hot on corn bread squares or with corn sticks. Serves 12 to 14.

This may be a Country Stew, but how city folks will love it.

Mrs. W. Blanton McBride, Jr.

CRABMEAT SOUP

2 cans tomato soup
1 can green pea soup
1 can cream of mushroom soup
4 soup cans milk

1 can consomme
1 can water
1 can crabmeat
3 tablespoons Parmesan cheese

Combine all ingredients thoroughly and heat. Sprinkle with more cheese when serving.

A can-opener soup of superior flavor. Add another can of crabmeat if you prefer a meatier, thicker texture and flavor.

Mrs. R. W. Orr

MARGARET EMENS' CORN SOUP

13 cups water
2 pounds brisket beef or stew beef
1 teaspoon salt
1 teaspoon pepper
3 large onions, chopped

3 large Irish potatoes, chopped
1 28-ounce can tomatoes, cut up
1 12-ounce can tomato sauce
6 ears corn

Trim excess fat off beef, add to water and other ingredients, except corn. Bring to boil, reduce heat to simmer for 1 hour. Cut corn off cob and add to pot. Simmer an additional 2 hours. Serve over rice.

A thick corn chowder from Louisiana. Fresh corn makes the difference here!

Mrs. Frank T. Richardson, Jr.

CHICKEN SOUP

6 to 8 pieces chicken (boney
  pieces may be used)
5 cups water
¾ cup chopped celery or 1
  teaspoon celery seed
1 carrot, finely shredded
  (optional)

8 whole cloves
2 teaspoons salt
¼ teaspoon pepper
Rice or noodles, as preferred

Place chicken pieces in large, heavy kettle or dutch oven. Add water and remaining ingredients, except rice or noodles. Over high heat, bring to a boil. Cover and reduce heat to simmer and allow to cook about 1 hour or until chicken is tender and can be removed from the bone. Remove bones and cut chicken into small pieces and return to the broth. Remove whole cloves and add rice or noodles and cook until they are done. Correct seasonings to taste. Garnish with parsley.

Chicken soup "cures" colds and mends broken hearts every time.

Mrs. L. Denton Cole

LOUISIANA CREOLE GUMBO

6 quarts water
1½ pounds stewing beef cut
   in 1-inch cubes
1 pound sliced raw ham cut
   in 1-inch cubes
3 tablespoons bacon drippings
2 heaping tablespoons flour
2 pounds okra (fresh or frozen)
1 can tomatoes (28-ounce size)

6 medium onions
2 cups parsley
2 cups celery
6 garlic cloves, or to your taste
2 pounds crabmeat
2 pounds shrimp
2 tablespoons file powder
Salt and pepper to taste
Cayenne pepper to taste

Chop onions, parsley, celery and garlic. Heat bacon fat and brown stew meat and ham. Remove to a side platter and add flour to the drippings making a dark roux. Add okra and onions and cook five minutes. Add tomatoes, water, parsley, celery and garlic and boil for 1 hour. Add shrimp, which has been shelled and cleaned; boil 1 hour. Add crabmeat and cook 15 minutes. Add file powder, stir well; season with salt and pepper and cayenne pepper. Serve with white rice. Serves 24.

Jambalaya, crawfish pie and . . . This is not a "dish", but an experience.

Mrs. Frank T. Richardson, III

ONION SOUP AU GRATIN

2 tablespoons butter
6 small onions, sliced
¾ teaspoon sugar
2 tablespoons flour

6 cups chicken stock or consomme
Salt
Thick slices French bread
Grated Romano cheese

Melt butter, add onion and cook slowly until onion is soft. Add sugar and flour. Stir and cook one minute. Add chicken stock or consomme. Season and simmer at least 30 minutes. Toast French bread and sprinkle with cheese. Put a slice of bread in each of 6 bowls and pour soup over the toast and set bowls in 400° oven to melt and brown cheese.

Anyone who traveled to Paris prior to the demise of Les Halles knows the wonder of eating this specialty at 4 o'clock in the morning. Duplicate the taste, if not the atmosphere, in your own kitchen. Great for Christmas Eve after Santa has finished his ride!

Mrs. William A. Sims

BLENDER GAZPACHO

1 clove garlic	1½ teaspoons salt
½ small onion	¼ teaspoon pepper
1 stalk celery	2 tablespoons olive oil
½ small green pepper, seeded	3 tablespoons wine vinegar
3 ripe tomatoes	1 cup V-8 juice, chilled
1 small cucumber, peeled	Dash Tabasco

Place all ingredients, chopped a little, in blender container. Cover and blend 3 seconds or until last slice of cucumber is pulled down — NO LONGER. Chill and serve with croutons as a garnish.

This cold soup compares with the best Spain has to offer. Served icy cold in chilled cups, few things are so refreshing on a hot summer day, when all the vegetables are happily at the peak of flavor.

Mrs. William E. Shinn, Jr.

SPLIT PEA SOUP

1 stalk celery	3 medium onions
3 fresh carrots	1 ham bone
1 cup dried yellow or green split peas	1 quart water
Salt and pepper	1 pint chicken broth

Cook all ingredients except chicken broth together until vegetables are tender — about two hours. Put through a sieve and add chicken broth. Season to taste and if consistency seems too thick, a small amount of water may be added.

Mrs. George Hansberry

CHILI

2 slices bacon	1 16-ounce can kidney beans, undrained
1 pound ground beef	
1 large onion, chopped	2 tablespoons chili powder
1 green pepper, chopped	1½ teaspoons salt
1 clove garlic, whole with skin	1/3 teaspoon cumin
1 6-ounce can tomato paste	¼ teaspoon ground cloves
1 8-ounce can tomato sauce, plus 2 cans water	

Brown bacon in heavy pan. Remove when crisp and brown ground beef and onion in grease. Add green pepper and garlic and cook, stirring constantly, for two or three minutes. Add tomato paste, tomato sauce, water, kidney beans and all the spices. Bring to simmer and cook for two hours in covered pan. Stir at least every 15 minutes, mashing clove of garlic as it softens. If chili thickens too quickly, add another ½ can of water. Before serving remove garlic and crumble bacon to be used as a garnish.

Serve this Spicy Chili with corn chips, guacamole, beer, and a good football game on T.V.

Mrs. Herbert Street

EASY "AMERICAN" CHILI

1 pound ground beef
1 can tomato soup
1 chopped onion
1 garlic clove or ¼ teaspoon garlic
   salt

1 16-ounce can kidney beans
1 1-ounce jar Mexene Chili
   powder (use ½ to ¾ of the jar)
Salt to taste

Saute chopped onion in small amount of fat. Add ground meat and saute until meat is browned. Add garlic. Salt meat very slightly as it is browning. After meat is browned, add chili powder and stir well, coating all the meat with the chili powder. Add tomato soup, plus ¾ soup can of water and stir well. Add drained kidney beans and simmer at low temperature for 10 to 15 minutes. Longer cooking is not necessary since the meat was coated in the chili powder.

This may be a short cut "American" chili, but it tastes like it belongs on the other side of the Rio Grande.

Mrs. E. J. Phillips

CHILI

3 pounds ground beef
6 to 8 large onions
6 16-ounce cans tomatoes

6 16-ounce cans kidney beans
12 to 14 tablespoons chili powder
Salt and pepper, to taste

Saute beef and onions in heavy skillet until beef is browned. In a large, heavy pot put 3 cans tomatoes and 3 cans kidney beans. Add the beef and onions and bring to a boil. Reduce heat to simmer and cook for 30 minutes. Add another two cans of tomatoes and two cans kidney beans and the chili powder. Let chili continue to simmer and when it has cooked down sufficiently add the remaining cans of tomato and kidney beans. The mixture should be stirred often and should simmer all day.

With a cold crisp salad or slaw and cornbread — in front of a roaring fire — this makes a very successful Sunday night supper for a group of congenial friends.

Mrs. Frederick S. Hunt, Jr.

VEGETABLE SOUP

Really great vegetable soup just happens when the cook has a real love affair with cooking, so it's difficult to give more than a basic recipe.

With a little advance planning you can produce a spectacular soup. A container in the freezer labeled "soup pot" is a good idea for collecting all the bits and dabs of leftovers — gravy or drippings from roasts or baked hams; trimmings from steaks; those tiny amounts of leftover vegetables that you hate to throw away but haven't enough to keep. Just dump it all in and keep frozen until THE DAY. Once the basic soup is begun, add the contents (still frozen) of the container to the pot.

Let your own taste and imagination dictate seasonings. Try various combinations of herbs, beginning with a light hand. Don't be afraid to experiment, for you will probably just make it better. Let the soup simmer slowly for several hours and let the aroma fill the kitchen with the promise of delectable eating ahead.

The following recipe is more than just a basic recipe and makes a good soup as is. But how much more fun you'll have adding to or taking away to find your own special soup thing!

Ingredients:
1 soup bone
1 pound of lean brisket, cut in 2-inch cubes or 1 pound lean stew meat
1 28-ounce can tomatoes
1 16-ounce can tomato juice
4 large stalks celery, chopped
2 large onions, chopped
1 16-ounce can okra and corn in tomato sauce

4 large carrots, diced
1 7-ounce package vegetable soup mix
1 cup chopped parsley
2 bay leaves
1 teaspoon crushed red peppers
1 tablespoon celery salt
2 tablespoons Worcestershire
2 tablespoons salt
1 gallon water

Sear meat cubes and bone in hot skillet until brown. Add the water followed by all the other ingredients. Cook as long as desired (from 6 to 12 hours). Place soup in a cool place until orange colored grease forms crust on top. Remove the grease crust with wide cooking spatula. Reheat and serve.

Other ingredients such as potatoes, butterbeans, string beans may be added if desired. If potatoes are added, do not freeze.

Mrs. R. W. Orr, Jr.

BEAN SOUP

2 ham hocks, or pieces of ham approximately 4 x 4 inches. (sugar cured)
1½ pounds dried navy beans

6 cups water
2 teaspoons salt
1 very large onion, chopped
Pepper to taste

Put ham hocks, water and beans in a heavy pot or kettle. Add salt and chopped onion. Bring to boil rapidly, then reduce heat to simmer and cook for several hours (approximately 3 hours). Remove ham from pot on to plate and cool. Continue simmering other ingredients. When ham is cooled, trim fat and skin and cut the meaty part into bite sized pieces. Return chopped ham to soup pot, stir well to break up some of the beans and continue to simmer until soup is the desired consistency. Correct seasonings. This correction is necessary because salt content of ham varies. If soup is too salty, add a little sugar. Total cooking time should be about 4 to 5 hours. If soup is too thick when reheated, add a little water.

A good excuse to get out grandmother's tureen.

Mrs. L. Denton Cole, Jr.

FRANNIE'S PINTO BEAN SOUP

2 pounds dried pinto beans (soak
  overnight in water to cover)
1 pound salt pork, ham or bacon
  (if bacon is used, fry very
  crisp and crumble)

½ cup fat (bacon drippings will do)
4 teaspoons cumin seeds (crushed)
2 cups chopped onions
3 cloves garlic, minced

Put soaked beans in pottery, enamel or glass cooking pan with soaking water. Add remaining ingredients and cook on low heat (simmer) for 4 or 5 hours. Stir occasionally with wooden spoon to prevent sticking. If more water is needed, add boiling water — cold water darkens beans. Salt to taste and cook a few minutes longer. Salting too soon hardens beans. A dash of hot sauce may be added if desired. Serve with corn bread or soft tortillas.

The cumin seed in this recipe gives bean soup an entirely new flavor.

Mrs. O. E. Kirby, Jr.

POTATO SOUP

4 to 6 medium potatoes
3 tablespoons butter
2 teaspoons salt
½ teaspoon pepper

3 cups milk
½ of one small onion, grated
  or finely chopped
Parsley to garnish

Slice potatoes thinly and cook in water to cover until tender. Drain off the water, and with a potato masher, mash the potatoes until they are smooth. Add all other ingredients except parsley and quickly bring to a boil. Stir constantly to prevent sticking. Immediately reduce heat and simmer for about 15 minutes. Add parsley as a garnish, or chopped, as you prefer.

For the busy gal on the go, or when luncheon guests arrive unexpectedly, a marvelous quick version can be made in 10 minutes as follows: In a saucepan measure 4 cups milk, 4 tablespoons butter, 2 teaspoons salt, ⅛ teaspoon pepper, 1 tablespoon instant parsley flakes, 1 teaspoon instant onion. Bring to boil. Add 1 cup instant potatoes just as mixture boils. Boil 1 minute and soup is ready. Mmm, delicious!

Mrs. Robert H. Hosey

PIMENTO CHEESE

½ pound sharp Cheddar cheese
½ cup Kraft mayonnaise
½ teaspoon salt
2 dashes Accent
1 tablespoon sugar

1 ounce pimentos, finely chopped
1 tablespoon sweet pickle, chopped
¼ teaspoon garlic or onion salt

Allow cheese to reach room temperature. Cream grated cheese in electric mixer, adding mayonnaise until soft and fluffy. Then add salt, Accent, sugar. Mix well. Add pimentos and mix until pimento is barely visible. Add pickles and garlic salt. Very important to beat in electric mixer much longer than you think necessary to make smooth and fluffy. Refrigerate. Makes about 1 pint.

If you think pimento cheese is a spread you buy at the grocery in a plastic carton with dear Mrs. Doe's name on top, please think again. Then whip up a batch of Mrs. McCrary's. She advises that for family, you use very little garlic salt (if any) — but that you pour on the garlic for parties.

Mrs. George L. McCrary, Jr.

PIMENTO CHEESE

1 pound mild Cheddar cheese
¾ cup Hellman's mayonnaise
Juice of 1 lemon

1 2-ounce jar pimentos, diced, with juice
½ teaspoon salt
¼ teaspoon Tabasco

Grate cheese into 1 quart mixing bowl. Add mayonnaise, lemon juice, pimento with juice, salt and Tabasco. Mix well. Makes 2 2/3 cups.

An excellent basic pimento cheese to always have on hand — for school lunches, after school snacks, and before dinner nibbles.

Mrs. Robert T. McWhorter, Jr.

MOTHER'S COOKED PIMENTO CHEESE

1 pound Cheddar cheese, grated
1 13-ounce can evaporated milk

1 7-ounce can pimentos, chopped

Mix together in a saucepan over low heat until melted. Cool slightly and refrigerate.

Mrs. John E. Wilks, Jr.

SAUCY HOT DOGS

3 slices diced bacon
1/3 cup chopped onion
2 tablespoons chopped bell pepper
¾ cup unsweetened pineapple
  juice

½ cup catsup
⅛ teaspoon chili powder
10 hot dogs
10 buns

Cook bacon slightly, but do not crisp. Add onions and pepper; cook until tender but not brown. Combine juice, catsup, and chili powder. Add to bacon mixture. Score hot dogs diagonally at 1 inch intervals. Add to sauce. Cover and bring to boil. Lower heat and simmer 8 to 10 minutes. Serve in warmed buns.

An end-of-the-month specialty, but good anytime. We suggest you serve these, too, for teenage parties. (Do make a lot.)

Mrs. John F. Manning

SHRIMP SALAD SANDWICH

Lettuce
Holland Rusk
Blue cheese
1 tomato, sliced

4 hard boiled eggs, sliced
2 strips bacon (per serving),
  sauteed
3 pound bag frozen shrimp, cooked

Shred lettuce and place on plate. Place 1 round Holland Rusk on top of lettuce. Spread with blue cheese. On top of this place I thick slice of tomato, 3 slices hard-boiled egg, and 2 slices bacon. Place shrimp on top. Pour dressing over sandwich.

Dressing:

1 pint jar mayonnaise
½ bottle chili sauce

Onion salt to taste

Mix well.

A sure success.

Mrs. William S. Coles

CRABBURGERS

6 small hamburger buns
2 cans crabmeat
6 stalks celery, chopped
Lemon juice, to taste

Salt and pepper, to taste
Mayonnaise
Sharp Cheddar cheese, grated

Mix crabmeat, celery, juice, salt and pepper. Add enough mayonnaise until right consistency is reached. Spread salad mixture on top and bottom of buns, making 12 open faced sandwiches. Top with cheese and heat in 350° oven until cheese melts. Serves 6.

Grand for impromptu entertaining — or for family when you've had one of those days.

Mrs. R. W. Orr, Sr.

CRABMEAT SANDWICH

1 6½ ounce can crabmeat
1 small onion, grated
2 8-ounce packages cream cheese, softened
Lemon juice, to taste

Dash Worcestershire
Salt, to taste
Tomatoes, sliced
Holland Rusk
Cheddar cheese, grated

Mix crabmeat, onion, cream cheese, and other seasonings. Put tomato slice on Holland Rusk. Pile crabmeat mixture on, sprinkle with grated cheese. Broil until cheese is melted. Serves 6.

For your next bridge foursome, try this.

Mrs. Richard D. Williams

HAM AND ASPARAGUS ROLL-UPS

4 slices boiled ham
12 asparagus spears
4 slices toast, buttered

½ pound American cheese
2 tablespoons milk

Roll a slice of ham around 3 or 4 asparagus spears. Fasten with wooden toothpick. Broil 3 inches from heat for 6 minutes, turning once. Melt cheese over low heat, gradually stirring in milk. Serve ham rolls on toast, with cheese sauce poured over each roll. These rolls can be made ahead of time and placed on broiler tray until time for cooking. Serves 4.

Mrs. R. W. Orr, Sr. varies her "Roll-ups" with a medium white sauce to which grated Cheddar cheese has been added.

Mrs. Albert P. Brewer
Pike Road, Alabama

BAKED CHICKEN SANDWICH

2 cups cooked chicken, cut in small dice
1 cup grated Cheddar cheese
½ cup mayonnaise
12 slices trimmed bread

6 eggs
3 cups milk
¾ to 1 teaspoon salt
Almonds

Mix first three ingredients together and spread between slices of bread; place in 9" x 13" dish. Beat eggs, add milk, salt and pour over sandwiches. Let stand overnight. Bake at 350° for 50 minutes. Keep covered first 35 minutes, then remove cover, sprinkle almonds over top and continue cooking, uncovered, the remaining 15 minutes.

This does not fall into the peanut butter and jelly category, and is perhaps even a bit too glamorous to be called a sandwich. It's very, very good and since doing the day before is a strict requirement here, it's a smart girl's luncheon favorite. Serve with "Heavenly Carrots" (see Vegetables).

Mrs. Robert Allen
Livonia, Michigan

ROAST BEEF OR CORN BEEF SANDWICH

Rye bread	Roast beef or corned beef
Butter	Sauerkraut
Mustard	Swiss cheese

Warm rye bread. Butter 1 piece and spread mustard on the other piece. Place beef next to mustard side of bread, add sauerkraut and Swiss cheese. Proportion amounts to own taste. Place sandwiches in pan, cover with foil to prevent drying, bake in 250° oven 7 to 8 minutes or until cheese melts or softens.

Fix this Bavarian specialty right at home — and simply, too. Beer to drink.

Mrs. Charles Eyster, Jr.

VEGETABLE SANDWICH SPREAD

2 tomatoes	1 envelope plain gelatin
1 cup celery	¼ cup cold water
1 small onion	¼ cup boiling water
1 bell pepper	1 pint Kraft mayonnaise
1 cucumber	1 teaspoon salt

Chop all vegetables very finely and drain well on paper towels. Soften gelatin in cold water, add boiling water. Cool. Then fold in mayonnaise and salt. Add vegetables and spread on bread.

You'll seldom taste anything this good! On bread, on crackers, generously stuffed in a tomato, or by the spoonful everytime you pass the refrigerator — it gets better with every bite.

Mrs. J. Bruce Ballentine

Chapel Hill, North Carolina

ENGLISHMAN'S DELIGHT SANDWICH

4 English muffins	Sliced, fresh tomatoes
2 onions, sliced and boiled in water until tender	8 slices bacon, sauteed
	8 slices American cheese

Split muffins with fork, butter generously and toast in oven approximately 15 minutes at 300°. Remove from oven and place onions in small heaps on each muffin. On top of this put tomatoes, bacon, and cheese, in that order. Place under broiler until cheese begins to bubble. Serve open faced with salad greens. Serves 4.

Any man's delight.

Mrs. A. Julian Harris

56

SARDINE SANDWICH BAKE

12 bread slices
2 tablespoons margarine, melted
2 cups (½ pound) grated sharp
  Cheddar cheese
2 cans small sardines, drained
1 onion, minced

1 cup milk
1 teaspoon salt
½ teaspoon dry mustard
¼ teaspoon Worcestershire
⅛ teaspoon pepper
2 eggs

Heat oven to 350°. In 13" x 9" baking dish, arrange 6 bread slices. Brush bread with half of butter; sprinkle with cheese. Arrange drained sardines on cheese; sprinkle with onion and rest of butter. Cover with remaining bread. In bowl mix milk, salt, mustard, Worcestershire and pepper. Add eggs. Beat until blended and pour over sandwiches. Bake uncovered for 40 minutes, or until brown. Yields 6 servings. You may substitute sauteed and drained bacon slices for sardines and/or add tomato slices on top.

Sardines and saltines have been a thing for so long that the little fish won't recognize himself in these new surroundings. You'll be glad he made the change.

Mrs. John R. Guice

CHEESE AND HAM SPREAD

1 tablespoon finely chopped onion
3 tablespoons chili sauce
3 tablespoons drained sweet
  pickle relish

1 2¼-ounce can deviled ham
½ cup mayonnaise
2 cups (½ pound) shredded
  American cheese

Combine ingredients, blending well. Use as sandwich spread or for stuffing celery. May substitute Cheddar cheese for American. Yields 2 cups.

Another good spread for quick sandwiches or to serve with crackers.

Mrs. William S. Coles

Salads and Dressings

APRICOT CONGEALED SALAD

Salad:

1 large can whole peeled
   apricots (or 2 17-ounce cans
   apricot halves)
2 envelopes Knox gelatin
½ cup cold water

½ cup sugar
3 cups liquid (apricot juice,
   water, apricot nectar, orange
   juice, etc.)
1 lemon

Soak gelatin in cold water. Add sugar to the juice from the apricots plus enough water or other liquid to make 3 cups. Bring this mixture to a boil and pour over the softened gelatin to dissolve. Cool. Add juice and grated rind of the lemon. Add sieved or mashed apricots and congeal in a two quart dish. Makes 10-12 servings.

Dressing:

4 egg yolks
¼ cup sugar
¼ cup vinegar
Pinch salt

½ pint cream, whipped
6 or 7 large marshmallows
½ cup toasted slivered or
   crushed almonds

Beat egg yolks, sugar, vinegar and salt together in top of double boiler and cook over hot water until thick. Add marshmallows and stir to melt. Cool. Fold in whipped cream and then almonds.

The salad is good; the dressing — like ambrosia — is food for the gods! Don't make this unless you do the dressing too, for the sweet, sweet salad needs the tangy topping.

Mrs. John S. Key

MRS. GREENE'S AVOCADO SALAD

A favorite salad served at the old Lyon's Hotel.

1 3-ounce package lime gelatin
1 cup hot water
1 avocado mashed to a smooth
   pulp

1 3-ounce package cream cheese
½ cup crushed pineapple

Dissolve gelatin in hot water. Cool and let almost set. Add avocado, pineapple, and cheese and beat in mixer until fluffy and cheese dissolves. Do not overbeat. Congeal. Serves 4-6.

CONGEALED BLUEBERRY SALAD

Quite different from the usual congealed fruit salad, you'll get requests for seconds from even your most timid guests — men and women.

Salad:

2 3-ounce packages of blueberry
   gelatin (A & P brand)
2 cups boiling water

1 15-ounce can blueberries
   (drained, but reserve juice)
1 8¼-ounce can crushed pineapple
   (drained, but reserve juice)

Dissolve gelatin in boiling water. Combine juices of the blueberries and the pineapple, and if necessary add enough water to make 1 cup. Add the cup of juices to the gelatin mixture. Now stir in the drained fruit. Pour into a 2 quart flat pan and let stand in the refrigerator until firm.

Dressing:

1 8-ounce package cream cheese	½ pint sour cream
½ cup sugar	½ teaspoon vanilla
	½ cup chopped pecans

Combine softened cream cheese, sugar, sour cream and vanilla and spread over congealed gelatin. Sprinkle with the chopped nuts. Makes 10-12 servings. (Blackberry gelatin may be substituted for the blueberry.)

Mrs. James D. Moore

BING CHERRY SALAD

Salad:

2 envelopes gelatin	1 20-ounce can pineapple chunks
1 cup cold water	(reserve juice)
1 16-ounce can pitted black	¾ cup sugar
cherries (reserve juice)	½ cup lemon juice

Dissolve gelatin in cold water. Add enough water to the cherry and pineapple juices to make 2 cups. (May add ¼—½ cup sherry wine as part of 2 cups liquid). Bring this to a boil and pour over dissolved gelatin. Add sugar and lemon juice, then fruit. Mix thoroughly and pour into 2 quart shallow dish. Congeal. Serve with the following dressing:

Dressing:

½ cup heavy cream whipped	½ cup mayonnaise
1 3-ounce package cream cheese	12 large marshmallows cut up
	½ cup chopped pecans

To the whipped cream add the softened cheese beaten with the mayonnaise. Fold in marshmallows and nuts. Serves 10-12.

Mrs. James P. Smartt, Jr.

CRANBERRY SALAD

1 pound cranberries (ground)	1 6-ounce package cherry gelatin
2 oranges (ground)	4 cups hot water
¾ cup chopped pecans	1 cup sugar
4 stalks celery, diced	1 teaspoon salt
1 8¼-ounce can crushed	1 envelope unflavored gelatin
pineapple	½ cup cold water

Combine cranberries, oranges, pecans, celery and pineapple. Set aside. Dissolve cherry gelatin in hot water; add sugar and salt. Dissolve unflavored gelatin in cold water and stir in cherry gelatin mixture. Combine all ingredients and pour into two large molds or 20 to 25 individual molds. Chill until firm. Serves 25.

Mrs. Gordon Mummert

COCA COLA BING CHERRY SALAD

2 3-ounce packages black cherry gelatin
1 20-ounce can crushed pineapple
1 20-ounce can pitted black cherries
2 small Coca Colas
1 cup pecans

Drain fruit and reserve juices. Measure juices and heat to boiling to dissolve gelatin. Add as much of the 2 Cokes as needed for required liquid (4 cups total). Cool until syrupy. Cut cherries into fourths and cut pecans into large pieces. When gelatin has begun to set, stir in fruit and nuts.

Pour into oiled ring mold and congeal. When ready to serve, fill center of ring with cottage cheese.

A sophisticated salad version of a popular childhood drink, cherry coke. Good with ham or turkey.

Mrs. David E. Bowers

CHERRY SALAD

1 16-ounce can red pie cherries (reserve juice)
1 3-ounce package lemon gelatin
1 cup sugar
1 envelope gelatin
¼ cup water
1 orange
1 lemon
1 8¼-ounce can crushed pineapple
1 cup chopped pecans

Heat cherry juice and pour over the lemon gelatin and sugar. Add the package of gelatin dissolved in ¼ cup cold water, juice of one orange and the grated rind, juice of the lemon and grated rind, crushed pineapple, cherries and pecans. (A few drops of red food coloring may be added). Mix thoroughly and pour into shallow 2 quart dish and congeal. Makes 12-14 individual molds.

A colorful congealed salad that everybody likes. Top with cottage cheese if you want.

Mrs. Joseph W. Walker

CRANBERRY WINE SALAD

Serve this cranberry salad with your Christmas turkey, but don't stop there. Because it's made with canned cranberry sauce, you can have it all year 'round. Delicious and exceptionally easy too!

2 teaspoons Knox gelatin
¼ cup cold water
1 6-ounce package raspberry gelatin
¾ cup boiling water
1 16-ounce can whole berry cranberry sauce
Small 8¼-ounce can crushed pineapple
¾ cup port wine
1 orange
1 lemon
½ cup chopped pecans

Dissolve plain gelatin in cold water. Pour boiling water over this and the raspberry gelatin. Stir in cranberry sauce, crushed pineapple and wine. Combine juice of the orange and juice of the lemon plus enough liquid to make one cup. Add this juice mixture to the cranberry mixture. Add grated rind of the orange and ½ cup chopped pecans. Chill in 2 quart dish. Serves 10-12.

Mrs. James P. Smartt, Jr.

GOLDEN SALAD

1 cup hot water
1 3-ounce package orange gelatin
1 cup crushed pineapple
  (drained)

1 cup grated cheese
1 cup evaporated milk
½ cup mayonnaise

Dissolve gelatin with hot water in a bowl and cool. Add other ingredients and mix well. Pour into 9 x 9 pyrex dish. Congeal. Serves 6-8.

Unusual and easy to make.

Mrs. John C. Bragg

LANDIS' SALAD

1 3-ounce package lime gelatin
1 cup hot water
1 8¼-ounce can crushed pineapple
  (drained)

1 pint vanilla ice cream

Dissolve gelatin in hot water. Dissolve ice cream into this by adding a spoonful at a time. Stir in pineapple and refrigerate. Serves 6-8. Very easy and quick.

Vary this salad using any flavor gelatin. It is very sweet and a favorite with children.

Mrs. Robert C. McAnnally

PEACH PICKLE SALAD

1 large jar peach pickles
1 3-ounce package orange gelatin
1½ cups hot water
½ cup peach pickle juice

1 3-ounce package cream cheese
  (softened)
Ground nuts

Dissolve gelatin with hot water and juice. Cool. Remove seed from pickles. Roll cream cheese into tiny balls and roll in nuts. Stuff pickles with cheese balls and place one in each individual mold. Pour gelatin mixture over each and congeal. Serves 6.

Best made with homemade peach pickles, but still good using the canned ones. Wouldn't this be nice with baked ham, or any meat for that matter?

Mrs. Ralph Huff

LIME GELATIN WITH BANANA NUT DRESSING

A tangier layered version of the lime gelatin and cottage cheese mold with an unusual and unusually good dressing. Time consuming — yes — but worth the extra effort.

1 20-ounce can crushed pineapple
½ cup lemon juice
2 3-ounce packages lime gelatin
1 cup chopped walnuts
2 tablespoons grated lemon rind

2 cups cottage cheese
1 cup diced celery
2 teaspoons horseradish
(optional)
½ teaspoon salt

Drain pineapple juice into 4 cup measure. Add lemon juice and enough boiling water to make 3 cups liquid. Add gelatin and stir until dissolved. Chill mixture until syrupy. Spoon about 1½ cups gelatin into bowl. Fold in pineapple, nuts, lemon rind and pour into 9 x 9 x 2 inch pan. Chill until sticky on top. Keep remaining gelatin at room temperature. When layer in pan is firm, beat remaining gelatin until it is fluffy. Blend in cottage cheese, celery and salt. Spoon over layer in pan and chill until firm. Top with banana nut dressing.

Banana Nut Dressing:
½ cup mayonnaise
1 cup mashed bananas
½ cup chopped walnuts

3 tablespoons heavy cream
1 tablespoon lemon juice

Blend all the above together.

Mrs. John A. Woller

PINEAPPLE PARTY SALAD

1 20-ounce can crushed pineapple
1 3-ounce package lemon gelatin
1 3-ounce package lime gelatin
¼ teaspoon salt

1 cup cottage cheese
1 cup mayonnaise
½ cup blanched & chopped
almonds or chopped nuts

Drain syrup from pineapple. Add enough water to syrup to make 2 cups. Heat to boiling point. Dissolve lemon and lime gelatin in boiling liquid. Add salt. Cool. Fold in cottage cheese, mayonnaise, crushed pineapple and nuts. Pour into molds or 2 quart dish. Chill. Serves 10-12.

Another version of the Pineapple Party Salad uses 2 cups of cottage cheese instead of 1 cup, a whole cup of pecans instead of half a cup and has one half can (2/3 cup) of Eagle Brand condensed milk added. It is perhaps a bit creamier, and serves 12 to 16 people.

How pretty either version would be made in a ring mold and served with mayonnaise in the center and surrounded by fresh fruits — strawberries, clusters of white grapes, orange sections or slices, blueberries, and julienne fresh pineapple garnished here and there with sprigs of fresh mint.

Mrs. Harold Pilgrim, Jr.

MANDARIN ORANGE SALAD

1 3-ounce package orange gelatin
1 8¼-ounce can crushed
   pineapple
1 can mandarin oranges
2 cups liquid (juice from
   oranges, pineapple & water)

1 8-ounce package
   cream cheese
1 small package of "tiny"
   marshmallows
½ pint heavy cream, whipped

Heat the liquid and pour over gelatin. Stir until dissolved. Add softened cream cheese and marshmallows and stir to dissolve. Let cool. Stir in pineapple and oranges. Cool until syrupy. Fold in whipped cream and refrigerate in 2 quart dish. Serves 8 to 10.

A good summer congealed salad — almost like a dessert. A delightful concoction!

Mrs. James P. Smartt, Jr.

ORANGE SHERBET GELATIN

1 6-ounce package orange gelatin
2 cups boiling water
1 pint orange sherbet
1 11-ounce can mandarin
   oranges, drained

1 20-ounce can crushed pineapple
   and juice
2 large bananas

Dissolve gelatin in boiling water. Add sherbet and stir to melt. Add fruit and chill. Serves 10-12.

The sherbet gives this salad a cool, refreshing air. Top with mayonnaise and a sprig of mint.

Mrs. Harold Michelson

RED RASPBERRY SALAD

Salad:

1 6-ounce package red raspberry
   gelatin
½ envelope gelatin
2½ cups boiling water

3 small packages frozen red
   raspberries, slightly thawed,
   undrained
1 cup applesauce or 1 8¼-ounce
   can crushed pineapple

Soak gelatin in small amount cold water. Dissolve softened gelatin and raspberry gelatin in boiling water. Add raspberries and applesauce or pineapple. Congeal and serve with dressing.

Dressing:

½ pint sour cream

16 large marshmallows cut
   into small pieces

Mix sour cream and marshmallows. Let stand in refrigerator over night.

A shimmering red mold, full of raspberries, it is expensive but so good. The dressing will surprise you, for the marshmallows lose their identity when allowed to stand in the sour cream over night.

Mrs. John S. Key

65

STRAWBERRY-CRANBERRY SALAD

1 pound frozen strawberries
1 8¼-ounce can crushed
  pineapple
1 16-ounce can "whole berry"
  cranberry sauce
1 3-ounce package lemon gelatin
1½ envelopes plain gelatin
  (dissolved in ½ cup cold water)

1 6-ounce can undiluted frozen
  orange juice
Juice of two lemons
½ teaspoon salt
Drop red food coloring
1 cup red wine

Thaw and drain in colander the strawberries, pineapple, cranberry sauce. To the strained and heated juices, add lemon gelatin and dissolved plain gelatin. Add orange juice, lemon juice, salt, wine and red food coloring. Mix all ingredients and pour into ring mold or individual molds.

Dressing:

One carton sour cream (8 ounce) with 5 chopped large marshmallows folded in. Let stand 12-24 hours. Top with Poppy Seed Dressing.

Poppy Seed Dressing:

Mix ½ cup sugar, 1 small grated onion, one teaspoon dry mustard, one teaspoon salt and one teaspoon poppy seed with three tablespoons wine vinegar. In mixer slowly add one cup cooking oil beating continually, and 3 more tablespoons wine vinegar and a little drop of green food color. Serves 12-14.

Everything good in a pretty congealed salad with not one, but two scrumptious dressings.

Mrs. F. D. Peebles

LUSCIOUS STRAWBERRY SALAD

1 6 ounce package strawberry
  gelatin
1½ cups boiling water
2 packages frozen strawberries
  (10 ounce size)

1 can crushed pineapple (10
  ounce size)
1 cup dairy sour cream

Dissolve gelatin with boiling water. Add frozen strawberries immediately and mix gently. Chill until slightly congealed. Add pineapple and mix. Put ½ of gelatin mixture into lightly oiled mold. Congeal slightly. Fold sour cream into remaining gelatin mixture and pour carefully into mold and chill until set. Serves 8-10.

Mrs. Ralph Huff

FRUIT CUP SALAD AND BANANA DRESSING

Salad:

1½ cups diced pineapple
1½ cups seeded white cherries

1½ cups fresh orange sections
¼ cup chopped nuts

Arrange 3 small cup like leaves of lettuce on each salad plate. In one place pineapple, another cherries and in the third the oranges. (any other three fruits may be substituted.) Sprinkle with nuts and garnish with Banana Salad Dressing.

Dressing:

1 small banana
2 tablespoons confectioners' sugar

½ teaspoon vinegar
½ cup mayonnaise

To mashed banana add sugar and vinegar. Fold mayonnaise into this. A few tablespoons of whipped cream may be added to produce a fluffy dressing. Makes 3 servings.

Mrs. James B. Odom

FROZEN FRUIT SALAD

1 cup mayonnaise
2 3-ounce packages cream cheese
1 cup heavy cream whipped
½ cup maraschino cherries
    quartered
½ cup green maraschino cherries
    quartered

1 28-ounce can fruit cocktail
    drained
24 large marshmallows diced
Lemon juice to taste

Soften cream cheese with mayonnaise. Add other ingredients. Pour into 9 x 13 pan. Freeze. Remove from freezer a few minutes before serving. Can be frozen in a bread pan so it is easily sliced.

Delicious for ladies luncheon — colorful for Christmas brunch. Serves 10-12.

Mrs. Rex Rankin

PINK ARCTIC FROZEN FRUIT SALAD

1 8-ounce package
    cream cheese
2 tablespoons mayonnaise
2 tablespoons sugar
1 8-ounce can whole cranberry
    sauce

1 cup crushed pineapple, drained
½ cup English walnuts (or
    chopped pecans)
1 cup prepared Dream Whip

Soften the cream cheese. Blend with the mayonnaise, sugar, cranberry sauce, crushed pineapple and nuts. Fold in Dream Whip. Place paper muffin cup in muffin tins and fill with salad mixture. Freeze. When frozen they can be placed in a plastic bag and kept in freezer till ready to use. Serves 8-10.

Mrs. C. W. Belt

PARTY SALAD

Salad:
2 cups canned white cherries,
    halved and seeded
2 cups diced pineapple
2 cups fresh orange sections
¼ pound chopped almonds
2 cups chopped large
    marshmallows

Cooked Dressing:
2 eggs
2 tablespoons sugar
1¼ cups whipping cream
Juice of one lemon

Beat eggs until light and add sugar gradually, ¼ cup of the cream, and the lemon juice. Mix thoroughly and cook in double boiler until smooth and thick, stirring constantly. Remove from heat and cool; fold in remaining cup of cream which has been whipped.

Pour cooked dressing over fruit mixture and mix lightly. Put in ring mold or pyrex pan and let stand in refrigerator at least 24 hours. Serve on lettuce with homemade mayonnaise, whipped cream or any fruit salad dressing you may prefer. Serves 8-10 generously.

Mrs. E. J. Phillips

FROZEN PINEAPPLE SALAD

1 pound miniature marshmallows
1 pint whipping cream
1 cup chopped nuts

2 cups crushed pineapple
1 cup maraschino cherries

Cut nuts and cherries. Add drained pineapple and marshmallows. Fold in salad dressing. Stand in refrigerator 10 to 12 hours. Remove and fold in whipped cream. Pour into molds and freeze.

Salad Dressing:
6 tablespoons sugar
¼ cup vinegar

2 tablespoons flour
½ cup pineapple juice

Cook together until consistency of white sauce. Let cool before adding to your salad mixture. May add food coloring to mixture if desired. Serves 12-14.

Mrs. William B. Eyster

MARINATED ARTICHOKE AND MUSHROOM MOLD

1 6-ounce package lemon gelatin
1 14-ounce can plain artichoke
    hearts
2 3-ounce cans sliced
    mushrooms

1 package Italian Good Seasons
    Dressing
4 tablespoons chopped pimento

Drain artichokes and cut them in half. Drain mushrooms. Mix salad dressing according to directions on package. Add artichokes and mushrooms to Italian Dressing and marinate overnight. Dissolve gelatin in 2 cups boiling water. Add cup of cold water. Drain the marinated artichokes and mushrooms. When the gelatin has begun to congeal, slightly, add artichokes, mushrooms, and pimento. Congeal and serve with the following dressing: Serves 12-16.

Dressing: One cup homemade mayonnaise
  Blend: ¼ cup Italian Good Seasons Dressing

Mrs. G. W. Adams

CONGEALED ASPARAGUS SALAD

1 cup water	½ cup diced celery
1 cup sugar	½ cup chopped pecans
½ cup vinegar	1 small jar pimento, chopped
½ teaspoon salt	1 medium can cut asparagus
2 envelopes unflavored gelatin	Juice of one lemon
½ cup cold water	Small amount of grated onion

Boil water, sugar, vinegar and salt. Dissolve gelatin in ½ cup cold water. Combine all ingredients and place in refrigerator to congeal.

A sweet-sour salad with an interesting combination of flavors and textures. Pretty and colorful too! Good with chicken or ham.

Mrs. Dan M. Crane

CONGEALED ASPARAGUS — BOUILLON SALAD

1 envelope gelatin	Red pepper
1 can medium asparagus spears	Crumbled cooked bacon
1 can beef bouillon or	Capers
consomme	Mayonnaise
Lemon juice	

Soften gelatin in juice from asparagus. Heat to boiling the bouillon plus enough water so that total liquid (asparagus juice, bouillon and water) used is 2 cups. Pour over gelatin to dissolve. Add lemon juice and red pepper to taste — at least a whole lemon and several dashes of pepper. Arrange asparagus spears in pan or mold. Pour gelatin mixture over and congeal. Serve topped with crumbled bacon and capers topped with mayonnaise and paprika. Serves 4 to 6.

We suggest serving it with cheese souffle and ham biscuits or with Quiche Lorraine for lunch.

A word of warning: Do not be tempted to serve this salad without the capers and bacon and hopefully homemade mayonnaise. Without the accompaniments, it's very blah! With them, it's an interesting taste experience.

Mrs. William E. Shinn, Jr.

69

CUCUMBER ASPIC SALAD

1 cucumber
1 teaspoon salt
1 teaspoon white pepper
1 cup sour cream
3 tablespoons vinegar

2 tablespoons minced chives
2 tablespoons minced onion
1 envelope unflavored gelatin
1/4 cup cold water

Peel and quarter a cucumber, removing any large seed. Dice very fine or grate to make 1 cup. Add salt and pepper. Mix sour cream vinegar, chives, and onion. Soften gelatin in cold water, heat to dissolve, and add to cucumber and sour cream mixtures. Mold and chill. In bottom of each mold, place a thin slice of cucumber. Makes 6 molds.

Is there anything, on a hot summer day, quite as cool and crisp as a cucumber? Cucumber congealed salad is, and if possible is even better — and prettier. Good with chicken casseroles, chicken salad, or any summertime lunch or dinner.

Mrs. Bill Sexton

CUCUMBER ASPIC

2 envelopes Knox gelatin
2 tablespoons sugar
3/4 tablespoon salt
2/3 cup boiling water
3—4 tablespoons lemon juice
   (about 2 lemons)
2 cups cucumber chopped fine,
   seeded and drained well.

1 8-ounce package cream cheese,
   softened
1 cup mayonnaise
1/4 teaspoon minced onion
Chopped parsley (optional)

Mix gelatin, sugar, and salt. Pour boiling water over this and stir until dissolved. Add lemon juice. Add chopped and drained cucumber, mayonnaise, onion and parsley to softened cream cheese. Blend well and stir cucumber mixture into gelatin mixture. Congeal. Serves 6-8.

Mrs. Gilmer Blackburn

DILL PICKLE SALAD

2 envelopes gelatin
1 cup cold water
1 20-ounce can crushed pineapple
   (drained, but reserve juice)
1/2 cup sugar
1/4 cup vinegar

1/4 teaspoon salt
1 large jar pimento, chopped
1 large dill pickle grated (the
   kind you buy individually
   packaged)
1 cup chopped nuts

Dissolve gelatin in cup of cold water. Heat juice from pineapple, sugar, vinegar and salt. Pour over gelatin. Add pimento, pineapple, grated pickle, and chopped nuts. Mix and pour into 2 quart dish. Serves 10-12.

Whether you are fond of dill pickles or not, you'll like this sweet and tart congealed salad. We bet you won't guess what you're eating.

Mrs. John E. Wilks, Jr.

HELEN APPLETON'S BROCCOLI SALAD

2 packages chopped frozen
  broccoli
2 envelopes gelatin, unflavored
3 ounce package cream cheese
  (or more)
1 cup mayonnaise
1 can beef consomme

3 tablespoons lemon juice
1½ teaspoons salt
½ teaspoon pepper
½ teaspoon Tabasco sauce
3 tablespoons Worcestershire
1 cup chopped pimento
4 hard boiled eggs (sliced)

Cook, drain broccoli. Heat consomme and add gelatin which has been added to ¼ cup water. Cool. Mash cream cheese, mayonnaise and seasoning. Combine all ingredients except eggs and pimento. Arrange eggs and pimento in mold and pour mixture over. Congeal. Serves 10-12.

Broccoli Salad?? Indeed! This one brings rave notices from all who indulge, and would be good with any meat dish. Amazingly pretty too!

Mrs. John F. Manning

PIMENTO CHEESE SALAD

1 3-ounce package lemon gelatin
½ teaspoon salt
1 cup hot water
1 5-ounce jar pimento cheese
  spread
½ cup mayonnaise
¾ cup cold water

2 to 3 teaspoons vinegar
Dash Tabasco
½ cup chopped celery
¼ cup finely chopped onion
2 tablespoons finely chopped
  green pepper

Dissolve gelatin and salt in hot water. Add cheese spread and mayonnaise. Beat with electric mixer until smooth. Stir in cold water, vinegar and Tabasco. Chill until partially set. Add remaining ingredients. Pour into mold and refrigerate until firm. Serves 4 to 6.

From an Alabama First Lady comes this unusual recipe, which Mrs. Brewer suggests you serve with cold cuts.

Mrs. Albert P. Brewer
Pike Road, Alabama

COLE SLAW MOLD

1 cup hot water
1 3-ounce package lemon gelatin
½ cup cold water
2 tablespoons vinegar
½ cup mayonnaise
¼ teaspoon salt

Dash pepper
2 cups shredded cabbage
2 tablespoons minced green
  pepper
1 tablespoon minced onion

Pour hot water over gelatin. Dissolve; add water, vinegar, mayonnaise, salt and pepper. Beat with mixer until blended. Place in refrigerator and chill until begins to firm. Beat until fluffy. Fold in cabbage, pepper and onion. Congeal. Serves 8-10.

A glamorous version of everybody's favorite.

Mrs. William A. Sims

QUICK TOMATO ASPIC

A good and very easy tomato aspic made with tomato juice.

1 cup water
2 envelopes plain gelatin
3 cups tomato juice
1½ cups diced celery
1½ cups stuffed olives, diced
1 tablespoon grated or finely
   chopped onion

1 teaspoon sugar
Juice of 1 lemon
Dash of red pepper
1 teaspoon chili powder

Soak gelatin in water until dissolved. Heat tomato juice to boiling point and pour over gelatin. Stir until well blended. Add remaining ingredients. Stir to blend well. Place in refrigerator until congealed. Serves 12.

Mrs. Barrett C. Shelton, Jr.

TOMATO ASPIC

4 envelopes unflavored gelatin
½ cup cold water
2 1-pound cans of stewed or
   plain tomatoes
1 small bunch celery
1 small bottle stuffed olives

1 tablespoon very finely chopped
   or grated onion
1 tablespoon salt
1 scant teaspoon cayenne pepper
3 tablespoons vinegar

Dissolve gelatin in cold water, mash tomatoes to a pulp, removing any stems and hard pieces. Add finely chopped celery, thinly-sliced olives, and onion. Mix well with salt and cayenne pepper. Heat gelatin over (not in) hot water until it is completely melted; add to tomato mixture blending well. Add vinegar and stir thoroughly. Pour into a 1½ or 2 quart mold which has been rinsed with ice water. Refrigerate over night. Serves 10-12.

Really good tomato aspic is a rarity, and this one is good! It is a little more trouble than most because it begins with canned tomatoes instead of juice, but don't pass it by. Crunchy, tangy, and hot, serve it in a ring mold with cottage cheese or a bland dressing.

Mrs. Randolph Pickell

V-8 TOMATO ASPIC

4 cups V-8 juice
2 tablespoons gelatin (when
   doubling recipe, use
   additional envelope)
1 teaspoon salt
½ teaspoon paprika

½ teaspoon sugar
2 tablespoons lemon juice
3 tablespoons chopped onion
4 stalks chopped celery
2 tablespoons chopped green
   pepper

Place gelatin in ½ cup V-8 juice to soften. Heat remaining 3½ cups juice with salt, paprika, sugar, lemon juice. Dissolve gelatin in heated juice. Add onion, celery and green pepper and chill until firm.

Because this aspic is made with V-8 juice, it has a little extra umph! If you like aspic hot, add red pepper to taste.

For company, if it's still early in the month and your bank account isn't depleted, try this variation:

Add the onion, celery and green pepper to the 3½ cups of V-8 before you heat it. Cook over low heat until vegetables are quite soft. Strain, add seasonings, including red pepper to taste, and dissolve softened gelatin in it.

Pour into ring mold, and when partially congealed, drop marinated artichoke hearts into the aspic, all the way around the ring. When firm, unmold and serve with either of the following dressings in the center:

1. Mayonnaise mixed half and half with sour cream and well laced with horseradish.
2. Mayonnaise and sour cream, again mixed half and half, with curry powder to taste stirred in.

The aspic with horseradish dressing goes nicely with roast beef. The curry flavored dressing is good when you serve your aspic with shrimp, chicken or lamb.

Mrs. John F. Manning

SLAW

A good basic slaw.

½ large cabbage	2 tablespoons mayonnaise
½ large onion	1 heaping tablespoon Durkee's
2 large stalks celery	dressing
1 tablespoon sugar	1 teaspoon salt
1 heaping tablespoon Miracle	Pepper to taste
Whip Salad Dressing	½ cup milk
	2 tablespoons vinegar

Shred cabbage; chop onion and celery and mix with cabbage. Mix rest of ingredients together and pour over vegetables. Refrigerate and stir occasionally. This slaw is better made several hours ahead or the day before serving.

Mrs. John Eyster

FAVORITE SLAW

1 head cabbage sliced very thin	½ cup dill pickle vinegar
2 tomatoes (cut in bite sizes)	½ ounce salad oil
1 cucumber sliced	Salt to taste
1 onion cut fine	Paprika to taste
1 dill pickle grated	Cayenne to taste
1½ ounces vinegar	

Mix all ingredients, let stand several hours before serving.

The cucumber and dill pickle make this an unusual and tasty slaw. This recipe was made to accompany Brunswick Stew.

Mrs. Thomas A. Caddell

73

STAY CRISP SALAD

8 cups shredded cabbage
  (use knife)
2 carrots (shredded or grated)
1 green pepper cut in thin strips
½ cup chopped onion
¾ cup cold water
1 envelope unflavored gelatin

2/3 cup sugar
2/3 cup vinegar
2 teaspoons celery seed
1½ teaspoons salt
¼ teaspoon pepper
2/3 cup salad oil

Mix cabbage, carrots, green pepper and onion; sprinkle with ½ cup cold water — Chill. Soften gelatin in ¼ cup cold water. Mix sugar, vinegar, celery seed, salt and pepper in saucepan; bring to boil. Stir in softened gelatin. Cool until slightly thickened. **Beat well.** Gradually beat in salad oil. Drain vegetables; pour dressing over top. Mix lightly until well coated. May be served immediately or stored in refrigerator. Toss before serving. Serves 8.

GUARANTEED to live up to its name, this slaw brought cheers from all who tasted it. It is unusually delicious!

Mrs. Lindsay A. Allen

TURMERIC SLAW

1 small head cabbage
1 medium sized bell pepper
1 teaspoon salt
1 medium size onion

Dressing:
1 cup vinegar
1 cup sugar
1 teaspoon turmeric

Shred, grate or chop the head of cabbage; cut bell pepper into small pieces and chop onion. Mix all of this together with the teaspoon of salt.

Dressing:
Bring just to a boil the vinegar, sugar and turmeric. **After vinegar mixture is cool,** pour this mixture over cabbage. Mix all together well and chill before serving.

If turmeric is your thing, you'll like this piquant slaw with its pretty yellow color. Good with barbequed chicken or pork or with ham.

Mrs. David Bowers

AUNT SADIE'S POTATO SALAD

10 potatoes (boiled in jackets,
  peeled and sliced)
1 head cabbage — green or red
  or mixed (shredded)
1 quart jar mayonnaise or salad
  dressing
Onions — in rings (about 3)
Green peppers — in rings
  (about 3)

Hard boiled eggs — sliced
Celery seed
Salt and pepper (on
  each layer of potatoes)
Paprika — for decorating top of
  salad

Begin with layer of shredded cabbage in bowl. Add layer of sliced potatoes. Salt and pepper, and sprinkle with celery seed. Add onion rings and pepper rings (your own preference for onion and pepper will determine how much to use. Men love lots of onion!) Add sliced eggs and then spread mayonnaise over all. Be sure to use enough to cover mixture. This is the magical ingredient. Now — start all over and add as many layers as needed; ending with mayonnaise and eggs. The above amount will serve about 10. This mixture **must** be refrigerated at least 24 hours before serving.

A Decatur favorite, Aunt Sadie's Potato Salad never fails to be a crowd pleaser. Watch the men — they sometimes even go for thirds!

Mrs. Michael D. Scroggins

GERMAN POTATO SALAD

8 large potatoes (boiled, sliced ahead of time)
1 pound of bacon
2 medium onions, chopped
¾ cup brown sugar

½ cup vinegar
4 tablespoons flour
2 cups water
½ teaspoon salt

Fry bacon and onion until bacon is brown and crisp. Remove bacon from fat; add sugar to fat and stir over low heat until thick. Add vinegar and stir until sugar is dissolved. Then add flour and enough water to make thick gravy. Simmer for 30 minutes and stir frequently. Add salt and pour over potatoes. Crumble bacon and mix thoroughly. Serve warm or at room temperature. Serves 8-10.

The Germans really scored when they thought this one up!

Mrs. Joe D. Burns

POTATO SALAD

6 medium potatoes, boiled
6 boiled eggs
2 tablespoons celery seed
1 tablespoon minced onion
1 medium can mushrooms, drained

½ cup mayonnaise
Salt to taste
4 slices bacon, fried crisp, drained and crumbled.

Cool, peel and dice potatoes into small cubes. Add finely chopped boiled eggs and next five ingredients. Mix well. Refrigerate a few hours, covered, to blend flavors. Before serving, top with crumbled bacon. Serves 6.

An original version of potato salad, this is delicious, unusual, easy to make and attractive. What more could you ask?

Mrs. Billy W. Payne

ASPARAGUS VINAIGRETTE

3 tablespoons vegetable oil	3 tablespoons vinegar
4 tablespoons chopped parsley	1 teaspoon salt
2 tablespoons chopped chives	⅛ teaspoon pepper

Mix together all ingredients as listed above. Beat with rotary beater until well blended. Pour over 1½ pounds cooked and cooled asparagus (may be fresh, frozen or canned). Refrigerate several hours or overnight. Serves 6. If dried chives and parsley are used, more liquid may be needed. Can add Italian Good Seasons for more liquid.

Served in crisp lettuce cups, this is an excellent salad to accompany a hot casserole. This is said to be a favorite recipe of Jackie Kennedy Onassis.

Mrs. John R. Taylor

CORN SALAD

2 1-pound cans LeSueur corn	1 small onion, chopped
½ cup oil	1 small green pepper, chopped
¼ cup vinegar	½ small jar pimento, chopped
¼ to ½ teaspoon dry mustard	Salt and garlic salt to taste

Drain corn. Add salt and garlic salt. Let stand overnight in above mixture. Like marinated beans, this should be drained somewhat before serving.

Good with barbeque!

Mrs. Walter M. Penny

24 HOUR VEGETABLES

2 cups canned peas, drained	Salt to taste
2 small jars pimento, diced — and juice	Combine:
1 16-ounce can French style green beans and liquid	1½ cups sugar
	1 cup vinegar
1 cucumber, diced	3 teaspoons water or juice from peas
1 green pepper finely diced	1 teaspoon paprika
1 small onion finely diced	½ cup cooking oil
1 small bunch celery finely diced	1 teaspoon garlic salt

Mix vegetables and sprinkle with salt. Mix remaining ingredients and pour over vegetables. Refrigerate overnight. Drain before serving. 8-10 servings.

Crisp and colorful, this can double as a salad or cold vegetable, and looks pretty served with roast beef or chicken.

Mrs. Dalton Guthrie

VIRGINIA HARRIS' MARINATED GREEN BEANS

Marinated Beans:
2 pound can tiny whole green beans
1 cup olive or salad oil
½ cup white vinegar
2 cloves garlic cut in halves or
  thirds
½ teaspoon powdered mustard
½ teaspoon salt
1 teaspoon sugar
⅛ teaspoon Tabasco
½ teaspoon Worcestershire
⅛ teaspoon pepper

Drain liquid from beans. Combine remaining ingredients and pour over beans. Marinate overnight. Remove garlic and drain off marinade. Serve with Sour Cream Cucumber Sauce. Serves 6.

Sour Cream Cucumber Sauce

2 medium cucumbers
½ pint sour cream
¼ teaspoon salt
⅛ teaspoon pepper
⅛ teaspoon Tabasco

Peel and remove large seeds from cucumbers. Chop finely and cover with iced salt water for 10 minutes. Drain well. Fold cucumbers into sour cream with salt, pepper and Tabasco. Serve from small bowl and top with paprika or crushed red peppers.

The cool, bland cucumber sauce is a perfect contrast for the sour, spicy cold beans. The sauce is also good with seafood.

WILTED FRESH SPINACH SALAD

½ pound of fresh spinach leaves
  (stems broken off)
½ small onion (sliced — pulled
  apart to thin rings)
3 bacon slices diced
2 tablespoons of vinegar
¾ teaspoon sugar
⅛ teaspoon salt
⅓ teaspoon pepper

In salad bowl combine spinach and onions. Fry bacon until crisp, pouring fat off as it cooks. Drain bacon; add to salad bowl. Return fat to skillet; add rest of ingredients. Bring to a boil; stirring constantly. Pour over salad; toss. Serve immediately. Two servings.

A delicious change from the usual tossed salad. Even spinach haters love this and don't know it's spinach.

Mrs. Frank T. Richardson, III

GREEN WONDER SALAD — MARINATED VEGETABLES

Bean salad with an oriental flair!

1 16-ounce can early English peas
1 can Blue Lake cut green beans
1 can Chinese fancy mixed
   vegetables
1 cup chopped celery
1 bell pepper, chopped

1 onion, chopped
1 4-ounce can pimento, chopped
1 cup vinegar (white)
1 cup sugar
½ cup Wesson oil

Mix all ingredients and marinate 24 hours. Can be kept in tightly covered container several days.

Mrs. Lindsay Allen

CAESAR SALAD

2 heads romaine lettuce
1 clove of garlic
Juice of 3 lemons (at least
   3 tablespoons)
2 teaspoons Worcestershire
1 teaspoon salt
¼ teaspoon pepper

1 can anchovies, drained
¼ cup blue cheese
¼ cup Parmesan cheese
½ cup salad oil
1 raw egg
2 cups white bread croutons

Wash lettuce and drain well. Combine remaining ingredients, except croutons, in blender. Blend well and toss with lettuce and croutons. Six generous servings.

Mrs. Bruce Flake

DAY-AHEAD SALAD

Lettuce, torn or chopped
1 1-pound can LeSueur peas
1 cup chopped celery
Thinly sliced onions or chopped
   green onions

Hellman's mayonnaise
Red pepper
Parmesan cheese

Layer each ingredient in 12" x 9" dish. Repeat so that you have two layers of each ingredient. Best if made one day ahead. Serves 10 to 12.

Mrs. Gilbert J. Key
Birmingham, Alabama

WEST INDIES CRAB SALAD

1 pound lump crabmeat
1 large onion, chopped
Pepper to taste

4 ounces salad oil
4 ounces cider vinegar
4 ounces ice water

Place ½ onion in bottom of bowl. Top with crabmeat. Add rest of onion. Pour liquids over **only** in following order: Salad oil, vinegar, water. **Do not mix.** Marinate 48 hours in refrigerator. May need to drain. Mix just before serving.

"Marinate 48 hours" is the trouble here. Once you've tasted this creation, how can you possibly resist "just a little pinch" everytime you open the refrigerator? For the hostess with self discipline this is easy and wonderful.

Mrs. Lloyd Nix

CRAB LOUIS

Dressing:
1 cup salad dressing
¼ cup chili sauce
¼ cup chopped green pepper
¼ cup sliced green onions
1 teaspoon lemon juice
¼ cup heavy cream, whipped

Salad:
4 Bibb lettuce cups
1 large head iceberg lettuce, shredded
2 7½-ounce cans crabmeat, chilled
2 large tomatoes, cut into wedges
2 hard boiled eggs, sliced

Combine all the ingredients for the dressing except cream. Fold in cream and chill. To serve, arrange in the lettuce cups, the shredded lettuce, the crabmeat, tomatoes and eggs. Top with the dressing. Serves four. Extra dressing may be passed. Garnish with a little paprika.

A hearty full-meal crab salad named for some Louis or other. Pretty too!

Mrs. James D. Moore

SHRIMP SALAD ON AVOCADO RING

1 pound cooked shrimp
1 cup chopped celery
2 fresh tomatoes, peeled and diced
¼ cup chopped green pepper
2 tablespoons chopped pimento
1 tablespoon chopped green onion
½ teaspoon salt
Dash pepper
8 avocado rings, ½ inch thick

Combine first eight ingredients and mix lightly with sour cream dressing. Arrange avocado rings on crisp salad greens. Fill center of each ring with shrimp salad.

Sour Cream Dressing:
1 cup sour cream
½ cup catsup
1 tablespoon soy sauce
1 tablespoon grated onion
1 tablespoon lemon juice
2 teaspoons horseradish
1 teaspoon salt
½ teaspoon dry mustard

Blend ingredients together. Pour over shrimp salad and mix lightly. Serves 8.

Shrimp and avocado have a natural affinity for each other as Mrs. Brewer proves beautifully. A must for your list of favorites!

Mrs. Albert P. Brewer
Pike Road, Alabama

CONGEALED SHRIMP SALAD

1 3-ounce package lemon gelatin
1 cup undiluted tomato soup
1 3-ounce package cream cheese
1 cup mayonnaise

1 cup diced celery
1 medium onion, grated
1 cup English peas
1 pound cooked shrimp

Dissolve lemon gelatin in heated tomato soup. Cool slightly. Add softened cream cheese and beat with mixer at high speed until smooth. Fold in remaining ingredients and mix thoroughly. Place in mold or square pan and congeal. Serves 8.

Mrs. John E. Wilks, Jr.

VERMICELLI SALAD

1 12-ounce pkg. vermicelli
  (spaghetti)
5 hard boiled eggs (chopped)
5 stalks celery (chopped)
6 good sized sweet pickles
  (chopped)

Paprika and salt to taste
$\frac{1}{4}$ small onion (chopped fine)
$1\frac{1}{2}$ cups mayonnaise
1 pound shrimp and crab

Break vermicelli in half and boil as directed on package. Drain thoroughly in colander and run under cold water well to prevent sticking. When cooled, add ingredients and mix well. Refrigerate. Add shrimp and crab and toss. Sprinkle with paprika. Serves 10-12.

An extremely simple salad that brought raves at a tasting luncheon.

Mrs. Jimmy E. Brown

CONGEALED TUNA FISH

1 envelope gelatin, softened in $\frac{1}{4}$
  cup cold water
$\frac{1}{4}$ cup hot water, poured over
  gelatin
2/3 cup mayonnaise
2 teaspoons prepared mustard
2 tablespoons lemon juice

1 7-ounce can tuna fish
  (drained, washed and mashed)
$\frac{3}{4}$ cup chopped celery
1 cup canned English peas
2 tablespoons minced pimento
1 teaspoon salt
1 hard boiled egg, chopped
  (optional)

Combine mayonnaise, mustard and lemon juice. Add this to the dissolved gelatin. Mix tuna, celery, peas, pimento, salt and boiled egg together. Combine the two mixtures and pour into mold that has been rinsed with cold water.

Mrs. George L. McCrary, Jr.

MARIE'S CRABMEAT AND BEANSPROUT SALAD

1 cup mayonnaise
4 tablespoons soy sauce
2 tablespoons lemon juice
3 tablespoons mild curry powder
1 pound can beansprouts
1 pound crabmeat
1 cup celery, diced

3 tablespoons green onions, chopped
½ cup toasted slivered almonds
Salt to taste
Pepper to taste
Lettuce
Paprika (sprinkle)

Mix mayonnaise, soy sauce, lemon juice, and curry powder and refrigerate overnight. Mix crabmeat, beansprouts, celery, green onions and almonds. Mix salad and dressing together and add salt and pepper to taste. Arrange on lettuce leaves and garnish with a sprinkle of paprika. Serves 8.

A curried crabmeat salad with several unusual additions. When a man with a preference for bland foods asks for seconds of this not-at-all-bland salad, you know it's good.

Mrs. William A. Sims

PRESSED CHICKEN

1 fryer — 3 pounds
2 cups or 1-10-ounce package cooked frozen green peas
2 cups finely chopped celery
1 cup minced onion

4 tablespoons chopped sweet pickle
1 cup Miracle Whip Salad Dressing
3 tablespoons Knox unflavored gelatin (dissolved in 6 tablespoons chicken broth)

Boil chicken and remove meat from the bones. Cut into small pieces. Cook frozen peas according to directions on package. Drain. Mix all ingredients together. Pour into 8" x 11" flat glass pyrex dish and chill. Cut in squares. Serve on lettuce. Serves 12.

A cool congealed chicken and vegetable salad, reminiscent of days gone by. Before air conditioning, pressed chicken was one of the few things that heat-stifled appetites could handle.

Mrs. Ben Stevens

CHICKEN SALAD

For a basic chicken salad mix one cup chopped celery to every 2 cups of chopped cooked chicken. Add homemade mayonnaise to make a moist salad and season to taste with salt and white pepper. A dash of cayenne pepper and lemon juice may be added for more seasoning.

Cook your chicken with celery, carrots and onions. You'll be amazed at the difference it will make.

Use your imagination when it comes to garnish: capers, hard boiled eggs, or toasted nuts are a few of our ideas.

Mrs. John S. Key

PARTY CHICKEN SALAD

4 cups cubed cooked chicken
  breasts
1 cup chopped celery
1 cup halved seedless green grapes
1 package slivered almonds, toasted

1 teaspoon salt
¼ teaspoon pepper
¾ cup mayonnaise
¼ cup sour cream

Combine ingredients and add mayonnaise and sour cream. Mix thoroughly and chill. Serves 10-12.

The very best chicken salad imaginable! Serve in cold crisp lettuce cups or stuff in a chilled and peeled ripe red tomato, if homegrown ones are available. For a really spectacular spring or summer luncheon, cut whole pineapple (including leaves) in half lengthwise, remove hard core, and top each half with a generous serving of chicken salad.

Mrs. James P. Smartt, Jr.

GILLAM'S SALAD DRESSING

1 10½-11-ounce can condensed
  tomato soup
¾ cup cider vinegar
1½ teaspoons salt
½ teaspoon paprika
1 tablespoon Worcestershire
  sauce

½ teaspoon black pepper
1/3-½ cup sugar
1 teaspoon minced onion (can use
  dehydrated)
1 teaspoon prepared mustard
1½ cups salad oil
1 peeled clove of garlic

Make a paste of mustard, Worcestershire, salt, pepper and paprika. Stir in tomato soup. Add other ingredients. Drop clove of garlic into mixture. Shake and store for 24 hours in a dark cabinet. Makes 1 quart.

Mrs. William H. Nabors

HONEY FRENCH DRESSING

1 lemon
1 cup Wesson Oil
2 cups sugar
1¾ cups catsup

2/3 teaspoon salt
1 cup white vinegar
1 onion grated (optional)

Beat all ingredients in electric mixer for 5 minutes. Can be made in blender (and don't have to grate onion). Yield: 2 pints.

A sweet French dressing. Good on fruit as well as on lettuce or a tossed salad.

Mrs. William G. Stone, Jr.

ITALIAN SALAD DRESSING

1½ cups Wesson Oil
½ cup vinegar
¼ cup sugar
½ cup tomato catsup

¾ teaspoon salt
Clove of garlic
Paprika

Mix all ingredients except clove of garlic together in a bowl and beat well with egg beater. Keep in a glass jar in the refrigerator (leave garlic clove in the jar). This is better after a day or two.

This is excellent for salads of all kinds. It is also good to marinate shrimp, tomato, avocado, and artichokes. Marinate only 15-30 minutes. If left too long they become soggy.

Mrs. James P. Smartt, Jr.

HITCHING POST SALAD DRESSING

1 cup grated hard boiled eggs
1 cup chopped parsley
1 cup chopped pecans

1 cup olive or Wesson Oil
1 cup tomato catsup
1 cup tiny pickled onions

Mix and let stand overnight. Serve on lettuce wedges or with grapefruit sections.

Mrs. Frank T. Richardson, Jr.

THOUSAND ISLAND DRESSING

1 cup catsup
1 tablespoon ground sweet pickle
1 tablespoon pickle relish
Dash Tabasco
1 clove of garlic
3 tablespoons grated cheese

1 tablespoon sugar
2 tablespoons chili sauce
2 tablespoons salad dressing
½ cup red wine vinegar
1 boiled egg, grated

Mix all ingredients; chill.

An unusual 1000 Island Dressing. Delicious on a head of lettuce.

Mrs. Ralph Huff

KUM-BAC SALAD DRESSING

½ cup oil
1 teaspoon black pepper
1 tablespoon salt
2 cups mayonnaise
¾ cup chili sauce and catsup
   mixed
1 clove of garlic, grated

1 teaspoon Worcestershire
1 teaspoon prepared mustard
Juice of one lemon
2 tablespoons of water
1 small onion grated (very fine)
1 dash of Tabasco
1 dash of paprika

Mix all ingredients well and store in refrigerator.

A good tart dressing which improves with age. Especially good on chef's salad or shrimp.

Mrs. James B. Odom

RUSSIAN DRESSING

1 cup mayonnaise
½ cup catsup
½ cup chili sauce
½ pimento, minced
1 tablespoon minced parsley
2 tablespoons chopped chives

1 hard cooked egg, chopped
1 tablespoon lemon juice
2 tablespoons Caviar
Salt
Dash cayenne pepper
Paprika

Mix all ingredients together. Chill. Serve with salads, seafood, avocado or on plain lettuce. Yield: 1 pint.

Mrs. William S. Coles

FAVORITE SALAD DRESSING

1 teaspoon salt
½ teaspoon pepper
1 teaspoon dry mustard
¾ cup salad oil
½ teaspoon basil leaves

¼ cup wine vinegar
1 teaspoon lemon juice
1 medium red onion sliced into
  rings

Mix all ingredients. Put into jar and shake. Chill. Makes 2½ cups.

A very unusual dressing. Serve on lettuce, fresh spinach or any mixed greens.

Mrs. Lindsay A. Allen

CREAMY ROQUEFORT DRESSING

1 pint sour cream
1 3-ounce Philadelphia cream
  cheese
2 tablespoons mayonnaise
1 tablespoon Worcestershire

Salt and pepper to taste
Dash of Accent
Small piece of Roquefort
¼ cup milk or more.

Combine all ingredients in blender.

Mrs. William A. Sims

ROQUEFORT OR BLUE CHEESE DRESSING

1¼-ounce package of Roquefort
  or blue cheese
½ pint commercial sour cream
½ teaspoon garlic salt
½ teaspoon minced onion (dried)
¼ teaspoon celery salt
1 teaspoon parsley flakes

Dash of black pepper
Juice of ½ lemon
1 teaspoon vinegar
2 teaspoons Wesson Oil
1 tablespoon Worcestershire
1 tablespoon water

Crumble cheese. Add above ingredients and mix. Thin to desired consistency by adding the tablespoon of water (more or less as desired). Chill well before serving.

Mrs. James Hurst

84

BAY'S RED ROQUEFORT

½ cup brown sugar
½ cup vinegar
1 cup salad oil
½ cup catsup
½ teaspoon garlic powder
  (or 1 clove of garlic, crushed)
¾ tablespoon onion juice

Juice of ½ lemon
½ teaspoon salt
¼ teaspoon pepper
½ cup water
Package of Roquefort cheese,
  crumbled

Mix all together (do not blend in blender) and allow to stand at least 3 hours with Roquefort in it. Will store for 3 months in refrigerator.

Mrs. William A. Sims

GRANDMOTHER'S CREAMY SALAD DRESSING

1 cup mayonnaise
½ cup sugar

¼ cup vinegar

Place all ingredients in mixer or blender and mix until smooth. Pour into covered jar and refrigerate. Keeps indefinitely.

This dressing is exceptionally good on chopped cabbage and Waldorf Salad.

Mrs. John R. Taylor

FLUFFY HONEY DRESSING

2 eggs
½ cup honey
¼ cup lemon juice
2 tablespoons frozen orange juice
  concentrate

⅛ teaspoon salt
½ cup heavy cream, whipped
2 teaspoons grated lemon peel

Beat eggs, stir in honey, lemon juice, orange juice and salt. Cook over low heat until thickened. Cool. Fold in whipped cream and lemon peel. Serve with fresh fruit. Makes 2 cups.

Mrs. Thomas A. Caddell

PINEAPPLE SALAD DRESSING

1 cup pineapple juice
1 lemon
½ cup sugar

2 tablespoons flour
2 eggs
1 cup heavy cream, whipped

Beat eggs; add sugar and flour. Heat pineapple juice and pour over the mixture. Cook in double boiler until very thick. Chill; fold in whipped cream when ready to serve.

Delicious on fresh fruit salad.

Mrs. James P. Smartt, Jr.

POPPY SEED DRESSING

¾ cup sugar
1 teaspoon dry mustard
1 teaspoon salt
1/3 cup vinegar

1½ tablespoons onion juice
1 cup salad oil
1½ tablespoons poppy seeds

Mix sugar, mustard, salt and vinegar. Add onion juice and stir thoroughly. Add oil slowly, beating constantly and continue to beat until thick. Add poppy seeds and beat for a few more minutes. Store in refrigerator. Makes 3½ cups.

It is easier to make with electric mixer or blender at medium speed. If the dressing separates, pour off clear part. Start over by slowly adding clear mixture to poppy seed mixture.

Delicious with fresh fruits, melons, pineapple, bananas, etc.

Mrs. Lynn Fowler

FRUIT SALAD DRESSING

1 teaspoon celery seed
1 teaspoon grated onion
1 teaspoon paprika
1 teaspoon salt

1 teaspoon dry mustard
1/3 cup sugar
¼ cup vinegar
1 cup cold Wesson Oil

Mix dry ingredients with 1 tablespoon of vinegar. To this mixture, add remainder of vinegar and oil alternately while beating with rotary egg beater. Refrigerate. Let stand 24 hours. Serves 8.

Good on any fruit or frozen salad.

Mrs. Norman Harris, Jr.

COOKED SALAD DRESSING

¼ teaspoon salt
1 teaspoon dry mustard
3 tablespoons sugar
2 tablespoons flour

1 egg
¾ cup milk
2 tablespoons butter
¼ cup vinegar

Mix salt, mustard, sugar and flour together in top of double boiler. Beat in the egg. Stir in milk and add butter. Cook over boiling water stirring constantly until thick. Then add vinegar. May have to beat with egg beater to remove lumps.

This is a handy dressing to make and keep in refrigerator (will keep for ages). It's excellent for slaw, chicken salad (mix half and half with mayonnaise) and other salads. It's less fattening and sweeter than mayonnaise. I've even mixed it with prepared mustard for an emergency sauce for broccoli.

Mrs. William E. Shinn, Jr.

MAYONNAISE (BLENDER RECIPE)

1 egg (whole)
1 scant teaspoon dry mustard
1 teaspoon salt
Dash of red pepper

½ teaspoon sugar
1¼ cups salad oil
3 tablespoons lemon juice

Put in blender the egg, mustard, salt ,red pepper, sugar and ¼ cup salad oil. Cover and blend until thoroughly combined. Remove cover and with blender still running, add slowly ½ cup salad oil and the lemon juice. Blend about a minute longer, then slowly add ½ cup salad oil. Blend until thickened. Use spatula to scrape down sides of blender.

Blender mayonnaise is much more stable than the hand-mixed type. This one is quite tart.

Mrs. A. Julian Harris

ANN ANDERSON'S BASIC MAYONNAISE

1 egg
2 tablespoons cider vinegar
¾ teaspoon salt

½ teaspoon dry mustard
Dash white pepper
1 cup Mazola

In blender combine all ingredients except oil. Blend at high speed for 5 seconds. Add ¼ cup oil and beat at low speed 5 seconds. Remove cover, turn blender to high and add rest of oil in a steady stream in a matter of 20 seconds. Makes 1 1/3 cups.

NOTES

Cheese and Eggs

CHILES RELLENO CASSEROLE

2 4-ounce cans Ortega green
   chiles
Strips of sharp Cheddar cheese
2 eggs, slightly beaten

½ cup flour
2 cups milk
½ to ¾ pound cheese, grated

Slit one side of chiles, remove seeds and rinse. Place thick strips of sharp cheese inside chilies. Place in buttered pan. Do not layer. Mix eggs, flour and milk; pour over the rolled peppers. Add much grated cheese to top. Bake at 350° for 55 minutes. Serves 4 adults.

Brighten your menu with a touch of Mexico. Good with tacos or toastados.

Mrs. Harold Pilgrim, Jr.

MACARONI AND CHEESE

1 cup cooked macaroni
½ cup grated sharp Cheddar
   cheese
½ cup grated onion
2 eggs, beaten

1½ cups milk
¼ cup butter
½ cup (or less) bell pepper,
   chopped
¼ cup chopped pimento

Mix all ingredients. Pour into a buttered 10" x 10" casserole. Bake at 325° for 30 to 40 minutes.

Easy, economical and an everybody pleaser — this one made a bit special with bell pepper and pimento. The perfect answer when you've forgotten to take the meat out of the freezer (and also happen to be out of tuna fish).

Mrs. John S. Key

SPAGHETTI AND CHEESE

12 ounces spaghetti
1 cup milk
1 egg
2 teaspoons butter

8 ounces sharp cheese, grated
½ teaspoon salt
Dash of pepper

Put spaghetti into rapidly boiling, salted water. Bring back to rapid boil. Cook, stirring constantly, for 3 minutes. Cover with tight fitting lid, remove from heat, and let stand for 10 minutes. Rinse with hot water and drain. Combine milk and egg. In greased, oblong baking dish, place alternating layers of spaghetti, dots of butter, cheese, salt, pepper and milk-egg mixture. Bake 30 minutes at 350°. Serves 6.

Mrs. Jimmy E. Brown

MACARONI MOUSSE WITH MUSHROOM SAUCE

1 cup macaroni, broken into
  2-inch pieces
1½ cups scalded milk
1 cup soft bread crumbs
¼ cup butter or margarine, melted
1 pimento, chopped
1 tablespoon parsley, chopped

1 tablespoon onion, chopped
1½ cups cheese, grated
½ teaspoon salt
⅛ teaspoon pepper
Dash of paprika
3 eggs, beaten

Cook the macaroni in boiling, salted water; Rinse in cold water and drain. Pour the scalded milk over the bread crumbs, add the butter, pimento, parsley, onion, grated cheese and seasonings. Then add the well beaten eggs and macaroni. Pour into a thickly buttered loaf pan (or ring salad mold if desired). Bake about 50 minutes at 300° or until the loaf is firm and will hold its shape when turned out on a platter. Serve with "Mushroom Sauce":

Mushroom Sauce:

1 tablespoon butter or margarine
4 tablespoons flour
¼ teaspoon salt
⅛ teaspoon pepper

Dash of paprika
1½ cups milk
½ cup reserved mushroom liquid
1 4-ounce can mushroom pieces

In a double boiler over boiling water, melt butter; add flour and seasonings. Combine milk and mushroom liquid and gradually add to sauce, stirring constantly until sauce thickens. When thick, add the mushroom pieces. This mousse serves 8 to 12.

From the owner of King's Inn, Highlands, North Carolina, renowned for its good food, comes this recipe for a sauced mousse — a pretty accompaniment to most meats, hot or cold.

Mrs. Barrett Shelton, Jr.

QUICK CHEESE FONDUE

2 cans Cheddar cheese soup
1 tablespoon Worcestershire

1/3 cup Kirsch

Heat ingredients until soup is completely melted and serve hot in fondue dish. Serve with bread cubes, celery sticks and hot dogs, wrapped and cooked in crescent roll dough.

Fondue "economique"!

Mrs. George M. Douthit

CHEESE FONDUE

1½ cups Sauterne (white wine)
½ clove garlic, finely chopped
2 pounds natural Swiss cheese,
  grated (may use Gruyere or
  Emmentaler or both)

1 tablespoon cornstarch
3 tablespoons Kirsch
2 teaspoons butter
½ teaspoon dry mustard
Dash of nutmeg

Rub pan (one that allows little sticking) with crushed garlic clove. Heat wine until warm in pan. Add chopped garlic. Add grated cheese slowly, stirring constantly. When this mixture begins to bubble, add cornstarch which has been mixed with Kirsch. Add butter, mustard and nutmeg. When thick, remove from stove and put over alcohol flame in chafing dish. Serve with hard bread which has been cut into bite-sized pieces so that each piece has a partial crust.

A chalet is not required to entertain the Swiss way. You'll need only cheese, wine, a fondue pot (pottery is preferable for the cheese fondue) and several game friends. Have a fun, late supper with a cold, crisp green salad and a beautiful white wine; or serve the fondue in front of a roaring fire for a late evening snack. "Bon appetit!"

Mrs. William G. Stone, Jr.

CARBONARE

1 pound linguini
5 large eggs
1 to 1¼ cups Parmesan cheese

2/3 pound bacon, sauteed and
  broken into small pieces
½ bunch parsley
6 green onions, minced

Cook linguini according to directions. Do not overcook. Beat eggs in bottom of deep, large bowl which has been warmed by rinsing in hot water. Add Parmesan cheese and mix well. Very quickly add the linguini to egg mixture and stir rapidly to avoid cooking the eggs (noodles will be coated with egg mixture). Add bacon, parsley, green onions and stir. Serve immediately to 4 people.

When the impromptu hospitality urge strikes try this exceptionally tasty pasta. Too, "Carbonare" lends itself well to variations, depending upon what you do have on hand. Some saute a large chopped onion in the bacon drippings, mix in ¼ to ½ cup cream, a few dried red pepper flakes, and pour the bacon dripping-cream mixture over the linguini just before tossing (omitting the parsley and green onions). Some also declare that it's not made properly without a liberal sprinkling of freshly ground black pepper. We leave the making up to your creative genius!

Mrs. A. Julian Harris

MRS. GEORGIA MILLER'S CREOLE EGGS

½ cup butter	Worcestershire, to taste
3 tablespoons flour	Salt and pepper, to taste
2 cups milk	10 hard-boiled eggs, chopped

Make rich cream sauce with butter, flour and milk. Season with Worcestershire, salt and pepper. Add chopped eggs and set aside.

Creole Dressing:

3 bell peppers, seeds removed	Bay leaf
3 onions	Salt and pepper, to taste
½ cup butter	Cayenne pepper, to taste
2 tablespoons flour	Buttered cracker crumbs
1 29 ounce can tomatoes	

Grind peppers and onion; put in skillet with butter and cook until tender. Add flour and stir. Add tomatoes, bay leaf and seasonings to taste. Cook until thick. In a greased baking dish, alternate layers of the creole dressing and creamed eggs. Top with buttered cracker crumbs and bake at 350° until well heated and browned, approximately 20 minutes.

Creole Eggs was a popular item in Decatur years ago and has recently been rediscovered by the younger set of cooks. A really good brunch dish with hot fruit casserole and ham.

Mrs. Charles Eyster, Jr.

EGGS SUE KING

1 dozen hard-boiled eggs, sliced	1 to 1½ cups bread crumbs

In top of double boiler, make rich white sauce of:

8 tablespoons margarine	½ teaspoon white pepper
6 tablespoons flour	Dash of red pepper
2 teaspoons salt	2¾ cups milk

Alternate layers of eggs, white sauce, and bread crumbs in buttered, oblong baking dish. Bake uncovered at 300° until bubbly and slightly browned. Serves 8 people.

Expecting weekend guests? Make this good egg dish the day before and refrigerate to heat for breakfast or brunch. Accompany with link sausage, biscuits and sweet rolls.

Mrs. A. Julian Harris

BRUNCH CASSEROLE

2 cups croutons
1 cup shredded cheese, natural
  or sharp
4 eggs, slightly beaten
2 cups milk
½ teaspoon salt

½ teaspoon prepared mustard
½ teaspoon onion powder
Dash of pepper
4 slices bacon, crisped, drained
  and crumbled

Preheat oven to 325°. In bottom of a greased 10" x 6" baking dish, combine croutons and shredded cheese. Combine eggs, milk, salt, mustard, onion powder and pepper. Mix until blended. Pour over crouton mixture. Sprinkle bacon over top of casserole. Bake 55 to 60 minutes or until eggs are set. Garnish with bacon curls if desired. Serves 6 amply if served with other dishes. Serves 4 generously, otherwise.

For an after-the-ballgame supper, or Saturday morning brunch, or even for Christmas morning breakfast — serve with fresh fruit, hot rolls or sweet rolls, and lots of hot coffee.

Mrs. Jack F. McLaughlin
Mrs. Barrett Shelton, Jr.

QUICHE LORRAINE

Pastry for 1 pie shell
6 slices bacon
½ cup sliced onion
¼ pound natural Swiss cheese,
  diced
4 eggs, beaten

1 cup milk
1 cup heavy cream
1 teaspoon salt
⅛ teaspoon pepper
⅛ to ¼ teaspoon nutmeg

Heat oven to 450°. Roll out pastry to 12' circle and fit into 9" pie pan. Make a high collar and flute it. Cover inside of shell with waxed paper, fill shell with rice or dried beans. Bake for 10 minutes. Remove rice or beans and paper and allow to cool.

Fry bacon until crisp; drain and crumble. Saute onion in 1 tablespoon bacon fat until transparent. Put diced cheese, crumbled bacon, and onion in pastry shell. Combine eggs, milk, cream, salt, pepper and nutmeg. Pour into shell. Bake 15 minutes at 450°. Reduce oven to 350°; bake 10 to 15 minutes longer until knife inserted halfway between center and edge comes out clean. Let stand 10 to 15 minutes before cutting into 6 or 8 pieces.

The French cheese and onion pie that is an excellent luncheon dish. How about a pretty fresh fruit salad to accompany this. For entertaining, you can have it all done except for pouring the custard into the pie shell and baking.

Mrs. William E. Shinn, Jr.

CHEESE AND RICE SOUFFLE WITH SHRIMP SAUCE

1 cup cooked rice
2 tablespoons butter
3 tablespoons flour
¾ cup milk
½ pound sharp Cheddar cheese

4 slightly beaten egg yolks
½ teaspoon salt
Dash cayenne pepper
4 egg whites, stiffly beaten

One hour before serving, heat oven to 325°. Cook rice. Melt butter and stir in flour until smooth. Slowly add milk, stirring constantly, and cook until thickened. Slice cheese and cook until melted and smooth. Stir in egg yolks, salt and pepper. Remove from heat, fold in cooked rice. Put into large bowl and fold in egg whites. Turn mixture into greased 1½ quart souffle dish. Bake uncovered for 40 minutes. Serve at once with shrimp sauce.

Shrimp sauce:
3 tablespoons butter
3 tablespoons flour

1 teaspoon Lawry's seasoned salt
1½ cups milk
1 pound cooked shrimp

In saucepan melt butter and stir in flour and salt until smooth. Slowly add milk, stirring constantly until smooth and thick. Stir cooked, cleaned shrimp into mixture. (Shrimp may be split lengthwise if desired.) Serve hot from sauce boat over cheese and rice souffle.

A no-fail cheese souffle served interestingly with a sauce of creamed shrimp. Beginners, take note! We guarantee success and your guests will declare you've been cooking for years.

Mrs. Norman Self

CHEESE SOUFFLE

¼ cup butter
¼ cup flour
1 cup milk

1 cup grated Cheddar cheese
3 eggs, separated
1 teaspoon salt
½ teaspoon cayenne pepper

Preheat oven to 300°. In saucepan melt butter, add flour and cook slightly. Remove from heat; gradually add milk, stirring constantly. Return to heat and cook until thickened. Add cheese. Let cool. Add beaten egg yolks, salt and pepper. Beat egg whites until stiff, but not dry. Carefully fold whites into cheese mixture. Pour into greased casserole and place casserole in pan of boiling water in oven. Bake at 325° for 30-45 minutes or until firm. Serves 4 to 6.

You really can, you know — make the prettiest and most versatile of cheese dishes, and you needn't even hold your breath. It really works! (Just be ready to serve as soon as the souffle comes out of the oven.) And what a marvel it is: for lunch with hot Smithfield ham biscuits and a cold vegetable salad; for supper with boiled shrimp or crab; or even for brunch underneath creamed chicken full of water chestnuts and toasted almonds.

To make a pretty "high hat," with a rubber spatula make an indentation about 1½ inches deep all around the top about an inch from the edge of the dish — just before cooking the souffle.

Mrs. William Sexton

MAKE-AHEAD CHEESE SOUFFLE

4 eggs
2 cups milk
1 teaspoon dry mustard, optional
1 teaspoon salt

½ pound sharp
   Cheddar cheese, grated
5 slices bread, cubed

Grease casserole. Blend together first five ingredients. Pour over bread cubes in casserole and refrigerate at least one hour or overnight. Place casserole in shallow pan of water. Bake for 1 hour in preheated 350° oven. Serves 6.

Doesn't this sound like a good thing to know? Sometimes called "cheese strata" — we've also heard "cheese pudding" — it tastes great no matter what the name, and really gets puffier and better the longer it's refrigerated prior to baking. Why not make one now? You know you have the ingredients.

Mrs. Harold Pilgrim, Jr.

GARLIC CHEESE GRITS

1 cup quick grits
1 teaspoon salt
4 cups water
1 roll garlic cheese, cut up

½ cup butter
½ cup milk
2 eggs, beaten
Grated Cheddar cheese

Cook grits slowly in 4 cups salted water. Add cheese and butter. Stir in milk and eggs; mix well. Pour into greased casserole and bake at 350° for 40 minutes. Remove from oven, top with grated cheese and cook an additional 5 minutes. Yields 8 to 10 servings.

A great way to introduce Yankees to grits.

Mrs. Richard Rouquie
Bluefield, West Virginia

CHEESE GRITS SOUFFLE

1 cup quick grits
4 cups water
1 teaspoon salt
¼ cup butter

3 tablespoons flour
3 teaspoons dry mustard
3 eggs, separated
2 cups grated sharp cheese

Preheat oven to 350°. Cook grits in 4 cups boiling salted water. In 1½ quart double boiler melt butter. Blend in flour and mustard. Add egg yolks, butter mixture and 1¾ cups cheese to cooked grits. Fold in stiffly beaten egg whites. Put in buttered 1½ or 2 quart casserole and bake 30 to 40 minutes. During the last 5 minutes, sprinkle the top with the remainder of the cheese. Serves 8.

An excellent and very cheesy cheese souffle with the added substance and texture of grits.

Mrs. Robert T. McWhorter, Jr.

Meats

LAMB LOUISE

1 boned leg of lamb (about 6 pounds—reserve bones—butcher will bone it for you)	1 teaspoon garlic powder
	1 teaspoon Accent
	1 teaspoon salt
	1 teaspoon cayenne pepper
¼ pound butter, room temperature	Fresh chopped parsley
	Gravy—See following recipe

Day before you plan to serve, cut off most of fat with sharp knife. Cream together butter, garlic powder, Accent, salt and pepper and spread over roast, inside and out. On double thickness of aluminum foil, place the bones with the lamb roast on top. Wrap tightly and refrigerate overnight. On following day, remove from refrigerator 2 hours before time to roast. Do not unwrap. Bake, wrapped, in shallow roasting pan in 375° oven, allowing 35 minutes per pound for medium or 45 minutes per pound for well done. Thirty minutes before roast is done, remove from oven. Unwrap carefully and strain juices into saucepan. Turn oven up to 400°, discard bones, place roast in open aluminum foil in the pan and return to oven to brown for 30 minutes. Make gravy.

When ready to serve lamb, (let stand on hot platter for at least 15 minutes before serving) sprinkle with chopped parsley.

Gravy For Lamb Louise:	1 teaspoon cornstarch
1 cup sour cream	3 tablespoons water
¾ teaspoon saffron	1 bottle capers, drained

To the strained juices from the roast, add the sour cream and saffron. Bring to boil stirring constantly. Mix cornstarch and water, add to juice mixture and boil gently for about 4 minutes. Add drained capers and cook for a minute more, then reduce to lowest possible heat and cover gravy until ready to serve. Pour into warmed gravy boat and sprinkle with paprika.

A tender, juicy, delicious lamb roast, with its own unusual gravy that even sworn lamb haters will like. Lamb Louise is a good company entree because it requires little last minute work, and is no carving problem since it is boned. Serve with poppy seed noodles. (See Vegetable and Accompaniments Section).

NOTE: Saffron is difficult to find, and quite expensive even when you do. The gravy is almost as good without the saffron, although the presence or absence really makes two different dishes.

Mrs. William E. Shinn, Jr.

LEG OF LAMB ROAST

Rub lamb with garlic, flour, salt and pepper. Brown in 500° oven for about 20 minutes. Reduce heat to 350° and cook, uncovered, about 15 minutes per pound for medium-rare.

Roast leg of lamb is an Englishman's delight. To please him—and **your** man, if he likes lamb . . . serve with potatoes roasted around the leg (pare potatoes and parboil for 5 minutes or so and arrange around roast while it cooks), fresh or frozen green peas (but not canned ones!) and mint jelly, or better yet, fresh mint sauce.

To make mint sauce: Mix about 1/3 to ½ cup very finely chopped fresh mint leaves with a cup of vinegar and as much sugar as will dissolve in the vinegar. The sauce needs to be made at least an hour before you serve it. It will keep in refrigerator indefinitely, and gets better as the days go by.

Mrs. Robert G. McNelly

BARBECUED LAMB CHOPS

4 to 8 lamb chops
2 tablespoons butter
Juice from ½ lemon
Sauce:
  3 tablespoons vinegar
  1½ teaspoons dry mustard
  3 tablespoons molasses

3 tablespoons wine (cooking
  or Burgundy)
Dash cayenne pepper
Dash salt
⅛ teaspoon garlic powder
⅛ teaspoon basil

Mix mustard with a little of the vinegar until smooth; add other ingredients. Broil lamb chops over grill or in oven, brushing with butter and lemon juice. Baste with heated sauce. Basting sauce should not be used until near the end of cooking time so chops will not burn. Serve drippings and remaining sauce over chops.

Mouthwatering cooked inside or out. A really good way to cook Spring lamb, and perfect if you suspect the lamb was approaching adolescence, for the sauce removes even a hint of the stronger mutton taste.

Mrs. Herbert Street

VEAL a la MADELON

1 clove garlic, minced
½ cup butter
2 pounds boneless veal, in bite
  sized pieces
2 tablespoons flour

1 teaspoon salt
¼ teaspoon pepper
2 1-inch wide strips lemon peel
1 cup boiling water
1 cup heavy cream

Saute garlic in hot butter in heavy skillet. Remove garlic and brown veal in butter. Sprinkle flour, salt and pepper over meat. Brown again. Add lemon peel and water. Cover. Simmer about 1 hour until tender. Remove lemon peel. Stir in cream; heat, and serve over hot buttered new potatoes.

A gourmet's delight is Veal a la Madelon: the subtle flavor of veal, a hint of garlic, and served, interestingly, over boiled new potatoes. Add a bright green vegetable . . . broccoli or spinach perhaps . . . and a fresh fruit salad, for color.

Mrs. Frank T. Richardson, III

VEAL SCALLOPINI

2 pounds veal
1 tablespoon fat
1 tablespoon chopped onion
1½ cups fresh parsley
½ teaspoon paprika
½ teaspoon dry mustard
¼ teaspoon black pepper
½ cup (small can) mushrooms
 with liquid or 1 box fresh
 mushrooms, cut in pieces and
 sauteed in butter

2 teaspoons or 2 cubes beef
 bouillon
2 cups water
1 tablespoon flour, dissolved
 in water
1 cup sour cream
Cooked rice or noodles
Chow mein noodles

Cut veal in finger size wedges. Melt fat in skillet. Brown veal and add next six ingredients. Dissolve bouillon in water and add to veal. Simmer for at least one hour, covered. This can be done day before. Five minutes before serving, stir in flour, blending well, then add sour cream. Serve over noodles or rice and top with chow mein noodles. Serves 8.

Veal is expensive and hard to find, but this recipe is superb if your pocketbook feels fat and you know a butcher who can find veal for you.

Mrs. Frank T. Richardson, Jr.

CATALONIAN POT ROAST

3-4 pounds chuck roast (or any
 good cut of roast)
2 bay leaves
¼ teaspoon marjoram
1 garlic clove
1 bell pepper, minced
1 small onion, chopped
¼ cup olive oil

1 16-ounce can tomatoes
1 tablespoon sugar
¼ teaspoon cinnamon
⅛ teaspoon ground cloves
1 cup red wine (Cabernet or
 Burgundy)
1 tablespoon red wine vinegar
2-3 teaspoons salt

Crush together marjoram, bay leaves and garlic. Mix this with green pepper and onion and rub over meat. Let stand 1 hour. Place olive oil in Dutch oven or heavy cooker, place meat in oil and sear over high heat. Then add tomatoes, sugar, cinnamon, cloves, wine, vinegar and salt. Cover tightly, cook at lowest temperature on top of stove 3 or 4 hours until tender with fork. Remove meat, thicken gravy and serve with noodles. Serves 8.

A spicy pot roast that is good for family or company.

Mrs. Frank Troup

MARINADE SAUCE

½ cup soy sauce
½ cup water
2 tablespoons Worcestershire

1 tablespoon sugar
½ to 1 teaspoon garlic salt

Mix well. Marinate meat at least 2 hours before cooking.

Mrs. Lindsay A. Allen

MARINATED ROAST OR STEAK

4 pounds round roast or
round steak
1 bottle separating French
dressing (Good Season's
Riviera French)

½ cup red cooking wine with
garlic or white cooking wine
1 package Adolph's Meat Marinade
2 tablespoons Worcestershire

Mix together and marinate for 24 hours, turning and basting occasionally. Cook on grill, with cover, using indirect cooking until it is as done as desired.

Mrs. Jim L. Thompson, Jr.

FRESH MUSHROOM SAUCE

½ cup butter or margarine
¼ teaspoon seasoned salt
1 pound fresh mushrooms, halved
or whole or 2 8-ounce cans,
drained

3 to 4 tablespoons flour
1 can beef consomme

Melt butter in a skillet over medium heat. Add salt and saute mushrooms until slightly cooked. Push mushrooms aside and add flour to make a smooth paste. Add consomme and stir constantly until sauce has thickened slightly.

This original sauce greatly adds to the flavor of beef kabobs, steaks, or beef roasts.

Mrs. E. Bruce Flake

ROAST BEEF
STANDING RIBS OR ROLLED RIBS
Cook in 325° Oven

This method can only be used with a tender cut of meat such as the rib portion. You can leave meat on the ribs or the butcher will bone and roll it. It is a little easier to slice if it is rolled; however, I prefer the standing rib roast. This type roast is just as juicy and tender as the most choice steak, but it is a lot cheaper and easier. Your guests will think you are a great cook, and really all you have to do is buy the correct amount of meat and roast it in a slow oven. Do not buy a rump roast, chuck roast or sirloin tip and expect to have the same results; they just aren't the same. I prefer a roast of 7 to 10 pounds. Allow ½ pound per person with the bone, a little less if it is rolled. If I am having guests, I allow 1 to 2 pounds more than this. Example: I would buy 8 pounds for 14 people. Tell the butcher what you want and he will trim the excess fat. Leave some fat on. Buy U. S. Choice meat for this roast.

Place the roast, fat side up, in an open shallow pan without the addition of water. Do not cover. The low temperature (325°) allows this meat to cook evenly, shrink little and be juicy. A standing rib roast will rest on the bones. Use a rack for the rolled roast. The roast may or may not be rubbed with salt and pepper. They do not penetrate the meat and may interfere with the browning. I do not put salt and pepper on mine.

You can use a meat thermometer or use the time chart below. I use the chart below. If you use the thermometer, be sure and read the directions accompanying it. The tip must be in the center of the thickest part of the roast and not touching the bone. The temperature scale should be visible without moving the pan. Before deciding the roast is done, wiggle the thermometer slightly; if the indicator drops, continue to roast until it returns to the desired temperature.

The temperature of the meat thermometer that corresponds to rare is 140° F., to medium, 160° F., and to well done, 170° F. I never cook this meat well done. If you do not use a thermometer, the time of cooking will be on the basis of the size and shape of the roast. The following table is set up for meat taken from the refrigerator and baked in a 325° oven.

Ribs, standing (6 pounds)
rare, 2 ¼ hours
medium, 2 ½ hours
well done, 3 ¼ hours

Ribs, standing (8 pounds)
rare, 3 hours
medium, 3 ½ hours
well done, 4 ½ hours

Ribs, rolled (4 pounds)
rare, 2 ¼ hours
medium, 2 ½ hours
well done 2 ¾ hours

Ribs, rolled (6 pounds)
rare, 3 hours
medium, 3 ¼ hours
well done, 4 hours

Roast can be carved more easily if it has been out of the oven for 15 to 30 minutes. Use the juice from the pan for spooning over the meat as it is served. Heat this juice and add salt if you like.

Sounds better if you call it au jus. This is really the way to a man's heart. I've never met one yet that would rather have apple pie.

Mrs. George W. Hansberry

EYE OF ROUND

(ROASTED)

Have eye of the round roast at room temperature. Sprinkle with coarse black pepper or other seasoning. Preheat oven to 500° and bake 5 minutes per pound. Turn off and do not open oven for 2 hours. Roast will be pink.

What great news for the hostess! Imagine "do ahead" roast beef that will still be pink and juicy at serving time.

Mrs. John E. Wilks, Jr.

ANN ANDERSON'S PERFECT POT ROAST

3 pounds sirloin tip roast
2 tablespoons all purpose flour
2 tablespoons cooking oil
1 cup chopped onion
1 cup water

1 6/10 ounce envelope Italian salad dressing mix
1 teaspoon salt
Carrots and potatoes
2 tablespoons flour
½ cup water

Coat roast with the first 2 tablespoons flour. Sprinkle with salt. Brown in hot oil. Add onions and saute 3 minutes. Combine water, salad dressing mix and salt; pour over meat. Cover; simmer 2½ hours until meat is almost tender. Add pared potatoes and carrots. Cover and simmer ½ hour or until vegetables are tender. Remove meat and vegetables to platter. Combine remaining flour and water; add to broth. Cook and stir until thickened and bubbly.

Pot roast lovers everywhere — rejoice! This original was a Better Homes and Gardens Honor Roll winner, and after one taste you'll know why.

GRILLED ROAST BEEF

3-5 pound sirloin tip roast
or boneless rump roast

Italian dressing (bottled)
Lemon-pepper marinade

Place roast in glass or plastic container. Pour in Italian dressing, about ½ inch deep. Sprinkle with lemon-pepper marinade. Cover and refrigerate for 24 hours, turning once. Grill over coals, as you would a steak. Time depends on how well done you like your meat. I have found that a 3 to 3½ pound roast takes about 1 to 1½ hours. Be sure to sprinkle with lemon-pepper marinade before grilling.

Almost anything tastes better cooked outside. This roast is no exception, and it is SO much more fun to cook.

Mrs. Michael D. Scroggins

POLYNESIAN BEEF

3 or 4 pound beef pot roast
1 large onion, sliced
1 cup unsweetened pineapple
  juice
¼ cup soy sauce

½ teaspoon salt
1½ teaspoons ground ginger
1 cup sliced mushrooms
1 tablespoon cornstarch
2 tablespoons cold water

Trim excess fat from roast. Place meat in shallow dish; cover with sliced onion. Mix unsweetened pineapple juice, soy sauce, salt and ginger. Pour over meat. Let stand 1 hour; turn once. Place onion and meat in Dutch oven. Pour marinade over. Cover and cook at 350° for 2½ hours or until tender. Remove meat to platter; place mushrooms on top of meat. Skim fat from liquid. Blend cornstarch and water and stir into liquid. Cook until thick and pour over meat.

The Polynesians really have a way with meat. A super easy, super delicious roast.

Mrs. William A. Sims

SUKIYAKI

1 can sukiyaki vegetables,
  drained
1½ pound standing rib roast,
  boned, frozen and sliced paper
  thin on butcher's bacon slicer
4 stalks celery, cut diagonally
  in ½ inch pieces
2 onions, sliced lengthwise
1 bunch green onions, including
  tops, cut in 2 inch lengths

1 pound fresh spinach
1 pound fresh mushrooms
1 piece beef suet
Sukiyaki Sauce:
  ¼ cup Japanese soy sauce
    (no substitute, please)
  ½ cup water
  2 tablespoons white wine or
  Saki
  4 tablespoons sugar

Arrange vegetables and raw meat attractively on large platter. (This can be done in advance and set in refrigerator). Place electric skillet at center of table and heat to 260°. Melt piece of beef suet in skillet. Put 1/3 meat into skillet. Pour ½ sauce over meat, add 2/3 vegetables. Turn ingredients gently, with chop sticks if possible, while cooking 5 to 6 minutes. Serve directly into salad sized plates or bowls. Replenish with fresh ingredients as the cooking proceeds. Add sauce as required for proper moisture. Serve with rice, Japanese pickles and hot tea. Serves 6.

Good fun for family or company, but ingredients such as real Japanese vegetables and Japanese soy sauce are unavailable except in special stores.

Mrs. Barrett Shelton, Jr.

TERIYAKI SAUCE

¾ cup soy sauce
½ cup sugar
1 clove garlic, grated
  or ⅛ teaspoon garlic powder

½ teaspoon Accent
1 teaspoon grated fresh ginger
  or ¼ teaspoon powdered ginger

Mix all ingredients. Marinate beef, chicken, fish or shrimp for a few hours. After marinating, heat sauce to boiling and serve on baked potatoes or over meat at table. Any leftover sauce can be refrigerated to pour over hamburgers later.

Mrs. John R. Guice

SWEET AND SOUR BEEF

3 tablespoons fat
1½ pounds lean beef, cut in
  small strips
¼ cup water
1 20-ounce can pineapple chunks
¼ cup brown sugar

2 tablespoons cornstarch
¼ cup vinegar
1 tablespoon soy sauce
½ teaspoon salt
¾ cup green pepper strips
¼ cup thinly sliced onion

Brown beef slowly in hot fat. Add water; cover and simmer until tender, about 1 hour. Drain pineapple, reserving syrup. Combine sugar and cornstarch; add pineapple juice, vinegar, soy sauce and salt. Cook and stir over low heat until thick. Pour over hot cooked beef; let stand 10 minutes. Add pineapple, green pepper and onion 2 or 3 minutes before serving time. Serve over rice or noodles. Yields: 6 servings.

If you prefer beef to pork, or if your diet does not permit pork, we recommend sweet and sour beef.

Mrs. Sage Copeland

STEAK PIQUANTE

⅛ to ¼ pound blue or Roquefort
  cheese
3 teaspoons butter
4 tablespoons A-1 sauce
4 tablespoons Worcestershire

Dash Tabasco
4 teaspoons catsup
2 teaspoons prepared mustard
Steak, 4 servings, T-bone or sirloin

Mix ingredients. Broil steak in oven or outside grill. After steak has been turned to cook on second side, coat top with sauce. You may wish to season steak with salt and pepper as usual. A blender mixes the sauce smoothly, but is not essential.

Children may not particularly care for this, but adults most certainly do!

Mrs. Herbert Street

"SPECIAL" STEAK

1½ pounds round steak
1 teaspoon salt
1 medium onion

1 tablespoon cooking oil
1 can mushroom soup
1 cup white wine

Cut steak in serving pieces. Brown in oil. Place in Dutch oven or roasting pan. Top with sliced onion which has been cooked until tender.

Pour wine over steak. Cover and bake 1 hour at 325°. Add soup and continue cooking 1 hour. Serve with liquid from pan as gravy.

This dish is delicious served with rice, a tossed salad and French bread.

Mrs. Lester H. Smith

STEAK IN RED WINE SAUCE

2 thin round steaks
1 cup onions, finely chopped
1 cup mushrooms
1 cup hard-cooked eggs, diced

1 cup cracker crumbs
1 egg, beaten
Salt and pepper
2 cups dry red wine

Salt and pepper steaks; pound well. On one of the steaks, place onions, mushrooms, hard-cooked eggs and crumbs. Pour beaten egg over mixture. Place second steak on top of first. Roll as for jelly roll and tie with heavy string at several places along roll. Brown in butter or drippings. Place in covered dish with wine. Bake 1 hour at 350°.

Very different and appealing.

Mrs. Frank T. Richardson, III

SAUERBRATEN

2 pounds sirloin
1 tablespoon fat
1 envelope brown gravy mix
2 cups water
1/3 cup white vinegar
¼ cup brown sugar, packed

1 tablespoon Worcestershire
2 teaspoons ground ginger (less if fresh ginger is used)
1 teaspoon dry mustard
1 teaspoon black pepper
2 bay leaves

Cut meat in small pieces and saute in fat. Pour off fat. Dissolve brown gravy mix in water and add the remaining ingredients. Add gravy mixture to meat and simmer slowly for 1½ hours. Serve on hot buttered egg noodles. Serves 4.

One usually thinks of sauerbraten — German for sour beef — as a rather large roast which has been marinated for days in a vinegar-wine-spice marinade before cooking.

We give you a short cut version using small pieces of sirloin (or chuck), that is an excellent fix-ahead meal since the flavor improves with time. You may serve it a day or two after it is cooked . . . if you can wait!

Mrs. Frank T. Richardson, Jr.

FILET MIGNON IN WINE SAUCE

4 filet mignon (6 or 8 ounces)
Toasted bread rounds
½ cup dry white wine
2 teaspoons tomato paste or
    catsup

1 clove garlic (unchopped)
½ teaspoon finely chopped
    tarragon

Saute filets in butter to desired doneness. Remove to plates. Place on toasted bread rounds. Add wine and other ingredients to butter left in skillet. Heat thoroughly, season to taste and remove garlic. Pour over filet. Garnish with parsley and an anchovy, if desired.

An expensive and elegant but simple little dinner for four.

Mrs. William A. Sims

BEEF IN RED WINE

6 slices bacon
4 pounds lean stew beef,
    cut small
½ teaspoon dry mustard

1/3 cup flour
1 teaspoon salt
⅛ teaspoon pepper

Fry bacon, cut in squares, put in large casserole, cover. Leave bacon fat in pan. Roll meat in flour mixed with salt, pepper and mustard. Use all of flour mixture. Brown meat in bacon fat and add to bacon in casserole.

Put in pan:

1 cup claret or Burgundy   1 cup consomme

Mix with fat and drippings, scraping all from bottom and sides of pan. Bring to boil, lower heat and simmer, stirring constantly. Cook 5 minutes and pour over meat in casserole.

2 tablespoons chopped parsley
4 cloves
2 bay leaves
1 teaspoon thyme
Salt and pepper, to taste

1 cup claret or Burgandy
16 small white onions (canned or
    fresh)
Large bunch carrots, sliced
½ pound mushrooms

Add above ingredients, except mushrooms, to meat mixture and bake at 300° to 325° for 3 hours. Last ½ hour of baking, add ½ pound sliced, cooked mushrooms. Serve on rice. Serves 8-10. (If cooked, canned onions are used, add with mushrooms instead of earlier.)

A variation of the French classic Beef Bourguignonne, this recipe may sound complicated and time consuming, but it's not difficult and the finished product is superb! Make it early in the afternoon and serve eight that night. A salad, homemade French bread (see bread section) and a good red wine will complete your dinner.

Mrs. Whit King, Jr.

BEEF KABOBS

Sauce:
Juice of 2 lemons
½ cup margarine
¼ cup Worcestershire
¼ cup soy sauce
1 teaspoon garlic salt

Kabobs:
2 pounds sirloin steak
   (1½ inches thick)
1 large red onion
1 large bell pepper
12 small red potatoes
4 strips bacon, uncooked
Salt and pepper

Bring the above sauce ingredients to a boil in small sauce pan and simmer a minute.

Kabobs:

Wash and boil potatoes (with peels on) until partially done. Cube steak into 12, or desired number, cubes. Cut bacon into squares and onion and bell pepper into hunks. Alternate meat, potatoes and hunks of onion and pepper on individual skewers putting a square of bacon on each side of meat. Salt and pepper to taste and baste generously with sauce. Broil in oven, 7 to 8 inches from broiler, to desired doneness (approximately 20 to 30 minutes). Baste frequently and turn at least four times while cooking. Serves 4, and is also very tasty cooked on grill.

Good with tomato aspic ring full of artichoke hearts, or a tossed salad with lots of tomatoes.

Mrs. James Hurst

MARINATED BEEF KABOBS

Sirloin steak, cut in large
   cubes
Small whole onions, parboiled
   until tender-crisp
Fresh tomatoes, quartered
Fresh mushrooms
Bell pepper, cut in large squares

Marinade: (for 4 to 5 pounds meat)
Good Season Italian dressing
¼ cup soy sauce
¼ cup bourbon

Marinate sirloin and mushrooms for an hour or longer. Bell pepper may be parboiled for a few seconds if desired. Alternate ingredients on skewers. Grill over hot coals.

Serve on bouillon rice. A salad of hearts of lettuce with crumbled Roquefort cheese and French dressing is good.

Mrs. Thomas Caddell

EASY-BAKE STEW

2 pounds lean beef stew meat
Salt
Pepper
Paprika
2 tablespoons dry onion soup
   mix

6 medium sized potatoes
8 white boiling onions
3 carrots, quartered
1 can cream of celery soup
½ cup water
½ cup California sherry

Season meat with salt, pepper, paprika and onion soup mix. Place meat in Dutch oven. Add whole potatoes, onions and carrots. Blend celery soup with water and sherry. Pour over meat. Cover. Bake in 250°-300° oven for 5 hours.

No browning, no watching! This easy bake stew is the answer to that meal in a dish every cook dreams about.

Mrs. John Manning

BEEF STEW

Another put-everything-in-the-pot-and-forget stew, this one tomato flavored.

3 pounds cubed lean beef
   stew meat
As many as desired of:
   Small onions
   New potatoes, cut in chunks
   Carrots

1 package frozen peas
1 can tomato soup
¼ cup dry red wine
Dash of sugar
Salt and pepper, to taste
Chopped parsley

Put meat and vegetables in casserole or Dutch oven with tight lid. Add tomato soup and remaining ingredients. Cover and bake at 250° for five hours. Serves at least 6 to 8 people.

Mrs. W. D. Gilchrist, III

BEEF STROGANOFF

1½ pound sirloin tip
Salt and pepper, to taste
1 large onion, chopped
3 tablespoons butter
2 tablespoons flour
2 cups beef bouillon

3 tablespoons sherry
2 tablespoons tomato paste
1 teaspoon dry mustard
1 cup sliced mushrooms
2/3 cup sour cream

Cube beef and tenderize, if necessary. Salt and pepper. Melt butter in heavy skillet and saute onion and beef; add more butter, if needed. Remove beef and onion to plate. Slowly brown flour in skillet and add beef bouillon to make a smooth gravy. Add sherry, tomato paste, dry mustard and blend well. Return beef and onions to skillet; add mushrooms and allow to simmer slowly until beef is of desired tenderness. Five minutes before serving, add sour cream. Serve over rice or noodles. Makes 4 to 6 servings.

Mrs. William Sexton

TROUP STROGANOFF

¼ cup butter or margarine
½ cup minced onion
1 clove garlic, chopped
1 pound ground chuck
1 teaspoon Bouquet Garni
Salt and pepper

1 8-ounce can mushrooms, including liquid
1 can mushroom soup
½ pint sour cream
¼ cup minced parsley

Melt butter in skillet. Add onion and garlic and cook until lightly browned. Add beef and cook until redness disappears. Add Bouquet Garni, salt and pepper lightly. Add mushrooms and soup. Stir and cook for 10 to 15 minutes on low heat. Add sour cream and parsley. Serve over small noodles or rice. Serves 4 or 5.

For economy minded stroganoff lovers.

Mrs. Frank Troup

CREAM CHEESE LASAGNA

1½ pounds ground lean beef
1 clove garlic
1½ teaspoons salt
1 teaspoon sugar
1 8-ounce can tomato sauce

1 10-ounce can tomato and chili peppers or plain tomatoes
1 teaspoon chili powder
¼ teaspoon basil

Brown meat and garlic; add other ingredients, cover and simmer for 15 to 20 minutes.

1 package wide egg noodles

Cook noodles 15 to 20 minutes, in boiling, salted water.

Cheese Sauce:
  10 green onions
  3 ounces cream cheese

1 cup sour cream
½ cup grated American cheese

Mix all four ingredients and let stand until very soft.

Put a layer of noodles in a casserole dish, cover with meat sauce, add a layer of cheese. Repeat layering process. Can be made ahead and stored in refrigerator. Bake at 350° for 25 to 30 minutes.

The name is a bit misleading, since this dish doesn't use lasagna noodles. Taste it, though, and you know you are headed in the right direction . . . not for Italy, but surely for a good dinner.

Mrs. Thomas Caddell

LASAGNA

Tomato Sauce (see below)
1 tablespoon salt
1 tablespoon oil
½ package (1 pound size) lasagna noodles
1 pound ricotta cheese

1 pound mozzarella cheese, thinly sliced
1 3-ounce jar grated Parmesan cheese (or grated fresh Parmesan)

Make tomato sauce. When sauce is done, bring 3 quarts water and salt to boiling in large kettle. Add oil. Add noodles, 2 or 3 pieces at a time. Return water to boiling. Cook noodles, uncovered, 15 minutes. Drain noodles and rinse under hot water.

Preheat oven to 350°. Grease a 13 x 9 x 2 inch baking dish. Spoon 1/3 of sauce over bottom of dish. Layer 1/3 each of noodles, ricotta, mozzarella and Parmesan. Repeat, beginning with sauce and ending with Parmesan until you have 3 layers of each. Bake uncovered 45 to 50 minutes. Let stand 10 to 15 minutes before cutting. Serves 9.

Tomato Sauce for Lasagna:
¼ cup oil
½ cup finely chopped onion
1 clove garlic, crushed
2 tablespoons finely chopped fresh parsley
½ pound ground chuck
¼ pound ground pork
1 35-ounce can Italian tomatoes, undrained

2 6-ounce cans tomato paste
1 teaspoon dried basil leaves, crushed
2 teaspoons dried oregano leaves, crushed
1 tablespoon salt
¼ teaspoon pepper
2 tablespoons sugar

Slowly heat oil in large, deep, heavy skillet. In hot oil, saute onion, garlic and parsley until onion is tender, about 5 minutes. Add chuck and pork. Saute until well browned, stirring occasionally. Add rest of ingredients. Stir to mix well. Bring to boiling, reduce heat and simmer, covered, for 3 hours.

To make ahead, make sauce and cook noodles as directed. Assemble lasagna. Refrigerate, covered, until 2 hours before serving. Let stand 1 hour at room temperature. Bake and serve as directed.

If ricotta is not available, you may substitute cottage cheese (1 pound) pushed through a sieve and beaten together with an egg.

An authentic Italian recipe, this takes time, but is really delicious! Let the sauce simmer during siesta!

Mrs. William E. Shinn

111

AMERICANIZED LASAGNA

1½ teaspoons salt
1½ pounds ground chuck
1 8-ounce can tomato sauce
1 16-ounce can tomatoes
1½ teaspoons oregano
1½ teaspoons basil

9 lasagna noodles
1 teaspoon salt
8-ounces mozzarella cheese, grated
1 carton cottage cheese
Parmesan cheese

Sprinkle salt in bottom of 10 inch skillet. Heat and add ground chuck. Brown. Add tomatoes, tomato sauce, oregano and basil. Let simmer 30 minutes. While meat sauce is simmering, cook lasagna noodles in 2 to 3 quarts boiling, salted water for 20 minutes. Drain noodles and add approximately 2 tablespoons of oil and swish around to keep them from sticking.

Place 3 noodles in bottom of 1½ quart greased baking dish (13x9 inch) and sprinkle ½ of grated mozzarella cheese over them. Spread ½ of cottage cheese over this and spoon ½ of the meat sauce on top of cheeses. Sprinkle Parmesan cheese liberally and add another layer of noodles (3). Repeat the above, ending with the remaining 3 noodles. Place in 425° oven and bake for approximately 20 minutes or until bubbly and cheeses have melted.

A great recipe to double. Serve half now and freeze other half for later. A quicker version of lasagna which suits the fast paced life style of the American.

Mrs. Otis E. Kirby, Jr.

BERNIE'S SPAGHETTI

An Army bachelor, who spent a summer living in New York with an Italian family, serves the most delicious spaghetti. When he was asked for the sauce recipe, he submitted the following:

"5 cans peeled tomatoes
4 or 5 cans paste
1 or 2 pounds bottom round and/or pork chops
1 onion
1 bell pepper
1 bunch parsley
1 clove of garlic
1 bay leaf

Italian spices to taste
Salt and black pepper
Optional:
  Mushrooms
  Soy sauce
  Beef bouillon cubes
  1 dried red pepper or equivalent

Brown meat in any oil (olive or beef fat). Brown vegetables. Add spices; add paste and tomatoes. Bring to boil and simmer. Add no water. Simmer until it has boiled down enough and tomatoes have dissolved into the sauce. I simmer 2 or 3 hours or longer."

Bernie boiled his spaghetti in lots of water until just tender, drained it, put it in a huge mixing bowl and poured the sauce over and tossed it well. Then he passed a large bowl of freshly grated Parmesan cheese.

We have worked out proportions for Bernie's sauce. It is good!

3 28-ounce cans tomatoes, preferably Italian Plum
4 6-ounce cans tomato paste
2 pounds round steak or a combination of round steak and pork chops, cut in bite sized cubes
2 medium onions, chopped
1 bell pepper, diced
¼ cup chopped fresh parsley
1 clove garlic, pressed
1 bay leaf
4 teaspoons Italian seasoning
2 carrots, grated
1½ to 2 teaspoons salt
½ teaspoon pepper
1 4-ounce can mushrooms or sauteed fresh ones, if you can get them
1 cube beef bouillon
1 dried red pepper

Follow Bernie's cooking instructions. The longer the sauce simmers, the better. This recipe makes four quarts of very thick spaghetti sauce, which really should be tossed with the noodles rather than served on top. This recipe will serve 8-10, generously.

Mrs. William E. Shinn, Jr.

SPAGHETTI CASSEROLE FOR 20

6 tablespoons olive oil
6 cloves garlic, minced
6 onions, chopped
1 cup celery, chopped
2 bell peppers, chopped
2½ pounds ground beef
4 8-ounce cans tomato sauce
3 6-ounce cans tomato paste
3 tomato paste cans of water
¼ teaspoon garlic powder
½ teaspoon onion salt
1 teaspoon parsley flakes
Dash of Tabasco
1½ teaspoons salt
¼ teaspoon pepper
Other seasoning, as desired:
    ½ teaspoon cayenne pepper
    1 teaspoon paprika
    1 teaspoon oregano
    1 teaspoon celery salt
    1 teaspoon Accent
1½ pounds mushrooms
4 tablespoons butter
1½ pounds spaghetti
Grated Parmesan cheese

Pour oil into large pot. Saute garlic, onion, pepper and celery until brown. Add meat and saute until meat cooks through, stirring occasionally. Add sauce, paste, water and seasonings. Cook over medium heat until sauce comes to a boil. Simmer for 45 minutes.

Wash and slice mushrooms and cook lightly in butter for about 15 minutes. Add mushrooms to sauce and simmer about 45 minutes more, stirring occasionally. Cook spaghetti and mix well with sauce. Turn into casserole. Sprinkle cheese on top. Freeze if desired or bake at 400° for 15 minutes. Makes approximately three 2-quart casseroles.

Handy for the hostess is our spaghetti casserole for 20. How nice to know that it freezes beautifully, too!

Mrs. John R. Guice

CHEESY MEAT LOAF

1 to 1½ pounds ground chuck
2 slices bread, crumbled
1 pound can tomatoes or 1½
    cups catsup
1 egg, beaten
1 small onion, finely chopped
¼ cup celery, finely chopped
½ teaspoon salt
Dash pepper
½ cup chopped bell pepper
½ to 1½ cups grated Cheddar
    cheese

Mix all ingredients together, except cheese, and form a loaf. Place in baking dish or loaf pan. Bake in preheated 350° oven for 1 hour. Remove and sprinkle with cheese. Return to oven until cheese melts. Serves 4-5.

A melted Cheddar topping — the amount depends on your fondness for cheese — makes this meat loaf different.

Mrs. David C. Harris

MARY'S MEAT LOAF

2 slices rye bread
2 slices white bread
1 cup water
1 pound ground beef
1 onion, chopped
Dash of parsley flakes
3 tablespoons Parmesan
    cheese
1 egg, beaten
1 teaspoon salt
¼ teaspoon pepper
2 tablespoons butter
1 8-ounce can tomato sauce
1 teaspoon oregano

Soak rye bread and white bread in water. Mix ground beef, bread, onion, parsley, Parmesan cheese, egg, salt and pepper. Shape in a loaf and top with butter. Bake at 375° for 30 minutes. Remove from oven and pour tomato sauce over the top. Sprinkle with oregano and bake 20 minutes longer. Serves 4.

Meat loaf with an Italian flair.

Mrs. James B. Odom

MEAT LOAF WITH SWEET AND SOUR SAUCE

1 8-ounce can tomato sauce
¼ cup brown sugar, packed
¼ cup vinegar
1 teaspoon prepared mustard
1 egg, slightly beaten
1 onion, minced
¼ cup crackers, crushed
2 pounds ground beef
1½ teaspoons salt
¼ teaspoon pepper
¼ teaspoon Accent

In a saucepan, mix tomato sauce with brown sugar, vinegar and mustard. Stir until the sugar is dissolved. Combine egg, onion, crackers, meat, salt, pepper and Accent and ½ cup of the tomato sauce mixture. Mix lightly but thoroughly and shape into loaf. Put into a shallow baking dish and pour the remainder of the tomato sauce mixture over it. Bake in 350° oven for one hour, basting occasionally. Serve sauce separately. If sauce appears too thick, add ¼ cup of water. Serves 6.

Comment from a tester: "This is the best meat loaf I've ever tasted. My children do not really care for meat loaf, but they loved this. It's good sliced cold for sandwiches the next day . . . if you have any left."

Mrs. Judson E. Davis, Jr.

MORE-MORE

(CASSEROLE)

2 tablespoons salt
4-6 quarts boiling water
1 pound medium egg noodles
1 cup chopped onion
2 tablespoons butter
4 pounds ground beef (or chuck)
2 cups celery (more or less)

1½ cup chopped bell pepper
6 8-ounce cans tomato sauce
1 pound can whole kernel corn, drained
Salt to taste
1 pound Cheddar cheese, grated

Add the 2 tablespoons salt to boiling water. Gradually add noodles so that water continues to boil. Cook, uncovered, stirring occasionally until just tender. Drain thoroughly. Meanwhile, saute onion and celery in butter in large skillet until soft. Add meat and cook until browned, stirring to break up large pieces. Add pepper, tomato sauce, drained corn and salt to taste. Mix well. Combine meat mixture with drained, cooked noodles. Turn into 6 quart baking dish. Cover and cook at 350° for ½ hour and then cook uncovered for ½ hour. Top with cheese for last ten minutes of cooking time. Yields 20 portions.

An economical but hearty way to serve twenty!

Mrs. Sage Copeland

MEXICAN BEEF HASH

½ cup chopped onion
½ cup chopped bell pepper
½ pound lean ground beef
2 teaspoons chili powder

1 teaspoon salt
¼ teaspoon pepper
½ cup uncooked rice
1 16-ounce can tomatoes, chopped

Saute first three ingredients until meat is browned. Add remaining ingredients, mix well and bake in a covered casserole at 350° for about 1 hour. Makes 4 generous servings.

If you want to freeze this casserole (or half of it), cook it about 20 minutes, let cool completely, then freeze. When you take it out of the freezer, let it thaw, then cook about 1 hour.

Mrs. George L. McCrary, Jr.

CUBAN HASH

2 tablespoons oil
½ cup diced bell pepper
¼ cup diced onions
¼ cup chopped mushrooms
1 pound ground round steak
1 29-ounce can tomatoes,
  mashed, including juice

¼ cup sliced stuffed olives
¼ cup seedless raisins
¼ cup slivered almonds
1 teaspoon salt
⅛ teaspoon pepper

Heat 2 tablespoons oil or margarine in heavy skillet or Dutch oven. Add green pepper, onions and mushrooms. Saute until onions are golden, stirring occasionally. Add meat and cook over moderate heat, stirring constantly, until browned. Add tomatoes, olives, raisins, almonds, salt and pepper. Cover and simmer gently for about 20 minutes. Serve over plain cooked rice or saffron rice.

Surprisingly good. A delightful change from stew or other basic "family" stand-bys. How colorful it is served with bright yellow saffron rice!

Mrs. A. C. Bailey

CHEROKEE CASSEROLE

1 pound ground beef
1 tablespoon oil
¾ cup finely chopped onion
1½ teaspoon salt
Dash pepper
⅛ teaspoon each of garlic
  powder, thyme, oregano

½ small bay leaf
1 16-ounce can tomatoes
1 can cream of mushroom soup
1 cup Minute Rice
6 stuffed olives, sliced
2 or 3 slices Cheddar cheese, cut
  in strips

Brown meat in oil, add onions and cook until tender. Stir in ingredients in order given, reserving three olives and cheese. Bring to a boil; reduce heat and simmer for 5 minutes, stirring occasionally. Spoon into a 2 quart greased baking dish and top with cheese and remaining olives. Bake at 350° for 25 minutes. Serves 4 to 6.

Why not keep a Cherokee casserole in your freezer . . . providin' you can think far enough ahead to get it in there. Take it out for that after-the-little-league-game dinner, or take it to a sick friend (if you are of a generous heart).

Mrs. Benjamin C. Stevens

TATER TOT CASSEROLE

1½ pounds ground chuck
1 small to medium onion, minced
1 can cream of chicken soup

1 small package of frozen Tater Tots
1 can cream of celery soup
½ can water

Cream of asparagus soup and cream of mushroom soup may be substituted for chicken and celery soups.

Line pan with hamburger meat (uncooked). Sprinkle minced onion on top of meat. Add chicken soup, one layer of Tater Tots (frozen or thawed), celery soup and water. Bake at 350° for 1½ hours.

This takes about 5 minutes to fix and children love it (which may or may not speak well of the casserole, but is music to a mother's ears!)

Mrs. Joe D. Burns

"QUICKIE" SPANISH RICE CASSEROLE

1 pound ground chuck
1 medium onion

1 cup grated mild Cheddar cheese
1 16-ounce can Spanish Rice

Brown ground chuck in large skillet, add can of Spanish rice. Slice onion and add to mixture. Mix and warm slightly. Pour mixture into a 2 quart casserole dish and sprinkle grated cheese over top. Bake 25 to 30 minutes in preheated 325° oven.

When you drag in after that last carpool and know there's no hope for dinner, put this dish together and toss a salad or cook a quick green vegetable while it's baking. They'll never know how tired you were!

Mrs. Fletcher Eddens
Wilmington, North Carolina

RHEA LEWIS'S
LUXURY HAMBURGER CASSEROLE

3 pounds lean ground beef, round preferred
2 medium onions, chopped
1 bell pepper, diced
1 stalk celery, diced

1 large can sliced mushrooms
3 cans tomato soup
½ pound sharp cheese
1 8-ounce box wild rice, cooked

Saute onion, pepper and celery. Season meat and add to mixture and brown. Mix together meat mixture, mushrooms, soup, cheese and rice. Put in casserole and cook 30 minutes at 350°. Serves 16-18.

This casserole is not for the end of the month. Good for a crowd.

Mrs. Barrett Shelton, Jr.

FRIED RICE WITH MEAT

1 cup rice, cooked and cooled
6 tablespoons vegetable oil
2 eggs
2 tablespoons soy sauce
¼ teaspoon Accent
Salt to taste

1 small garlic clove, crushed
4 green onions, chopped
½ cup diced roast pork
or
cooked shrimp, lobster, chicken or turkey

Place oil in heavy skillet, 10 inches or more, and saute rice over high heat for 3 or 4 minutes. Break eggs and stir rapidly into rice. Reduce heat. Add remaining ingredients, heat thoroughly and serve. Serves 3 to 4 people.

Another Chinese specialty that is a grand way to use leftover roast pork, chicken or other meat without anyone's suspecting it's leftover.

Mrs. A. J. Coleman, III

117

RICE BALLS

2 medium onions
½ cup chopped celery
1½ pounds ground round steak
Salt and pepper, to taste
2 to 3 tablespoons chili powder
2 8-ounce cans tomato sauce

1½ cup rice (short grained, only)
Margarine
Cooking oil
1 egg
Bread crumbs, as needed

Chop onion and celery. Saute until soft in small amount of cooking oil. Add the ground meat. Mix well. While meat is browning add salt, black pepper and chili powder. When meat is brown, add tomato sauce and cook until the mixture is thick. Stir often to avoid sticking.

While meat mixture is cooking, boil rice until it will mash between fingers. When rice reaches this consistency, drain in colander, running hot water over it to wash off excess starch. Place rice on large platter and add margarine generously. Allow both rice and meat mixture to cool enough to handle. Pat some of the rice out in your cupped hand, then add about one tablespoon of meat mixture on rice and cup rice around meat into a ball.

When all the rice and meat have been rolled into balls, roll rice balls in beaten egg (seasoned with salt and pepper) and then in bread crumbs. Fry in deep fat until brown. Serves 6 to 8.

A truly unusual dish of unknown origin, rice balls resemble old fashioned rice croquettes but have a surprise filling of chili flavored beef. Good for lunch or dinner with salad and French bread; you may vary the size of the balls to suit yourself. The smaller the balls, the crisper they will be. Serve two or three per person and have plenty in reserve for seconds!

This definitely does not fall into the quick and easy category, but happily the balls may be made ahead, frozen between sheets of waxed paper, and then dipped in egg, rolled in crumbs and fried at the last minute.

Mrs. James Hurst

STUFFED CABBAGE

1 pound ground lean pork
1½ cups rice
2 small onions, chopped
　(or 1 large)

Salt
Pepper
1 head cabbage
Allspice (ground)

Place rice over boiling water for a few minutes until swollen but not cooked (just steamed). Separate about 10 cabbage leaves from head and steam in boiling water. Do not cook . . . just steam so as not to break when rolled. Mix well together: uncooked pork, rice, onion, salt and pepper and place large cooking spoonful in a cabbage leaf. Roll leaf up and secure with toothpicks. Place in roaster, on rack, with water in roaster and sprinkle generously with ground allspice. Cook on top of stove for 1½ hours on low heat. Add water to roaster as necessary so cabbage will steam. Serve with hot pepper sauce.

Complicated . . . time consuming . . . very old world. But good!!!

Mrs. Frank Troup

BAR-B-CUE PORK CHOPS

Place pork chops in baking pan lined with foil. Cook in preheated 450° oven for 30 minutes. Slice onion and lemon on each. Bake at 350° for 60 minutes, basting every 15 minutes with sauce.

Sauce:	1 teaspoon salt
1 cup catsup	2 dashes Tabasco
1/3 cup Worcestershire	2 cups water
1 teaspoon chili powder	

Mrs. Elmer S. Loyd, Jr.

SWEET AND SOUR PORK CHOPS

6 pork chops	1 cup catsup
Salt and pepper, to taste	Juice of ½ lemon
6 slices lemon	¼ cup brown sugar
6 teaspoons brown sugar	

Place chops in deep baking pan; sprinkle with salt and pepper. On each chop place a slice of lemon and a teaspoon of brown sugar. Mix remaining ingredients and pour over chops. Cover baking pan with foil. Seal to make airtight. Bake in 350° oven for one hour.

Easy to make — easy to eat!

Mrs. Malcolm L. Prewitt, Jr.

PORK CHOPS WITH WILD RICE

1 6-ounce box long grain and wild rice	Salt and pepper
2 cups hot water	1 can cream of mushroom or celery soup
6 lean pork chops	½ cup milk

Combine rice and water in 2½ quart casserole. Salt and pepper pork chops to taste. Arrange on top of rice mixture. Bake covered 1¼ hours at 350°. Combine soup and milk. When casserole is done, pour soup mixture over casserole. Return to oven, uncovered, and bake until soup is bubbly. Serves 4-6.

Plan to keep pork chops in the freezer and a box of this rice in the cabinet. You probably always have mushroom soup on hand, and if you don't, you should, for it solves many a cooking crisis. Then, when the phone rings and you hear, "we're in town," you can calmly put this together and toss a salad . . . they'll think you're a genius!

Mrs. Jolly McKenzie

POLYNESIAN SPARERIBS

4 pounds pork spareribs
1 cup brown sugar, packed
3 tablespoons cornstarch
1 teaspoon celery salt
1 teaspoon ground ginger
¼ cup soy sauce
½ cup water

1 8-ounce can crushed pineapple,
  undrained
¼ cup minced onion
2 tablespoons Worcestershire
4 dashes Tabasco
1/3 cup wine or cider vinegar
1 tablespoon shredded orange
  rind

Cut ribs into serving pieces, 3-4 ribs wide. Arrange spareribs in shallow roasting pan. Cover pan with aluminum foil, crimped tightly to edge of pan. Bake in 350° oven for one hour. Mix brown sugar, cornstarch, celery salt and ginger. Stir in remaining ingredients. Cook over low heat, stirring constantly, until mixture thickens slightly. Drain drippings from baking pan. Brush ribs generously with sauce, turn and spoon remaining sauce over ribs. Cover pan with foil and crimp to pan edge. Return ribs to oven and bake 30 minutes. Remove foil and continue baking until tender and brown. Makes 4-6 servings.

Spareribs . . . any style . . . have always been a cotton country special. Until you've tried spareribs Polynesian, though, you cannot discuss the subject of ribs with any authority.

Mrs. Randolph Pickell

SWEET AND SOUR PORK

1½ pounds lean pork, cut in ½
  by 2 inch strips
2 tablespoons fat
¼ cup water
2 bell peppers, cut in strips
1 large onion, thinly sliced

1 20-ounce can pineapple
  chunks
¼ cup vinegar
2 tablespoons soy sauce
1 teaspoon salt
¼ cup brown sugar
2 tablespoons cornstarch

Brown pork in the melted fat in skillet over medium heat. Add water, peppers and onion and simmer 1 hour, or until tender. (You may add a bit more water, if needed.) Add pineapple with syrup, vinegar, soy sauce, salt and brown sugar mixed with cornstarch. Bring to boiling point and simmer until sauce is thick and meat is fork tender. Serve on steamed rice. Serves 6.

You DON'T have to wait to find a Chinese restaurant to eat this favorite.

Mrs. J. B. Charlton
Pensacola, Florida

ANN GRATWICK'S SAUSAGE AND SAUERKRAUT

2 Kolbase Polish sausages
1 large or 2 regular cans
  sauerkraut

Dash of salt and pepper
½ cup brown sugar
5 or 6 apples

Rinse sauerkraut with cold water and drain. Peel, core and slice apples and put in baking dish with sauerkraut. Add about 1/3 of the brown sugar and toss apples, sauerkraut and sugar. Place scored sausages on top of the mixture and arrange a few additional apple slices around the sausages in an attractive pattern. Add remaining brown sugar over the top of the sausages. Place covered in a 400° oven for about 25 minutes.

So you don't like sauerkraut? Try this! We think you'll change your mind.

Mrs. L. Denton Cole, Jr.

SAUSAGE CASSEROLE

6 slices bread
1 pound sausage
1 teaspoon prepared mustard
1 cup slivered Swiss cheese
3 eggs, slightly beaten
1 cup milk

¾ cup light cream
¼ teaspoon salt
Dash pepper
Dash nutmeg
1 teaspoon Worcestershire

Place bread in well buttered 9 x 13 inch casserole to cover bottom. Cook sausage in skillet until done. Drain off fat. Mix with mustard. Sprinkle sausage evenly over bread, sprinkle cheese over sausage. (Can stop here and freeze.) Combine eggs, milk, cream, and seasonings. Pour over casserole. Bake in 350° oven, 30-35 minutes, or until set in middle.

Great for breakfast, brunch or Sunday night supper, with hot curried fruit, perhaps. Keep one of these casseroles in your freezer. Then add the eggs and milk for a delicious late breakfast treat for your next weekend guests . . . or maybe even just for yourself.

Mrs. Thomas A. Caddell

BAKED HAM

12 pound ham
Cloves
Brown sugar

Black pepper
Nutmeg
Paprika (on top)

Cut all fat off ham; skin. Coat ham with spices, with paprika on top, very thick. Leave in refrigerator uncovered at least two weeks. When ready to cook, put in turkey roaster on rack. Use 3 or 4 glasses of water to cover rack. Cook covered for 2 hours at 350°. Leave in oven until oven is cold.

If you are a country ham buff, yet find a country ham hard to come by, try this method of cooking a store-bought'n ham. You are actually curing your own and will be surprised to find it tastes almost like a country one when you're through.

Mrs. Henon Pearce

121

"SOMETHING SPECIAL" HAM

½ precooked boneless ham,
   5 or 6 pounds
1 medium onion
1 large or 2 small apples,
   cored
½ teaspoon thyme
½ teaspoon cinnamon

½ teaspoon marjoram
6 cloves
10 peppercorns
½ cup sherry (or white wine)
1 beef bouillon cube, dissolved in
   1 cup water

Preheat oven to 300 degrees.

Place thickly sliced onion and apple over bottom of a heavy casserole or Dutch oven. Sprinkle with ¼ teaspoon thyme, cinnamon, marjoram and all the cloves and peppercorns. Place ham in pot and rub remaining spices into top surface. Pour sherry or white wine slowly over the ham. Place in oven and bake for two hours. As ham bakes, frequently baste with the beef broth. Use about ½ cup altogether. Be sure to ladle pan juices over ham as you baste. Ham may be covered with pot lid or foil for the last 30 minutes of cooking time. (See following sauce recipe). Ham should be removed from pot and allowed to "rest" for 30 minutes before slicing.

The "something special" is definitely an understatement when used to describe this creation!

Mrs. Herbert Street

SAUCE FOR "SOMETHING SPECIAL" HAM

Pan juices from ham
½ cup beef broth
   (see ham recipe)
2 tablespoons brown sugar
2 tablespoons grape, apple
   or currant jelly

1 tablespoon sherry or wine
   (or more to taste)
1 teaspoon cornstarch
1 teaspoon mustard (Dijon
   preferred)
¼ cup currants

Pour pan juices from ham (including cooked apple and onion) through a sieve or wire strainer into a saucepan. Mash the onion and apple slices through the strainer. Be sure to remove any peppercorns or cloves that might slip through. Any fat on top of the pan juices should be ladled off. Add beef broth, brown sugar, jelly to pan juices and bring to a boil. Mix the cornstarch and mustard with the sherry and quickly stir this into simmering mixture. Stir for several minutes until all ingredients appear to be blended. Add currants and let sauce barely simmer for about 10 or 15 minutes before serving.

Mrs. Herbert Street

RAISIN SAUCE FOR HAM

1 cup raisins
1 cup water
5 whole cloves
¾ cup brown sugar
1 tablespoon cornstarch

¼ teaspoon salt
Dash pepper
1 tablespoon butter
1 tablespoon vinegar
¼ teaspoon Worcestershire

Cover raisins with water, add cloves and simmer for 10 minutes. Add sugar, cornstarch, salt and pepper which have been mixed. Stir until slightly thickened, then add remaining ingredients.

Mrs. William B. Eyster

PASTE FOR BAKED HAM

½ cup brown sugar
2 teaspoons dry mustard
¼ cup flour
2 tablespoons vinegar

1 ham, 8 to 10 pounds (or portion may be used)
2 tablespoons whole cloves

Combine brown sugar, mustard and flour and mix with vinegar to make a thick paste. Rub paste over entire surface of ham and stud with whole cloves about 2 inches apart. Place on rack and bake uncovered until ham is done. Paste will form a crust. Remove cloves, slice and serve ham hot or cold.

Mrs. L. Denton Cole

BROCCOLI, HAM AND MACARONI CASSEROLE

1 8-ounce package macaroni
3 quarts boiling water
1 tablespoon salt
1 package frozen chopped broccoli, cooked
2 cups ham, cubed
½ cup butter
¼ cup flour

2½ cups milk
¾ cup grated cheese
1 teaspoon grated onion
½ teaspoon dry mustard
1 cup mayonnaise
2 teaspoons salt
⅛ teaspoon pepper
Buttered bread crumbs (optional)

Slowly add macaroni to boiling salted water. Allow water to return to boil and cook for 7 to 9 minutes, stirring occasionally. Cube ham. Melt butter in saucepan and blend in flour. Add milk and stir until sauce thickens. Add grated cheese, onion and mustard to sauce mixture and fold in mayonnaise. Combine macaroni, cooked broccoli, ham and sauce; season with salt and pepper. Pour into a 2 quart casserole, top with buttered bread crumbs, if desired, and bake at 375° for 25 to 30 minutes.

It has been said that a ham and two people equal eternity. Sometimes it seems that a ham and any number short of an army equals the same. So when the left-over ham is getting the best of you, cube two cups of it and stir up this casserole.

Mrs. John R. Guice

HAM CASSEROLE

¼ cup butter or margarine
¼ cup flour
1½ cups milk
½ cup salad dressing
½ teaspoon salt
2 cups cooked ham, cubed
2 cups cooked rice

½ cup chopped bell pepper
½ cup sliced water chestnuts
  OR slivered almonds
¼ cup grated Parmesan
  cheese
2 tablespoons chopped pimento

Make a cream sauce with margarine, flour and milk; stir in salad dressing and salt. Add remaining ingredients and mix well. Pour in a 2 quart casserole, cover and bake in a 350° oven for 30 minutes.

Dressy enough — and good enough — for a luncheon.

Mrs. J. P. Smartt, Jr.

HAM SHORTCAKE

Sauce:
4 tablespoons butter
4 tablespoons flour
2 cups milk
2 teaspoons dry mustard
2 cups cooked and cubed ham
2 tablespoons Worcestershire
2 tablespoons chopped parsley
4 tablespoons chopped pimentos
Salt and pepper to taste

Potato Cakes:
4 cups raw potatoes, grated
3 eggs, well beaten
¼ teaspoon baking powder
2 teaspoons salt
3 tablespoons grated onion
4 tablespoons flour
Bacon drippings

Melt butter in saucepan. Combine flour and mustard and stir into butter until smooth. Add milk and cook gently until smooth and thick, about 10 minutes. Add ham, pimentos, parsley and seasonings; mix thoroughly. Keep hot; if it gets too thick, add a little milk. Mix potatoes with remaining ingredients in order given with the exception of bacon drippings which are to be placed in frying pan and heated. When fat is hot, drop potatoes by large spoonfuls into fat and cook until brown on both sides. For each "shortcake" alternate potato cakes and sauce, finishing with sauce. Serves 6.

Another excellent recipe for left over ham! These potato pancakes layered with zippy creamed ham would be grand for brunch, served with lots of coffee.

Mrs. Charles B. Howell

LUNCHEON CHIPPED BEEF CASSEROLE

12 slices bread, frozen
¾ pound sliced American
  cheese
2 packages broccoli spears
2 cups chipped beef, diced
8 eggs, beaten

5 cups milk
2 tablespoons instant onions
½ teaspoon salt
¼ teaspoon dry mustard
Parmesan cheese

Trim and discard edges from frozen bread slices. Using doughnut cutter, cut rounds of bread, saving scraps. Put scraps in bottom of greased 13 x 9 inch pan. Lay cheese over this, then broccoli (cooked) and a layer of meat sprinkled with the instant onion. Place bread rings on top. Beat eggs, milk, salt and dry mustard together and pour over all. Refrigerate for 6 hours or longer. Remove from refrigerator and allow to sit at room temperature for 30 minutes before baking. Bake at 325° for 55 minutes. Sprinkle with Parmesan cheese and return to oven for 5 minutes.

A delicious casserole for 12 . . . broccoli, dried beef and cheese in a puffy souffle. Since it must be refrigerated for at least 6 hours before baking, you can get your house in order and your table set before guests arrive and still have time to be beautiful! A fresh fruit salad and rolls would be good company.

Mrs. J. Bruce Ballentine
Chapel Hill, N. C.

GAME

YUMMY DOVE

12 to 14 dove breasts
Flour—fat as desired
2 cans beef consomme
1 carrot, minced

3 stalks celery, finely chopped
1 medium onion, minced
4 tablespoons dry sherry
Cornstarch

Flour dove and brown in hot fat. Drain well. Pour consomme in a 2-quart casserole. (An electric skillet also may be used.) Stir in carrot, celery, onion and sherry. Thicken with a little corn starch and water to consistency of gravy. Place browned dove in gravy. Cover. Place in oven for about 1½ hours at 325 degrees. Serve with brown rice and mushrooms or wild rice. Serves 6.

Using the breast only is easier for the cook and the consumer.

Mrs. Harold Pilgrim, Jr.

TOBY'S DOVE PIE

3 doves per serving
Margarine or butter

Salt and pepper
1 box pie crust mix

Drop doves into boiling water (use only enough water to cover), seasoned with salt, pepper, and margarine. (Use ½ stick margarine for 8 doves and increase accordingly.)

Boil doves just until tender. Remove meat from bones and set aside. Save the broth.

Make pie crust according to directions on package or use your own pie crust recipe. Line a casserole (size depends on number of servings desired) with pie crust rolled thin. Add cooled meat and enough broth to cover. Top with pie crust. Bake at 325 degrees until pie is bubbly and crust is brown, about 45 minutes.

This recipe never fails to delight. Even "confirmed dove haters" succumb to the subtle flavor of doves prepared in this way. An excellent way to use last season's doves that are possibly suffering from freezer burn.

Mrs. William E. Shinn, Jr.

TYLER'S DOVE SUPPER

Dove
Salt
Pepper
Flour
Butter

Worcestershire
Lemon juice
Boiling water
Wine, if desired

Wash dove; pat dry and roll in flour after salting and peppering. Place in black iron skillet in melted butter that generously covers bottom of skillet. Cover and cook over medium heat until nice and brown. Shake Worcestershire generously over dove and squeeze lemon juice heavily over all. Continue cooking until done — about an hour. Time will depend upon how many birds you have in skillet. When done the dove may be held in oven about 45 minutes and still will be moist and delicious.

This makes a delightful Sunday night supper when served on a bed of rice garnished with parsley and fruit. Serve gravy separately. A broccoli salad with wine or beer completes the meal nicely.

Mrs. John D. Davis, Jr.

WILD DOVE DELICIOUS

Dove breasts
Salt and pepper
Flour

1 cup butter or margarine
½ teaspoon thyme
1 cup heavy cream

126

Use dove breasts only. Salt and pepper and dredge with flour. Heat butter in heavy skillet and brown dove nicely. Sprinkle with thyme and add cream. Cover tightly and simmer very slowly until tender — about 1½ hours. This gravy may be thinned with milk and served on wild rice.

Lots of butter and heavy cream do marvelous things to dove breasts.

Mrs. James B. Odom

OVEN QUAIL

Quail
Salt and pepper
¼ cup lemon juice (per 6 quail)

¼ cup butter or margarine
(per 6 quail)
Bacon slices

Salt and pepper quail. Make a split down the back of the bird. Mix lemon juice and margarine. Put mixture inside and outside quail. Wrap each quail with a piece of bacon and put in baking pan. Bake 350° about 30 minutes or until tender. (Young birds cook more quickly.) Baste with lemon mixture while baking. You may want to brown birds and bacon under broiler before serving.

If your man will clean his birds, this is the easiest dish imaginable— and tastes great, too. If he won't, we guess there's not an easy method.

Mrs. W. P. Dozier

QUAIL WITH SAVORY RICE

½ cup butter
12 to 14 quail
Salt and pepper
¾ cup sauterne
¼ cup butter
¾ cup finely chopped celery
¼ cup chopped celery leaves
1/3 cup chopped onion
2 tablespoons chopped parsley

1 teaspoon salt
½ teaspoon sage
¼ teaspoon marjoram
⅛ teaspoon pepper
1½ cups cooked rice
1½ cups chicken stock, or
2 chicken bouillon cubes
dissolved in water

Melt ½ cup butter in heavy dutch oven. Season quail and brown on all sides. When browned, pour sauterne over quail and cover tightly and simmer for 30 minutes. Meanwhile, melt ¼ cup butter in skillet and saute celery, onion, parsley, and other seasonings. Add rice and chicken stock, mix thoroughly and pour into casserole dish. Place quail on top of rice mixture in casserole and cover tightly with aluminum foil. Place in 350° oven until rice has absorbed liquid. This should take about 45 minutes. Remove foil and serve.

A rice and quail casserole with a very definite sage flavor.

Mrs. L. Denton Cole, Jr.

CHICKEN FRIED QUAIL

Quail   Bacon fat
Flour   Salt and pepper

Split quail down backs and salt several hours before cooking. Shake quail in seasoned flour in bag to coat evenly. Put floured quail in heated bacon fat and cook quickly until brown. Cook with cover on pan until tender. These may be cooked in any fat, but bacon fat makes them tastier. Drain well on paper towel.

Nothing could be this good. Serve them to yourself on a lazy morning, and feel like a queen. The king will be pleased too!

Mrs. W. P. Dozier

BRAISED QUAIL

12 quail or dove   ½ cup chopped onion
2 cups flour   ½ cup chopped celery
Salt and pepper   2 tablespoons vinegar
1 can beef bouillon or 2 cups
 water and 2 cubes bouillon

Roll birds in flour seasoned with salt and pepper. Melt butter in frying pan. Brown birds in butter. Add beef bouillon, onion, celery, vinegar. Turn to low temperature. Cook covered for 1½ hours.

To make these quail extra special, add several glugs of sherry or white wine to the bouillon mixture.

Mrs. William D. Gilchrist, III

ROASTED WILD DUCK

4 ducks, cleaned   1 whole onion, skinned
¼ cup bacon fat   1½ cups each grape wine and
2 teaspoons salt   water, mixed
½ teaspoon pepper   Gravy:
2 oranges, sliced very thick 3 tablespoons flour
3 carrots, sliced very thin 6 teaspoons water

Rub breasts of ducks with bacon fat. Salt and pepper ducks inside and out. Place ducks breast side up in roaster. Put a thick orange slice on the top of each duck. Put carrots and onion in roaster. Then pour the water and wine mixture in roaster, being careful not to pour on the seasoned ducks. Cook covered in 325 degree oven for 1½ hours, basting every 30 minutes. After the 1½ hours, throw away the orange slices and the onion and turn duck breast side down. Now cook covered another 30 minutes. Remove ducks to a warm platter. With a fork mash the carrots in the broth. Make a gravy of the broth by adding the flour mixed with water and stirring until thick. Serves 8.

Mrs. James D. Moore

PHIL'S FAVORITE ROAST RARE WILD DUCK

2 ducks
Salt and pepper
4 stalks celery
4 sliced, peeled onions

½ cup melted butter
Paprika
½ cup brandy
Sauce prepared in advance

Salt and pepper inside of ducks. Place 2 celery stalks and 2 onion slices in each. Place in roasting pan and pour melted butter over them. Sprinkle lightly with salt, pepper, and paprika. Roast 20 minutes in pre-heated 450 degree oven. Remove pan from oven, pour brandy over birds and ignite. Carve and serve with sauce. Makes 4 servings.

Roast Wild Duck Sauce
4 tablespoons butter
1 2½-ounce jar mushrooms, chopped
3 green onions, thinly sliced
⅛ teaspoon thyme

2 tablespoons browned flour
½ cup hot consomme
2 tablespoons catsup
¾ cup red wine
Dash of cayenne
½ cup green olives, chopped

Melt butter in saucepan and saute mushrooms, onions, and thyme for 2 minutes. Stir in browned flour. Stir in consomme mixed with catsup. Mix well. Add wine gradually. When very hot and bubbling, add cayenne and olives. Stir and cook until thickened. Serve with wild duck. Makes about 2 cups sauce.

Men particularly like the rare method of presentation and certain gourmets believe this is the only way to cook duck. Serve these and their sauce with wild rice, a congealed fruit salad, a simple green vegetable, and a full bodied red wine.

Mrs. William A. Sims

ROASTED GOOSE

Goose
Strong vinegar water
Salt
½ cup margarine

1 onion
1 apple, peeled
1 stalk celery

Soak goose in strong vinegar water about 2 hours before cooking. When ready to cook, rub well with salt and margarine. Place in roaster. Put onion, apple, and celery inside goose. Cover and cook in oven at about 325° until tender. Age of bird will determine length of cooking time. Discard onion, apple, and celery. Make gravy.

To cook your own goose, we suggest this method. (If you'd rather stay cool, calm and collected, take the big bird to the nearest barbecue stand and ask the proprietor to do it along with his chickens. Great that way, too!)

Mrs. W. P. Dozier

MARINADE FOR DOVE OR VENISON (CHARCOALED)

½ cup butter
Juice of 2 lemons

1 tablespoon Worcestershire
½ teaspoon soy sauce

Melt butter and add other ingredients. Marinate dove for several hours in mixture. Charcoal until just pink at breast bone.

This marinade kills the wild or "livery" flavor in dove. Try for a patio party.

Mrs. Robert McWhorter

VENISON SWISS STEAK

¼ cup flour
¾ teaspoon salt
⅛ teaspoon EACH cayenne
  pepper, thyme, nutmeg, and
  cloves
2 pounds venison round steak
¼ cup cooking oil
2 large onions, thinly sliced

2 cups stewed tomatoes
1½ tablespoons Worcestershire
1 cup good red wine
1 garlic clove, crushed
1/3 cup EACH chopped carrots,
  green pepper, and celery
1 4-ounce can mushroom pieces

Make a seasoned flour by mixing the flour, salt, pepper, thyme, nutmeg, and cloves. Pound this into round steak, and then cut steak into 1-inch by 3-inch strips. Brown all sides of strips in oil. Add onion slices and let onion cook about three minutes. Then add all other ingredients in order given. Cover and cook in 350 degree oven for about 2½ hours. Good served with red currant jelly. Yield: 6-8 servings.

Mrs. James D. Moore

CORNISH GAME HENS WITH WILD RICE STUFFING

8 Cornish game hens
¾ cup margarine
1 1/3 cups canned mushroom
  pieces, drained
½ cup chopped onion

¼ cup bell pepper
3 cups cooked wild rice OR mixed
  long grain and wild
1½ teaspoons salt
¼ teaspoon pepper

Preheat oven to 325 degrees. Lightly sprinkle cavity of hens with salt. Melt ¼ cup margarine in large skillet. Saute mushrooms, onions, and green pepper. Add rice and pepper and toss. Stuff hens. Fasten with skewers. Place breast side down on rack and brush with margarine. Bake, uncovered, for 1 hour at 325 degrees. Then cover and bake 1 hour longer. If you prefer to wrap each bird in aluminum foil instead of using skewers, cook for 1½ hours covered with foil and ½ hour with foil open so that birds can brown. Serves 8.

An impressive "splurge" entree.

Mrs. William D. Gilchrist, III

CORNISH HENS IN WINE SAUCE

8 Cornish game hens
Margarine
Salt and pepper
Paprika
Sauce:
  1 tablespoon margarine
  ½ cup port wine

1 small jar currant jelly
3 cloves
1 teaspoon salt
Juice of 1 lemon
Cornstarch
Cayenne pepper

Thaw hens; wash thoroughly. Melt margarine; roll hens in melted margarine. Salt and pepper inside and out. Place in a pan two inches deep with breast side up. Sprinkle paprika on hens to help them brown. Cook slowly, 325 degrees, until meat begins to fall off wing. (Cook neck and livers from hens for broth.) Toward end of cooking baste with the wine sauce as needed.

SAUCE: Cook ingredients in double boiler. Mix a little broth with cornstarch for thickening. Yield: 1 cup of sauce; enough for 8 hens.

Currant jelly and port sauce these little hens to perfection.

Mrs. Bill Sexton

CORNISH HENS

2 Cornish game hens
¼ cup margarine
4 pieces bacon

Salt and pepper
½ cup water
½ cup white wine

Thaw hens to room temperature. Wash thoroughly and rub outside and cavity with margarine. Wrap two pieces of bacon around each hen. Salt and pepper as desired. Place breast side up on meat rack in baking pan. Pour water and wine over hens. Cook in 325 degree oven covered with foil for 1 hour; remove foil and cook 1½ hours more or until tender, basting often.

Brown, bacon wrapped, succulent. Put the children to bed early tonight and surprise him — and yourself — with your culinary expertise.

Mrs. David C. Harris

131

POULTRY

FRIED CHICKEN

1 fryer cut in pieces or equivalent
   in selected parts
Buttermilk
All-purpose flour

Salt and pepper
Lawry's seasoned salt
Shortening for frying

Wash chicken pieces, remove skin, place in large bowl and pour buttermilk over to cover. Allow to soak as long as possible, normally 1 to 3 hours or overnight for a better taste. The buttermilk tenderizes the chicken and helps pick up the seasoned flour.

When ready to cook, melt shortening in electric skillet set at 360 degrees, so that you have ½-inch to ¾-inch melted shortening. (You can store the shortening, adding to it each time to fry chicken.) Into paper or plastic bag put about 1½ cups flour, 1 teaspoon salt, ½ teaspoon Lawry's seasoned salt, and ½ to 1 teaspoon pepper. Shake well. Shake chicken pieces, **one at a time,** in flour mixture until thoroughly coated. Place in hot shortening. When all chicken is in pan, cover and cook until golden, about 15 minutes. With tongs, turn chicken pieces over, replace top of pan, and cook about 5 to 10 minutes longer until well browned. Remove from fat and drain well on paper towel or brown paper sack. Serve while still hot.

MOCK CHICKEN LEGS — Use main portion of wing and cook by above method.

To many, Alabama hospitality means fried chicken. Don't be one of those who says, "I just can't fry chicken." Follow these instructions and it will be perfect — every time.

Mrs. William E. Shinn, Jr.

BAKED CHICKEN, QUAIL OR DOVE

Birds
Salt and pepper
Lemon juice
Margarine

Sherry
Gravy
Almonds

Salt and pepper your birds. Then squeeze lemon juice over them. Brown birds in margarine. Place birds in roasting pan with ¼ cup sherry per whole chicken or ⅛ cup per quail or dove. Bake until tender. Add thickening (water stirred into flour or cornstarch) to the juice after baking for a thick gravy. Always top with almonds and serve with yellow rice. (Use sherry to individual's taste.)

This is good served with Coke salad and a green vegetable. There's your meal.

Mrs. William Sexton

ROAST CHICKEN

1 whole (2-2½ pound) chicken

Wash chicken inside and out thoroughly. Sprinkle with salt and pepper.

Stuffing:

¼ cup margarine	2 cups cooked rice
¼ cup celery, diced	1 teaspoon salt
¼ cup onion, diced	Dash of pepper

Melt margarine in skillet. Add celery and onion. Cook until tender, but not brown. Remove from heat; add other ingredients and mix well.

Fill neck cavity with stuffing. Hook wing tips into back. Fill body cavity with remaining stuffing. Tie legs together with string. Rub entire body with soft margarine. Place chicken on rack in shallow pan and roast at 375° 30 minutes per pound or until done. May be covered with foil part of roasting time.

Mrs. Ralph Huff

ROAST TURKEY

To cook the noble bird.

12-15 pound turkey	½ cup margarine
(Self basting is not necessary.)	1 soft rag or cheesecloth

Thaw turkey at least 24 hours ahead of cooking time. When thawed, wash well — inside and out. Take out giblets (liver, gizzard, neck, heart) and put in saucepan with water. Cook on low heat until tender. Salt the turkey **well** inside and out. Stuff dressing in both openings, close with skewers, place on rack in large flat pan. Melt ½ cup margarine. Take large pieces of cheesecloth or soft rag and dip into butter. Soak well and drape over turkey. Make sure the wings and legs are covered. Place in oven at 300 degrees. Cook 1 hour; turn oven down to 250 degrees for four hours. Test to see if done by moving leg. If leg moves freely the turkey is done. The turkey will be browned and more moist if you baste it every 30 minutes after the first hour. Even the "self-basting" turkeys are better this way. Remove from rack to large plate. (Cooking time should be about 1 hour less if turkey is not stuffed.) **Gravy:** Skim off some of the grease. Put aside in cup. Sprinkle ½ cup of flour over drippings in pan. Work into drippings with a fork. **Get all lumps out!** Add a small amount of water and stir. Keep adding water or stock from cooking giblets until gravy is thick. Cut up cooked giblets and pour into gravy. Add salt and pepper to taste. All this is done over low heat.

Mrs. Benjamin C. Stevens

CORNBREAD DRESSING FOR TURKEY

1 box of cornbread mix or 1 recipe cornbread
½ large loaf bread or 1 small loaf
2 good-sized onions, chopped
1 small bunch of celery, chopped
Cooking oil
½ to 1 pint oysters

The day before cooking turkey: Make cornbread and crumble to allow to harden. Put bread out to get hard or stale.

The day of cooking: Mix cornbread and bread by crumbling together. Saute onion and celery in enough oil to cover. Cook until soft. Pour celery and onion into bread-cornbread mixture. Toss well and add salt and pepper. If desired, add oysters to ¾ of dressing. Cut oysters in pieces. Use juice to moisten a little. Stuff large end of turkey with oyster dressing. Use plain dressing to stuff small end. This gives a choice. Stuff turkey well, but do not pack. Then use skewers to sew ends together. You may sew ends with threads if you don't have skewers. The dressing will make the turkey more moist.

Mrs. Benjamin C. Stevens

CORN BREAD DRESSING

Make a recipe of cornbread and crumble into a large bowl.

Neck, gizzard and liver of chicken or turkey
1½ cups water
3 chicken bouillon cubes
1 cup chopped onion
1 cup chopped celery
½ teaspoon poultry seasoning
¼ teaspoon pepper
1 teaspoon salt
3 eggs, slightly beaten

Stew together the neck, gizzard, liver, salt, pepper and chopped vegetables in a stock made of the bouillon cubes and water. Save pieces of the chicken or turkey for the gravy. Add the remaining ingredients and mix thoroughly. If necessary, use additional stock of the chicken or turkey. Place in a greased 2" deep pan and cook for 20 minutes at 450°.

Mrs. Harold Pilgrim, Jr.

BARBECUED CHICKEN

3 small fryers (split down the middle)
Salt, pepper and red pepper to taste
½ cup margarine
1 quart white vinegar
Hickory chips, soaked in water

Wash chickens thoroughly. After sprinkling with salt, pepper and red pepper, marinate with 1 quart vinegar in which you have melted ½ cup margarine.

When ready to cook, start charcoal fire and place chickens in covered container in 350° oven for 30 minutes. When coals turn white, add hickory chips and place chickens on grill away from direct heat. Cook with grill cover down for 2½ hours or until tender. Baste frequently with marinating liquid to which you have added more red pepper. Serve with accompanying white sauce.

Flavor of chicken is improved if marinated overnight, but may be cooked same day. If grill does not have a hood, cook shorter time, basting frequently.

White Sauce:

Add sugar to taste

1½ cups mayonnaise
2 cups white vinegar

¼ cup black pepper (more if desired)

Shake ingredients together and pour over chicken. Sauce will keep at least two weeks in refrigerator.

This recipe was devised in an attempt to duplicate the chicken from a local barbecue establishment which does cook the best chicken anybody has ever eaten. This method probably won't put them out of business but is an excellent imitation. The secrets are a slow fire, long cooking time and lots of hickory smoke. Don't forget the white sauce.

Mrs. David C. Harris

OVEN BARBECUED CHICKEN

3 tablespoons catsup
2 tablespoons vinegar
1 tablespoon lemon juice
2 tablespoons Worcestershire
4 tablespoons water
1 teaspoon paprika
3 tablespoons brown sugar

1 teaspoon salt
1 teaspoon chili powder
½ teaspoon red pepper
2 tablespoons margarine
1 teaspoon dry mustard
1 2½-3 pound chicken

Mix all ingredients. Dip chicken in sauce. Bake covered in aluminum foil at 500 degrees for the first 15 minutes and 350 degrees for 1 hour. Remove cover so chicken can brown, and cook uncovered for 15 minutes more.

Superior oven-barbecued chicken with a nippy sauce.

Mrs. S. Britt Owens

TANGY BARBECUED CHICKEN

1 chicken (2½-3 pounds)
  quartered, skin removed
¼ cup melted margarine
2 teaspoons salt
½ teaspoon pepper

½ teaspoon paprika
2 tablespoons sugar
2 tablespoons lemon juice
1 teaspoon Worcestershire

Combine all ingredients before placing chicken on grill. Turn and brush chicken with sauce mixture several times during cooking period. Allow about one hour for cooking. Yield: 4 servings.

If you're out of charcoal, cook chicken in the oven at 350-375 degrees. If you're out of chicken, pork chops will do.

Mrs. Jolly McKenzie

BARBECUED CHICKEN
OR
PORK CHOPS FOR GRILL

Broiling chicken or pork chops
1 bottle Italian dressing
½ cup margarine

½ cup lemon juice
1 teaspoon garlic salt
2 tablespoons Worcestershire

Marinate chicken or chops for several hours in Italian dressing. Grill on a slow fire for an hour or longer, turning as needed. Baste often with barbecue sauce made of left over salad dressing and other ingredients.

Crisp outside, juicy inside, extra easy. Corn on the cob, sliced home-grown tomatoes, and tangy slaw would make ideal platemates.

Mrs. Gilbert Key

CHICKEN OR TURKEY CASSEROLE

8 slices day-old bread
2 cups cooked chicken or turkey,
  diced
½ cup chopped onion
½ cup chopped bell peppers
½ cup finely chopped celery
½ cup mayonnaise

¾ teaspoon salt
Dash of pepper
2 eggs, slightly beaten
1½ cups milk
1 can cream of mushroom soup
½ cup shredded sharp cheese

Butter 2 slices bread; cut in ½" cubes and set aside. Cut remaining bread in about 1" cubes; place ½ of **unbuttered** cubes in bottom of 13"x 9"x2" baking dish. Combine chicken, vegetables, mayonnaise, and seasoning; spoon over the bread cubes. Sprinkle remaining **unbuttered** cubes over chicken mixture. Combine eggs and milk; pour over all. Cover and chill one hour or overnight. After well chilled, spoon soup over top. Sprinkle with **buttered cubes**. Bake in slow oven (325 degrees) for about 50 minutes or until set. Sprinkle cheese over top the last few minutes of baking. Yield: 6-8 servings.

A mock souffle of chicken or turkey you'll want to try.

Mrs. James E. Brown

"CAN OPENER" CASSEROLE

4 large whole chicken breasts
1 can cream of mushroom soup
1 can cream of chicken soup
1 small can evaporated milk
1 small can mushrooms, cut

1 cup celery, diced rather largely
1 medium bell pepper, chopped
Pimento
1 can sliced almonds
1 cup Chinese Noodles

Cook chicken breasts, cool, and cut into chunks. Mix mushroom soup, chicken soup, evaporated milk, mushrooms, chicken, celery, green pepper, pimento, and almonds. Put into casserole dish and cover with Chinese Noodles. Bake 325 degrees for 1 hour.

A terrific solution to that last minute call from husband who is bringing unexpected guests home for dinner. Don't wilt, cry, or threaten hari-kari. Run quickly to the emergency shelf (and if your male companion is in the habit of doing such things, surely you have one) and reach for all the ingredients. You can even use Swanson's canned chicken.

Mrs. Claude Carter
Omaha, Nebraska

CHICKEN CURRY

3 whole chicken breasts
2 tablespoons onion, chopped
2 tablespoons celery, chopped
½ cup margarine
½ teaspoon salt
1 tablespoon curry powder

½ cup flour
3 cups milk, or half milk and half chicken stock
1 cup cream
2 tablespoons sherry

Simmer chicken breasts in salted water for 1 hour. Debone chicken and dice. In a double boiler saute onion and celery in margarine until onions are yellow; add salt and curry powder; mix thoroughly. Add flour and stir until thoroughly mixed with above. Add milk and cream, stirring briskly until smooth and thick; cook until starch flavor has disappeared. Add sherry and chicken. Serve with rice cooked with a bit of curry powder in the water. Serves 6-8.

Curry Condiments:

Chutney
Crisp bacon
Diced hard-boiled egg
Onion rings

Shredded coconut
Tart jelly
Chopped peanuts
Chopped sweet pickle

A grand curry for eight! Pretty and good with a fresh fruit salad of many colors — greens, oranges, reds, purples — topped with poppy seed dressing.

Mrs. Norman Harris, Jr.

MILD CHICKEN CURRY

½ cup onion, finely chopped
½ cup celery, finely chopped
¼ cup oil
1/3 cup flour
2 cups chicken stock
1 cup tomato juice

½ teaspoon Worcestershire
Salt and pepper
1 teaspoon curry powder
4 cups cooked chicken, diced
4 cups hot cooked rice

Lightly brown onion and celery in hot oil. Add flour and blend. Add stock; cook till thick, stirring constantly. Add tomato juice, Worcestershire, seasonings, and chicken. Heat thoroughly. Serve over rice. Serves 4-6.

Tomato juice instead of milk makes this very mild chicken curry very different.

Mrs. John R. Taylor

CHICKEN ITALIAN

1 3-pound fryer, cut into pieces
Cooking oil
4 tablespoons chopped onions
½ clove garlic, thinly sliced
½ pound canned mushrooms

1 29-ounce can tomatoes
¾ cup Chianti wine
2 tablespoons tomato puree
Salt and pepper
1 bay leaf

Flour chicken; brown in hot oil. When brown, remove from pan. Saute onions, garlic, and mushrooms in oil. Return chicken to skillet and add remaining ingredients. Cover skillet and simmer until chicken is tender, approximately 35 minutes. Remove chicken. Serve the gravy with brown rice.

Again the Italians score in the kitchen — this time with a best-ever way to fix chicken. Chalk up points for yourself too, when you put this on the table.

Mrs. Charles W. Belt

COUNTRY CAPTAIN CHICKEN

1 5-pound hen
2 medium onions, chopped
1 clove garlic, finely chopped
1 bell pepper
3 tablespoons olive oil or any
    vegetable oil
2 29-ounce cans tomatoes
2 teaspoons curry powder
1 teaspoon thyme, powdered

1 teaspoon sugar
1 teaspoon salt
⅛ teaspoon red pepper
½ cup currants
1 cup chicken stock
¼ cup flour dissolved in small
    amount of water
1 can blanched almonds

Cook hen until tender. Cool and bone, cutting into bite-size pieces. Save stock. Saute onions, garlic, bell pepper in oil. Add tomatoes and cook five minutes. Add curry powder, thyme, salt, sugar, and red pepper. Cook 10 minutes. Add chicken, currants soaked in chicken stock, flour dissolved in water, and almonds. Cook in 350 degree oven for 45 minutes. Serve over rice with curry condiments. Yield: 12 servings.

Mrs. Lynn Fowler uses 8 chicken breasts instead of whole chicken. Plan an evening with your favorite friends, and serve our favorite chicken — a wondrously seasoned curry with tomatoes, currants, and almonds. The condiments make the meal, even if you don't have the seven boys to serve them.

Mrs. William A. Sims

SHERRY CHICKEN IN SOUR CREAM

6 medium chicken breasts
1 can mushroom soup
1 3-ounce can mushrooms and liquid OR fresh mushrooms sauteed in butter

1 cup sour cream
½ cup cooking sherry
Seedless white grapes or white raisins
1 cup cubed ham (optional)

Place chicken breasts in baking dish. Combine ingredients and pour over the chicken. Sprinkle with paprika. Bake covered at 350 degrees for 1½ hours until tender. Makes 4 to 6 servings.

Mrs. S. Britt Owens

GOURMET CHICKEN

6 large chicken breasts
1 teaspoon salt
¼ teaspoon pepper
¼ teaspoon paprika
4 tablespoons margarine
1 tablespoon onion, minced

Dash garlic powder
¾ cup white wine or sherry
¾ cup mushrooms
1 cup sour cream
½ cup toasted almonds

Sprinkle chicken with salt, pepper and paprika. Melt half of the margarine in a baking dish. Roll chicken in melted margarine until coated and place skin side down. Bake at 400 degrees until browned, about 20 minutes. Turn chicken. Combine onion, garlic powder, and ½ cup of wine and pour over the chicken. Return to oven and bake about 40 minutes or until tender. Saute sliced mushrooms in remaining butter. Add drippings from chicken to sour cream and remaining wine. Heat slowly, blending well. Add toasted almonds. Place chicken on serving dish. Pour sauce over it and sprinkle with a few toasted almonds.

The most versatile of birds goes gourmet in this creation; you go gourmet with it.

Mrs. Otis E. Kirby, Jr.

139

MARINATED BAKED CHICKEN BREASTS

2 cups sour cream
¼ cup lemon juice
4 teaspoons Worcestershire
2 teaspoons celery salt
2 teaspoons paprika
½ teaspoon garlic salt

1 tablespoon salt
1 teaspoon pepper
12 chicken breasts
1½ cups Ritz cracker crumbs
1½ cups soda cracker crumbs
1 cup margarine

Combine first eight ingredients. Add chicken, coating well. Let stand in refrigerator overnight. Remove chicken from sauce, roll in crumbs, and arrange in shallow pan. Melt margarine. Spoon half of it over chicken. Bake at 300° for one hour. Spoon rest of margarine over chicken. Bake 45 minutes more.

A grand metamorphosis — from plain chicken to chicken extra-ordinaire — takes place overnight in your very own refrigerator.

Mrs. Bill Lovin
Mrs. Allen Hamilton

CHICKEN BREASTS BAKED IN CREAM

2 whole (about 2 pounds) chicken breasts
3 tablespoons bacon fat
½ cup chopped onions
1 small garlic clove, minced

¾ cup chicken broth
¾ cup cream
1½ teaspoons salt
⅛ teaspoon pepper
1 teaspoon Worcestershire

Heat oven to 300 degrees. Cut chicken breasts, making 4 pieces. Brown breasts in bacon fat until golden brown. Heat onion, garlic, broth, cream and seasonings in saucepan. Place chicken in pyrex casserole and pour sauce over. Cover and bake 2 hours. Uncover and bake 15-20 minutes more. Serve with or on wild rice. Serves 4.

This recipe, along with a small collection of other exceptional ones, was a wedding gift to its contributor. We take pleasure, now, in giving it to you.

Mrs. Frank T. Richardson, III

CHICKEN PIQUANT

4 chicken breasts (8 halves)
½ cup margarine
1 clove garlic, mashed
1½ teaspoons salt
2 teaspoons chili powder

Dash pepper
Dash dry mustard
Juice of 3 lemons
2 teaspoons Worcestershire

Melt margarine in a small saucepan; blend in remaining ingredients. Place chicken in shallow baking dish with tight fitting cover or use foil.

140

Pour margarine mixture over chicken and cover. Bake at 350 degrees 2 hours with cover on; then remove cover, baste, and cook for 15 minutes. Place on heated platter and spoon sauce over chicken. Serves 8.

A simple-to-fix-and-let-the-oven-do-the-rest chicken dish that won all the blue ribbons at a tasting luncheon.

Mrs. Lloyd Nix

CHICKEN BREASTS AND RICE

4 chicken breasts (8 halves)
1½ cups instant rice
1 can cream of celery soup
1 can cream of mushroom soup

1 8-ounce can mushroom stems and pieces
¾ cup white cooking wine
1 envelope dry onion soup mix

Put uncooked rice in shallow baking dish. Mix two soups together, add mushrooms which you have sauteed in a tablespoon of margarine. Spoon this mixture over dry rice; then spoon the wine over this. Place the breasts in next, skin side up. Over the breasts sprinkle dry onion soup. Seal tightly with heavy duty foil and bake 2 hours in 325 or 350 degree oven. Do not open while baking.

If you are one of those rare gems who still cooks Sunday dinner (the noon variety), this is your kind of dish. Put it in a slow oven when you leave for Sunday School. Toss a salad when you get home, and serve before the family has a single chance to grumble.

Mrs. William D. Gilchrist, III

LUNCHEON CHICKEN BREASTS

8 boned chicken breasts
8 strips of bacon
8 slices of chipped beef
1 can mushroom soup

1 can chicken consomme or 2 cubes of chicken bouillon dissolved in 1 cup hot water
1 cup sour cream
Bread crumbs

Line casserole with sliced chipped beef. Wrap chicken breasts in strips of bacon to hold together. Place on chipped beef. Mix soup, consomme and sour cream together. Pour over chicken. Cook slowly—225 degrees—for two hours, adding bread crumbs and paprika at last to give a pretty brown crust.

A combination of chicken, chipped beef and bacon that is superb. What a gorgeous luncheon headliner this would be.

Mrs. Richard Rouquie

141

CHICKEN MADRID

6 chicken breasts
2 tablespoons margarine
½ teaspoon salt
¼ teaspoon pepper
1 package (2½-ounces) Lawry's spaghetti sauce mix with mushrooms

1½ cups water
1 medium onion, sliced
1 3-ounce can sliced mushrooms
½ cup ripe olives, sliced, optional
¼ cup red wine, optional

Saute chicken breasts in margarine in skillet over medium heat until browned. Sprinkle with salt and pepper. Stir together sauce mix and water. Pour over chicken, cover and let simmer for 30 minutes, stirring occasionally. Add onions, undrained mushrooms, olives, wine, and let cook 15 minutes longer. Serve over rice.

Mrs. David B. Cauthen

CHICKEN SIMMERED IN WINE

4 chicken breasts
4 chicken thighs
1 tablespoon salt
¼ teaspoon pepper
1 teaspoon rosemary

1 teaspoon marjoram
1 teaspoon oregano
¼ cup lemon juice
1 cup white wine OR 1 cup chicken broth

Remove skin from chicken. Mix together salt, pepper, rosemary, marjoram, and oregano. Sprinkle over the pieces of chicken. Saute the chicken in margarine until golden brown. Add ¼ cup lemon juice and white wine, or broth. (A combination of wine and broth may also be used). Cover and simmer until tender. Serves 6.

This can simmer a long time and just be better, so you can serve anytime your guests are ready.

Mrs. Whit King, Jr.

BREAST OF CHICKEN—DELUXE

6 chicken breasts
Flour
Egg wash (to each egg add ¼ cup water and beat)
Parmesan cheese, grated
½ cup sherry wine

Rice Colette:
    1 cup rice
    1 cup celery, chopped
    1 bell pepper, chopped
    1 onion, chopped
    1 pound chicken livers
    Kitchen Bouquet

Sherry Sauce:
    2 tablespoons margarine
    2 tablespoons flour
    1 cup milk
    ½ cup American cheese
    3 tablespoons sherry wine
    Chopped pecans
    Seeded bing cherries

Dip chicken breasts in flour, then in egg wash, then in Parmesan cheese. Mash cheese into breasts so that a good quantity is on each. Fry breasts in cooking oil just as you fry regular fried chicken. The last ten minutes of frying remove most of oil and add ½ cup sherry wine to skillet. The chicken is served on Rice Colette.

Rice Colette: Boil and steam rice. Saute finely chopped celery, onion, bell pepper, and raw chicken livers in oil until done. Mix in well with rice. When this is done, color rice slightly with Kitchen Bouquet. Chicken breast is placed on rice and covered with Sherry Sauce.

Sherry Sauce: Melt margarine and stir in flour until blended. Add milk, heat and stir until thickened. Add ½ cup grated American cheese. Stir and mix well. Add sherry. Pour sauce over chicken, already on rice. Serve with chopped pecans sprinkled over and topped with a seeded bing cherry.

Beautiful — delicious — The girl who really loves to cook will find this great fun; the girl who doesn't will meet her Waterloo.

Mrs. Claude Carter
Omaha, Nebraska

CHICKEN WITH SHRIMP AND WINE SAUCE

6-8 chicken breasts or a 3-pound chicken
½ cup margarine
3 tablespoons flour
1 cup chicken broth
1 can mushroom slices
1 teaspoon paprika
½-¾ teaspoon grated lemon peel

1-2 tablespoons freeze-dried chives
2 cups sour cream
2-4 tablespoons chopped parsley or parsley flakes
2 cans cream of shrimp soup
2-4 tablespoons sauterne
½ cup chopped boiled shrimp (optional)

Cook chicken in margarine until browned lightly. Transfer to large casserole. Blend flour into margarine. Add broth and stir constantly until thick and boiling. Add mushroom slices and juice. Add paprika, grated lemon peel, and chives. When blended add **1 cup** sour cream. Pour over chicken in casserole. To shrimp soup add remaining cup sour cream and chopped shrimp, if desired. Pour over chicken and gravy. Cook covered 350 degrees about an hour. When chicken is tender, add sauterne and parsley and cook 10 minutes uncovered. May be served with rice.

Keeps well overnight and may be warmed and served again. You have only to add a little more wine and parsley before serving.

Mrs. John D. Davis, Jr.

CHICKEN ALOHA

1 chicken breast for each person
1 small bottle catsup
1 can tomato soup or tomato paste
1 bell pepper, chopped

¼ cup brown sugar
1/3 cup vinegar
1 teaspoon dry mustard
1 can pineapple chunks and juice

Mix sauce and pour over chicken. Bake at 375 degrees for 1 hour covered. Remove cover and bake an additional 15 minutes. Serve over rice.

Although the islands would probably make no claim to it, this is a sumptuous and different way to fix chicken.

Mrs. Frank T. Richardson, Jr.

CHICKEN LIB A LA LYNNE

1 4-ounce can mushrooms
1 tablespoon Wylers instant
   chicken bouillon
4 chicken breasts
Margarine
Celery salt

White Pepper
Salt
Tarragon leaves
Basil leaves
1 can cream of chicken soup

In glass mix juice of mushrooms and 1 tablespoon of bouillon. Butter the bottom of casserole. Sprinkle the bottom of breasts with celery salt and white pepper. Dot margarine on top of breasts and sprinkle with salt and white pepper: sprinkle with Tarragon leaves and Basil leaves. Spoon on chicken soup. Add ½ of bouillon mixture. Cook 1 hour in 350 degree oven uncovered. After cooking 1 hour add the rest of bouillon mixture and 1 can mushrooms. Cook for 15 minutes more.

Subtle herb flavor makes this a great party dish.

Mrs. William S. Coles

CHICKEN KIEV

4 large whole chicken breasts
Salt and pepper
½ cup chilled margarine
¼ cup flour

¼ cup milk
* 1 cup fine fresh bread crumbs
1 quart corn oil for 3 quart pan

Cut breasts in half, remove skin and bone. Place each piece of meat between waxed paper, pound with flat side of wooden mallet until meat spreads out in a thin slice. Sprinkle meat with salt and pepper. Cut chilled margarine into eight equal crosswise pieces. Place a piece of margarine off center toward narrow thick end of chicken piece; fold thick end over margarine; roll over piece tightly and press down edge; turn under side edges, press down and fasten with toothpick. Dust rolls with flour, roll in milk, then in crumbs. Refrigerate 1 hour or more before frying.

144

Heat oil in heavy skillet to 375 degrees. Add rolls slowly; turn with spoon to cook and brown all over — 3 to 5 minutes. Lower temperature if rolls get too brown. If rolls are fried in two batches, keep first batch warm in slow oven, 250 degrees. Drain on absorbent paper. Makes 4 servings.

*To make fine fresh crumbs: Cut crusts from slices of day-old firm-type white bread; cut into small squares; use electric blender to make crumbs.

Of Russian origin, these delicate morsels are numbered among the world's great chicken dishes. As you cut into your first crisp bite, watch the melted butter ooze out, and feel your mouth begin to water.

Mrs. Billy W. Payne

COQ AU VIN

2½ pound broiler-fryer, quartered or cut in pieces
6 bacon slices, diced before cooking
2 tablespoons margarine
8 small white onions, peeled
8 large fresh mushrooms or canned mushrooms
2/3 cup sliced green onions
1 clove garlic, crushed

2 or more tablespoons flour
1 teaspoon salt
⅛ teaspoon pepper
¼ teaspoon dried thyme
2 cups Burgundy or California Mountain Red Wine
1 cup canned chicken broth
Chopped parsley
8 small new potatoes, peeled

Day before: Wash chicken and dry with paper towel. In at least a 3-quart Dutch oven over medium heat saute diced bacon until crisp. Remove bacon and drain. Add margarine to bacon fat. Heat. In hot fat, brown chicken on all sides. Remove and set aside. Pour off all but 2 tablespoons fat from the Dutch oven. Add onions, mushrooms, and green onions and garlic. Over low heat, cook covered, stirring occasionally for 10 minutes. Remove from heat. Stir in flour, salt, pepper and thyme. Gradually add Burgundy and chicken broth, scraping bottom of pan well. Bring mixture to boiling, stirring constantly. Remove from heat. Add potatoes, chicken, and bacon. Mix well. Cover and refrigerate overnight.

Next day: About 2 hours before serving time, preheat oven to 400 degrees. Bake Coq Au Vin, covered, about 1 hour and 50 minutes or until chicken and potatoes are tender. Sprinkle top with chopped parsley before serving and serve right from Dutch oven. Serves 4. Increase amount of all; you are limited only by the size of Dutch oven. Increase cooking time for larger amount.

French country cooking inspires cotton country cooks. Coq au Vin is a hearty chicken stew with red wine. Fix the stew in a colorful enamel Dutch oven today, let it spend the night in the refrigerator, cook and serve tomorrow night from the same vessel. You'll need only a loaf of your OWN French bread and a good red wine.

Mrs. William E. Shinn, Jr.

GOOD-BYE CHICKEN CASSEROLE

1 can mushroom soup	½ cup grated cheese
½ cup water	1½ cups cooked asparagus
1 1/3 cups instant rice	2 cups sliced chicken
1½ cups chicken broth	2 tablespoons slivered almonds

Pour Minute Rice from box into 2 quart shallow pan and sprinkle half of cheese over rice. Top with asparagus, then chicken. Pour mushroom soup and water which have been mixed together over entire mixture. Pour broth over the soup mixture; top with remaining cheese. Bake at 375 degrees for 20 minutes. Add almonds during last 10 minutes of baking. Serves 6.

Designed, as the name implies, to get rid of the left over chicken or turkey, this meal-in-a-dish is so easy and so good that you may even cook some chicken just for the occasion.

Mrs. John A. Woller

CHICKEN DIVAN

1 package frozen broccoli, cooked	½ cup mayonnaise
2 whole chicken breasts, cooked	1 teaspoon lemon juice
½ cup shredded sharp cheese	Dash curry powder
1 can cream of chicken soup	Bread crumbs

Place cooked broccoli in shallow baking dish. Top with sliced chicken. Sprinkle with cheese. Combine chicken soup, mayonnaise, lemon juice and curry powder and pour this mixture over the chicken. Sprinkle bread crumbs on top along with additional shredded cheese, if desired. Bake in a 350° oven for 30 minutes or until heated through.

An easy method for fixing that pretty and tasty chicken and broccoli dish that is a meal in itself.

Mrs. Paul E. Hargrove
Mrs. Norman Harris, Jr.

QUICK CHICKEN AND ASPARAGUS CASSEROLE

4 chicken breasts, deboned	1 lemon
1 can asparagus tips	Salt and pepper
1 can cream of chicken soup	½ cup buttered cracker crumbs
½ cup mayonnaise	

Boil chicken breasts until tender, debone, and cut into pieces; put into a greased casserole dish and place asparagus on top. Make a sauce of the soup, mayonnaise and juice of the lemon, mixing mayonnaise and lemon juice together before mixing this with soup. Pour the sauce over the chicken and asparagus and sprinkle cracker crumbs on top. Bake at 350 degrees for 30 minutes.

Mrs. James P. Smartt, Jr.

CHICKEN ALMOND POLYNESIAN

2 cups cooked chicken, diced
½ cup mushrooms, sliced
½ cup bamboo shoots, sliced
½ cup water chestnuts, sliced
2 cups celery, sliced

½ cup Chinese pea pod,
  if available
1 teaspoon salt
2 tablespoons cornstarch
2 cups chicken stock
Toasted almonds

Saute cut up chicken in small amount of oil in large skillet until browned lightly. Add mushrooms, bamboo shoots, water chestnuts, celery, and pea pods and 1 teaspoon salt. Saute another 5 minutes. Place cornstarch in sauce pan. Slowly stir in chicken stock. Cook over medium heat, stirring constantly until mixture thickens and boils. Boil 1 minute. Add chicken stock mixture to other ingredients; stir. Cover and simmer additional 5 minutes. Serve with white rice and soy sauce. Sprinkle with almonds.

A beautiful and inviting chicken entree of oriental influence, with the intriguing variety of textures so often found in Polyneslan foods.

Mrs. Frank T. Richardson, III

FIRST PLACE CHICKEN CASSEROLE

2 to 3 cups cooked chicken, diced
4 hard-boiled eggs, chopped
2 cups cooked rice
1½ cups celery, chopped
1 small onion, chopped
1 cup mayonnaise
2 cans mushroom soup

1 3-ounce package slivered
  almonds
1 teaspoon salt
2 tablespoons lemon juice
1 cup bread crumbs
2 tablespoons margarine

Mix all ingredients except bread crumbs and margarine. Place mixture in buttered 9"x12" pan or casserole. Brown bread crumbs lightly in margarine. Sprinkle over casserole, refrigerate overnight. Remove from refrigerator 1 hour before cooking. Bake 40-45 minutes at 350 degrees. Serves 8.

Superlatives are definitely in order for this make-ahead dish — which came to us already aptly named. We suggest cooking the rice in the broth left from the chicken. We promise rave notices to you too!

Mrs. Garner Pride
Mrs. Lewis C. Brown

CHICKEN-ALMOND CASSEROLE

2 cups cooked chicken, diced
½ cup mayonnaise
1 can cream of chicken soup
2 hard-boiled eggs, chopped

1 cup celery, chopped
½ cup slivered almonds
Potato chips

Combine first six ingredients in casserole. Top generously with crushed potato chips. Bake at 350 degrees for 20 minutes.

Mrs. Charles W. Belt

CHICKEN TETRAZZINI

1 medium onion, chopped
¾ cup bell pepper, chopped
1 cup celery, chopped
½ cup margarine
1 tablespoon flour
1 cup sharp cheese, grated
1 can mushroom soup
2 cans chicken broth or milk

1 teaspoon salt
½ teaspoon celery salt
2 to 3 cups chicken
1 4-ounce can mushrooms
½ cup slivered almonds
1 2-ounce jar pimento, chopped
1 small package spaghetti, cooked

Saute onion, bell pepper, and celery in margarine. Add flour, cheese, and soup. Stir to blend well. Add broth or milk. Blend till smooth. Stir in remainder of ingredients. Pour into large casserole or flat baking dish. Sprinkle top with cracker crumbs. Bake at 400 degrees for 15-20 minutes. Serves 8.

A standard for entertaining, tetrazzini is always well received and is easily stretched as the crowd increases.

Mrs. Herbert Street

CHICKEN SPAGHETTI

1 4 to 5 pound chicken
1½ cups celery, chopped
½ cup cooking oil
3 small onions, chopped
1 medium bell pepper, chopped
2 16-ounce cans tomatoes

1 4-ounce can mushrooms
2 tablespoons Worcestershire
Chicken broth
1 package spaghetti
Salt and pepper
¼ pound New York State cheese

Cook chicken in 2 quarts water with celery. Heat cooking oil in large skillet and cook onions and pepper until half-done. Add tomatoes, mushrooms, Worcestershire, cut-up chicken, and some broth, if necessary. Simmer for 30 minutes. Cook spaghetti in chicken broth. Add cooked spaghetti, salt and pepper to taste to mixture. Place in large casserole with cheese grated on top. Heat in oven until hot throughout. Serves 8.

Are you in a rut with spaghetti and meat sauce? Climb out of your rut with our chicken spaghetti — good for everyday or company suppers.

Mrs. Norman L. Self

MARY'S SPAGHETTI

2 whole chicken breasts
2 cups chopped celery
1 cup chopped onion
2 bell peppers, chopped
2 pounds ground beef
3 tablespoons oil
Salt and pepper, to taste
1 tablespoon garlic powder

½ cup stock
3 26½-ounce cans Franco American spaghetti
1 15-ounce can tomato sauce
1 4-ounce can mushrooms, drained
Parmesan cheese
½ cup almonds

Boil chicken breasts until tender and cut into pieces. Reserve stock. Cook celery, onions and peppers in oil until clear. Salt and pepper beef to taste and brown in oil. Add garlic powder. Add stock and remaining ingredients. Put in layers with Parmesan cheese between layers. Top with slivered almonds. Bake at 350° until bubbly. Serves 10 to 12.

Mary combines ground beef and chicken breasts with canned spaghetti for a treat which is good today, better tomorrow and which freezes beautifully.

Mrs. James B. Odom

CHICKEN A LA KING

(Serves 48)

4 quarts cooked chicken (about 3 whole fryers or 6 whole chicken breasts)
1 2/3 cups chicken fat
1⅛ cups butter
3¾ cups flour
1 gallon chicken stock
1 quart milk
8 egg yolks, slightly beaten
5¾ cups mushrooms

1 onion, chopped
2 cups pimentos
Salt and pepper to taste
Lemon juice
Worcestershire
Accent
Sherry (if desired)
7 9½-ounce cans Chow Mein noodles

Undercook chicken so it will not be stringy. Cut in big hunks. In saucepan melt chicken fat and butter. Stir in flour and cook slightly. Slowly add milk and egg yolks. Cook until thickened. Saute onion and add with remaining ingredients except noodles and heat. Serve over warmed noodles.

Keep this recipe in mind. The results are marvelous, and we can think of many times you may need to cook in this quantity, even though, at this moment, you can not imagine it.

Mrs. William B. Eyster

149

ANN ANDERSON'S LOW FAT CHICKEN TETRAZZINI

6 ounces extra fine spaghetti, cooked
1 can (4 ounces) sliced mushrooms
3 tablespoons flour
1 cup skim milk
1 cup undiluted evaporated skim milk
2 tablespoons sherry
1 small green pepper, slivered

2 teaspoons salt
1/8 teaspoon white pepper
1 teaspoon Worcestershire
1 jar (2 ounces) pimentos, drained and slivered
4 cups cooked white chicken, diced
2 tablespoons Parmesan cheese

Arrange spaghetti in shallow 1½ quart pyrex pan. Drain mushrooms and blend flour with the liquid. Bring milk to boil in 3 quart saucepan. Stir in flour mixture and cook, stirring until thickened. Add mushrooms, sherry, next five ingredients and mix well. Fold in chicken. Pour over spaghetti and sprinkle with cheese. Bake in slow oven, 300 degrees about 45 minutes. Put under broiler to brown lightly.

BAKED CHICKEN SALAD

2 cups cubed cooked chicken or turkey
2 cups celery, chopped
½ cup toasted almonds, chopped
½ teaspoon salt
2 tablespoons grated onion
½ cup bell pepper, chopped

½ cup mayonnaise
2 tablespoons pimento, chopped
2 tablespoons lemon juice
½ can cream of chicken soup
½ cup American cheese, grated
3 cups potato chips, crushed

Combine all ingredients except cheese and potato chips. Toss lightly; spoon into a 1½-quart casserole. Spread chips and cheese on top. Bake at 350 degrees for 25 minutes or until heated through and browned. Serves 8 to 10.

Mrs. George Godwin, Jr.

CALIFORNIA HOT CHICKEN SALAD

3 cups cooked chicken, diced
½ cup chicken broth
2 cups celery, chopped
1 cup slivered almonds
1 pimento, cut in strips
1½ cups mayonnaise
1 tablespoon lemon juice

1 tablespoon onion juice
½ teaspoon pepper
1 teaspoon salt
½ cup green stuffed olives, sliced
½ cup mild cheese, grated
1 cup potato chips, crushed

Heat chicken and broth in covered pan over low heat; remove from heat and add celery, almonds, pimento, and mayonnaise (the mayonnaise blended with the lemon and onion juices). Toss with fork. Add seasonings and olives and pour in buttered casserole. Mix cheese and chips into mixture, leaving a little of both to sprinkle over top. Bake in oven at 450 degrees for 15 minutes or until brown.

You'll be missing an awfully good thing if you don't try this for a wintertime luncheon. Sliced green olives make the hot salad different and extra special.

Mrs. James P. Smartt, Jr.

SEAFOOD

FISH IN FOIL

2 packages, 1 pound each, frozen cod, whiting, ocean perch or haddock, completely thawed
Salt and pepper

1/3 cup melted margarine
1 thinly sliced onion
2 crushed bay leaves
½ cup chili sauce

Divide fish into six portions and drain on paper towels. Arrange each portion in center of 11-inch square of heavy foil and sprinkle lightly with salt and pepper. Add remaining ingredients, dividing equally. Seal foil. Bake at 400° for 25 minutes. This may be prepared ahead and refrigerated until baking time. Serves six.

We wonder how any cook really managed before the advent of that multi-use marvel, aluminum foil. Here, thanks to foil, is a very good, very easy way to fix fish which leaves no fishy smell in the air and no grease spatters on the stove.

Mrs. William G. Stone, Jr.

FRIED CRAPPIE

Crappie
Cornmeal (plain)

Salt and Pepper
Corn Oil

Cleaning crappie: Never skin a crappie — scale a crappie with a tablespoon. Cut at 45 degree angle from gill to anus. Split down toward tail. When the head is pulled off, the entrails will be removed.

Score on both sides, 1 time for small crappie, 2 times for larger crappie. Salt and pepper both sides. Cover both sides with cornmeal. Use a 5-6" deep, iron Dutch oven, 9 to 10" in diameter. Fill ½ full of corn oil. Heat on high until corner of bread bubbles and browns immediately. Put fish in, a few at a time. Lower heat between high and medium high. May be necessary to raise heat. Turn fish occasionally so that they do not brown too much. They are done when they float freely in oil.

Mrs. George Howell, Jr.

151

RED SNAPPER WITH ALMOND SAUCE

6 to 8 snapper fillets, the size of
   your hand
Salt, to taste
Fresh lemon juice
Cornmeal

½ cup Sauterne
Almond Sauce:
½ cup margarine
1 tablespoon Worcestershire
1 6-ounce package sliced almonds

Sprinkle snapper liberally with lemon juice. Salt each piece to taste and roll lightly in cornmeal. Using a heavy skillet, brown fish in hot oil. Remove from skillet and place in an ovenproof dish with a tight fitting lid. When all pieces are browned, sprinkle with the wine, making certain that wine touches each piece in casserole. Cover casserole and place in oven to steam for approximately 1 hour at 300°. This time may be adjusted to individual convenience.

Almond Sauce: Melt butter in small skillet and brown very slightly. Add Worcestershire and almonds. Simmer for a minute or two. Arrange snapper on a serving platter and pour sauce over fish. Garnish with lemon wedges and parsley sprigs and serve. Size of snapper determines number recipe will serve.

A favorite salt-water fish cooked almost any way, red snapper with its browned butter and almond sauce is sure to please!

Mrs. L. Denton Cole, Jr.

BUTTER-COOKED SHRIMP

1 to 1½ pounds raw, cleaned
   shrimp
¾ cup butter or margarine

Juice of six whole lemons and
   rind
½ teaspoon salt

Melt butter in skillet on very low heat. Add juice of lemons and lemon rinds. Place shrimp in skillet and sprinkle salt over shrimp. Turn heat up slightly and cook shrimp until pink on both sides (about 2½ minutes on each side.) Serve immediately. It can be placed in a chafing dish to serve. Serve with a seafood sauce or pour the remaining butter and lemon juice over the shrimp. Serves six.

A very quick but delicious way to cook shrimp — the very freshest you can get — for those who really like the taste of shrimp and not just the sauce.

Mrs. David C. Harris

BROILED SHRIMP

2 pounds jumbo, unshelled raw
   shrimp
½ cup butter or margarine
½ cup salad oil
¼ cup chopped parsley

4 to 6 garlic cloves, crushed
1 teaspoon salt
Dash cayenne pepper
¼ cup lemon juice

152

Rinse shrimp, remove shells leaving tails on. Devein using a sharp knife and cut shrimp open (butterfly). Wash, drain, and pat dry on paper towels. Melt butter in shallow broiler pan without rack (13 x 9 x 2 baking pan). Add oil, 2 tablespoons parsley, garlic, salt, cayenne and lemon juice. Mix well. Add shrimp, tossing in butter mixture to coat well. Arrange in single layer in pan. Broil 4 to 5 inches from heat about five minutes. Turn shrimp, broil five to ten minutes longer or until lightly browned. Remove shrimp to heated platter and pour garlic mixture over all. Sprinkle shrimp with parsley and garnish platter with lemon slices. Makes eight servings.

Magnifico!

Mrs. John E. Wilks, Jr.

BAKED STUFFED SHRIMP

1½ pounds cleaned raw shrimp
¾ cups prepared toasted bread
crumbs
¾ cups rolled Ritz crackers
½ teaspoon garlic salt
½ teaspoon celery salt
½ teaspoon parsley flakes
Dash or two of lemon juice
½ cup melted butter

Place shrimp in a buttered baking dish. Mix all other ingredients and cover shrimp with mixture. Bake at 400-450° for 30 minutes. Baking shells may be used for individual servings if preferred. Bake only 25 minutes. Serves 4.

Sounds complicated, but it's not. Sounds good, and it is.

Mrs. Arthur F. Jordan

SHRIMP CREOLE

¼ cup salad oil
1 cup thinly sliced onion
1 cup thinly sliced celery
1 cup bell pepper strips
(2 inches long)
3½ cups canned tomatoes
1 8-ounce can tomato sauce
2 bay leaves
1 tablespoon sugar
1 tablespoon salt
1 tablespoon chili powder
⅛ teaspoon Tabasco
2 pounds raw, cleaned shrimp
2 tablespoons flour
1/3 cup water

Preheat electric skillet to 300°. Pour in oil and saute onions, celery, bell pepper until tender but not brown. Add tomatoes, tomato sauce, bay leaves, sugar, salt, chili powder, Tabasco. Mix well, add shrimp. Cover and reduce temperature. Simmer 30 minutes or longer. Mix flour and water. Add to mixture and cook about 5 minutes until thickened. Serve over rice. Serves six generously.

Many tasters declare this is the best shrimp creole they've ever eaten.

Mrs. Joe D. Burns

SHRIMP CREOLE

1¼ cups bacon drippings
2 cups flour
2 6-ounce cans tomato paste
4 large diced onions
1 small bell pepper, chopped
¾ diced lemon

4 garlic cloves, pressed
Water
¼ teaspoon oregano
3 bay leaves
Salt and pepper
5 pounds raw shrimp

Make paste or roux of the drippings and flour. Cook until dark brown, stirring constantly. Roux should be very brown but not burned. Add tomato paste, stirring frequently. Combine onions, pepper, lemon, garlic and add to roux. Stir in water until mixture is consistency of gravy. Add oregano, bay leaves. Salt and pepper to taste. Cook about 1 hour. Add 5 pounds raw shrimp and cook an additional 30 minutes. Serve over rice. Serves 12 to 14.

This recipe is from Louisiana, where Creole cookery began.

Mrs. George McCrary, Jr.

CURRIED SHRIMP

½ cup butter
1 cup chopped onions
½ cup chopped celery
1 cup chopped apples
2 tablespoons curry powder
3 tablespoons flour
3 tablespoons butter
2 cups milk

¼ teaspoon salt
½ teaspoon allspice
½ teaspoon nutmeg
5 pounds shrimp, cooked
3 small boxes instant rice, cooked
1/3 cup sherry
Parmesan cheese

Saute onions, celery and apples in butter. Add curry powder. Make a thick cream sauce by mixing flour with melted butter over medium heat. Stir until smooth and cook until frothy. Add two cups milk and stir constantly until thick. Add salt, allspice and nutmeg. Combine sauteed onion, celery and apples with cream sauce. Add shrimp and sherry to this mixture and stir well. Combine with rice and place in casserole. Sprinkle Parmesan cheese on top. Put in 350° oven only long enough to get hot. (Shrimp mixture may be served in chafing dish and poured over hot rice.)

Don't forget the condiments. Any or all of the following are particularly good with shrimp: chopped peanuts, sieved hard-boiled eggs, grated coconut, sliced green onions, chopped tomatoes, crumbled crisp bacon and chutney.

Mrs. William B. Eyster

154

SHRIMP OR CHICKEN CURRY

3 tablespoons butter
¼ cup minced onion
3 tablespoons flour
1½ teaspoons curry powder
¾ teaspoon salt
¾ teaspoon sugar
⅛ teaspoon ground ginger

1 cup chicken broth (or 1 chicken
   bouillon cube in 1 cup water)
1 cup milk
2 cups cooked, cleaned shrimp
   (or 2 cups cut-up chicken)
½ teaspoon lemon juice

Melt butter over low heat in saucepan. Saute onion in melted butter. Blend in flour and seasonings. Cook over low heat until mixture is smooth and bubbly. Remove from heat. Stir in chicken broth and milk. Bring to a boil, stirring constantly. Boil 1 minute. Add shrimp or chicken and lemon juice. Heat. Yields 4 servings. Serve over rice with accompaniments.

Curry Accompaniments

Chutney — Slivered, salted almonds — Diced, hard-boiled eggs Flaked coconut — Raisins — Chopped peanuts — Bacon bits — Sliced avocado — Currant jelly — India relish.

Curried dishes have become quite popular for entertaining, and rightly so. They're delicious — and it's such fun to fix your own plate with all those enticing little bowls of interesting bits of things to sprinkle on top. This is an excellent shrimp curry — or chicken curry, if you prefer.

Mrs. Frank T. Richardson, III

SHRIMP PARMESAN

2 cloves garlic, chopped fine
¼ cup salad oil
¼ cup butter or margarine
3 cups cooked shrimp (2½ pounds
   raw)
½ teaspoon salt
⅛ teaspoon pepper

1 tablespoon flour
½ cup dry white wine
½ teaspoon dried oregano
½ cup grated Parmesan cheese
4 teaspoons parsley (optional)
½ cup fresh bread crumbs
3 cups hot cooked rice

Let garlic stand in oil overnight, then remove garlic 45 minutes before using. In large skillet, melt butter, add cooked shrimp, salt and pepper. Spoon shrimp into 2 quart casserole, leaving butter in skillet. In small bowl mix flour with a little of the wine. Stir into butter in skillet. Simmer until light brown. Stir in oregano, rest of wine and garlic oil. Pour over shrimp. Combine parsley, Parmesan cheese and crumbs. Sprinkle over shrimp. Bake 30 minutes in 350° oven. Serve over hot rice.

This is a good party dish and doubles or triples nicely.

Mrs. Fletcher Eddens
Wilmington, North Carolina

BEVERLY ANN'S SHRIMP IN WINE SAUCE

1 two or three pound package frozen shrimp

Cook shrimp according to directions on package adding a few celery flakes and 3 or 4 bay leaves to cooking water. Drain and add to thickened wine sauce.

Wine Sauce:

6 tablespoons butter	1 cup shrimp stock
6 tablespoons flour	¼ cup dry sherry
1½ cups milk	1 teaspoon nutmeg
	Paprika to color

Melt butter in saucepan, blend in flour, stir until smooth. Now stir in the next three ingredients gradually and cook over direct heat, stirring constantly until sauce becomes thick and smooth. Add nutmeg. Stir in cooked shrimp, add paprika for color. Serve over rice. Serves 6 to 8.

This easy to stir up sauce does marvelous things to the easy-to-cook frozen shrimp. No one will guess it isn't fresh! Serve with lots of color: fresh asparagus, perhaps dressed with lemon butter, and a tomato and avocado salad.

Mrs. Harold Pilgrim, Jr.

SHRIMP FLORENTINE

2 pounds raw or frozen shrimp	Salt and pepper to taste
2 packages frozen, chopped spinach	Pinch of nutmeg
	2 tablespoons minced onion
4 tablespoons butter or margarine	2 teaspoons chopped parsley
4 tablespoons flour	¼ to ½ cup grated Parmesan cheese
4 cups milk	
8 egg yolks, slightly beaten	

Clean and cook shrimp. Cook spinach and drain. Melt butter in saucepan, stir in flour until smooth. Gradually pour in milk and cook until thick, stirring constantly. Stir in beaten egg yolks and cook to the boiling point, but do not boil. Remove from heat and season to taste with salt and pepper. Add nutmeg, onion and parsley. Place a layer of cooked spinach in bottom of buttered 2 quart casserole. Add a layer of cooked shrimp and pour sauce over shrimp. Sprinkle with Parmesan cheese, then paprika. Bake at 400° (hot oven) about 10 minutes or brown in broiler. Serves 6-8.

Mrs. David C. Harris

EGG FOO YONG

6 eggs
2 cups drained bean sprouts
1 cup finely chopped cooked
  shrimp
½ teaspoon salt

¼ teaspoon pepper
½ cup chopped green onions
2 tablespoons chopped parsley
1 tablespoon soy sauce
2 tablespoons cooking oil

Beat eggs for one minute. Add bean sprouts, shrimp, salt, pepper, onion, parsley, soy sauce; mix lightly. Heat oil in skillet, drop in mixture to form small pancakes and saute until golden brown on both sides.

Chinese Brown Gravy:

6 tablespoons shortening
4 tablespoons flour
1 beef bouillon cube
2 tablespoons soy sauce
1 tablespoon brown gravy sauce

1 teaspoon salt
½ cup water
1½ cups hot water or mushroom
  juice

Melt shortening, add flour. Add remaining ingredients except hot water. Mix thoroughly. Add hot water. Cook until smooth, stirring constantly. Serve over Egg Foo Yong. Serves 6.

Mrs. John Power
Miami, Florida

SHRIMP AND SAUSAGE

1 4-ounce can sliced mushrooms
2 chicken bouillon cubes
2 cups water
⅛ teaspoon crushed saffron
1 1/3 cups instant rice
¼ cup butter

½ cup chopped onions
1 pound cleaned, cooked shrimp
1 cup diced cooked ham
¼ pound brown-and-serve
  sausages, sliced
¼ cup grated Parmesan cheese

Drain mushrooms, measuring the liquid. Combine 1/3 cup mushroom liquid, the bouillon cubes, water and saffron in a sauce pan. Bring to a boil. Then add instant rice. Mix just enough to moisten the rice. Cover. Remove from heat. Let stand for 5 minutes. Meanwhile, melt the butter in large skillet. Add onions, mushrooms, shrimp, ham and sausages. Saute until lightly browned. Add the seasoned rice and cheese; then mix gently with fork. Makes four or five servings.

An American variation (you know, that implies it's quick) of Paella, that heavenly concoction of chicken, sausage and seafood the Spaniards boast about.

Mrs. Frank T. Richardson, Jr.

157

SHRIMP JAMBALAYA

8 pieces of bacon
2 medium onions
1 cup chopped celery
1 large chopped bell pepper
1 cup uncooked rice
1 pound raw, cleaned shrimp

2 cups beef bouillon
1 ounce New Orleans Hot Sauce
1 ounce Worcestershire
1 bay leaf
Black pepper, to taste
Lawry's seasoned salt, to taste

Fry bacon. Saute onion, celery and bell pepper in ¼ inch of bacon grease. Add rice and brown slightly. Add bouillon which has been heated to boiling point and all other ingredients except shrimp. Cook until rice is tender and add shrimp. Continue to cook until shrimp is done, about ten minutes. Do not overcook shrimp. Serves six.

Cajun cooking at its best. Very hot shrimp and rice flavored with bacon. A green salad or tomato aspic, French bread, and a dessert of fresh fruit are our recommendations.

Mrs. William A. Sims

SHRIMP IN WINE SAUCE

1 pound shelled, raw shrimp
¼ cup flour
¼ cup olive oil
¼ cup dry white wine
2 teaspoons canned tomato paste
1 tablespoon snipped parsley

1 scallion, chopped
2 tablespoons warm water
½ teaspoon salt
¼ teaspoon pepper
Dash cayenne pepper

Coat shrimp with flour. Saute in skillet with hot oil until golden. Into saucepan, pour excess oil from skillet. Set aside. Add wine to shrimp in skillet, cook uncovered, over low heat about three minutes. Meanwhile, to oil in saucepan, add tomato paste, water, salt, pepper and cayenne. Cook over low heat five minutes, then pour over shrimp. Sprinkle with parsley and chopped scallion (use tops, too) and cook five minutes. Makes two servings.

Want a special dinner for just the two of you? This is perfect for a cozy anniversary or birthday celebration. A word of caution: He may never take you out to dinner again!

Mrs. John Manning

SAUCY SHRIMP CASSEROLE

¼ cup margarine
¼ cup flour
1 teaspoon salt
½ teaspoon Worcestershire
2 cups milk

1 8-ounce wedge sharp Cheddar
   cheese, shredded
6 hard-boiled eggs, sliced
1 pound cooked shrimp

Make a cream sauce with margarine, flour, seasonings and milk. Add cheese, stirring until melted. Alternate layers of egg slices, shrimp, and sauce in a casserole. Bake at 350° for 20-25 minutes.

Mrs. Julian Bibb

SHRIMP GRUYERE

¾ cup plus 2 tablespoons butter
¾ cup flour
3 cups milk
12-ounces Gruyere cheese
¼ teaspoon garlic powder
3 teaspoons salt
1 teaspoon white pepper
¼ teaspoon monosodium
   glutamate
¼ teaspoon dry mustard
2 teaspoons tomato paste
2 teaspoons lemon juice
2 pounds cooked, cleaned shrimp
2 tablespoons diced bell pepper
½ pound sliced mushrooms

Make a cream sauce in top of double boiler with ¾ cup butter, flour and milk. Cut cheese into pieces and add to sauce. Cook and stir until cheese melts. Add other ingredients except last three. Saute mushrooms and bell pepper in remaining 2 tablespoons butter and add to sauce with the shrimp. Heat 10-15 minutes. Serves 8. Serve over rice.

A sauce too smooth to be true — beautiful in a silver chafing dish garnished with bell pepper. Get out that bottle of dry white wine you've been saving for a special occasion.

Mrs. Whitfield King

CONNIE ESTRIDGE'S SHRIMP CASSEROLE

2 tablespoons butter
1 medium onion minced
1 4-ounce can drained mushrooms
1 16-ounce can drained whole
   tomatoes
1 pound cleaned, cooked shrimp
½ teaspoon salt
¼ teaspoon pepper
1 teaspoon paprika
½ cup thin cream or half and half
2 tablespoons flour
1 tablespoon Worcestershire
¼ cup sherry

Saute onion in butter but do not brown. Add tomatoes and simmer for 10 minutes. Blend cream and flour and add along with sherry and seasonings. Add mushrooms and shrimp and put in casserole. Top with buttered bread crumbs and bake 20 minutes in preheated 350° oven. Serves 4.

Once tried, you'll use this over and over again.

Mrs. Frank T. Richardson, Jr.

159

SHRIMP ETOUFFEE

1 medium onion, finely chopped
2 finely chopped green onions
and blades
3 or 4 cloves garlic, minced
1 tablespoon Worcestershire
¼ cup celery, finely chopped
4 drops Tabasco
½ cup butter
1 teaspoon salt
½ teaspoon sugar

2 tablespoons flour
½ teaspoon crushed thyme
2½ cups water
⅛ teaspoon pepper
1 10 ½-ounce can tomato puree
2 bay leaves
1 pound (3 cups) cleaned raw
shrimp
2 hard-boiled eggs, quartered

In large skillet saute onion, green onion, garlic and celery in butter until tender. Add flour; cook and stir until lightly browned. Add 2½ cups water, tomato puree, bay leaves, Worcestershire, Tabasco and seasonings. Simmer uncovered, stirring occasionally for 25 minutes or until sauce is almost desired consistency. Add shrimp and continue cooking for 15 minutes. Garnish with quartered boiled eggs. Serve over herbed rice.

Herb Rice:

3 tablespoons margarine
1 cup uncooked white rice
1 cup finely chopped onions
½ teaspoon marjoram
½ teaspoon summer savory

1 teaspoon rosemary
½ teaspoon salt
3 chicken bouillon cubes
2 cups water

Melt margarine in a two-quart saucepan. Add the onion and rice. Cook until it begins to brown. Add marjoram, summer savory, rosemary, salt and bouillon cubes. Add water. Bring to a boil, stir to dissolve bouillon cubes, turn heat as low as possible, cover with lid and leave over heat for 14 minutes. Remove the saucepan from heat, but leave lid on for 10 minutes or until ready to serve. Serves 6 adults.

Straight from a Louisiana bayou comes this marvelous mixture to be served over its own herbed rice.

Mrs. David E. Bowers

SHRIMP LE MAISTRE

2 cans mushroom soup
1 cup mayonnaise
1 pound cleaned, cooked shrimp
3 hard-boiled eggs, chopped
2 sliced or cut pimentos

½ cup slivered almonds
2 teaspoons Worcestershire
1 clove garlic, minced
Salt and pepper, to taste
Buttered bread crumbs

Mix all ingredients, sprinkling bread crumbs on top. Bake at 350° for 30 minutes. Serves 8-10.

The prayers of many a hostess are herewith answered! Mixing time is almost nil, frozen shrimp works beautifully, (though, of course, fresh may be used if you're up to the peeling). The casserole may be served in a variety of ways — on rice, wild rice mixture, in patty shells or in individual scallop shells topped with buttered crumbs. Too, Shrimp Le Maistre is good for the cook who likes to play with ingredients. Try adding a glug of sherry and sliced water chestnuts and leaving the eggs in the refrigerator.

Mrs. A. A. Jones, Jr.

WILD RICE AND SHRIMP

1½ pounds cooked shrimp
½ cup margarine
½ large chopped onion
½ cup chopped bell pepper
1 large can sliced mushrooms
1 tablespoon Worcestershire
6 drops Tabasco
1 can cream of chicken soup
2 tablespoons cream
Buttered bread crumbs
1 small box wild rice cooked as directed (makes 3 or 4 cups)

Saute onion, pepper and mushrooms in margarine. Add shrimp, Worcestershire and Tabasco. Heat soup with cream. Fold all together with cooked rice. Pour in greased casserole. Cover with bread crumbs. Bake at 325° for 30 minutes. Serves 10 to 12.

An excellent and easily put together (if you use frozen shrimp) casserole that will satisfy even the most sophisticated palate.

Mrs. W. H. Tankersly
Birmingham, Alabama

DEVILED EGGS AND SHRIMP

Devil 6 eggs, with lots of mustard, sweet pickle juice, little mayonnaise, Worcestershire.

Sauce:

½ cup margarine
4 tablespoons flour
2 cups milk and cream, or half and half
2 4-ounce cans mushrooms
1 tablespoon Worcestershire
1 tablespoon tarragon vinegar
Dash of Tabasco
Salt, to taste
1 pound medium shrimp, cooked
Buttered crumbs
1 cup grated New York cheese

Make cream sauce of first three ingredients. Add mushrooms, Worcestershire, vinegar, Tabasco, salt and shrimp. Layer the sauce and eggs in a 9"x13" casserole. Top with buttered crumbs and cheese. Cook at 350° until bubbly. Serves 8 to 10.

This has been a popular dish in Decatur for many years.

Mrs. George Wallace

161

MARY LOUISE'S SHRIMP DISH

6 slices bacon
1 chopped onion
1 16-ounce can tomatoes

1 cup seashell macaroni
1 small can shrimp or small package frozen cooked shrimp

Fry bacon, remove from pan. Add onion, cook until slightly brown. Add macaroni, tomatoes, and chopped bacon. Cook until macaroni is tender. Add shrimp and heat thoroughly but do not cook. Serves four.

Serve four in a hurry with this simple little dish using canned shrimp.

Mrs. Ralph Huff

IMPERIAL DEVILED CRAB

1 pound crabmeat
1 medium bell pepper
1 pimento
1 teaspoon dry mustard
½ teaspoon cayenne pepper

½ teaspoon Worcestershire
2 tablespoons mayonnaise (or more)

Chop bell pepper and saute in butter until tender. Add to other ingredients and mix as gently as possible to prevent breaking crab lumps. Place in individual crab shells or a casserole and bake at 400° until golden brown. Serves four.

"Imperial" designates something of superior quality. This dish is aptly named.

Mrs. Noble Russell

CRABMEAT ASPARAGUS

2 15-ounce cans asparagus spears
6 hard-boiled eggs
2 6½-ounce cans crab meat
6 tablespoons butter
6 tablespoons flour

3 cups milk
2 packages Old English cheese
Red pepper, to taste
Almonds

In a shallow casserole, place asparagus, sliced eggs and crabmeat. Make a cream sauce by melting the butter in a sauce pan. Stir in the flour and cook slightly. Pour in the milk and stir continually until thick. Add cheese and red pepper. Pour cheese sauce over and sprinkle almonds over top. Bake 30 minutes at 350°. Serves 6 to 8.

A simple to make people pleaser! Seafood lovers with fat pocketbooks may consider doubling the amount of crab, but more crab or not, we can't think of a better luncheon dish.

Mrs. Bill Sexton

MARYLAND CRAB CAKES

1 pound lump crabmeat
1 tablespoon mayonnaise
1 teaspoon mustard
¼ cup melted butter or margarine

1 piece bread soaked in milk
1 egg
Salt and pepper, to taste

Mix all ingredients and form into cakes. Place in refrigerator about one hour before frying. Fry in shortening until golden brown.

An old family recipe from Maryland — and that's where the crabs are! Served with slaw and sliced homegrown tomatoes, everybody likes them, even children. And do try crab cake sandwiches sometimes.

Mrs. Noble Russell

CRAB BLUE MOON

4 large onions
3 large bell peppers
4 cloves garlic
1 cup olive oil
¼ teaspoon pepper

½ teaspoon salt
Hot sauce, to taste
2 6-ounce cans tomato paste
18 ounces water
1 pound crabmeat

Chop onions, bell peppers and garlic and put into olive oil. Let saute until tender. Add tomato paste, water and hot sauce. Add salt and pepper. Let cook about two hours on low heat. Add flaked crabmeat about one-half hour before serving. Serve hot on rice. Serves eight.

Fresh crab meat in a well-seasoned tomato sauce from Montgomery's Blue Moon Inn. A taste treat like this, you'll find only once in a . . .

Mrs. Richard Bryson

CRAB CASSEROLE

6 slices bread
1 pound crab
½ cup bell pepper, chopped
½ cup onion, chopped
½ cup celery, chopped
½ cup butter

1 cup mayonnaise
2 cups milk
3 tablespoons Worcestershire
1 teaspoon salt
4 eggs, beaten
1 can cream of mushroom soup

Butter bread on both sides and cut in half. Place half the bread on bottom of 9"x13" casserole. Place crabmeat over bread. Saute bell pepper, onion and celery in butter. Cool and pour over bread and crabmeat. Add mayonnaise, milk, Worcestershire, and salt to beaten eggs. Pour on top of casserole. Cover with remaining bread. Place in refrigerator for 24 hours. Before baking, allow casserole to return to room temperature. Pour undiluted soup over top, and place in cold oven. Bake at 350° from 45 to 60 minutes. Serves 12.

No recipe instruction catches the eye of the organized hostess any faster than "refrigerate for 24 hours." When the recipe is for a dish this good, she can only rejoice.

Mrs. Bill Sexton

CRABMEAT CASSEROLE

6-ounce package shell macaroni, cooked and drained

For cheese mixture, combine the following:

1 8-ounce package cream cheese
1 cup sour cream
½ cup cottage cheese

½ cup sliced green onions and tops
¼ teaspoon garlic salt

2 7½-ounce cans flaked crabmeat
2 medium tomatoes, peeled and
   thinly sliced
1½ cups shredded sharp Cheddar
   cheese

In a 2 quart casserole, layer half the macaroni, half the cheese mixture, all the crabmeat, then the remaining macaroni and cheese mixture. Cover with tomatoes and shredded cheese. Bake for 30 minutes at 350°.

A ticker-tape parade should be in order for whoever conjured this one up. Add something green for color and you're in!

Mrs. S. Britt Owens

HOT SEAFOOD CASSEROLE

1 pound crabmeat
1 pound cooked and deveined
   shrimp
1 cup mayonnaise
2 tablespoons diced pimento
½ cup chopped bell pepper
¼ cup minced onion

1½ cups chopped celery
¾ teaspoon salt
2 teaspoons parsley
1 tablespoon Worcestershire
2 tablespoons lemon juice
2 cups crushed potato chips

Lightly toss all ingredients, as you would a cold salad, reserving enough potato chips for topping. Preparation can be done the night before and mixed in the morning. Cover with potato chips, sprinkle with paprika and bake at 400° for 25 minutes. Serves 12 for luncheon.

A toss-it-all-together dish — really a hot crab and shrimp salad — said to have been a favorite of President Kennedy. Serve it to your three tables of bridge next month.

Mrs. John R. Guice

LOBSTER THERMIDOR

2 boxes frozen African lobster
   tails (20 ounces of tails)
¼ cup margarine
1½ tablespoons grated onion
1½ cups milk
2 teaspoons Worcestershire

¼ cup flour
2 teaspoons prepared mustard
½ cup grated Cheddar cheese
1 teaspoon salt
¼ teaspoon pepper

Cook lobster according to package directions. Shell. Saute lobster and onion in margarine for 5 minutes. Stir in 1 cup of the milk and the Worcestershire. Blend flour with the remaining ½ cup milk. Add this to lobster mixture and cook on low heat until thickened, stirring constantly. Add mustard and cheese. Stir until cheese is melted. Add seasoning and serve on rice.

The perfect entree for the time you wish to entertain lavishly.

Mrs. James D. Moore

ARTICHOKE AND LOBSTER CASSEROLE

3 packages frozen artichokes, cooked with 1 bay leaf
2 cans mushroom soup
5 teaspoons chopped onion
6 tablespoons sherry
1 teaspoon salt
¼ teaspoon garlic salt
¼ teaspoon pepper
4 cups cooked lobster, cut in bite-size pieces (2 or 3 frozen packages)
1 cup grated Cheddar cheese

Mix soup, onion, sherry, salt, garlic salt, pepper. Arrange artichokes and lobster in casserole. Top with soup mixture and grated cheese. Bake at 400° for 15 minutes. Serves 8.

A casserole truly fit for a king. Most commoners will love it too, but unless you are on an unlimited budget, you'd better save it for royalty. Believe it or not, it's easy.

Mrs. Barrett C. Shelton, Jr.

BAKED OYSTERS

1 pint oysters
1 chopped onion
½ cup diced celery
1 egg, beaten
10 to 12 saltine crackers
1 teaspoon Worcestershire
Salt and pepper, to taste
Butter

Drain oysters to remove excess liquid. Saute chopped celery and onion slowly in butter until cooked but not brown. Add oysters to celery and onion. Increase heat and cook the oysters until edges curl. Remove skillet from stove and add the beaten egg, stirring constantly. Crumble crackers into mixture until excess liquid is taken up. Season to taste. Pour into a greased casserole. Sprinkle with crumbs. Dot with butter and bake in 350° oven for about 25 minutes. Serves four.

An excellent basic oyster dish — main course for lunch, good side dish for dinner.

Mrs. Ralph Huff

OYSTERS NEW ORLEANS

1 8-ounce can fresh select oysters (16 to 18 if you shuck your own)
6 tablespoons butter
½ cup flour
Milk
2 tablespoons dried shallots
1 tablespoon dried minced onion
¼ teaspoon dried minced garlic
¼ teaspoon salt
¼ teaspoon seasoned salt
⅛ teaspoon white pepper
¼ teaspoon basil
¼ teaspoon marjoram
¼ teaspoon thyme
1 tablespoon dried parsley
6 canned artichoke hearts
Parmesan cheese
Pernod

Drain oysters well, reserving liquid. Cook in 3 tablespoons of the melted butter. Stir for only 2 minutes, then remove from butter with slotted spoon and drain again, saving liquid. Add rest of butter to pan and melt. Stir in flour and cook over low heat for a minute. Remove pan from heat and gradually stir in oyster liquid plus milk added to make one cup. Make a smooth, thick white sauce. Add the spices and cook over very low heat for a few minutes. Just before serving, return oysters to sauce. Add artichoke hearts cut in half and a dash or two of Pernod if it's handy. Pour mixture into 6 small oven-proof ramekins, or use a pie plate. Sprinkle top generously with grated Parmesan. Brown under preheated broiler and serve at once as an elegant first course.

A highly seasoned mixture of creole and French — typical New Orleans.

Mrs. Herbert Street

OYSTERS BIENVILLE

3 tablespoons butter
¼ cup chopped green onions
¼ cup flour
¾ cup fish stock
3 tablespoons white wine
1/3 teaspoon salt
¼ teaspoon cayenne pepper
1 egg yolk
½ cup boiled shrimp
½ cup chopped mushrooms
1½ teaspoons Worcestershire
3 teaspoons parsley
1½ dozen oysters and shells
Bread crumbs
Paprika
Butter (see below)
Box rock salt

Mix first 12 ingredients in blender until thoroughly blended. Cook slowly for about five minutes or until sauce is thickened. Set aside. Fill two pie plates with rock salt and place in 350° oven to preheat. Place oysters in shells and cover with sauce. Top sauce with bread crumbs, sprinkle with paprika and dot with butter. Place shells on preheated rock salt and bake until edges of oysters begin to curl and brown slightly (about 10 to 15 minutes.) Serves four to six depending on size of servings.

You may not find the pearl, but you'll find these a delight — as a first course or as hors d'oeuvres.

Mrs. L. Denton Cole, Jr.

OYSTERS KIRKPATRICK

4 dozen large fresh oysters
4 dozen half shells
Box of rock salt
1 cup chili sauce
¼ cup lemon juice

½ teaspoon Worcestershire
⅛ teaspoon black pepper
4 or 5 strips bacon cut in 1-inch
   lengths

Arrange oyster half shells on bed of rock salt in four 9" pie pans (12 shells to each pan.) Put a fresh oyster in each half shell, top with one teaspoon of sauce made by blending together the chili sauce, lemon juice, Worcestershire and black pepper. Put 1-inch piece of bacon on top of each oyster. Broil about six inches from heat for five to seven minutes or until bacon is done. Serve immediately. Serves four.

The original recipe for this famous dish came from San Francisco's Palace Hotel and got its name from the hotel's manager.

Mrs. Billy W. Payne

OYSTERS ROCKEFELLER

2 jars strained baby food spinach
2 tablespoons lemon juice
1 tablespoon grated onion
½ teaspoon pepper
1 tablespoon Worcestershire
1 tablespoon anchovy paste
½ teaspoon Tabasco
¼ cup Parmesan cheese

¼ cup melted butter
1 box frozen spinach, thawed,
   drained, chopped
½ cup bread crumbs
3 tablespoons parsley
¼ teaspoon garlic powder
1 tablespoon Pernod

Mix all ingredients. This may be frozen or stored in refrigerator for several days.

Preparation of Oysters:

Place about 2 dozen oysters on half shell in pan filled with rock salt. Place in 450° oven without sauce. When edges of oysters curl, remove and pour off water. Then cover each oyster with sauce and sprinkle with additional Parmesan cheese. Broil until brown.

This is a lot of trouble to go to for the little bivalve, but just the sight of a plate of Oysters Rockefeller does something to the oyster lover. Next time you entertain, try these as a first course before moving to the dining room. Please do have some carrot sticks handy for those who don't indulge.

Mrs. Thomas Caddell

ESCALLOPED OYSTERS

2 pints drained oysters
(reserve liquid)
3 to 4 cups coarse crumbled
saltine crackers
½ cup heavy cream or milk

¼ to ½ cup oyster liquid
1 teaspoon Worcestershire
Salt and pepper, to taste
½ cup butter

In buttered casserole dish, place layer of oysters, then cracker crumbs, repeating until oysters are used, finishing with cracker crumbs. Combine cream, oyster liquid, Worcestershire, salt and pepper. Pour evenly over casserole. Dot with butter over top of casserole. Bake at 350° about 30 to 40 minutes until liquid is absorbed. Serves 6-8.

What Christmas turkey feels complete without a casserole of escalloped oysters by its side?

Mrs. L. Denton Cole, Jr.

TUNA LOAF

2 cups milk
3 cups (¼-inch cubes) white
bread
2 7-ounce cans tuna, drained
and flaked
4 eggs, slightly beaten

¼ cup finely chopped onion
1 tablespoon chopped parsley
1 tablespoon lemon juice
1 teaspoon salt
1 teaspoon paprika

Combine milk and bread cubes; heat to a gentle simmer. Remove from heat; beat until smooth. Combine remaining ingredients in two-quart mixing bowl; stir in milk mixture. Pour into buttered loaf pan, 9x5x3 inches. Bake at 325° for 55 minutes, or until set. Let loaf cool in pan ten minutes before serving. Slice, serve with dill sauce. Serves 6.

Dill Sauce:
2 tablespoons butter
2 tablespoons flour
½ teaspoon salt
Dash paprika

1 cup milk
1/3 cup finely diced dill pickle
2 tablespoons dill pickle juice
1 tablespoon chopped pimentos,
optional

Melt butter in one quart saucepan. Blend in flour, salt and paprika. Add milk; cook, stirring constantly, until thick and smooth. Stir in dill pickle, juice and pimento. Heat, serve over tuna loaf. Makes 1½ cups.

The loaf stands alone . . . but sauced with dill, it becomes something special!

Mrs. Robert McWhorter, Jr.

TUNA LEMON LOAF

3 or 4 thin lemon slices
2 6½-ounce cans drained tuna fish
1 can condensed cream of celery
   soup
3 slightly beaten egg yolks
1 cup fine cracker crumbs

¼ cup chopped onion
2 tablespoons pimento
2 tablespoons parsley flakes
1 tablespoon lemon juice
Dash of pepper
3 egg whites, stiffly beaten

Place lemon slices on bottom of greased pan. Combine all ingredients except egg whites. Fold in egg whites, spoon over lemon slices, bake in moderate oven (350°) for 45 minutes. Serves six.

The whole family will enjoy this pretty loaf — and that always makes Mamma smile.

Mrs. James B. Odom

MACARONI-TUNA FLAKE

2 tablespoons butter
½ cup fine dry bread crumbs
1 6½-ounce can drained and
   flaked tuna

1 16½-ounce can macaroni and
   cheese
2 tablespoons chopped pimento
½ teaspoon Worcestershire
1 or 2 drops Tabasco

Heat butter in pan. Mix in bread crumbs and cook slowly until they are brown. Meanwhile mix all other ingredients in buttered 1½ quart casserole dish. Put bread crumbs over top and cook in 325° oven for 20 minutes.

This casserole for four requires little more effort than needed to open two cans. (If you have an electric can opener, you're home free!)

Mrs. Benjamin Stevens

TUNA-MACARONI CASSEROLE

½ cup chopped onion
¼ cup chopped bell pepper
3 tablespoons cooking oil
2 tablespoons flour
1¼ cups milk

1 can undiluted cream of
   chicken soup
½ cup chopped pimento
1 6½-ounce can tuna
1 cup macaroni, cooked according
   to directions

Saute onion and pepper in oil until tender. Add flour and blend. Add milk and cook over low heat until thick, stirring constantly. Add remaining ingredients. Pour into greased 1½ quart casserole dish. Bake in 350° oven for thirty minutes. Serves four.

A creamy and colorful dish.

Mrs. Charles W. Belt

TUNA SUPREME

2 tablespoons butter
2 tablespoons flour
¼ cup milk
1 29-ounce can Italian style
   tomatoes, cut in small pieces
1 can cream of celery soup
1 6½-ounce can tuna fish, drained

1 teaspoon catsup
1 teaspoon Worcestershire
½ teaspoon minced onion
6 ounces shredded Cheddar
   cheese
Chow mein noodles

Melt butter in saucepan. Blend in flour. Stir in milk slowly until creamy. Remove from heat; blend in tomatoes; mix in soup, tuna, catsup, Worcestershire, onion and Cheddar cheese. Heat until bubbly. Cool five minutes. Serve on chow mein noodles. Serves 6 to 8.

When your fisherman comes home without a catch, quickly stir up "Tuna Supreme" and serve over noodles, spaghetti or even toast with a lot of loving sympathy.

Mrs. Benjamin Stevens

SALMON CROQUETTES

1 large can pink flaky salmon
1 large onion finely chopped
Juice of two lemons
Salt and pepper, to taste

2 large eggs, slightly beaten
1 cup milk
3½ cups crumbled saltine
   crackers

Mix all ingredients reserving 1¾ cups crackers. Chill mixture for several hours. When ready to cook, shape mixture into balls or patties. Roll in remaining cracker crumbs until completely covered. Cook in preheated electric skillet at 375°. When croquettes are crispy, remove from skillet, drain, and serve with seafood sauce or white sauce.

White Sauce:

6 tablespoons butter or oleo
3 tablespoons flour

½ cup milk
Salt and pepper, to taste

Melt butter on low heat. Add flour and milk gradually. Stir continuously. Add salt and pepper. Pour over salmon and serve immediately. Serves 4 to 6.

If meal planning is an upstream battle for you, we suggest adding a can of salmon to your grocery list and trying these good croquettes.

Mrs. David C. Harris

SALMON SOUFFLE

1 can cream of celery soup
½ cup grated Cheddar cheese
⅛ teaspoon dill weed

1 7¾-ounce can salmon
6 eggs (separated)

Combine soup and cheese in medium sauce pan. Heat until cheese melts. Stir in dill and salmon. Beat egg yolks well and add to mixture.

Beat egg whites until stiff and fold into mixture. Bake in an ungreased 2 quart casserole at 300° for one hour. Serve immediately. Serves six.

A tall, light, beautiful souffle made with a minimum of effort. What could make you feel more accomplished!

Mrs. Charles W. Belt

CREOLE SAUCE

1 medium onion, finely chopped
1 bell pepper, finely chopped
1½ cups chopped celery
1 16-ounce can tomatoes
1 tablespoon Worcestershire

1 tablespoon lemon juice
Dash Tabasco
Salt and pepper, to taste
1 tablespoon butter or margarine
1 bay leaf

Combine all ingredients and simmer for 20 minutes. Remove bay leaf before serving over fish.

Mrs. David C. Harris

TARTAR SAUCE

1 cup mayonnaise
1 small sour pickle, finely minced
1 tablespoon finely minced parsley

2 stuffed olives, finely chopped
1 small onion, finely chopped

Mix all ingredients and serve with sliced lemon on fish, oysters, or clams.

Mrs. Thomas C. Bingham

SEAFOOD SAUCE

2 cups chili sauce or catsup (or combination of both)
2 tablespoons Worcestershire
3 tablespoons prepared horse-radish

Dash Tabasco (optional)
1 tablespoon vinegar
Juice of two lemons

Mix ingredients and chill. Good on shrimp and crabmeat cocktails.

Mrs. David C. Harris

COCKTAIL SAUCE FOR SHRIMP

1 cup catsup
½ cup mayonnaise
2 or 3 drops Tabasco
2 tablespoons vinegar
1 tablespoon prepared horseradish

1 teaspoon finely chopped celery
  leaves
1 teaspoon lemon juice
½ teaspoon sugar
½ teaspoon salt
1 teaspoon Worcestershire

Mix and serve cold with cooked shrimp.

Mrs. Elmer S. Loyd, Sr.

SPAGHETTI WITH WHITE CLAM SAUCE

3 tablespoons olive oil
½ cup margarine or butter
1 4-ounce can minced clams
1 tablespoon parsley flakes
¼ teaspoon salt

¼ teaspoon hot pepper sauce
2 garlic cloves, crushed
⅛ teaspoon ground black pepper
1 8-ounce box spaghetti

In skillet over medium heat, combine olive oil, margarine, minced clams with liquid, parsley flakes, salt and hot pepper sauce. Peel and crush garlic into skillet. Add coarse pepper and cook until mixture begins to bubble. Cook spaghetti according to directions on package and drain. Toss spaghetti and sauce together. Serves 6.

A hurry-up dish that is really good, spaghetti with clam sauce is an excellent side dish with steak.

Mrs. Harold Michelson

CLAM SAUCE

1 large clove garlic, chopped
1 tablespoon butter
3 tablespoons chopped fresh
  parsley
2 cups grated American cheese

2 small cans minced clams,
  drained (reserve liquid)
Milk or cream

Saute garlic in butter. Add juice from drained clams, and parsley and simmer about 5 minutes. Add clams and grated cheese and heat until cheese melts. Add enough milk or cream to dilute to creamy consistency. Serve over cooked spaghetti. Serves 6.

A cheesy clam sauce for spaghetti; a grand change from the usual tomato-meat routine. Picture this with French bread, a salad of everything green, and a good white wine.

Mrs. Dale Crites
Lakewood, Colorado

Vegetables and Accompaniments

APPLE RINGS

¼ cup butter
2 tablespoons sugar
1 tablespoon lemon juice

3 apples, cored, sliced in rings,
and dipped in lemon juice

Heat sugar, butter, and lemon juice in a skillet. Add apples and cook covered 5 minutes and uncovered 5 minutes.

Extremely simple. Yet what could taste better or look prettier on a breakfast tray next to ham, on a brunch buffet table with a good sausage dish or for dinner around a pork roast?

Mrs. Paul McCain

GLAZED APPLES

3 cups water
1½ cups sugar
9 or 10 small apples

Mincemeat, coconut, and cake
coloring for variety

Put sugar and water in skillet on top of stove. While syrup begins to boil, peel and core apples. Keep turning apples in skillet of syrup for 20 or 30 minutes. Remove from skillet but continue cooking syrup until consistency of jelly. Pour syrup over apples and garnish with coconut, or fill the holes with mincemeat, before glazing with the syrup.

Mrs. Frank Stone

CINNAMON APPLES

6 tart apples
1 cup sugar

2 tablespoons cinnamon candy
1½ cups water

Pare and core apples. Cook together sugar, water and cinnamon candy for about 5 minutes until candy is dissolved. Add apples, simmer until tender but not mushy, turning once. Baste several times with syrup in pan.

Serve warm with meat or as a dessert. For a truly special salad, top chilled cinnamon apples with cream cheese mixed with chopped pecans and a little mayonnaise to soften. Great with a ham sandwich.

Mrs. William E. Shinn, Jr.

HOT FRUIT COMPOTE

1 heaping cup dried prunes,
pitted and chopped
1½ cups pineapple chunks,
undrained
2 cups dried apricots, cut up

1 cup cherry pie filling
1½ cups water
½ to 1 cup sherry, as desired

Mix fruit well, place in buttered casserole. Combine pie filling, water and sherry. Pour over fruit and bake 1 hour at 350°. Serves 8-10.

Dried fruits combined with canned ones to make a hot compote in harvest colors.

Mrs. Frank W. Troup

HOT FRUIT CASSEROLE

1 16-ounce can sliced pineapple
1 16-ounce can peach halves
1 jar apple rings
1 16-ounce can pear halves
1 16-ounce can apricot halves
Green and red cherries

2 tablespoons flour
½ cup brown sugar
½ cup butter
1 cup sherry

Drain all fruit well and arrange attractively in casserole dish. Mix last four ingredients until well blended and free of lumps and pour over fruit. Bake in 350° oven until liquid bubbles and fruit is thoroughly hot. Serves 10.

Another pretty hot fruit — this one laced with sherry.

Mrs. L. Denton Cole

CURRIED FRUIT

1 29-ounce can pears
1 29-ounce can peaches
1 29-ounce can apricots
1 can pie cherries

1 16-ounce can chunk pineapple
½ cup butter
¾ cup brown sugar, packed
4 teaspoons curry powder

Drain fruit and arrange in baking dish. Melt butter, add sugar and curry to butter, blending well. Pour mixture over fruit. Cover and refrigerate for 24 hours. Uncover and bake at 350° for 1 hour. Serves 8 to 10.

A beautiful and mouthwatering accompaniment to any meat or cheese entree, for breakfast, brunch, lunch or dinner.

Mrs. Albert P. Brewer
Pike Road, Alabama

BAY NAYLOR'S ARTICHOKE CASSEROLE

1 package frozen prepared
   creamed spinach
1 14-ounce can artichoke bottoms
   (may substitute hearts)
½ teaspoon nutmeg, optional
Salt and pepper to taste

Hollandaise sauce:
   ½ cup butter, melted
   2 egg yolks
   Juice of 1 lemon
   Pinch salt

Cook spinach according to directions. Place artichokes on bottom of buttered casserole dish and pour spinach over. Sprinkle on nutmeg, salt and pepper. Top with hollandaise sauce. To make sauce, put melted butter, yolks, lemon juice and salt in blender and blend until firm. Place casserole in 250° oven for 5 minutes. Serves 4 or 5.

How could this be anything but marvelous with these ingredients. Aren't you hungry already?

Mrs. William A. Sims

ASPARAGUS SOUFFLE

2 tablespoons butter
2 tablespoons flour
¾ cup milk
Option: 1 can cream of mushroom
  soup may be substituted for the
  above ingredients
1 teaspoon chopped onion

1½ cups American cheese,
  grated
3 eggs, separated
1½ cups asparagus pieces
Salt and pepper, to taste
Blanched almonds, optional

Make cream sauce or use soup. Add onion and cheese, stirring until cheese is melted. Add beaten egg yolks and blend well. Add asparagus. Fold in stiffly beaten egg whites. Bake at 350° about 45 minutes. Use blanched almonds if desired. Serves 4.

A gourmet's delight.

Mrs. William A. Sims

ASPARAGUS CASSEROLE

2 tablespoons margarine
1 tablespoon flour
1 can cream of mushroom soup
¼ teaspoon dry mustard
1 15½-ounce can asparagus,
  drained

1 17-ounce can small English
  peas, drained
4 hard-boiled eggs, sliced
1 cup bread crumbs
¼ cup grated cheese

Melt margarine in small pan. Add flour, soup (undiluted), and mustard. Cook until thick and bubbly. Drain all liquid from the asparagus and English peas. In a 2 quart casserole, layer asparagus, peas and sliced boiled eggs. Pour sauce over this. Saute crumbs in as much margarine as it takes to lightly brown them. Place over top and sprinkle with grated cheese. Bake at 300° for 30 minutes. Serves 6-8.

This casserole has endless variations, all are up to you: If you prefer a cheese sauce, add ½ to ¾ cup grated Cheddar to the sauce and omit cheese on top; or leave out the peas and toss in a handful of toasted, slivered almonds. Just play with this.

Mrs. David E. Bowers

BROCCOLI GOURMET

2 packages frozen chopped
  broccoli
1 can cream of mushroom soup
2 tablespoons grated onion
2 eggs, beaten

1 cup sharp Cheddar cheese,
  grated
1 cup mayonnaise
Buttered bread crumbs

Cook broccoli until tender, then drain. Combine soup, onion, eggs, cheese and mayonnaise. Fold until mixed thoroughly. Layer broccoli and

176

sauce in a greased casserole. May add buttered bread crumbs. Place in a 350° oven for 20 to 30 minutes. Serves 8.

A broccoli dish for company or family that you can put together with hardly a thought. We've heard — from all quarters — "this is the best broccoli I've ever tasted."

Mrs. Lindsay A. Allen

BROCCOLI CASSEROLE

¼ cup margarine
1 medium onion, chopped
1 can cream of mushroom soup
1 3-ounce can sliced mushrooms
1 roll garlic cheese
1 teaspoon parsley flakes
½ teaspoon oregano

Salt and pepper, to taste
2 packages broccoli, chopped or whole
2 cups bread crumbs or stuffing
4 tablespoons butter
¼ cup almonds, optional

Saute onion in margarine until tender. Mix onions, soup, mushrooms, garlic cheese, parsley, oregano, salt and pepper. After mixing well, pour over partially cooked broccoli. Top with crumbs or herb seasoned stuffing and butter. May add almonds. Bake 20 to 30 minutes at 350°. Serves 6 to 8.

An excellent buffet dish.

Mrs. William Sexton

COMPANY BROCCOLI CASSEROLE

2 packages frozen broccoli
1 can cream of shrimp soup
1 teaspoon lemon juice

1 container whipped cream cheese with chives
½ cup slivered almonds

Cook and drain broccoli. Mix together and heat shrimp soup, lemon juice, and cream cheese with chives. Pour over broccoli in a 2 quart casserole. Top with ½ cup slivered almonds. Bake at 350° until it bubbles. Serves 6.

A convenient dish made with convenience items. Great taste with NO work.

Mrs. John S. Key

CURRIED BROCCOLI CASSEROLE

1½ pounds broccoli, or 2 packages frozen
½ teaspoon salt
Juice of 1 lemon
1 can cream of chicken soup

½ cup mayonnaise
½ teaspoon curry powder
½ cup bread or cracker crumbs
2 tablespoons melted butter

Cook broccoli with salt until tender. Drain and place in 1½ quart casserole. Squeeze lemon juice on top. Blend soup, mayonnaise, curry powder and pour over broccoli. Combine melted butter with bread crumbs and sprinkle on top. Bake 20 minutes at 350°. Serves 6.

A marvelous curried broccoli that adds finesse to any meal!

Mrs. Malcolm L. Prewitt, Jr.

BROCCOLI-RICE CASSEROLE

½ cup long grain rice, cooked
3 packages frozen chopped broccoli, cooked
2 tablespoons chopped onion
2 tablespoons margarine

1 can cream of chicken soup
¾ can water
1 8-ounce jar Cheese Whiz
Paprika

Saute onions in margarine. Add soup and water, then add drained broccoli, cheese and rice. Stir until cheese has melted. Arrange in casserole and sprinkle with paprika. Cook at 350° for 20 to 30 minutes. Yields 10 to 12 servings.

For the next covered dish supper at church, or potluck bridge in the neighborhood, try this good recipe.

Mrs. Jim L. Thompson, Jr.

BROCCOLI SUPREME

3 packages frozen broccoli
1 can cream of mushroom soup
1 can cream of shrimp soup
Salt

Tabasco
½ cup slivered almonds
1 cup grated cheese

Cook broccoli according to package directions. Drain well. Mix together soups and add a light sprinkle of salt and a couple dashes of Tabasco. Place broccoli in greased 2 quart baking dish. Sprinkle half the almonds and grated cheese on top. Pour the soup mixture in and spread evenly to cover all the broccoli. Sprinkle remaining cheese and almonds on top. Bake 350° oven for 30 minutes or until bubbly. Makes 8 servings.

Mrs. Herbert Street

QUICK HOME-STYLE BAKED BEANS

1 pound can baked beans (Boston style or in tomato sauce)
¼ cup onion, finely chopped
2 tablespoons molasses or dark brown sugar

1 tablespoon dry or prepared mustard
½ cup water
1 or 2 slices bacon for topping

Mix all ingredients except bacon in a small casserole dish. Lay strips of bacon on top (two tablespoons of bacon grease stirred into mixture also adds to flavor). Bake, uncovered, 30 to 40 minutes. Makes 4 servings.

Mrs Lindsay A. Allen

BARBECUED BEANS

1 pound can pork and beans
1 pound can kidney beans, drained
1 pound can green lima beans, drained
1 large onion, chopped
1 clove garlic, minced
1 tablespoon Worcestershire
2 tablespoons cumin seed (or 1 teaspoon ground cumin)

2 to 3 tablespoons strong cold coffee
¼ cup brown sugar
½ cup catsup
Pinch oregano
Pinch sweet basil
Dash Tabasco
3 strips bacon

Combine all ingredients in large shallow baking dish. Place bacon strips on top. Cover and bake for 1 hour at 350°. Remove cover and continue baking for 15 minutes. Serves 10.

Beans with a bite! An unusual combination of beans and flavors that is especially good with barbecued pork. Serve with a mild slaw.

Mrs. A. Julian Harris

COMPANY BEANS

1 package frozen French beans (or canned)
1 package frozen baby lima beans
1 package frozen English peas
1 cup mayonnaise
1 tablespoon vegetable oil

1 tablespoon Worcestershire
Dash Tabasco
1 medium onion, minced
4 hard-boiled eggs, sliced
Salt and pepper, to taste

Cook each package separately, according to directions and drain. Mix the remaining ingredients for a sauce and keep at room temperature. Place cooked, drained vegetables in a serving dish and top with sauce. Serves 8-10.

Imagine what good fortune it would be to find a really good vegetable dish you could serve warm, at room temperature or even cold. Here it is — it's YOURS! Enjoy it!

Mrs. John D. Davis, Jr.

THREE BEAN CASSEROLE

1 package frozen French green beans
1 package frozen lima beans
1 package frozen peas

1 cup mayonnaise
1 cup sour cream
Cheddar cheese
Paprika

Cook beans according to directions. Drain and place in casserole. Add mayonnaise, sour cream and mix. Sprinkle grated Cheddar cheese on top. Cook for 20 to 30 minutes at 350°. Serves 6.

Three legumes quickly mixed with handy items produce an excellent vegetable casserole for daily fare or very special dinners.

Mrs. John D. Wyker, II

ORIENTAL GREEN BEANS

1 pound fresh tender green beans
2 cups boiling water
½ teaspoon salt
1/3 pound pork tenderloin, cut in matchstick strips
½ garlic clove

1 tablespoon butter
½ teaspoon ginger
Salt and pepper, to taste
1 teaspoon soy sauce
½ cup bean liquid
4 servings cooked rice

Wash beans, remove strings and ends, break in 2-inch lengths. Drop beans in boiling salted water; cover and cook at low boil for 20 minutes only. Drain beans, reserving ½ cup liquid. Saute pork strips and garlic in butter until lightly browned. Sprinkle meat with ginger, salt, pepper and soy sauce. Add green beans and reserved liquid to meat in skillet. Stir. Cover and simmer 20 minutes. Taste, add more salt if needed. Scoop green beans and sauce over rice which has been cooked according to package directions. Serves 4.

What a great way to turn green beans into something really special.

Mrs. Billy W. Payne

SWEET AND SOUR GREEN BEANS

1 quart cooked green beans, fresh or frozen
1 medium onion, chopped
8 slices bacon, fried crisp and crumbled

½ cup vinegar
½ cup sugar
½ cup bacon grease

Place a layer of cooked beans in slightly greased, flat casserole, then a layer of onion and a layer of bacon. Repeat layers. Pour sauce of vinegar, sugar and bacon grease over casserole. Cook uncovered at 350° for 30 minutes, then cover and cook an additional 30 minutes. Eight servings.

Oh, so good with almost any meat — fried chicken or pork roast or chops particularly — are these tart sweet beans with bits of bacon. Once you've tried them, they'll be high on your list of favorite vegetables.

For a real hurry-up version (for days when you've been hungry for these beans all day, but didn't have the hour-plus required): for each 10 ounce package of frozen French style beans, cook 3 or 4 slices of bacon until crisp. Saute a small chopped onion in the drippings, add ¼ cup vinegar and ¼ cup sugar and add the package of frozen beans. Separate with fork, cook covered about 5 minutes, then uncovered, over high heat, until all liquid is gone, usually another 5 minutes. Great result!

Mrs. James D. Moore

180

FRENCH BEAN CASSEROLE

1 large onion
¼ cup margarine
1 can cream of mushroom soup
1/8 teaspoon Tabasco, or to taste
1 cup cheese, grated
Salt and pepper to taste

4 slices bacon, sauteed and
  crumbled
2 16-ounce cans whole or French
  style beans, drained
2 5-ounce cans water chestnuts,
  sliced
Almonds

Saute onion in margarine. Add soup, Tabasco, grated cheese, salt and pepper. Heat until cheese melts. Add crumbled bacon to sauce. In casserole layer beans, sliced water chestnuts and sauce. Repeat. Top with almonds and butter. Bake 350° for 30 to 45 minutes. French fried onion rings may be used on top. Serves 8.

Especially for the man — or men — in your life. Zip them up with added Tabasco.

Mrs. William Sexton

FRENCH GREEN BEAN CASSEROLE

1 package frozen French green
  beans
1 tablespoon flour
½ teaspoon salt
⅛ teaspoon pepper
1 teaspoon sugar

½ teaspoon grated onion
1 cup sour cream
½ cup Swiss cheese, grated
½ cup buttered bread crumbs

Cook and drain green beans. Place in another pan: flour, salt, pepper, sugar, onion, sour cream and cheese. Mix over low heat for a short time. Pour over beans in casserole and cover top with buttered bread crumbs. Bake in 350° oven about 20 minutes until bubbly. Serves 5. To make twice as much, double all ingredients except use 3 packages of beans.

Beans sauced with an unusual combo of sour cream and Swiss cheese — a pleasant variation!

Mrs. Joseph Walker

GRATED CARROTS

10 carrots, coarsely grated
¼ cup water
Salt and pepper to taste

½ teaspoon sugar
3 tablespoons butter

Put all ingredients in covered saucepan and bring to quick simmer over high heat, stirring occasionally. Cook, covered, 10 minutes without stirring over medium low heat. Serve what little juice remains with the carrots. Serves 6.

The most pleasant way we know to supply your family with vitamin A. Not only do these carrots taste good, but the cooking method destroys very little of the high vitamin content.

Mrs. William G. Stone, Jr.

HEAVENLY CARROTS

2 pounds carrots, scraped and cut into circles or cut on the diagonal, Chinese style (carrots may be fresh or frozen)
1 small bell pepper, sliced
1 medium onion, sliced
1 can tomato soup

½ cup salad oil
1 cup sugar
¾ cup vinegar
1 teaspoon prepared mustard
1 teaspoon Worcestershire
Salt to taste

Boil carrots until tender-crisp in salted water. Place cooked carrots, pepper and onions in layers and cover with the sauce which is made by blending well the remaining ingredients. Refrigerate at least overnight. Keeps well. Serves 16.

This one dish has converted more confirmed carrot haters than any other we know. It must be made ahead, so carrots can marinate; it keeps practically forever; and it's delicious with any meat or sandwich.

Mrs. Robert Allen
Livonia, Michigan

MARINATED CARROTS

5 cups carrot sticks (or about 2 lbs.)
1 medium onion, sliced
2 bell peppers, sliced
1 can tomato bisque soup

¾ cup vinegar
1 cup sugar
1 teaspoon dry mustard
1 teaspoon Worcestershire
Salt and pepper to taste

Cook carrot sticks slightly, allowing to boil 3 to 5 minutes. Drain at once. Place cooked carrots, raw onions and peppers in layers. Cover with marinade. Prepare at least 12 hours in advance. Will keep in covered container in refrigerator 2 weeks.

"Marinated Carrots" has all the good points of "Heavenly Carrots" and has the added advantage of having fewer calories because the marinade contains no oil.

Mrs. Henon Pearce

CHEESE FROSTED CAULIFLOWER

1 head cauliflower
½ cup mayonnaise

2 teaspoons prepared mustard
¾ cup shredded sharp cheese

Cook cauliflower, leaving whole. Drain well. Place it in a shallow pan and frost with mayonnaise mixed with mustard. Sprinkle on cheese. Bake at 350° until cheese melts, about 10 minutes. Serves 6.

An especially good buffet item — it's pretty, too!

Mrs. Julian Bibb

CAULIFLOWER WITH CREAM SAUCE

1 large head cauliflower
2 tablespoons butter or margarine
2 tablespoons flour
½ teaspoon salt
⅛ teaspoon pepper
1 cup milk or cream

1 cup grated processed sharp
cheese
1 teaspoon Worcestershire
½ cup chopped pimento, optional
¼ cup chopped parsley, optional

Remove leaves and stalk from cauliflower. Add 1 teaspoon salt to 1 quart cold water and soak, head down, ½ hour. Drain. Cook, covered, in 1 inch of boiling, salted water 15 to 20 minutes or until tender. Drain. Melt butter; blend in flour, salt and pepper. Add milk gradually and cook, stirring constantly, until thickened. Add remaining ingredients and cook over low heat until cheese is melted. Pour over hot cauliflower. For variation, add pimento or parsley to sauce. Serves 6.

Fresh cauliflower has its very own taste and nothing compliments that taste better than a nippy cheese sauce. The combination is one of the world's great vegetable dishes.

Mrs. Dalton Guthrie

CORN PUDDING

1 16-ounce can corn kernels or
the same amount of fresh corn
off the cob
2 heaping tablespoons flour
1 tablespoon sugar

½ teaspoon salt
2 eggs, well beaten
2 tablespoons margarine, melted
1¼ cups milk

Mix well the corn, flour, sugar and salt. Add the beaten eggs, margarine and milk. Bake, covered, 30 to 40 minutes in a pan of hot water at 400°. Serves 6.

Corn pudding is one dish that is delicious with fresh corn and just about as good with canned. Nothing tastes much better in the middle of the winter when the sight of corn, tassled and full of ears, is a vague summer memory.

Mrs. Elmer S. Loyd, Sr.

CREAMED CORN

12 ears corn
½ cup butter or margarine
2 teaspoons sugar
Salt and pepper, to taste

1 cup water
2 cups milk
2 tablespoons flour dissolved in
¼ cup water

Cut corn from the cob and place in pan. Add margarine, sugar, salt and pepper. Simmer gently for 15 minutes. Add milk and flour dissolved in water. Cook on medium low heat for 30 minutes, stirring to prevent sticking. If mixture becomes too thick, add additional milk or water.

Mrs. William A. Sims

CORN CASSEROLE

1 17-ounce can whole kernel corn	2 tablespoons corn starch
1 17-ounce can cream style corn	6 ounces sharp Cheddar cheese,
8 strips bacon, crisply fried and	grated
crumbled	1 2-ounce jar pimentos, chopped
2 tablespoons bacon drippings	(or to taste)
2 eggs, beaten	Bread crumbs or Fritos

Mix all ingredients except bread crumbs in a casserole. Place bread crumbs or Fritos on top. Bake at 350° for 25 to 30 minutes. Serves 6-8.

A hearty dish and a real husband pleaser. Some cooks add a little chopped bell pepper.

Mrs. Dan M. Crane

BAKED CORN WITH SOUR CREAM

6 strips bacon	½ teaspoon salt
2 tablespoons chopped onion	1 cup sour cream
2 tablespoons butter	2 12-ounce cans shoe peg corn
2 tablespoons flour	1 tablespoon chopped parsley,
	optional

Cook and crumble bacon. Cook onion in butter; blend in flour and salt. Add sour cream gradually, stirring to keep smooth. Bring just to a boil and add corn. Cook until heated through. Fold in half of bacon and pour in greased baking dish. Garnish with parsley and remaining bacon. Bake at 350° for 30 minutes or until bubbly. Yield 8 servings.

Mrs. William H. Nabors

FRIED CORN

12 ears corn	1 cup water
¼ cup sugar	½ cup bacon drippings
2 teaspoons salt	

Cut corn from ears with vegetable peeler. Stir in sugar and salt. Add about 1 cup water (adjust according to moisture in corn). Heat bacon drippings in iron skillet over medium heat. Pour corn in skillet and stir continually until done (about 15 minutes). Serves 8.

Mrs. John E. Wilks, Jr.

EGGPLANT OYSTER CASSEROLE

1 eggplant	Butter
Onion juice	Salt and pepper, to taste
Cracker or bread crumbs	1 10½-ounce can oyster stew

Cube eggplant and cook in water with a little onion juice. Drain well. Butter casserole dish. Layer cracker crumbs, eggplant, and dots of butter. Salt and pepper to taste. Repeat. Pour over top a can of oyster stew. Top with more cracker crumbs and dot with butter. Bake at 350° until bubbly. Serves 6.

Eggplant combined with oysters has long been a popular dish and in some sections is served with turkey on Christmas Day. This recipe produces an eggplant side dish which becomes a main dish with the addition of a small can of bay oysters.

Mrs. John F. Manning

EGGPLANT CASSEROLE

1 eggplant

Corn meal

1 egg or more (depending on size of eggplant), beaten

Slice eggplant no thicker than ¼ inch. Place slice in corn meal, then egg, then again in corn meal. Fry until brown, turning once.

1 16-ounce can tomatoes (or 29-ounce can if large eggplant), reserve liquor

1 bell pepper, sliced

1 onion, sliced

Parmesan cheese

Dash Lawry's salt

Dash pepper

2 tablespoons Worcestershire

Place layer of fried eggplant in dish. Cover with tomatoes, onion, and bell pepper. Sprinkle Parmesan cheese, salt and pepper over. Repeat. Put extra eggplant on top. Pour tomato liquor and Worcestershire over casserole until moist. Bake 40 to 45 minutes at 350°. Serves 8.

It will be a LONG, LONG time before you taste anything this good again. It is simply superb — even to certain husbands we know who would choke if they knew what they were eating. Amazingly enough, it's even good leftover and cold.

Mrs. Thomas Caddell

LOUISE BRADFORD'S LIMA BEANS WITH WATER CHESTNUTS

3 packages frozen Fordhook lima beans

1 cup sour cream

1 can water chestnuts, drained and sliced

1 can cream of mushroom soup

1 teaspoon salt

1 teaspoon soy sauce

½ package slivered, blanched almonds

Cook lima beans in slightly salted water about 10 minutes. Drain. Toss with water chestnuts. Blend remaining ingredients together then stir into beans and chestnuts. Turn into buttered casserole. Bake at 300° about 35 minutes. Serves 8.

A pleasant way to dress up frozen limas.

Mrs. Frank T. Richardson, Jr.

185

FANCY LIMA BEANS

2 packages frozen lima beans
2 stalks celery, chopped
1 can cream of mushroom soup
½ cup almonds, blanched
¼ pound Cheddar cheese, grated
½ pound pimento loaf cheese, grated

Cook lima beans according to package directions. Drain. Add remaining ingredients. Pour into casserole dish and heat in 350° oven until hot. Serves 6-8.

Mrs. C. W. Belt

STUFFED MUSHROOMS

1 package frozen spinach
18 large mushrooms
¾ cup butter
¼ cup finely chopped onion
¼ cup fine bread crumbs
Garlic salt
¾ teaspoon salt
Dash pepper
¼ teaspoon nutmeg
½ cup grated Parmesan cheese

Cook spinach as directed on box. Drain and chop in blender until pulp consistency. Wash and dry mushrooms. Remove stems and chop. Dip mushroom caps in melted butter. Saute onions and mushroom stems. Add this to spinach, bread crumbs and spices. Mix well. Pile caps full of filling and sprinkle with cheese. Bake 350° for 20 to 25 minutes. Serves 6.

A delight for mushroom lovers, and anyone else for that matter. These delicacies can be made far in advance to freeze for future use.

Mrs. John R. Guice

FRIED OKRA

1 pound okra, cut in ½" pieces
½ cup corn meal
Salt, to taste
Vegetable oil

Toss okra with meal and salt until coated. Fry in ½ inch of oil over medium-high heat until brown and crisp. Serves 4.

Mrs. John E. Wilks, Jr.

OKRA CREOLE

1 pound can tomatoes
1 package frozen cut okra or ¾ pound fresh okra (fresh is better)
1 medium onion, chopped
¾ large bell pepper, chopped
3 stalks celery, chopped
3 tablespoons Worcestershire
1 bay leaf
Salt to taste
¼ teaspoon oregano
½ teaspoon sugar
4 strips crisply fried bacon, crumbled
¼ cup bacon grease

Mix all ingredients in saucepan and simmer until catsup consistency. This dish may be cooked without any spices except salt and Worcestershire and is still very tasty. If there is any leftover, add shrimp for another good meal. Serves 6.

An old, old recipe from the deep South for an exceptionally delicious summer time dish (though with frozen okra readily available, you can have it whenever your taste buds start jumping). It takes about 4 hours to cook down to the proper consistency, but your patience will be rewarded. Think about fried, crunchy chicken, fresh field peas, and "Okra Creole" — and drool!

Mrs. William Sexton

PEAS ELEGANT

6 slices bacon	1 16-ounce can Le Sueur peas,
1 medium onion, chopped	drained
2 tablespoons flour	Dash Lawry's salt
1 cup milk	Dash nutmeg
1 cup sliced mushrooms	Salt and pepper, to taste

Fry bacon and crumble. Brown onion in bacon drippings. Add flour (as in making cream sauce), then milk and other ingredients. Add crumbled bacon. Place in 1½ quart casserole. Bake 15 minutes at 350°. Serves 6.

The bacon does wonders for canned peas.

Mrs. William A. Sims

DEVILED PEAS

1 16-ounce can small English peas	1 tablespoon Worcestershire
1 can cream of mushroom soup	4 hard-boiled eggs, sliced
1 can cream of celery soup	1 cup grated cheese
3 or 4 tablespoons chili sauce	Ritz crackers

Drain peas. Mix soups, chili sauce, and Worcestershire. Alternate layers of peas, soup mixture, sliced eggs and grated cheese in casserole. Cover with Ritz cracker crumbs. Bake at 375° about 30 minutes. Serves 8.

Simple pea casserole that everybody — man, woman, child — will like.

Mrs. Ralph Huff

PEA CASSEROLE

1 17-ounce can English peas
1 can cream of mushroom soup
1 cup slivered almonds, toasted
1 4-ounce can pimentos, chopped
1 4-ounce can mushrooms

Brown mushrooms and pimentos in butter. Toast almonds at 350° for about 10 minutes. Layer: peas, soup, almonds, pimentos and mushrooms. Repeat. Top with dots of butter or may use cracker crumbs. Bake at 350° until bubbly. Serves 6-8.

A nice combination of textures, colors, and tastes.

Mrs. John F. Manning

TWICE-BAKED POTATOES

4 medium baking potatoes
4 to 5 tablespoons of butter
Salt to taste
½ cup milk, heated
4 tablespoons grated Cheddar cheese

Wash and grease potatoes. Bake. Scoop potatoes from jackets. Mash with butter, milk and salt. Fill shells. Top with grated cheese and bake ½ hour at 325°. Serves 4. For variation, add 1 tablespoon chopped chives and 4 strips crisp, crumbled bacon to mashed potatoes before returning to shells.

Why not make at LEAST 12 stuffed potatoes at once, as long as you have the oven on and the ingredients out? Use what you need and freeze the others — yes, they freeze beautifully — for future use or to take a puny friend. After that sales pitch, why not do 24?

Mrs. James R. Fite

BAKED POTATOES WITH HERBS

4 large Idaho potatoes
3 tablespoons butter
1/3 cup sour cream
½ teaspoon dried rosemary
½ teaspoon chives
½ teaspoon parsley
Pinch dried sage
Salt and pepper, to taste
Melted butter or margarine

Bake potatoes until done and slice lengthwise while hot. Scoop out potatoes and mash with butter. Add sour cream to make fluffy. Beat well. Blend in herbs, salt and pepper. Replace in jackets and brush top with margarine. Wrap in foil and place in refrigerator. About 30 minutes before serving, reheat potatoes 20 to 25 minutes or until thoroughly heated in 450° oven. Remove foil and serve. Garnish with parsley. Serves 8.

Mrs. Frank W. Troup

188

BAKED POTATO SUPREME

6 potatoes, baked
½ cup mayonnaise
½ cup melted butter

¼ cup Parmesan cheese
2 teaspoons chopped onion
¼ teaspoon Worcestershire

Mix all ingredients, except potatoes, in a small bowl and serve over baked potatoes. Serves 6.

Love baked potatoes and especially what goes on them? Ready for a little variety? What a good topping this is!

Mrs. T. S. Simms

POTATO CASSEROLE

1 can cream of mushroom soup
2/3 cup milk
4 cups thinly sliced raw Irish potatoes
3 or 4-ounce can pimentos,
  chopped

1 medium onion, thinly sliced
1 cup grated hoop cheese

Mix together soup and milk. In casserole layer potatoes, onion, pimento and soup mixture. Top with grated cheese and dot with pimento. Bake covered about 45 minutes and uncovered 15 minutes at 350°. Serves 6-8.

When a husband asks his wife to get the recipe for something, she's wise to get it — and serve it often! Many a husband has requested this simple potato dish. Here it is, with our compliments.

Mrs. George L. McCrary, Jr.

POTATO-OREGANO CASSEROLE

6 medium potatoes, pared and
  sliced
2 medium onions, thinly sliced
Oregano

Butter
Salt and pepper to taste

Place layer of sliced potatoes in buttered casserole. Sprinkle with just a pinch of oregano, then salt and pepper. Dot with butter. Top with layer of onions. Continue layering in this manner until all ingredients are used. Cover casserole and bake at 350° for 1 hour or until done. Serves 6.

Something new has been added to the spud — oregano this time!

Mrs. Billy W. Payne
Mrs. Jim L. Thompson, Jr.

189

SCALLOPED POTATOES

6 tablespoons butter
4 tablespoons flour
2 teaspoons salt

4 cups milk
6 cups sliced, raw potatoes

Melt 4 tablespoons butter, add flour and salt. Add milk slowly. Cook until sauce thickens. Add sliced potatoes and bring to a boil. Arrange in a 13" x 9" baking dish and dot with remaining butter. Bake at 350° for 1 hour and 15 minutes. Yields 12 servings.

A potato standard — always good. To turn this into the main part of a meal, top casserole with half-cooked link sausages for the last 20 to 25 minutes. Use about 24 sausages.

Mrs. Sage Copeland

CREAMY POTATO PUFF

1 8-ounce package cream cheese,
softened
4 cups hot mashed potatoes
1 egg, beaten

1/3 cup finely chopped onion
¼ cup chopped pimento
1 teaspoon salt
Dash pepper

Combine softened cream cheese and potatoes, mixing until well blended. Add remaining ingredients. Place in a quart casserole and bake for 45 minutes at 350°. Yields 6 to 8 servings.

Mrs. Charles B. Howell

CHANTILLY POTATOES

4 medium potatoes
Water to cover
1 teaspoon salt
4 tablespoons butter
⅛ teaspoon paprika
1/3 cup milk

½ cup heavy cream, whipped
½ cup grated American cheese
⅛ teaspoon onion salt
Freshly ground black pepper,
to taste
Paprika

Wash and pare potatoes. Cut in thirds crosswise. Cover potatoes in saucepan with cold water, add salt and boil until tender, about 30 minutes. Drain thoroughly. Return to lowest heat and shake pan to dry potatoes slightly. Add butter, cut in chunks, and stir to melt. Remove from stove and mash potatoes thoroughly. Add paprika and milk and beat until light and fluffy. Spread mashed potatoes in a buttered 9" x 9" baking dish. Fold grated cheese, onion salt and pepper into whipped cream. Spread this mixture over potatoes and sprinkle lightly with paprika. Bake at 350° for 6 to 8 minutes or until top is delicately brown. Serves 6.

The plain old Irish potato goes continental with this dressed up dish.

Mrs. Billy W. Payne

RAW POTATO PANCAKES

4 medium potatoes	2 tablespoons flour
1 tablespoon grated onion	½ teaspoon baking powder
2 eggs, separated	¼ teaspoon nutmeg
1 teaspoon salt	1 tablespoon parsley, optional
Pepper, to taste	3 to 4 tablespoons butter

Wash and pare potatoes. Grate at once and drain in sieve while grating onion. Beat egg yolks and add to potatoes, onion, and remaining ingredients, except butter. Mix batter thoroughly. Fold in stiffly beaten egg whites. Melt butter on griddle or in large iron skillet. When hot, drop batter by spoonfuls, baking 3 or 4 at one time. Cook until brown and crisp on each side, turning only once. Place cooked pancakes on hot dish in 200° oven while others are cooking on griddle. Serve immediately. Serves 4.

Potato pancakes may be topped with crisply cooked bacon or a spoonful of warm apple sauce, depending on your menu. Omit parsley, if applesauce is your choice.

From grandmother, a dish we mustn't forget — it's too good! You can make these pancakes with leftover creamed potatoes, too, though the texture is quite different.

Mrs. Billy W. Payne

GRATED RAW SWEET POTATO PUDDING

2 eggs	2 teaspoons vanilla
½ cup sugar	Pinch salt
1½ cups milk	1 cup coconut, grated
¼ cup melted butter	2 cups grated raw sweet potatoes

Beat eggs and sugar. Add remaining ingredients and pour into a buttered baking dish. Bake at 350° about 45 minutes or until solid. Serves 6.

Serve as a vegetable but do go easy on the dessert. Fresh fruit perhaps.

Mrs. Joseph W. Walker

LOLA'S SWEET POTATO CASSEROLE

5 sweet potatoes	Juice and grated rind of 1 orange
1 cup butter	4 eggs
1½ cups sugar	1 cup nuts, chopped and mixed
1 cup milk	with melted butter

Stew potatoes in jackets. Skin and mash. Add butter, sugar, milk, orange juice, rind and eggs. Put in buttered casserole. Sprinkle buttered nuts on top. Bake at 350° for 30 minutes.

This was enthusiastically endorsed at the tasting luncheon.

Mrs. Robert C. McAnnally

191

SWEET POTATO CASSEROLE

3 cups cooked sweet potatoes   2 eggs, slightly beaten
1 cup sugar   1 teaspoon vanilla
½ cup margarine   1/3 cup milk

Combine all ingredients and pour into casserole.

For topping mix: ½ cup flour
   1 cup brown sugar   1/3 cup butter

Sprinkle topping over casserole and bake at 350° for 25 minutes. Yields 8 to 10 servings.

Sweet potato casserole with a streusel topping.

Mrs. William S. Coles

SOUTHERN RICE CASSEROLE

1 cup uncooked rice   1 can beef consomme
½ cup butter   1 can water

Melt butter, add rice and cook for 5 minutes. Pour into casserole dish consomme, water, rice and butter. Bake uncovered at 350° for one hour. Serves 6.

In cotton country, rice is more than a staple — it's almost a necessity, and is served, in one form or another, VERY frequently. A favorite southern rice dish is made with beef bouillon or consomme — a modified pilaf. Add mushrooms, toasted almonds, or seedless green grapes the last 15 minutes if you want.

Mrs. Paul McCain

RICE CASSEROLE

½ cup margarine   1 mushroom can water
1 large onion, chopped   1 can beef bouillon
1 cup uncooked rice
1 4-ounce can sliced mushrooms,
   with juice

In skillet melt margarine, add onion and rice, brown until dark. Put this mixture in buttered casserole. Add undrained mushrooms and one mushroom can of water and bouillon. Cook covered at 400° about 45 minutes until all liquid is absorbed and rice is tender. Serves 6.

Mrs. Frank W. Troup

BAKED RICE

½ cup celery, chopped
1 small onion, chopped
1 small bell pepper, chopped
2 tablespoons butter
3 cups cooked rice
1 4-ounce can mushrooms, drained

1 2-ounce jar pimento, drained
1 can cream of celery soup
½ cup milk
Salt and pepper, to taste
Ritz cracker crumbs

Saute celery, onion, and bell pepper in butter. Combine with rice, mushrooms, and pimento. Add celery soup diluted with milk. Season to taste with salt and pepper. Top with Ritz cracker crumbs in greased casserole. Bake 45 minutes at 350°. Serves 6.

A flavorful, colorful rice dish.

Mrs. Lynn C. Fowler

DOUBLE BOILER RICE

1 cup Uncle Ben's long grained converted rice

1½ cups water
1 teaspoon salt

Mix rice, water and salt in top of double boiler. Cover. Place over boiling water and steam without removing top for 45 minutes to an hour.

This method of cooking rice is the only sure and positively fool-proof method of cooking rice we've ever found. The formula is simple: 1½ times as much water as rice.

Mrs. William E. Shinn, Jr.

WILD RICE CASSEROLE

1 8-ounce package wild rice
6 chicken bouillon cubes
6 tablespoons margarine
2 stalks celery, chopped
1 medium onion, chopped
1 4-ounce can mushroom pieces

3 tablespoons chopped pimento
¼ teaspoon salt
¼ teaspoon pepper
¼ teaspoon dehydrated parsley
1/3 cup sherry, optional

Cook rice according to directions, dissolving the bouillon cubes in the cooking water. Cook until rice is dry. In the margarine, saute celery, onion, and mushrooms until soft. Add the sauteed vegetables, pimento, seasoning and sherry to cooked rice. Put into greased casserole and set in a pan of hot water in 350° oven for 45 minutes. Yields 12 servings.

If your freezer is full of game and your pockets are full of lots of loose change — LARGE change, this dish is a perfect choice. Truly elegant!

Mrs. James D. Moore

HOPPIN' JOHN

1 cup uncooked rice
½ cup water
1½ cups tomato juice
1 small package pimento cheese, grated
1 medium sweet onion, chopped
1 teaspoon salt
1 teaspoon celery salt, optional
1 tablespoon Worcestershire

¼ teaspoon Tabasco or 1 dried hot pepper, chopped
½ stick butter, cut in pieces, or ¼ cup bacon drippings
3-4 slices of cooked crumbled bacon
1 15-ounce can blackeyed peas, undrained
Parsley
Pimento

Mix all ingredients to bacon. Pour into a 2-quart buttered casserole. Bake at 350°, tightly covered, for 1½ hours. Uncover, stir and toss lightly with blackeyed peas; cover and bake 30 more minutes. Garnish with bacon and parsley. Pimento is pretty with this, also. Serves 6.

A creole flavored variation of basic Hoppin' John. Good as a side dish with any kind of pork.

Mrs. Dalton Guthrie

POPPY SEED NOODLES

1 8-ounce package broad noodles
¼ cup real butter
½ cup slivered almonds

3 tablespoons poppy seed
2 tablespoons lemon juice
Dash cayenne pepper

Cook noodles according to instructions, undercooking slightly. While draining noodles, melt butter in small pan, add almonds and brown, watching closely. When nicely browned, add poppy seeds and lemon juice. Put noodles in ovenproof dish in which they will be served. Pour over the butter mixture and toss gently with two forks. Sprinkle lightly with cayenne. Serves 8-10.

If you are preparing this well ahead of time, cook noodles uncovered. Dot with butter, cover with foil and let stand. Just before ready to serve, place covered dish in 400° oven for about 30 minutes.

If you are preparing noodles shortly before serving time, of course it isn't necessary to let cool. Just dot with butter, cover and cook in oven 15 to 20 minutes.

Serve these marvelous noodles with any meal in place of rice or potatoes. Especially good with "Lamb Louise" (see Meats).

Mrs. William E. Shinn, Jr.

SPINACH WITH CREAM CHEESE

2 packages frozen, whole spinach
1 3-ounce package cream cheese
¼ cup butter

Salt and pepper, to taste
Parmesan cheese

Cook spinach according to directions and then chop into pieces. Melt cream cheese and butter in baking dish in oven. Mix spinach

194

with cheese and butter. Salt and pepper. Sprinkle with Parmesan cheese and heat thoroughly in 350° oven about 15 minutes. Serves 6.

A real spinach quickie for your family, so good that we've even seen children who "never touch the stuff" actually gobble.

For company, stir several good shakes of Parmesan into spinach-butter-cream cheese mixture. When slightly cool, fold in 2 stiffly beaten egg whites, and bake at 350° for 30 minutes for a souffle effect.

Mrs. Norman W. Harris, Jr.

SPINACH SOUFFLE

1 package frozen chopped spinach	1 cup milk
3 tablespoons butter	Salt and pepper
3 tablespoons flour	3 eggs, separated

Cook spinach according to directions and drain thoroughly. Melt butter over low heat and stir in flour. Remove from heat, add milk and stir until smooth. Return to low heat. Cook and stir constantly until thick and bubbly. Remove from heat. Add salt and pepper to taste. Beat egg yolks well and add a small amount of spinach. Return it all to the saucepan. Add rest of spinach. Cook and stir over low heat.

Beat egg whites until stiff. Fold into spinach mixture. Turn into buttered 1½ quart casserole. Place in a pan of very hot water. Bake in 350° oven for 30 to 35 minutes. Can be garnished with grated eggs. Serves 6.

Serve only when you know your guests will be prompt, or when you have good help in the kitchen to do the last minute work. A souffle WON'T WAIT! This souffle is delicious and worth any extra effort you make.

Mrs. Albert P. Brewer
Pike Road, Alabama

SPINACH CASSEROLE

Isn't it a shame that Popeye never knew about this dish! It's so easy as opening a can — and infinitely better.

3 packages frozen chopped spinach	1 package onion soup mix
1 cup sour cream	

Cook spinach according to package directions and drain. Then add sour cream and onion soup mix. Bake for 30 minutes at 350°. Yields 8 servings.

For variation, scoop out some pulp of tomatoes. Salt and pepper tomato. Fill with spinach. Bake 325° about 20 minutes. Garnish with bacon crumbles.

Mrs. William S. Coles

COMPANY SPINACH

2 packages frozen, chopped spinach
1/4 cup butter, melted
2 tablespoons chopped onion
2 tablespoons flour
1/2 cup evaporated milk
1/2 cup reserved vegetable liquor
1 roll garlic cheese

1/2 teaspoon pepper
3/4 teaspoon celery salt
1 teaspoon salt
1/2 teaspoon Worcestershire
Red pepper to taste
1 jalapeno pepper, finely chopped
Bread crumbs

Cook spinach according to directions, drain, and reserve liquor. Melt butter, add chopped onion and cook until soft. Add flour. Mix and add milk and vegetable liquor slowly. Cook until smooth and thick. Add cheese (which is cut into small pieces) and remaining ingredients. Stir until cheese is melted and add to spinach. Put in casserole and top with buttered bread crumbs. Bake at 350° for 30 minutes. Serves 8.

A zippy cheese and jalapeno pepper sauce gives this spinach its appeal!

Mrs. Lynn C. Fowler

SUNDAY SQUASH

1 pound yellow squash, sliced
1/4 cup boiling water
Salt, to taste
1 medium onion, grated
1/4 cup chopped, blanched almonds

1/4 cup margarine
1/2 cup fine, soft, fresh bread crumbs
1/2 cup sharp Cheddar cheese, grated

Cook squash with water and salt over medium heat until tender. Saute onions and almonds separately in margarine. Drain and mash squash. Add more salt if desired. Add bread crumbs and onion. Mix and arrange in a quart casserole. Top with almonds. Sprinkle with cheese. Heat in oven until cheese melts.

Good any other day of the week, too!

Mrs. Allen Hamilton

BAKED SQUASH

3/4 pound yellow squash, sliced
10 scallions, chopped (including tops)
2 tablespoons butter
Salt, to taste

1 can cream of celery soup
Cheese Ritz crackers, crumbled
1 egg, beaten
Parmesan cheese

Cook squash, scallions, and butter with salt until tender. (Add a little water, if needed.) Cool squash, add beaten egg and celery soup. Then add Cheese Ritz crackers (enough to thicken mixture for baking) and much Parmesan cheese. Pour in buttered casserole and bake at 350° until top is brown. Serves 4.

Thank Nabisco and their cheese Ritz crackers for this taste treat.

Mrs. William Sexton

SQUASH SOUFFLE

4 medium yellow squash, sliced
1 medium onion, chopped
Salt and pepper, to taste
4 crackers, crushed

4 tablespoons melted butter
2 eggs, separated
1/3 cup grated cheese

Steam onion and squash together until tender. Drain excess water and mash well. Add crushed crackers, salt, pepper, butter, 2 beaten egg yolks and cheese. Blend well. Fold in 2 stiffly beaten egg whites. Pour into greased baking dish and bake at 350° about 45 minutes or until set and slightly brown. Serves 4.

This recipe comes originally from the hostess at a very large church in Birmingham, who sometimes makes this souffle for as many as 80 people! You try it for four, or double it for eight, but remember — if you ever need to feed 80 — it CAN be done. Think big!

Mrs. Arthur F. Jordan

SQUASH CASSEROLE

1½ pounds fresh yellow squash
  or 2 16-ounce cans squash
Salt and pepper
1 2-ounce jar pimentos, chopped
1 medium onion, chopped finely
1 cup sour cream

1 can cream of chicken soup
4 small carrots, grated
1 package Pepperidge Farm
  cornbread stuffing (or herb
  stuffing)
½ cup margarine, melted

Cook squash in small amount of water until tender. Drain and mash. Season to taste. Stir in remaining ingredients, reserving half the stuffing which has been mixed with melted margarine. Line a casserole with reserved stuffing. Set aside enough stuffing to sprinkle on top. Fill casserole with squash mixture and top with remainder of stuffing. Bake at 350° for 30 minutes. May be prepared the day before and baked when needed. Serves 8.

A very pretty casserole with a delightful flavor.

Mrs. Dan M. Crane

LAYERED SQUASH PAPASAN

A thick layer of sliced, yellow
  squash
Layer of sliced, fresh tomatoes
Salt, pepper, and butter

Layer of onion
Layer of American cheese
Layer of croutons (cube either rye
  or white bread and fry in butter)

Butter a deep casserole dish. Layers may be repeated; if so, leave croutons until last. Cover and bake at 350° for 1 hour. Serves 6.

Layer after colorful layer of two favorite summer vegetables. And WONDERS occur in the oven.

Mrs. Lindsay A. Allen

STUFFED SQUASH

8 or 10 nice, tender yellow squash
1 small onion, grated
2 slices Roman Meal bread,
   crumbled

¼ cup butter
Salt and pepper, to taste
New York State Cheese, grated
Paprika

While boiling squash until tender, put bread in bowl with butter and onion. When squash are tender, remove from water and cut off tops. With spoon scoop out insides, add salt and pepper, and add to bread mixture. Fill shells with this mixture, top with grated cheese and paprika. Bake in 350° oven, 20 to 30 minutes. Serves 8.

When yellow squash is in season, nothing much tastes this good. An attractive vegetable, stuffed squash adds color to any luncheon plate, and color is so important in making a meal appealing.

Mrs. Frank Stone

SQUASH BALLS

2 cups yellow squash, finely cut
1 small onion, chopped
2 eggs

1 cup soft bread crumbs
Salt and pepper, to taste

Simmer squash until tender in a little salted water. Drain and mash to a fine pulp. Saute onion in butter. Add to squash with egg and soft bread crumbs. Salt and pepper. Add more bread crumbs if necessary to make a light but firm ball. Roll in more crumbs and chill 6 hours. Fry in deep fat until brown.

Trouble, yes, but a delicious and different way to serve squash!

Mrs. John D. Sherrill

ZUCCHINI AND TOMATOES AU GRATIN

2 pounds zucchini
3 tablespoons chopped onion
3 tablespoons bacon grease
2 cups canned, stewed tomatoes

½ teaspoon salt
⅛ teaspoon pepper
1 cup grated cheese, American or
   mild Cheddar

Wash and cut zucchini into ¼ inch pieces. Cook onion in bacon grease, add zucchini and cook slowly 5 minutes, stirring frequently. Add tomatoes, salt and pepper. Cover and cook 5 minutes longer. Turn into greased 1½ quart baking dish, sprinkle cheese over top and bake in 350° oven, about 20 minutes. Serves 6 to 8.

Mrs. Lindsay A. Allen

ZUCCHINI QUICK AND EASY

½ cup onion, thinly sliced
2 tablespoons butter
1 tablespoon Good Seasons Italian
   salad dressing mix

1 pound zucchini
½ cup water
¾ cup grated American cheese

Brown onion in butter. Wash and cut zucchini into about ¼ inch slices. Add zucchini, dressing mix, and water and cook together 15 minutes. Top with grated cheese. Serves 4.

Mrs. Lindsay A. Allen

ZUCCHINI SOUFFLE

2 cups peeled and sliced zucchini
1 cup salted water
½ onion, minced; or 1 clove
   garlic, crushed
Rich cream sauce of:
   2 tablespoons butter

2 tablespoons flour
1 cup light cream
¼ teaspoon cayenne pepper
¼ teaspoon pepper
Pinch salt
2 whole eggs

Cut peeled zucchini into 1 inch pieces. Cook in salted water until tender with onion or garlic. Drain and mash. Prepare the rich cream sauce. Stir over medium heat until thick and smooth. Remove from heat and stir in 2 whole eggs. Fold cream sauce into drained zucchini. Pour into a 1½ quart buttered casserole. Bake at 350° about 1 hour and 15 minutes until golden brown.

Zucchini is a squash that is often overlooked in cotton country because to most Southerners, "squash" is synonymous with "yellow squash." Zucchini has a good flavor and this is an excellent recipe which lets that flavor shine. Do try it — and broaden your horizons.

Mrs. R. W. Orr, Jr.

TOMATO PUDDING

1 20-ounce can tomatoes
1 cup brown sugar
1 teaspoon salt

3 cups white bread cubes, fresh
   or stale
½ cup melted margarine

Crush tomatoes through sieve to release every drop of juice. Add sugar and salt to tomatoes and juice and let cook rapidly for about 5 minutes. Place bread cubes (about ½" in size) in medium size casserole. Pour melted butter over cubes, stir, then add boiling tomato mixture. Stir again. Bake 50 minutes at 375°. Serves 6 or more.

A rich, fattening, and delicious side dish — a welcome change from baked beans with hamburgers, or other outdoor meals. This amount should serve six easily, but may not if you have a hungry bunch!

Mrs. William E. Shinn, Jr.

GLAZED CHERRY TOMATOES

1 pint, hard-ripe, cherry tomatoes
¼ cup water
¼ teaspoon salt

1 teaspoon light brown sugar
½ teaspoon freshly ground pepper

In a two quart saucepan, combine all ingredients. Heat to boiling point, tossing gently with fork or spoon to evenly cook tomatoes. Boil 5 to 7 minutes or until just tender. Serve immediately. Serves 6 to 8.

A quick and pretty hot tomato dish with the good bite of freshly ground black pepper.

Mrs. David C. Harris

SCOFFIELD

1 29-ounce can tomatoes
¼ cup oil
½ cup vinegar

½ cup sugar
Salt and pepper, to taste
¼ to ½ small onion, scraped

Mix all ingredients together and chill several hours before serving. Cut tomatoes in half. Serve in a bowl and use a spoon to drink the juice. (The juice is as good as the tomatoes.)

In midwinter, when the only fresh tomatoes available resemble small pink rubber balls, yet you die to taste a real tomato, season up a can as suggested, chill well, and serve as a cold soup, salad, vegetable, or whatever — in bowls. Perhaps it's not as good as a juicy red tomato right off the vine, but it will satisfy your craving for a while.

Mrs. David C. Harris

FRIED GREEN TOMATOES

3 green tomatoes, sliced ½" thick
Salt and pepper, to taste

½ cup corn meal
Fat

Slice tomatoes, salt and pepper, then coat with corn meal. Fry slowly in hot fat until brown, turning once.

Mrs. John E. Wilks, Jr.

FANCY TURNIP GREENS

1½ pounds turnip greens
1 teaspoon salt
½ to ¾ cup water
4 strips bacon

2 tablespoons onion, finely chopped
2 tablespoons cider vinegar
2 hard-boiled eggs, chopped
Salt and pepper, to taste

Discard withered leaves and stems from fresh turnip greens. Wash greens thoroughly 4 or 5 times to remove all undesirable matter. Cook, covered in salted water at low boil until tender, about 45 minutes. While greens are cooking, boil eggs and chop; fry bacon until crisp and then crumble. Reserve 2 tablespoons bacon drippings in skillet. When greens are done, drain and place in warm serving dish. Slightly saute onion in bacon drippings. Turn off heat and add vinegar to skillet. Blend. Pour sauce over greens and toss slightly. Garnish with chopped eggs and bacon and sprinkle with salt and pepper. Serves 4 to 6.

Soul food with more spirit.

Mrs. Billy W. Payne

ANN GRATWICK'S VEGETABLE SOUFFLE

1 package frozen spinach (asparagus may be used, but tastier with spinach)
10 slices Pepperidge Farm white bread
4 eggs
2 cups milk

1 teaspoon salt
1 16-ounce can tomato wedges, reserving liquid
Salt and pepper, to taste
1 can cream of mushroom soup
Grated Swiss or Parmesan cheese (Swiss is preferable)

Thaw spinach and drain. Slice crusts from bread and cut each slice into 4 squares. Place bread in buttered casserole, 13" x 9". Beat eggs, milk and 1 teaspoon salt. Pour this over bread, allowing time for bread to soak up all liquid, at least 1 hour. Arrange tomato wedges over bread evenly and pour remaining tomato liquid over all. Add salt and pepper to taste. Mix drained spinach with undiluted mushroom soup and spoon this mixture over tomatoes allowing the tomatoes to show through. Sprinkle cheese on top. Bake at 350° for about 1 hour, or at 375° for 30 to 45 minutes if in a hurry. Serves 8.

Ann does her souffle in a shallow copper casserole; it is unusually pretty AND super good. You'll need to have a meat and bread and this!

Mrs. L. Denton Cole

VEGETABLE CASSEROLE DELIGHT

2½ cups potatoes, coarsely grated
1½ cups carrots, coarsely grated
½ cup onion, coarsely grated
1 cup milk

1 can cream of celery soup
Salt and pepper to taste
½ cup grated cheese

Place all ingredients in buttered dish except cheese. Bake at 375° for 1 hour. Add cheese and bake 10 more minutes.

Mrs. Robert H. Hosey

MOCK HOLLANDAISE SAUCE

3 tablespoons margarine, softened   Dash salt
3 tablespoons mayonnaise   Dash pepper
2 tablespoons lemon juice

Mix margarine and mayonnaise with spoon until smooth. Add lemon juice and stir until completely mixed with other ingredients. Season with salt and pepper. Pour over hot vegetables.

Mrs. Norman W. Harris, Jr.

WHITE SAUCE

Ingredients	Thin	Medium	Thick
Butter or			
Margarine	1 tablespoon	2 tablespoons	3 tablespoons
Flour	1 tablespoon	2 tablespoons	3 tablespoons
Milk	1 cup	1 cup	1 cup

Melt butter or margarine. Remove from heat and blend in flour until smooth. Slowly stir in milk. Cook until thick, stirring constantly. Season to taste with salt and pepper.

Breads

JUNE WILSON'S WHITE BREAD

2¼ cups skim milk	3 tablespoons shortening
3 tablespoons sugar	2 envelopes dry yeast
1 tablespoon salt	5 to 6 cups unsifted all purpose flour

Combine milk, sugar, salt and shortening in heavy saucepan and stir well. Cook over medium heat until mixture is hot enough to form small bubbles at the edge of pan. Remove from heat and allow to cool until mixture is just on the hot side of lukewarm (so that you can touch the sides of the pan). Sprinkle the yeast onto mixture, and allow it to soften well before stirring it into mixture.

Gradually add flour, stirring in part at a time until it is well blended. Mixture should be slightly sticky. Turn onto a well floured surface and knead, adding additional flour to prevent sticking, until dough holds together in a big ball and becomes smooth. Place dough in large greased bowl, cover and set aside in warm place until dough doubles in bulk. Punch down, turn dough over in bowl and allow to rise again until doubled.

Punch down again and turn out onto lightly floured surface. Cut dough in half, shape into loaves and fit into 2 greased 9x5x3 loaf pans. Cover and allow to rise until doubled.

Bake at 400° for about 30 minutes until crusty brown. Butter tops of loaves. Turn out of pans and allow to cool on wire racks. Yields 2 loaves, which freeze well.

And all you need is a jug of wine and thou!

To our readers who have never made bread, or watched it being made, the term "knead" may be perplexing.

To "knead": turn dough onto floured surface (a wooden board is most satisfactory, but not essential). With the heel of both hands, push firmly into the dough, pushing away from your body and getting your body weight into the action. Then, with finger tips, lift dough from far side and pull it toward you, turning it partly over. Repeat the push-pull until the dough feels smooth or until you've met the recipe requirements. It won't take long to get a good kneading rhythm established.

Mrs. Whit King, Jr.

MY GRANDMOTHER'S HOMEMADE BREAD

If you prefer an old-fashioned, dump method, get-your-hands-into-the-dough recipe that always produces big, delicious golden loaves, please try this.

2 cups warm water (105° - 115°)	2 pounds all purpose flour (approximately; use a 2 pound bag or not quite half of a 5 pound bag)
3 tablespoons sugar	
1 package dry yeast	
	½ cup shortening
	2 teaspoons salt

Stir sugar into warm water. Sprinkle yeast over water and stir to dissolve. Set aside.

Place flour in large bowl. It is not necessary to sift. Add salt and shortening. Gradually add water-sugar-yeast mixture, and mix with hands until all the flour is mixed in and a stiff dough is formed. It may be necessary to add additional warm water to get all the flour taken up.

Turn onto floured board and knead well until the dough is smooth and elastic (at least 5 minutes — the more the better).

Place dough in bowl, cover with cloth and put in warm spot to rise until doubled in bulk. This generally takes 1½ to 2 hours.

Push dough down, turn onto board and knead again for a minute or two, put back in bowl, cover with cloth and allow to rise again until doubled. Push dough down, turn out of bowl and form into 2 loaves. Place each loaf into a greased 9x5x3 loaf pan, cover and let rise until smooth on top and well out of pan. A good test is to pick pan up and if it feels weightless, the loaves are ready to cook.

Bake in 350° oven for an hour. Turn out on wire rack to cool.

Bread making is good for the soul! The original mixing of dough takes care of all those pent-up mud-pie making desires, and kneading gets rid of anger and frustration. And you feel so accomplished when you see and smell those loaves — your very own creation. Watch out, though. It's fattening. Also it takes time to make bread. Do this on a day you plan to be at home.

For a special breakfast treat, try this bread toasted. Butter thin slices and bake in a 300° to 350° oven for a few minutes until medium crisp.

Mrs. William E. Shinn, Jr.

HERB BREAD

1 loaf unsliced day old bread	¼ teaspoon oregano
½ pound butter	¼ teaspoon basil
Garlic salt, to taste	¼ teaspoon rosemary
½ teaspoon paprika	¼ teaspoon salt

Remove crust from bread; cut into slices and down the middle. To softened butter, add the remaining ingredients. Let mixture stand for an hour or longer so flavors can blend. Frost bread, between slices and over top and sides with butter mixture. Bake at 350° for 15 to 20 minutes.

Mrs. Billy W. Payne

DILL BUTTER

1 teaspoon lemon juice
2 tablespoons melted butter
½ teaspoon dill seed

Blend and serve on hard bread or spread on pork chops.

WHOLE WHEAT BREAD

¼ cup sugar
1 cup warm water (105° - 115°)
1 package dry yeast
2 2/3 cup heated milk

½ cup honey or molasses
1 tablespoon salt
2 tablespoons margarine
7 cups whole wheat flour

Stir sugar into warm water in small bowl and sprinkle yeast over it. Stir until dissolved.

In large mixing bowl, stir together milk, honey or molasses, salt and margarine. When lukewarm, add yeast mixture. Sift in whole wheat flour, and stir until well mixed and a stiff dough is formed. It may be necessary to add additional whole wheat flour if dough seems sticky.

Turn out on floured board and knead well, until smooth and elastic. Place dough in clean bowl, cover with damp cloth and let rise for one hour or longer until almost doubled in bulk.

Turn out onto floured board and knead again. Shape into two loaves and place into greased 9x5x3 loaf pans. Cover with damp cloth and let rise for an hour or longer until smooth and out of pan.

Preheat oven to 450°. Place bread in oven, reduce heat to 350° and bake for one hour and 10 minutes. Cool on wire rack.

This is an absolutely delicious bread. Most whole wheat breads are made with part white flour and part whole wheat. This one, though, is 100% whole wheat. It's dark, moist, slightly coarse in texture and the flavor is unusually good.

If you find that your loaves are a bit dry, try adding additional margarine — say 2 or 3 tablespoons — and reduce the amount of milk a bit to compensate. Contrary to popular opinion, it's really very hard to ruin yeast bread. You can change ingredients to suit yourself without hurting a thing. Bread is not the temperamental prima donna many people think it is, and it is really worth your effort.

Mrs. A. Julian Harris

BRIOCHE

½ cup margarine (1 stick)
½ cup sugar
½ tablespoon salt
½ cup scalded milk

2 packages dry yeast
½ cup warm water
3 eggs, slightly beaten
5½ cups all purpose flour

Into large bowl put margarine, sugar and salt. Pour in scalded milk and stir to dissolve sugar and margarine. Set aside to cool.

In small bowl, sprinkle yeast into warm water and stir to dissolve.

When milk mixture is lukewarm, add dissolved yeast and eggs. Add half the flour and beat well, by hand or with electric mixer. Add remaining flour. Turn onto floured board and knead for ten minutes.

Divide dough into two equal portions. Cut each portion into three pieces and make a braid to fit a 9x5x3 loaf pan. Pinch each end of braid together and place in greased pan. Repeat for other half of dough. Let rise until doubled in bulk. Bake at 350° for 30 minutes. Makes two loaves.

These pretty, braided loaves look as if you've spent hours working, but since this bread rises only once, it takes less time than most bread. The texture is light and airy, the color a lovely pale yellow and the taste, sweeter than most bread, is good. Brioche would be nice for breakfast, if you are of a continental bent. How does sweet butter and tart plum jelly sound?

Mrs. John Power
Miami, Florida

REFRIGERATOR ROLLS

1 cup water
½ cup butter or margarine
  (1 stick)
½ cup shortening
¾ cup sugar

1½ teaspoons salt
1 cup warm water (105°-115°)
2 packages dry yeast
2 eggs, slightly beaten
6 cups all purpose flour

Boil 1 cup water in saucepan. Set off stove. Add butter and shortening and stir until melted. Add sugar and salt. Cool to lukewarm.

In large bowl, put 1 cup warm water. Sprinkle yeast over and stir to dissolve.

Add butter-sugar-shortening mixture and eggs to dissolved yeast. Add 6 cups flour or enough to make a thick dough, and mix thoroughly. Cover and put in refrigerator overnight.

About 2 to 2½ hours before serving rolls, turn dough out on floured board, roll to desired thickness, cut and shape. (For Parker House rolls, roll dough to a thickness of about 1/3 to ¼ inch, cut with round biscuit cutter and fold in half). Place on greased pan. Let rise about 1½ to 2 hours. Bake at 400° for 12 to 15 minutes until well browned.

The entire recipe will yield approximately four dozen large Parker House rolls. It is not necessary to use all the dough. Make out as many rolls as you need, re-cover the remaining dough and keep refrigerated. Dough will keep for several days.

Mrs. Lloyd Nix

207

MARY'S FRENCH BREAD

2½ cups warm water (105°-115°) 7 cups unsifted all purpose flour
2 packages dry yeast Cornmeal
1 tablespoon salt 1 egg white
1 tablespoon melted margarine 1 tablespoon cold water

Measure warm water into large warm bowl. Sprinkle in yeast; stir until dissolved. Add salt and margarine. Add flour and stir until well blended (dough will be stiff but sticky). Place in greased bowl, turning dough to grease top. Cover. Let rise in warm place until doubled in bulk. Turn dough onto lightly floured board. Divide into two equal portions. Roll each into an oblong shape, 15 x 10 inches. Beginning at wide end, roll up tightly toward you; seal edges by pinching together. Taper ends by rolling gently back and forth. Place loaves on greased baking sheets sprinkled with cornmeal. Cover. Let rise until doubled in bulk. Make diagonal cuts on top of each loaf with very sharp knife. Bake in 450° oven for 25 minutes. Remove from oven and brush with egg white beaten with cold water until frothy. Sprinkle with poppy or sesame seeds. Return to oven. Bake 10 minutes longer. Cool on wire rack.

This is a very simple bread to make and produces two beautiful loaves, as tasty as any you'll find in this country, and far superior to most so-called "French breads". Serve thick slices and plenty of butter — it's too good to doctor up with garlic butter and heat as one does with purchased French bread — and it won't last long.

Mrs. Thomas Bingham

FRENCH BREAD

Anyone who has spent any time in France knows of the French passion for bread — their bread. You also know the reason. The French look with disdain upon any attempt to duplicate their product, and more often than not they are justified in their appraisal. This recipe produces bread which is closer to the real thing than any we have found. It is more complicated and time consuming than most bread recipes, but the results are superb.

2 cups warm water (105°-115°) 1 tablespoon salt
1 package dry yeast (or 1 cake 6 to 6½ cups all purpose flour
  yeast) Cornmeal

Measure water into large warm bowl. Sprinkle (or crumble) in yeast. Stir to dissolve. Beat in salt and 4 cups flour until smooth. Add enough additional flour to make stiff dough, mixing with hands if necessary.

Turn dough onto floured board. Knead at least 5 minutes until smooth and elastic.

Place dough in large clean bowl with vertical sides instead of slanting ones. Cover with heavy towel folded in half. Set in warm spot

(75° to 80° but no higher) on board or towel, not on cold counter. Let rise 2½ to 3 hours or until dough triples in bulk.

Punch dough down. Let rise again 45 minutes to an hour, or until dough more than doubles in size.

Punch down again. Loosen from sides of bowl with rubber spatula. Turn dough out onto floured board. Cut into 3 or 4 equal pieces. To form loaves, roll each piece back and forth with palms, sliding hands gradually toward ends as dough lengthens. Roll each to about 15 inches long or to fit cookie sheet.

Sprinkle cookie sheet with cornmeal. Place loaves on cookie sheet. With razor blade, make 3 or 4 lengthwise slashes in each loaf, ¼ to ½ inch deep. Let loaves rise, uncovered, in warm spot for 2 hours or until doubled in bulk. While loaves rise, heat oven to 400°. Put a shallow pan of boiling water on bottom rack of oven to create steam. Boiling water will probably have to be added to pan as it steams away. When ready to bake, brush loaves with cold water with a soft brush (an artist's brush is good). Bake 20 minutes. Brush with cold water again, and bake for 20 minutes more. Transfer loaves to wire rack to cool. Yields 3 or 4 loaves.

Mrs. George Howell, Jr.

ANN ANDERSON'S

LOW FAT-LOW CHOLESTEROL DINNER ROLLS

¾ cup skim milk
¼ cup sugar
2½ teaspoons salt

1 package yeast
¾ cup lukewarm water
¼ cup Mazola oil
4 cups sifted flour

Scald milk. Add sugar and salt cooling to lukewarm. Sprinkle yeast over warm water, (105° to 115°) in large mixing bowl. Stir until dissolved. Add lukewarm milk mixture and oil. Beat in 2 cups flour until smooth. Add remaining flour or enough to make soft dough. Turn dough out on lightly floured board and knead until smooth.

Place in lightly oiled bowl and brush top lightly with oil. Cover and let rise in warm place about 1½ hours. Punch down dough, knead lightly, divide in half and roll ½ inch thick and cut into rounds. Crease heavily through center with dull edge of knife and brush lightly with oil. Fold over into pocketbook-shape. Place on greased baking pan. Cover and let rise until double in bulk, about 1 hour. Bake 400° about 12 minutes.

A surprisingly good substitute, especially for those dieters.

ICEBOX CLOVERLEAF ROLLS

1 cup shortening	3 eggs, slightly beaten
½ cup sugar	2 cakes yeast
1 cup boiling water	2 teaspoons salt
1 cup cold water	7 cups all purpose flour

Cream shortening and sugar. Add boiling water and stir until dissolved. Add cold water and eggs and mix well. Add crumbled yeast cakes and salt. Blend in flour and mix well. Dough will be slightly thicker than cake batter. Cover dough with wet dish towel, placing towel directly on dough, and refrigerate overnight.

About 3 hours before serving, flour hands very well and pinch off enough dough to form a ball about the diameter of a quarter. Place 2 or 3 balls in each cup of a greased muffin tin. Allow to rise about 2½ hours in a warm spot. Bake in 400° oven for 15 minutes or until lightly browned.

Remaining dough may be kept in refrigerator several days as long as covered directly with wet cloth. Yields 3 to 4 dozen rolls.

The flavor and texture of these rolls are great! Save this one for cloverleaf rolls, though, and don't try to roll out, for the dough is too soft.

Mrs. L. Denton Cole

EASY DROP ROLLS

¾ cup margarine (1½ sticks)	1 package dry yeast
¼ cup sugar	2 cups warm water
1 egg, slightly beaten	4 cups self-rising flour

Melt margarine and cool. Add all other ingredients and stir until blended. (Dough will be soft and sticky.) Place in air tight covered container and store in refrigerator several hours before using.

To serve, spoon into greased muffin tins and bake at 400° for 20 minutes.

The entire recipe will yield 3 dozen large rolls or 6 dozen small ones, and the ones made in small muffin tins are especially tasty.

This roll recipe is a handy one for your file. It is quite simple to make (even children can do it — if you dare), the dough can be kept a week and since there is no rising time to consider, it's a quick way to have hot rolls on the table. The results are surprisingly good.

Mrs. John E. Wilks, Jr.

FREEZER ROLLS OR BISCUITS

This is an indispensable recipe for those that like to think ahead.

5 cups self-rising flour	2 packages yeast
4 tablespoons sugar	2 tablespoons warm water
1 cup shortening	2 cups buttermilk

Cut shortening into combined sugar and flour. Dissolve yeast in warm water and add buttermilk. Stir milk and yeast into dry ingredients and mix well.

Turn on lightly floured board, knead lightly and roll out. Cut into desired size, and shape pocket-book style. Freeze on baking sheet and store in plastic bags.

When ready to serve, dip in butter and place on pan. Let rise about 1 to 1½ hours or longer. Bake 400° about 10 minutes.

For Biscuits: Use 1 package yeast and cut with biscuit cutter to desired thickness.

For Sausage Biscuits: Cook 2 pounds sausage stirring to separate. Allow to cool slightly in grease. Roll about a fourth of the dough into a rectangle 8 x 16 and sprinkle with a fourth of the cooled sausage. Salt lightly and roll up like cinnamon rolls. These may be frozen in rolls or cut into ¼ inch slices and frozen on cookie sheets. As soon as rolls are frozen on cookie sheets, place in plastic bag for storage. Bake 350° about 10 minutes until lightly browned.

Mrs. John E. Wilks, Jr.

LETA'S SOUR CREAM ROLLS

These are superb! Don't fail to try them.

3½ cups all purpose flour
1 cup margarine (2 sticks)
¼ cup warm water
1 package dry yeast

1 egg and 2 egg yolks, beaten well
¾ cup commercial sour cream
½ cup sugar

Cut margarine into flour with pastry blender or knives. Add yeast which has been dissolved in ¼ cup warm water, the beaten eggs and sour cream. Mix well. Cover bowl with damp cloth and place in refrigerator for at least 2 hours, or overnight if possible.

On well-floured board, roll dough into an oblong approximately ¼ inch thick. Sprinkle with half of the sugar. Fold one side three-fourths of the way over, then fold other side over. Roll to original size. Sprinkle with remaining sugar and repeat the folding process. Again roll into oblong, cut into strips ½ inch wide and about 5 inches long. Twist into small rolls. The shape is up to you; either figure eights, (tucking ends under so they won't separate during baking) small loops or even knots. Bake immediately in 350° oven for about 12 to 15 minutes. Yields about 3 dozen small rolls.

These rolls are sweet flaky dreams. They are simple to make, there is no kneading required, and they do not have to rise before cooking. This is an excellent party recipe. Make rolls out and refrigerate on baking sheet until time to bake.

Mrs. John A. Woller

BRAN ROLLS

1 cup boiling water	2 eggs, beaten
1 cup shortening	2 packages dry yeast
3 teaspoons salt	1 cup warm water
¾ cup sugar	6 to 7 cups sifted all purpose
1 cup Kellogg's All Bran	flour

Pour boiling water over shortening, salt and sugar in large mixing bowl. Stir to melt shortening. When melted, add All Bran. Add eggs and the yeast, dissolved in the cup of warm water.

Add 3 cups flour. Beat in well with electric mixer. Add 3 or more cups flour and beat in by hand.

Pour a small amount of oil on dough and spread over surface. Refrigerate covered, overnight. Make up into rolls on floured board and place on greased baking pan. Let rise about 2 hours. Bake at 450° for 10 to 12 minutes or until brown. Makes about 4 dozen rolls.

These rolls are light, airy and have a marvelous flavor — a nice change from "white" rolls.

Mrs. William E. Shinn, Jr.

BEER ROLLS

1 tablespoon sugar	3 cups Bisquick
1 can beer (12 ounce can)	

Mix ingredients together in bowl. Spoon into greased muffin tins. Bake at 400° for 12 to 15 minutes. Yields a dozen or more large rolls.

Don't laugh until you've tried these! These closely approximate yeast rolls, and talk about quick — you won't believe it.

Mrs. Robert H. Hosey

BISCUITS

2 cups sifted all purpose flour	¼ teaspoon baking soda
3 teaspoons baking powder	1/3 cup shortening
1 teaspoon salt	¾ cup buttermilk, approximately

Sift together flour, baking powder, salt and soda into bowl. Cut in the shortening with a pastry blender until mixture resembles coarse meal or crumbs. Make a hollow in flour mixture and pour in enough buttermilk to make a soft dough. Mix quickly with a fork only until dough clings together and leaves the sides of the bowl.

Turn onto lightly floured surface and knead lightly with heel of hand about 10 times, or until dough is manageable. Roll ¼ inch to ½ inch thick with floured rolling pin (¼ inch for crusty biscuits; ½ inch for high fluffy ones). Cut with floured biscuit cutter and place on ungreased baking sheet or pan. Place close together for soft sides or about an inch apart for crusty sides.

Bake in 450° oven for 10 to 12 minutes, or until golden. Makes 12 to 16 two-inch biscuits or 24 smaller ones.

There is just something about biscuits made with buttermilk! You can make them without it, though, if you must. Substitute sweet milk for the buttermilk and omit the baking soda.

Mrs. Robert H. Harris

FANTASTIC STIR AND ROLL BISCUITS

2 cups self-rising flour　　　1/3 cup vegetable oil
Pinch of salt　　　　　　　　2/3 cup milk

Place flour and salt in mixing bowl. Combine oil and milk in measuring cup. Pour combination into flour and stir quickly until dough clings together.

Turn out onto lightly floured board, knead lightly a few times, roll with floured rolling pin to ¼ inch to ½ inch thickness and cut with floured cutter. Place on ungreased baking sheet and bake at 450° for about 10 minutes. Makes 16 to 20 biscuits.

You may substitute buttermilk for the sweet milk if you'll add ¼ teaspoon soda to the flour.

Comments we've heard:

"This recipe should be made available to people like me, who can't cook but like homemade biscuits." and

"Only biscuits I've ever been able to make."

Mrs. Michael D. Scroggins

QUICK DROP MUFFINS

1 cup self-rising flour　　　　¼ cup mayonnaise
½ cup milk

Mix ingredients and drop in hot greased muffin tins. (Try greasing tins with mayonnaise, as long as you have it at hand.) Bake in 450° oven for 12 to 15 minutes or until brown.

This makes 6 large or 12 small muffins. We think the small muffin tins make these muffins a bit more special.

Win the mother-of-the-day award one day soon with hot muffins for breakfast. Mix quickly and put in oven. You'll have just enough time to cook the bacon and scramble the eggs before your bread is ready — and you'll still be able to get everyone off to school.

Mrs. Fred Sittason
Mrs. Jim L. Thompson, Jr.

DILLY BREAD

For an unusual bread treat — good warm or cold — make dilly bread. It is truly fool proof, and the aroma from your kitchen will buoy your spirits.

1 package dry yeast	1 tablespoon soft butter or
¼ cup warm water (105° to 115°)	margarine
1 cup creamed cottage cheese	2 teaspoons dill seed
1 egg, beaten slightly	1 teaspoon salt
2 tablespoons sugar	¼ teaspoon baking soda
1 tablespoon minced onion	2½ cups all purpose flour

In warm mixing bowl, dissolve yeast in warm water. In small saucepan, heat cottage cheese to lukewarm. Add to dissolved yeast. Add egg, sugar, onion, butter and dill seed. Mix well. Sift together flour, soda and salt and add to other ingredients and stir until blended. Dough will be quite soft.

Let dough rise about an hour. Spoon into 2 small loaf pans (8x3), well greased, or 1 large round pyrex casserole, well greased. Let rise for 1 hour and bake at 350° for 30 to 35 minutes for the loaf pans or 50 minutes for round casserole. Remove from oven, brush with melted butter and sprinkle with salt.

Mrs. Joe D. Burns

CORNBREAD

1 cup plain white cornmeal	1 cup buttermilk
1 tablespoon flour (optional)	1 egg, beaten slightly
2 teaspoons baking powder	3 tablespoons melted shortening
½ teaspoon salt	or bacon drippings
¼ teaspoon baking soda	

Preheat oven to 450°. Generously grease 6 to 7 inch round iron skillet with bacon grease or shortening, and heat in oven until very hot while mixing bread.

Place meal, flour, baking powder, soda and salt in mixing bowl. Mix buttermilk and egg and add to dry ingredients. Pour in melted shortening or bacon grease and mix well.

Pour batter into hot skillet, place in 450° oven and bake about 20 minutes or until brown on top.

Cut in wedges and serve with butter and um-m-m-m. There's not anything much better.

A point to remember: be sure the greased skillet is very hot before pouring in batter. If it is not, the bread will stick, you'll lose that wonderful crunchy bottom, and run the risk of ruining your skillet.

Mrs. John C. Eyster

EGG BREAD

If you prefer a cornbread with more flour:

1 egg
1 teaspoon salt
¼ cup flour

¾ cup plain white cornmeal
2 rounded teaspoons baking powder
1 cup sweet milk

Beat egg and salt together until light. Add remaining ingredients and stir until well blended. Pour into hot, well greased iron skillet (6 to 8 inch size). Bake in 450° oven for about 20 minutes or until brown.

To double recipe, double all ingredients except egg. Use 10-inch skillet.

Mrs. Randolph P. Pickell

EASY CORNMEAL BISCUITS

1½ cups self-rising flour
½ cup self-rising cornmeal

¼ cup shortening
¾ cup milk

Mix flour and meal. Cut in shortening. Stir in milk, and knead lightly. Roll ¼" to ½" thick. Bake 450° for 12 minutes.

Mrs. John Manning

CORNMEAL BISCUITS

¾ cup all purpose flour, unsifted
¼ cup plain white cornmeal
2 teaspoons baking powder
¼ heaping teaspoon salt

¼ teaspoon soda
2 tablespoons shortening
½ cup buttermilk

Sift flour, cornmeal, baking powder, salt and soda into bowl. Cut in shortening with pastry blender. Stir in buttermilk with fork until dough clings together. Turn out on lightly floured board; knead gently a few times. Roll dough to about ¼ inch thickness and cut with biscuit cutter.

Dip biscuits in melted butter or margarine and place buttered side up on ungreased baking sheet. Bake at 450° for 12 to 15 minutes until nicely browned. Yields 12 to 15 small biscuits.

This is an interesting quick bread variation — neither biscuit nor cornbread. You'll find it a delightful change from the norm. Really good with fried chicken.

Mrs. Paul E. Hargrove

CRUSTY CORN STICKS

1 cup sifted all purpose flour	1 cup yellow cornmeal
3 tablespoons sugar	2 eggs, slightly beaten
4 teaspoons baking powder	1 cup milk
¾ teaspoon salt	¼ cup melted shortening

Sift flour, sugar, baking powder and salt together into mixing bowl. Stir in cornmeal. Add eggs, milk and shortening. Beat with mixer until just smooth — about 1 minute. Do not overbeat.

Pour batter into hot, greased cornstick pans and cook at 400° to 425° for 15 to 20 minutes until a good brown. Makes 18 to 20 cornsticks, or small muffins, if you prefer.

The cornsticks are sweet, moist inside and very crusty on the outside. They are a bit different from ol' Southern cornbread and are great with vegetables and soups. Take two and butter 'em while they're hot.

Mrs. F. T. Richardson, III

CORN PONES OR HOT WATER BREAD

2 to 3 tablespoons shortening	½ teaspoon salt
1 cup plain white cornmeal, preferably water ground	Boiling water

Melt shortening in heavy iron skillet in 450° oven. Mix meal and salt in mixing bowl. Pour in enough boiling water to form stiff dough. Remove skillet from oven, turning it to coat bottom with shortening. Pour rest of melted shortening into dough and stir well.

With hands, quickly form small patties (about three-fourths the size of the palm of your hand), and place on hot skillet. Bake at 450° for 20 to 30 minutes until light brown and crisp. Makes 8 to 10 pones.

The meal, salt and water dough can also be cooked on top of the stove. Heat ¼ inch shortening or bacon grease in skillet and fry the patties until golden, turning once. These pones are crisp on the outside, but quite soft inside, while the oven baked ones are crisper all through.

Serve with a vegetable dinner, homemade vegetable soup, or chili. Hope you're feeling thin — because "I bet you can't eat just one!"

Mrs. William E. Shinn, Jr.

COLOSSAL CORN BREAD

2 cups milk, scalded	2 eggs, well beaten
1/3 cup sugar	1 package dry yeast dissolved in ¼ cup warm water
1/3 cup shortening	
1 tablespoon salt	1 cup yellow corn meal
3 cups sifted flour	4 to 4½ cups flour

In a large mixing bowl combine milk, sugar, shortening and salt; then stir in 3 cups flour until blended. Now add well-beaten eggs, yeast and corn meal; Gradually stir in 4 cups flour.

On lightly floured board, use remaining flour and knead dough 5 minutes. It should be smooth and plastic.

Turn dough into greased bowl and cover with a towel. Let rise until double in bulk, about 1½ hours.

Turn dough onto floured surface and knead a few minutes and shape into two loaf pans 9½ by 5 by 3 and place seam side down in pan. Let rise 20 minutes in warm place and bake 375° for 35 to 45 minutes. Turn out on side on wire rack to cool.

Excellent flavor — Simply colossal loaves.

Mrs. John E. Wilks, Jr.

HUSHPUPPIES

With fried fish, you know that hushpuppies are a must! Not for calorie counters though!

2 cups plain white cornmeal
1 tablespoon flour
1 teaspoon soda
1 teaspoon baking powder

1 teaspoon salt
6 tablespoons finely chopped onion
1 egg, beaten
1 cup buttermilk

Sift meal, flour, soda, baking powder and salt together into bowl. Add chopped onion (you may increase the amount of onion if you really like the onion flavor). Combine the beaten egg and buttermilk and add to dry ingredients. Drop by teaspoonfuls into hot deep fat (375° on thermometer). Cook until golden. When done the hushpuppies will float. Drain on paper towel or brown paper bag.

Makes 35 to 40 hushpuppies.

Mrs. George Douthit

SOUR CREAM CORNBREAD

½ cup margarine (1 stick)
1 cup cream style corn
1 cup sour cream

1 cup self-rising cornmeal
2 eggs, beaten
½ medium onion, grated, if desired

Melt margarine in 8 x 8 inch square pan or an 8-inch iron skillet in 350° oven. Coat pan with margarine.

Mix other ingredients until blended. Pour remaining melted margarine into batter and mix well. Pour batter into hot pan and bake at 350° for 35 to 40 minutes.

This is a very rich cornbread. So simple to stir together — and yet they'll ask for your recipe every time.

Mrs. Russell Lynne

PEPPER CORNBREAD

Another "cornbread-with-corn" recipe, with other additions, and a definite South of the Border flavor. It is almost a meal in itself; serve with a meat and a salad or slaw and eat away, amigo!

1 cup plain white cornmeal
¾ teaspoon baking soda
½ teaspoon salt
¼ cup vegetable oil
2 eggs, slightly beaten
1 medium onion, grated

1 cup buttermilk
1 small can cream style corn
1 small can El Chico Chiles
  (green), chopped
1 cup grated sharp cheddar
  cheese

Mix meal, soda and salt in bowl. Add oil, eggs, onion, buttermilk, corn and chile peppers.

Pour half the batter into greased 10 inch heavy skillet. Sprinkle half of cheese over batter. Pour in remaining batter and sprinkle remaining cheese on top. Bake in 425° oven for 25 minutes. Serves 6 to 8.

Mrs. Otis E. Kirby, Jr.

SPOON BREAD

1½ cups milk
½ cup yellow corn meal
2 tablespoons all purpose flour
3 tablespoons butter or
  bacon drippings

2 teaspoons sugar
3 egg yolks, beaten
1 teaspoon salt
3 egg whites, stiffly beaten

Heat milk. Add cornmeal mixed with flour slowly, stirring well; cook over low heat until mixture thickens (about 5 minutes), stirring constantly to prevent lumping. Remove from stove and beat until smooth. Add butter. When cool, add beaten yolks, sugar and salt.

Just before baking, beat egg whites until stiff and fold into cool cornmeal mixture. Pour into buttered 9x3 inch casserole, place casserole in a pan containing hot water. Bake in 350° oven for 45 minutes. Serve immediately. And pass the butter!

For those readers who have never eaten spoon bread, and wonder how you serve it, check the name again. You do just that: spoon it out of the serving dish onto your plate. You may eat it with a fork, though. This version is a West Virginia one.

Mrs. Paul E. Hargrove

VIRGINIA SPOON BREAD

For those who prefer white cornmeal, we suggest this unsweetened spoon bread. The recipe comes from Virginia, and evokes visions of George and Martha W. — you'll certainly share their fondness for this dish!

¾ cup white cornmeal
  (preferably water ground)
2 cups milk

3 tablespoons butter
3 eggs, separated
½ teaspoon salt

Scald milk. Add meal and cook over low to medium heat until thick, stirring constantly. Add butter and salt. Cool slightly. Beat in egg yolks until well blended. Beat egg whites until quite stiff and fold into meal mixture. Pour into buttered 1½ quart casserole. Place in pan of hot water in 300° oven. Bake 45 to 55 minutes, or until set. Serve with butter. Serves 4 to 6.

A nice, different idea for brunch: spoon bread topped with chicken or turkey hash.

Mrs. William E. Shinn, Jr.

SALLY LUNN

½ cup butter or margarine
  (1 stick)
1 cup sugar
2 eggs, well beaten

2½ cups sifted all purpose flour
¼ teaspoon salt
3 teaspoons baking powder
1 cup milk

Cream butter, add sugar and mix well. Add beaten eggs. Sift flour with salt and baking powder. Add to butter-sugar-egg mixture alternately with milk and beat until smooth. Grease and flour biscuit pan (7 x11), or an 8 x 8 inch pan will do. Bake about 30 minutes in 350° oven, starting on lower shelf and moving to upper shelf the last 5 or 10 minutes.

This is a very light, airy and sweet bread with a marvelous crusty brown outside. Cut in squares and serve hot with butter. Eating Sally Lunn is almost as sinful as eating cake for breakfast — but better!

Mrs. Randolph P. Pickell

ORANGE MUFFINS

2 cups sifted all purpose flour
¼ cup sugar
3 teaspoons baking powder
1 teaspoon salt
¼ cup shortening

½ cup chopped pecans
1 egg, slightly beaten
½ cup orange juice
½ cup orange marmalade

Sift flour, sugar, baking powder and salt into large bowl. Cut in shortening with pastry blender. Add pecans. Combine beaten egg, orange juice and marmalade. Pour this over dry ingredients and mix lightly until just blended. Spoon into paper lined or well greased muffin tins. Sprinkle streusel topping on muffins and bake at 375° for 20 to 25 minutes. Makes 18 muffins.

Streusel Topping:
3 tablespoons flour
¼ cup sugar

½ teaspoon cinnamon
½ teaspoon nutmeg
2 tablespoons butter, softened

Blend ingredients together to make crumbly mixture. Sprinkle over muffins.

Serve these unusually good muffins piping hot!

Mrs. Joe D. Burns

PARTY COFFEE CAKE

Batter:
1 cup butter (2 sticks)
1 cup sugar
3 eggs
1 cup sour cream
2½ cups sifted all purpose flour
2 teaspoons baking powder
1 teaspoon soda
1 teaspoon lemon juice
1 teaspoon vanilla
Topping:
2/3 cup sugar
1 cup broken pecans
1¼ teaspoons cinnamon

Cream butter (margarine will do, but butter is better) and sugar. Add eggs one at a time, beating after each addition. Add sour cream and blend. Sift flour, baking powder and soda and add to the mixture. Mix well. Beat in lemon juice and vanilla.

Spread half of batter into two greased 8 inch cake pans. Sprinkle with half of the topping. Spread remaining batter over this and finally sprinkle other half of topping over second layer of batter. Bake in 350° oven for 35 minutes or until cakes test done. Serve from pan in which cake was baked (do not invert).

This one is hard to resist while it's still warm, so how fortunate the recipe makes two cakes. Call a friend or two over for coffee while the cakes are in the oven; eat one right away, and freeze the other for later.

Mrs. J. P. Smartt, Jr.

BUTTERHORNS

1 package yeast
¼ cup warm water
1 teaspoon sugar
2½ cups sifted flour
1 cup shortening
1 whole egg, plus 2 yolks
1 teaspoon vanilla
½ teaspoon salt
Meringue:
2 egg whites
½ cup sugar
¾ cup finely chopped pecans
Glaze:
2 cups confectioners' sugar
¼ cup water

Dissolve yeast in water. Sprinkle sugar on top and let stand. Cut shortening into flour as for piecrust. Beat yolks and whole egg together and blend into pastry. Add vanilla and salt to yeast mixture and stir this into pastry until well blended. Cover and chill pastry just long enough to make meringue and prepare rolling pin. Make meringue by gradually beating sugar into egg whites. Sprinkle board and dust pin with confectioners sugar. Divide pastry into 3 portions. Work with one portion at a time. Keep "waiting" pastry refrigerated.

Roll each portion of pastry into a 9 inch circle. Spread 1/3 of the meringue to within ½ inch of circle edge. Sprinkle with 1/3 of the chopped pecans Cut into 16 pie shaped wedges. Carefully roll up wedges beginning at wide edge. Place pointed edge down, one inch apart, on foil covered baking sheet. Bake each portion as soon as completed in 350°

oven for 18 minutes. Watch carefully, butterhorns should not brown. Spoon glaze over butterhorns as soon as they come from the oven. Remove to rack in 3 minutes.

The secrets of success with this recipe are to concentrate thoroughly, follow directions exactly and work quickly. Dough must not be allowed to rise before going to oven.

Mrs. Billy W. Payne

SKILLET COFFEE CAKE

¾ cup butter or margarine
1½ cups sugar
2 eggs
1¼ cups sifted all purpose flour

Pinch of salt
1 teaspoon almond flavoring
Slivered almonds
Sugar

Melt butter and add to sugar in mixing bowl. Beat in eggs, one at a time. Add flour, salt and flavoring and mix well.

Pour batter into large iron skillet (9 to 11 inch) which has been lined with aluminum foil. (Leave excess foil on either side for later use.) Cover top with slivered almonds and sprinkle with granulated sugar. Bake 30 to 40 minutes in 350° oven.

Remove cake from the pan with the foil and when cool, wrap tightly in the foil to store. Do not try to peel the foil off while cake is still warm, for it will stick.

This is a very rich, heavy, unleavened coffee cake which is soooo good. If you like coffee cake for Sunday morning breakfast, though, forget this one or you'll kill yourself. It would be perfect, cut in tiny wedges or strips, for a coffee or tea. Pecans may be used instead of almonds.

Mrs. Randolph P. Pickell

ORANGE BUTTER

1 carton whipped butter
Frozen orange juice to taste (undiluted)
Powdered sugar

Blend all ingredients well.

When you want to add that special touch to pancakes or other hot breads, try this.

Mrs. William H. Nabors

221

ORANGE ROLLS

½ recipe of Mrs. Nix's refrigerator roll dough (in this section)
6 to 8 tablespoons butter, softened
¼ cup granulated sugar
1½ teaspoons grated orange rind
2 cups confectioners sugar
3 to 4 tablespoons orange juice

Make up recipe of roll dough. Use only half for the orange rolls. Divide this amount of dough into half again. Roll each portion, on lightly floured board, into a 12 x 8 inch rectangle.

Stir together the softened butter, granulated sugar and orange rind. Spread half of this mixture over each rectangle. Roll up each rectangle of dough like a jelly roll, beginning with the long side. Slice each into 18 equal slices.

Place rolls in cupcake papers in muffin pans (this helps hold the glaze) or use 3 greased 8 or 9 inch square baking pans.

Let rolls rise about 1½ hours. Bake at 375° for 15 minutes or until lightly browned.

Combine confectioners sugar and orange juice. Drizzle over warm rolls to glaze. Makes 36 rolls.

Wouldn't these be grand, made in disposable aluminum pans, for Christmas presents?

Mrs. Lloyd Nix

WAFFLES

2 egg yolks
2 teaspoons sugar
2½ cups sifted all purpose flour
2 teaspoons baking powder
1 teaspoon salt
½ cup melted margarine
2 egg whites
2 cups milk

In large bowl, beat egg yolks with mixer until light. Add sugar and milk and blend well. Sift together the flour, baking powder and salt; add gradually to egg mixture. Pour in margarine and stir to blend.

In separate bowl, beat egg whites until stiff. Fold into batter with rubber spatula. Cook in hot waffle iron until steaming stops.

This batter keeps well in refrigerator for several days. Makes about 6 to 8 waffles.

Have you been popping frozen waffles into your toaster lately, or using a pancake mix for your batter? Exert a little extra effort today, and make these from scratch. You may have even forgotten what real waffles taste like.

Mrs. A. Julian Harris

SUNDAY MORNING FLAPJACKS

For small, light, tender pancakes with, oh, such a good taste:

4 egg yolks
2 cups sifted all purpose flour
2 teaspoons baking powder
½ teaspoon salt
2 tablespoons sugar

6 tablespoons melted butter or margarine
2 cups milk
4 egg whites

Place all ingredients except egg whites in large mixing bowl, and beat with mixer until well blended.

In separate bowl, beat egg whites until stiff but not dry. Fold beaten egg whites into batter.

Cook on hot griddle. Make small cakes by using 1 tablespoon batter for each cake. Turn when top surface is dry. Serves 4 to 5 persons. And they're just as good on Monday through Saturday.

Use these cakes as a dessert by topping with shaved maple sugar and whipped cream, or with a fruit sauce — strawberry or cherry perhaps. For a really dressy occasion, these can be flamed.

Mrs. George Hansberry

APRICOT BREAD

½ cup dried apricots
2 cups sifted all purpose flour
1 teaspoon baking soda
2 teaspoons baking powder
¼ teaspoon salt
1 cup sugar
½ cup chopped dates

½ cup chopped nuts
   (pecan or walnuts)
Juice and grated rind of 1 large
   orange
Boiling water
1 egg, beaten
2 tablespoons melted margarine
1 teaspoon vanilla

Snip apricots into small pieces with scissors, and cover with cold water. Soak 30 minutes to soften; drain.

Sift flour, soda, baking powder, salt and sugar together into large bowl. Add nuts, dates and grated orange rind.

Add enough boiling water to juice of orange to make 1 cup liquid. Add this, together with apricots, beaten egg, margarine and vanilla to dry ingredients. Blend well.

Bake in greased and floured loaf pan (9x5x3) or tube plan in 350° oven for 50 minutes.

Rich, very moist, and full of fruit, this bread may be served hot with butter, cold with cream cheese, or may be frozen.

If you are fond of apricots, and prefer a less sweet loaf, you might omit the dates and use a whole cup of apricots.

Mrs. John R. Taylor

OVEN PANCAKE FOR TWO

¼ cup butter (½ stick)
½ cup sifted all purpose flour
½ cup milk
2 eggs

Dash nutmeg
Confectioners' sugar
Juice of half a lemon

Melt butter in heavy 8 inch iron skillet in 400° oven, being careful not to burn it.

In mixing bowl, stir slightly the flour and milk. In measuring cup beat the eggs with fork. Add to flour mixture and add nutmeg. Stir until blended but not smooth; batter should be a little lumpy.

Pour batter into skillet with melted butter. Bake in 400° to 425° oven for 15 to 20 minutes until puffy and lightly browned.

Sprinkle with confectioners sugar and lemon juice. Serve hot with marmalade, jelly or syrup.

An interesting cross between a pancake, an omelet and a chess pie. Try it for a late breakfast or even a midnight supper for just the two of you.

Mrs. Robert H. Hosey

BLUEBERRY BREAD

2 tablespoons butter
¼ cup boiling water
½ cup orange juice
3 teaspoons grated orange rind
1 egg
1 cup sugar

2 cups sifted all purpose flour
1 teaspoon baking powder
½ teaspoon soda
½ teaspoon salt
1 cup fresh blueberries

In saucepan, melt butter in boiling water. Add orange juice and rind.

In bowl, beat egg well. Add sugar and beat until fluffy. Sift flour, baking powder, soda and salt together and add to egg and sugar alternately with juice, rind and butter combination. Fold in blueberries.

Bake in paper lined 9x5x3 loaf pan at 325° for 1 hour and 15 minutes.

Remove from pan onto aluminum foil. While still hot, spoon glaze over top of loaf and immediately wrap in the foil until cold.

Glaze:

2 tablespoons honey
2 tablespoons orange juice

1 tablespoon orange rind

Fresh blueberries are best, but if they are out of season, frozen ones, thawed and drained, will do. If you're in a real pinch, used canned ones, but be sure to drain them and rinse them thoroughly to avoid having pale blue bread.

Mrs. Ralph Huff

BANANA NUT BREAD

This standard is a much nicer way to get rid of those overripe bananas than the disposal!

½ cup butter or margarine
  (1 stick)
1 cup sugar
2 eggs
3 large very ripe bananas, mashed

2 cups sifted all purpose flour
1 teaspoon baking soda
½ teaspoon salt
½ cup chopped nuts

Cream butter and sugar thoroughly. Add eggs one at a time, beating after each addition. Add mashed bananas and beat well. Sift flour, soda and salt together and add to butter-sugar-banana mixture, mixing well. Stir in nuts. Pour into greased and floured 9x5x3 loaf pan. Bake at 350° for 55 to 60 minutes. Allow to cool thoroughly before slicing.

For a short cut mixing method, melt butter and add with the mashed bananas to the well beaten eggs. Sift dry ingredients in and mix well. Stir in nuts. This makes a less fluffy, more compact moist loaf.

Mrs. Paul E. Hargrove

LEMON BREAD

6 tablespoons softened margarine
1 cup sugar
2 eggs
1½ cups sifted all purpose flour
½ teaspoon salt

2 teaspoons baking powder
½ cup milk
¾ teaspoon lemon extract
Grated rind of 1 lemon
½ cup chopped nuts

Cream margarine and sugar. Beat in eggs well. Sift together flour, salt and baking powder and add to sugar and eggs alternately with milk. Beat in lemon extract and grated rind. Stir in nuts. Pour into greased and floured 9x5x3 loaf pan. Let rise for 20 minutes.

Bake in 350° oven for 45 to 60 minutes or until loaf tests done. Cover with foil for first 20 minutes of baking; remove foil and continue baking until done.

While loaf is still warm, brush with glaze. Yields 1 loaf.

Glaze:
Juice of one lemon
½ cup confectioners' sugar

Very sweet and moist — almost like cake. Delicious with cream cheese.

Mrs. Lynn Fowler

PUMPKIN BREAD

This one is a surprise. Dark, moist and spicy, you'd never guess there is any pumpkin in this bread. Quick and easy to make, too!

3 eggs
1 pound can solid pack pumpkin
   (about 1 1/3 cups)
¾ cup vegetable oil
½ cup water
2½ cups sifted all purpose flour
2¼ cups sugar

1½ teaspoons soda
1¼ teaspoons salt
¾ teaspoon nutmeg
¾ teaspoon cinnamon
½ cup chopped pecans or walnuts
½ cup golden raisins

In large mixing bowl, beat together eggs, pumpkin, oil and water. Sift together flour, sugar, soda, salt and spices and fold into pumpkin mixture, mixing well. Stir in raisins and nuts.

Bake in two greased 9x5x3 loaf pans at 325° for an hour. Reduce oven to 275° and bake for another half an hour or until bread tests done.

The golden raisins give this bread such an interesting flavor, so don't be tempted to substitute dark ones just because you have them on hand.

Mrs. Jolly McKenzie

DATE NUT PUMPKIN BREAD

This second recipe for pumpkin bread is included because its flavor is completely different from that of the preceeding recipe. This bread is lighter in color, not as sweet, the pumpkin flavor is more distinct and this one has dates and dark raisins.

1 cup butter or margarine
   (2 sticks)
1½ cups sugar
4 eggs
2 cups canned pumpkin
3 cups sifted all purpose flour
1 teaspoon salt

2 teaspoons baking powder
½ teaspoon soda
1 tablespoon cinnamon
1 8-ounce package diced dates
½ cup seedless raisins
1 cup chopped pecans

Cream butter and sugar. Add eggs, one at a time, beating after each addition. Add pumpkin and mix well. Sift flour, salt, baking powder, soda and cinnamon together; add to pumpkin mixture and beat well. Stir in dates, raisins and pecans.

Bake in two greased 9x5x3 loaf pans or one tube pan at 375° for 60 to 75 minutes or until bread tests done (a knife blade inserted in center of loaf should come out clean).

Mrs. A. Julian Harris

ORANGE NUT LOAF

½ cup shortening, softened
1¼ cups sugar
2 eggs
2 cups sifted all purpose flour
1½ teaspoons baking powder

1 teaspoon salt
½ cup orange juice
1 tablespoon grated orange rind
½ cup chopped pecans

Cream shortening and sugar. Beat in eggs one at a time. Sift flour, baking powder and salt together and add to creamed mixture, blending well. Slowly add orange juice, beating constantly. Stir in orange rind and nuts.

Bake in greased and floured 9x5x3 loaf pan at 350° for 60 to 65 minutes. Cool for 10 minutes. Remove from pan, sprinkle with confectioners' sugar and wrap tightly in foil while still warm. If left out too long, loaf will dry out. Makes 1 loaf.

This is a very old recipe — a real treat for breakfast or dessert. Children, like Pooh Bear, love it, especially when spread with a blend of softened butter and honey.

Mrs. Norman Self

ORANGE BREAD

This is a superlative bread! It takes more time and effort than many of the fruit breads, but the results are worth every minute of your trouble. Firm and moist, it is full of tiny bits of candied orange peel. It freezes well — if you can keep it long enough to get to the freezer.

Peel of 3 oranges
1 teaspoon soda
Water
1 cup sugar
1 cup water
2 eggs
1 cup sugar

3½ cups sifted all purpose flour
2 teaspoons baking powder
Pinch salt
1 cup milk
3 tablespoons melted butter or
   margarine
1 cup chopped pecans, floured

Peel around oranges, cutting skin thin. Cover peel with water and add soda in saucepan. Bring to boil and boil slowly for 15 minutes. Pour off water and rinse with cold water. Drain.

Cut peel into thin slivers. Mix cut peel, cup of water and cup of sugar. Cook slowly to a syrup — about the consistency of maple syrup. Put aside to cool.

Beat eggs well in mixing bowl. Beat in sugar until fluffy. Sift flour, baking powder and salt together and add to eggs and sugar alternately with milk. Add butter and nuts. Add orange syrup and mix well.

Bake in greased and floured 9x5x3 loaf pan in 350° oven for 1 hour and 15 minutes or until center tests done. Cool in pan for 30 minutes. Turn out on rack and cool completely. Yields 1 loaf.

Slice thin and serve with butter or cream cheese.

Mrs. John Power
Miami, Florida

BRAN MUFFINS

2 cups boiling water
2 cups Kellogg's All Bran
1 heaping cup shortening
3 cups sugar
4 eggs
1 quart buttermilk

5 cups all purpose flour
5 teaspoons soda
1 tablespoon salt
4 cups Kellogg's All Bran
Raisins (optional)

Pour boiling water over 2 cups All Bran. Set aside.

Cream shortening and sugar in very large bowl. Add eggs and beat in well. Add buttermilk and scalded Bran. Sift flour, soda and salt together and add, with the 4 cups All Bran, to the liquid mixture. Beat until just blended. Add raisins if desired.

Bake in greased muffin tins for 15 to 20 minutes at 400°.

As you may have guessed from the large amounts of the ingredients, this is a farm recipe and makes an enormous number of muffins — six to seven dozen. Don't panic though! You don't have to cook them all at once. That is the greatest thing about this recipe. Not only does it make delicious muffins, but this batter will keep in the refrigerator in a tightly covered container, for a month or more, to be cooked whenever you want a few muffins.

Mrs. William E. Shinn, Jr.

BLUEBERRY LEMON MUFFINS

1¾ cups sifted all purpose flour
¼ cup sugar
2½ teaspoons baking powder
¾ teaspoon salt
¾ cup milk
1 egg, well beaten

1/3 cup vegetable oil
1 cup fresh blueberries or 1 cup
frozen berries, thawed and
drained
2 tablespoons sugar
1 teaspoon grated lemon rind

Sift together flour, sugar, baking powder and salt into mixing bowl. Make a well in the center of dry ingredients. Combine milk, egg and oil and add, all at once, to dry ingredients. Stir quickly with fork, just until dry ingredients are moistened. Toss together blueberries and 2 tablespoons sugar; gently stir into batter along with lemon rind.

Fill greased 2½ inch muffin pan 2/3 full. Bake in 400° oven for about 25 minutes. While muffins are still warm, dip tops in melted butter and then in a little granulated sugar.

Makes 1 dozen muffins.

Mrs. Frank Troup

Desserts

DAMA'S JELLY ROLL

¾ cup cake flour	3 egg yolks
1 teaspoon baking powder	2 tablespoons cold water
Pinch of salt	½ teaspoon lemon juice
3 egg whites	¾ cup tart jelly
¾ cup sugar	Confectioners' sugar

Sift together flour, baking powder, and salt. Beat egg whites stiff; gradually beat in ½ cup of sugar. Mix egg yolks and water. Beat until foamy. Add ¼ cup sugar and beat until thick. Add lemon juice. Fold egg yolk mixture into egg white mixture. Then gently fold in flour. Line bottom of 10" x 15" x 1" baking sheet with greased wax paper. Spread with batter. Bake in 350° oven for 25 minutes. Turn out on cloth dusted with confectioners' sugar. Quickly remove paper and spread jelly. Roll immediately while hot.

Watch their young eyes light up when they see this coming to the table! You may even spy a gleam in the eye of a member of the older generation. May we suggest that plum or quince jelly would be especially good.

Mrs. Gilbert J. Key
Birmingham, Alabama

SNOW WHITE CHOCOLATE ROLL

6 tablespoons cake flour	4 egg whites, stiffly beaten
6 tablespoons cocoa	4 egg yolks, beaten until thick
½ teaspoon baking powder	1 teaspoon vanilla
¼ teaspoon salt	Confectioners' sugar, sifted
¾ cup sifted sugar	

For filling, mix the following together:

1 cup whipping cream, whipped	½ teaspoon almond flavoring
1 3½ ounce can angel flake coconut	

Sift flour, cocoa, baking powder and salt together three times. Beat sugar gradually into egg whites. Beat in egg yolks and vanilla. Fold in flour gradually. Pour into a 10" x 15" x 1" cookie sheet that has been greased and lined with waxed paper. Bake in 400° oven for 13 minutes. After baking, turn onto a cloth covered with sifted confectioners' sugar. Quickly remove the crisp edges of cake with sharp knife, spread filling, and roll immediately, beginning at narrow side. Wrap in cloth and cool. Place in refrigerator until serving time.

Work quickly to successfully make this chocolate roll which is impressive looking and tasting!

Mrs. William A. Sims

PINEAPPLE DELIGHT

1 8¼ ounce can crushed pineapple	1 stick margarine, sliced in pats
1 9-ounce size yellow cake mix	Vanilla ice cream or whipped
1 cup chopped pecan meats	cream, optional

Preheat oven to 375°. Spread pineapple in 8" pie plate. Cover evenly with dry cake mix. Sprinkle pecans over top of cake mix. Place pats of margarine on top of pecans. Bake for 20 minutes or until top is brown and crusty. Serve warm. Cut pie-shaped wedges and top with vanilla ice cream or whipped topping. Makes 6 to 8 servings.

Two minutes to make — twenty to bake. Good news for harried housewives.

Mrs. Herbert Street

PEACH KUCHEN

2 cups sifted flour	12 peach halves, fresh or canned;
¼ teaspoon baking powder	or 2 packages of frozen slices
½ teaspoon salt	1 teaspoon cinnamon
¾ to 1 cup sugar	2 egg yolks
1 cup butter	1 cup heavy or sour cream

Preheat oven to 400°. Sift flour, baking powder, salt and 2 tablespoons of sugar together in mixing bowl. Cut in butter with 2 knives until mixture looks like coarse corn meal. Put an even layer of this crumbly paste over bottom and half way up the sides of an 8"x8" baking pan. Use your hands and press pastry firmly until it holds.

Peel fresh peaches and cut in half. Drain canned peaches or thaw and drain frozen peaches. Arrange on bottom pastry neatly and sprinkle with a mixture of remaining sugar and cinnamon. Adjust sugar to sweetness of peaches. Bake 15 minutes. Then pour a mixture of slightly beaten egg yolks and cream over the top. Bake 30 minutes longer. Serve warm or cold. Serves 6.

Mrs. John R. Guice

PEACH COBBLER

2 cups sliced, fresh peaches	2 teaspoons baking powder
2 cups sugar	¼ teaspoon salt
½ cup butter or margarine	¾ cup milk
¾ cup flour	

Mix peaches with 1 cup sugar; let stand. Put butter in a 2 quart casserole; place in a 325° oven to melt. Combine remaining sugar, flour, baking powder, salt and milk. Pour over melted butter. Do not stir. Spoon peaches on top of batter. Do not stir. Bake at 325° for 1 hour. Yield: 4 to 6 servings.

A perfect family dessert with many names — cobbler with sweetie crust is the most descriptive — and many faces — depending upon what fruit is in season or what can you grab from the cabinet. Don't stop with peaches, for any sweetened fresh fruit or canned fruit will do nicely. The crust is crisper when cobbler is made in a shallow, rectangular 2 quart casserole.

Mrs. Sage Copeland

OLD FASHIONED RICH SHORTCAKE

½ cup butter
½ cup sugar
1 egg
4 teaspoons baking powder
½ teaspoon salt

2 cups flour
Nutmeg to taste, about ¼ teaspoon
1/3 cup milk
Whipped cream

Cream butter and sugar well and add egg. Blend well, add sifted dry ingredients alternately with milk. Turn into greased cake pan or heavy skillet (batter will be very stiff). Bake at 450° for 12 minutes. Cool and split. Spoon your favorite fruit or berries between layers, and add whipped cream.

A grandmother recipe to use with any fresh berries or fruit.

Mrs. L. Denton Cole

FAT MAN'S MISERY

14 Oreo cookies
½ cup butter
1 cup confectioners' sugar
1 egg
Few drops almond flavoring

1 pint whipping cream
½ tablespoon sugar
1 teaspoon vanilla
1 cup chopped pecans

Crush Oreos. Line 9" pie pan or an 8" square pan with most of crushed cookies (save some for topping). Cream butter and sugar. Add egg. Cream again. Add almond flavoring. Spread this mixture on crumbs. Whip cream with sugar. Add vanilla and chopped pecans. Fold until well blended. Spread this on first mixture. Cover with crushed wafers. Let stand in refrigerator for 24 hours. Makes 6 to 8 servings.

Thin man's delight — though with very much of this number, he won't stay in that category very long.

Mrs. Ralph Huff

FUDGE PIE

1 cup sugar
½ cup butter, melted
2 eggs, beaten
1 teaspoon vanilla

½ cup flour
2 tablespoons cocoa
½ cup nuts, optional

Combine all ingredients. Put in buttered pie plate. Bake at 325° for 30 minutes. Serve with vanilla ice cream.

Mrs. Charles Belt substitutes 2 squares unsweetened chocolate for the cocoa and ¼ cup butter rather than a ½ cup.

This fudge pie is one of those sweets that you can resist just so long — eventually you know you'll break down — so why not go ahead and make it today? We bet you have all the ingredients on hand right now!

Mrs. Malcolm L. Prewitt, Jr.

DATE TARTS

3 eggs, separated
¾ cup sugar
1 pound dates
2 cups nuts

2 tablespoons flour
1 teaspoon baking powder
1 teaspoon vanilla
Whipped cream

Beat egg yolks until light. Add sugar and blend thoroughly. Cut dates and chop nuts. Combine flour and baking powder and sprinkle over dates. Add along with nuts to egg mixture. Fold in well beaten egg whites. Add vanilla. Bake in well greased muffin tins (or paper baking cups). Bake at 350° for 20 minutes. Serve warm or cold with whipped cream. Yields 16 to 18 tarts.

These wonderful little tarts — actually individual date puddings — are our answer to your "whatever can I serve for dessert since everybody will be eating on his lap?" Glad we could help!

Mrs. W. Blanton McBride

CREAM PUFFS

1 cup water
½ cup butter
¼ teaspoon salt
1 teaspoon sugar

Pinch nutmeg
1 cup sifted flour
4 large eggs

Boil water. Add salt, sugar, nutmeg and butter. Stir over heat until butter has melted. Remove from heat and immediately pour in all flour at once. Beat vigorously with a wooden spoon until thoroughly blended. Then beat over moderate heat for 1 or 2 minutes until mixture is smooth and forms a ball that doesn't separate. Cool slightly. Add eggs, one at a time. Beat vigorously after each egg until mixture is smooth. Drop batter on greased cookie sheet. Bake at 450° for 15 minutes, then reduce heat to 325° and bake 25 minutes. Remove from oven; make a small slit in side of each puff. Return to turned-off oven for 10 minutes. Cool on wire rack. Makes 12 puffs about 3 inches in diameter.

Unfilled, the puffs will keep in a tin for several days. They can also be frozen quite successfully, although you may need to run them in a slow (250°) oven a few minutes after they thaw in order to re-crisp.

The filling is up to you: thick custards, sweetened whipped cream, fresh fruit, or to get out of the dessert realm, even creamed chicken or other creamed dishes.

You are sure to win a prize with these flaky, tasty puffs — at least the "favorite Mommy" award.

Mrs. Thomas C. Bingham

ADA'S GINGERBREAD WITH LEMON SAUCE

2 tablespoons molasses
4 to 5 tablespoons melted butter
1 cup sugar
1 teaspoon salt
1 teaspoon cinnamon
½ teaspoon cloves

¼ teaspoon ginger
1 egg
2 cups flour
1 teaspoon baking soda
1 cup buttermilk

Add molasses and butter to sugar. Add salt and spices and stir together. Beat in egg. Sift flour and soda together and add alternately with buttermilk. Grease and flour an 8" square baking pan. Pour in batter and bake at 400° for 35 minutes. Remove from oven. Let pan sit about 5 minutes; then remove gingerbread. Serve warm with lemon sauce. Best when served fresh and warm. Does not keep well.

Lemon Sauce:
½ cup sugar
1 tablespoon cornstarch
Dash salt
Dash nutmeg

1 cup boiling water
2 tablespoons butter or margarine
1½ tablespoons lemon juice, fresh, frozen or canned

Mix first 4 ingredients. Gradually stir in water. Cook over low heat stirring constantly until thick and clear. Blend in butter and lemon juice. Makes 1 1/3 cups.

Can't you smell it baking?

Mrs. A. Julian Harris

BAKED APPLE PUDDING WITH RUM SAUCE

1 cup sifted flour
1 teaspoon soda
1 teaspoon cinnamon
¾ teaspoon nutmeg
¼ teaspoon salt

¼ cup butter
1 cup sugar
1 egg, beaten
2 medium apples, grated, peel included

Sift dry ingredients together. Cream butter and sugar. Add egg and grated apples. Fold in dry ingredients. Bake in greased and floured pan (8" x 8"), 25 to 30 minutes at 400°.

Rum Sauce:
½ cup butter
1 cup sugar
½ cup light cream
   or canned evaporated milk

1 teaspoon vanilla
¼ teaspoon rum flavoring
Dash nutmeg

Mix butter, sugar and cream in top of double boiler. Cook 10 to 12 minutes or until slightly thickened. Add flavorings and nutmeg. Serve warm on apple pudding.

This pudding, sauced with rum, brought nothing but compliments to its cook. Though fresh apples are better, chopped canned ones (not pie filling) will do.

Mrs. Dan M. Crane

LEMON SPONGE

1 cup sugar
4 tablespoons flour
¼ teaspoon salt
5 tablespoons lemon juice
Grated rind of 1 lemon

3 or 4 eggs, separated
1½ cups milk
2 tablespoons melted butter
Coconut, optional

Sift sugar, flour, and salt. Add lemon juice and rind. Beat until creamy and smooth. Beat egg yolks until lemon-colored and add milk. Mix thoroughly. Add yolk-milk mixture and melted butter to the flour mixture. Beat until fluffy and smooth. Beat egg whites until stiff and fold into mixture. Pour into buttered 1½ quart baking dish. May sprinkle top with coconut. Place in pan of water and bake at 350° for 45 to 60 minutes until firm.

Light as a cloud lemon pudding which develops its own cake-like topping in the oven. Don't let that fool you — it's still a pudding and must be served with a spoon. Good to take to sick folks!

Mrs. John R. Guice

BANANA PUDDING

½ cup sugar
2 tablespoons flour
Dash salt
1¾ cups milk
1 egg

1 teaspoon vanilla
2 tablespoons butter
Graham crackers or vanilla wafers
2 bananas

Mix sugar, flour, and salt in top of double boiler. Measure milk and add enough milk to moisten the sugar, flour and salt mixture. With whisk, beat in egg. Turn heat to medium high, adding the rest of milk gradually. Stir constantly with spatula or wooden spoon. Cook until sauce thickens and boils. Take off stove. Add vanilla and butter. Put lid on boiler while butter melts. In a deep casserole dish, put one layer of graham crackers and one layer of sliced bananas. After the butter has melted, stir custard carefully, and spoon the custard (does not need to cool) over the sliced bananas. Make two more layers like the first. Top the pudding with a layer of graham crackers or vanilla wafers. Chill. May add meringue if desired. Makes 6 servings.

Mrs. Jimmy E. Brown

SUGAR PLUM PUDDING

1 cup flour
¾ teaspoon soda
¾ teaspoon cinnamon
1½ teaspoons nutmeg
½ cup butter
¾ cup sugar
½ cup buttermilk

1 egg, beaten
½ cup chopped, cooked prunes
Topping:
¼ cup butter
¼ cup buttermilk
½ cup sugar
1 teaspoon vanilla

Blend flour, soda, cinnamon, nutmeg. With a pastry blender mix butter and sugar into the above mixture. Mix together butter, milk, egg and prunes. Add to first mixture. Stir until well blended. Bake in 9" square pan 25 minutes at 350°.

Topping: Bring to a boil butter, ¼ cup buttermilk, and ½ cup sugar. Remove from heat and add 1 teaspoon vanilla. Serve over fresh-from-the-oven plum pudding.

Neither you nor your children will ever be satisfied with the proverbial dancing visions again after you've eaten the real thing — hot with mounds of whipped cream.

Mrs. Robert C. McAnnally

SWEET POTATO PUDDING

4 medium raw sweet potatoes,
   peeled and grated
3 eggs, beaten
½ cup butter or margarine, melted

2/3 cup sugar
½ teaspoon nutmeg
½ cup milk or cream

Mix all ingredients together. Bake in greased casserole or pan in 375° oven until brown, about 1 to 1¼ hours. Serve hot or cold (we prefer hot and plain). If cold, may top with whipped cream.

If you prefer a crunchy rather than a custard texture, stir pudding several times during baking. The top will brown, and you will stir it down into the pudding where it will stay.

Mrs. George W. Hansberry

ANGEL FOOD CAKE WITH LEMON FILLING

6 egg yolks, well beaten
¾ cup lemon juice
¾ cup sugar
1½ tablespoons grated lemon rind
1 tablespoon plain gelatin
¼ cup cold water

6 egg whites
¾ cup sugar
2 small angel cakes or one large
   (10") cake, crumbled
Whipped cream
Cherries or other fruit

Cook first 4 ingredients in double boiler until thick. Add gelatin which has been dissolved in cold water. Beat egg whites until stiff and gradually add ¾ cup sugar. Fold into custard. Oil angel food cake pan, and crumble bits of cake into pan. Pour in some filling. Alternate until pan is filled. Chill overnight in refrigerator. Unmold when ready to serve. Cover with whipped cream. Garnish with cherries or fruit. Serves 10 to 12.

An excellent airy lemon dessert. Not at all difficult to prepare and perfect for three tables of bridge. Be sure to make it the night before, and leave the finishing touches for the last minute.

Mrs. Lloyd Nix

APRICOT NECTAR DESSERT

1 round, large angel food cake (10" diameter)
1 quart apricot nectar (2 12-ounce cans may be sufficient)
1½ cups sugar
7 tablespoons cornstarch
1 tablespoon plain gelatin
1 pint whipping cream

Break cake into **very** small pieces and place in large, flat pan (9x13). Combine in a sauce pan the nectar, sugar, cornstarch and gelatin (may add a pinch of salt). Cook until it thickens, stirring continually. While hot, pour over cake and let stand all night in refrigerator (or a few hours). The sauce makes a marbled effect as it seeps through the pieces of cake. Whip the cream and spread over cake. Cut into squares. Serves 12 to 15.

How can you go wrong with anything calling for apricot nectar? You cannot make a mistake with this dessert which has at least four other things going for it: it's easy, it must be done ahead, it serves a large number, and it's really delicious.

Mrs. Whit King, Jr.

MOTHER'S BOILED CUSTARD

1 quart milk
3 eggs, well beaten
1 scant cup sugar
½ teaspoon salt
1 tablespoon vanilla

Heat milk in heavy saucepan or in double boiler. In mixing bowl beat together the eggs, sugar, and salt. Add to milk. Using a wooden spoon, stir constantly over medium heat until custard thickens and coats the spoon. Pour custard into a mixing bowl and beat with a rotary beater or low-speed electric mixer until slightly cool. Add vanilla. Refrigerate.

If you're lucky enough to have a cooking blender, boiled custard is a cinch. If you don't, a little patience will do.

Mrs. A. Julian Harris

BAKED CUSTARD

8 eggs
1 1/3 cups sugar

1 quart milk
1 teaspoon vanilla

Beat eggs well. Add sugar, milk, and vanilla. Strain (to avoid egg parts) into a greased tube pan or a 2 quart souffle dish and set in a pan of hot water. Place in 325° oven and bake for 1 hour or longer until set (silver knife inserted in middle will come out clean). When cold, invert and serve.

Baked custard is an old favorite and a must in the dessert file of any cook who is catering to an ulcer — her own or someone else's.

To turn a plain Jane dish into a Cinderella dessert, try this variation:

Caramelize 1 cup sugar in a heavy skillet, stirring slowly and constantly until thoroughly melted and golden brown. Pour the caramel into the dish or pan, turning pan to permit caramel to spread evenly over bottom. You may have to work with a spoon to get the whole surface covered.

Pour the custard mixture into the prepared dish and bake as directed. When cold, invert onto platter. If desired sprinkle with toasted, slivered almonds and serve with whipped cream.

Mrs. Robert H. Hosey

QUICK BOILED CUSTARD

1 quart plus ½ cup milk
½ cup butter
1 cup sugar

4 eggs
3 teaspoons vanilla

Heat 1 quart milk, butter and sugar in covered, 2 quart double boiler until bubbles form on top. Beat 4 eggs and ½ cup milk until foamy. Add slowly to heated mixture. Stir for 1 minute over boiling water. Pour through strainer into crockery pitcher. Cover with foil. Let stand. When partially cool, add vanilla. Makes 1½ quarts.

Mrs. Robert T. McWhorter, Jr.

POTS de CREME

1 egg
1 6-ounce package semisweet
   chocolate morsels
1 teaspoon vanilla
1 teaspoon instant coffee

Dash salt
1 pat butter
2/3 cup milk
Whipped cream
Semi-sweet chocolate

Put all but last three ingredients in blender. Heat milk just to boiling and add to mixture in blender. Blend for 1 minute. Pour into small dessert dishes. Chill several hours. Serve with whipped cream on top, and grate semi-sweet chocolate on top of cream. Serves 4.

If this mocha custard doesn't prompt you to buy some pretty, individual pots de creme, nothing will. A pretty and delicious do-ahead dessert.

Mrs. T. S. Simms

PARTY CUSTARD

1 package chocolate wafers, crushed
¼ cup butter or margarine, melted
4 eggs, separated
¼ cup sugar
1¼ cups milk
3 tablespoons flour

1 envelope plain gelatin
¼ cup water
Vanilla to taste
¼ cup sugar
1 cup heavy cream, whipped

Mix crushed wafers with melted butter. Beat egg yolks and add ¼ cup sugar and milk. Stir in flour. Put in the top of a double boiler and add gelatin which has been dissolved in ¼ cup water. Cook, stirring until thickened or until mixture coats a spoon. Cool over water, stirring occasionally. Add vanilla to taste. Beat egg whites until stiff. Add ¼ cup sugar. Fold into custard mixture. Line custard cups with chocolate-butter-crumb mixture. Fill with custard. Refrigerate several hours or overnight. To serve, top with whipped cream and sprinkle on additional dry crumbs. Fills 8 to 10 5-oz. containers.

Mrs. Otis E. Kirby, Jr.

CHERRY CRUNCH

1 can red, sour pitted cherries
   (water packed)
Juice of two large lemons
1 can Eagle Brand condensed milk
1 cup whipping cream

1 cup chopped nuts
1½ cups finely crushed vanilla
   wafers

Drain cherries well and place in refrigerator at least 4 hours or overnight. Mix lemon juice and condensed milk. Whip cream and fold into mixture. Add well drained cherries and nuts. Spread wafer crumbs out in 9"x13" pan, reserving ¼ cup crumbs for topping. Pour in filling and top with crumbs. Chill 4 to 6 hours before serving.

A pretty cherry dessert with pecans that is a natural for a Valentine dinner or for celebrating Washington's birthday if you are of a patriotic disposition.

Mrs. Norman L. Self

CHERRY DELIGHT

2 cups flour
1 cup butter
1 cup chopped pecans
3 cups confectioners' sugar

1 8-ounce package cream cheese
2 packages Dream Whip, prepared
  according to directions
1 can cherry pie filling

Mix flour, butter and pecans together. Mixture will be crumbly. Spread over bottom of 13" x 9" pan and bake at 350° for 15 to 20 minutes or until golden brown. Cool. Cream the confectioners' sugar and cream cheese. Add beaten Dream Whip and spread over cooled pastry. Refrigerate for 1 hour. Spread cherry pie filling over cheese mixture. Refrigerate again.

This speaks for itself.

Mrs. John A. Woller

CHERRY DESSERT

2 cups Ritz crackers, crumbled
  in blender
1 cup nuts
2 cups sugar

6 egg whites
¾ teaspoon cream of tartar
1 can pie cherries
Whipped cream

Preheat oven to 350°. Put crackers and nuts in blender. When thoroughly crumbled, remove and add sugar. Beat egg whites and cream of tartar until stiff. Fold all ingredients together. Bake for about 25 minutes in a pie pan or brownie pan. Check to see if middle is done before removing. When cool, add cherries or an equal amount of any fruit (fresh, frozen or canned) and whipped cream. Makes 10 to 12 servings.

The taste will surprise you — and pleasantly!

Mrs. Garner Pride

STRAWBERRY ICE BOX CAKE

1 pound vanilla wafers
1 cup butter
1½ cups confectioners' sugar
2 eggs

1 quart strawberries, sliced (fresh,
  if possible)
1 cup heavy cream, whipped

Crush wafers fine, putting more than half on bottom of 8"x12" pan. Cream butter and sugar. Add eggs one at a time, beating well after each addition. Spread this mixture over the crumbs and cover with berries. Spread whipped cream over the berries and top with reserved crumbs. Cover and refrigerate overnight. To serve, cut in squares and top with a teaspoon of whipped cream and a berry. Raspberries may be substituted for strawberries.

Mrs. William A. Walker

CHOCOLATE ICE BOX DESSERT

¾ cup margarine
2 cups confectioners' sugar
2½ squares dark chocolate melted

Vanilla wafers
2/3 cup chopped pecans
3 eggs (if eggs are small, use 4)
Whipped cream

Cream margarine and sugar. Add melted chocolate. Add eggs, one at a time, beating thoroughly after each addition. Add chopped nuts to creamed mixture. Put a layer of crushed or whole vanilla wafers in a greased 8" square pan. Pour in creamed mixture. Top with large pieces of pecans or crushed wafers. Chill overnight or longer. Serve plain or with whipped cream. Serves 8, 10 or 12, depending on size of portion you wish.

So-o-o rich! Make portions small.

Mrs. E. J. Phillips

NUTTY PINEAPPLE ICE BOX DESSERT

½ cup butter
1 cup sugar
2 eggs, separated
1 tablespoon cream
1/3 cup pineapple juice

1 cup drained pineapple
25 graham crackers, crushed
½ cup pecans, chopped, added to
   cracker crumbs
Whipped cream

Cream butter and sugar. Beat egg yolks with cream; stir over hot water until thick and smooth. Add to butter-sugar mixture. Cool. Add pineapple and juice; fold in beaten egg whites. Line shallow tin with waxed paper. Layer: cracker crumbs, ½ mixture, cracker crumbs, remaining mixture. Place in refrigerator 5 or 6 hours. Serve with whipped cream.

Mrs. T. S. Simms

CHOCOLATE ICE BOX CAKE

1 package Baker's German Sweet
   Chocolate
1½ tablespoons water
1 egg yolk, unbeaten
1 tablespoon confectioners' sugar

½ cup cream, whipped
1 egg white, stiffly beaten
9 double ladyfingers or 18 strips
   sponge cake or angel food cake
¼ cup chopped pecans, optional

Melt chocolate in top of a double boiler. Add water and blend. Remove from boiling water, add egg yolk, and beat vigorously with rotary beater until smooth. Add sugar and mix well. If desired, add ¼ cup chopped pecans. Fold in whipped cream; then fold in stiffly beaten egg white. Line bottom and sides of an 8" x 4" loaf pan with wax paper. Separate lady fingers and arrange on bottom and sides of pan. Pour in chocolate mixture. Arrange remaining ladyfingers on top. Chill 12 to 24 hours in refrigerator, then unmold. Slice and serve with additional whipped cream, if desired. Makes 4 or 5 delicious servings.

A dessert standard — one of those that there's hardly anything better than and probably never will be.

Mrs. John D. Davis

241

GRAHAM CRACKER DESSERT

1 cup sugar
1 cup brown sugar
3 tablespoons flour
3 tablespoons water

1 cup broken pecans
3 eggs
1 8¼-ounce can crushed pineapple
Graham crackers

Mix all ingredients except granam crackers together and cook in a double boiler, stirring constantly until thick. When cool, spread ½ mixture on graham crackers placed on a cookie sheet or platter. Add another layer of graham crackers and spread on remaining filling.

A speedy dessert which is grand to keep in the refrigerator for those always hungry little people.

Mrs. William G. Stone, Jr.

FROZEN LEMON DESSERT

1 13-ounce can Pet milk, chilled
1/3 cup lemon juice

1 cup sugar
1 cup graham cracker crumbs

Whip milk in deep bowl. Add lemon juice and sugar. Pour into a 9"x13" pan. Sprinkle graham cracker crumbs on top. Freeze. Yields 12 servings.

A really quick-to-mix dessert to make with ingredients you'll usually have on hand.

Mrs. William S. Coles

FROSTY STRAWBERRY SQUARES

1 cup sifted flour
¼ cup brown sugar
½ cup chopped pecans
½ cup melted butter
2 egg whites

1 cup sugar
1 10-ounce package frozen strawberries, partially thawed
2 teaspoons lemon juice
1 cup heavy cream, whipped

Stir flour, brown sugar, pecans and butter together. Spread evenly in shallow baking pan. Bake 20 minutes at 350° stirring often. Sprinkle 2/3 of this crumbled mixture in 13"x9" baking pan. Combine egg whites, sugar, berries and lemon juice in a large bowl (if possible, chill bowl and beaters). Beat at high speed until stiff peaks form, about 10 to 12 minutes. Fold in whipped cream. Pour into pan. Top with remaining crumbled mixture. Freeze at least 6 hours before serving. Cut in squares and top with fresh or frozen berries. Serves 10 to 12.

A luscious luncheon or dessert bridge treat. Clean the house, set up the tables and run get those tallies you forgot while it's freezing.

Mrs. Lindsay A. Allen

ALMOND MOUSSE

2 eggs, separated
1/3 cup sugar
1 tablespoon water
1 teaspoon vanilla

1 teaspoon almond flavoring
1 cup heavy cream, whipped
1 dozen stale almond macaroons

Beat egg yolks. Add sugar and water. Cook to thin custard in a double boiler. Cool. Add vanilla and almond flavoring. Whip egg whites until stiff. Fold in whipped cream and stiffly beaten whites. Crumble almond macaroons to cover the bottom of the pan and the top of the mixture. Use a 6" x 9" casserole or an old-fashioned, deep metal freezer tray and freeze mixture until solid. Cut and serve. Makes 8 to 10 servings.

A creamy, delicately flavored, frozen dessert that falls into the "best I've ever eaten" category. Make yesterday for today's luncheon.

Mrs. John D. Wyker, II

WINE JELLY AND CHARLOTTE RUSSE

Wine Jelly:
2¼ tablespoons gelatin
½ cup cold water
1 2/3 cups boiling water
1 cup sugar

1 cup sherry or Madeira
1/3 cup orange juice
3 tablespoons lemon juice
Red food coloring

Soak gelatin in cold water. Dissolve in boiling water. Add sugar and stir until dissolved. Add wine, orange juice and lemon juice; color with a few drops of red food coloring. Strain, pour into mold (preferably a deep, narrow one — 8 to 9 cup capacity) and chill. Allow jelly to almost set, then put Charlotte Russe over it and let all congeal.

Charlotte Russe:
2 eggs
½ cup sugar
1 cup scalded milk

1 envelope gelatin
¼ cup cold water
1 teaspoon vanilla
1 pint cream, whipped

Beat eggs in saucepan. Add sugar and mix well. Gradually add the scalded milk and cook over low heat until custard is thick enough to coat a silver spoon. Soften gelatin in ¼ cup cold water. Dissolve in hot custard and set aside to cool. Add vanilla and chill, but watch carefully. When custard mixture is ready to set, fold in the whipped cream. Turn into mold on top of the almost-congealed wine jelly. Chill all until well set. Unmold to serve. Serves 12 or more.

For a spectacular and unusually delicious finale to Christmas dinner, make this two-part dessert in your prettiest mold to turn out on a silver tray and surround with sprigs of holly. Be forewarned that this takes time to prepare — but it needs to be done the day ahead anyway.

Mrs. William E. Shinn, Jr.

ORANGE CHARLOTTE

1 1/3 tablespoons gelatin
1/3 cup cold water
1/3 cup boiling water
1 cup sugar
3 tablespoons lemon juice

1 cup orange juice and pulp
3 egg whites, stiffly beaten
1 cup whipping cream, whipped
Orange sections

Soak gelatin in cold water, dissolve in boiling water. Add sugar, lemon juice, orange juice and pulp. Chill in pan of ice water. When quite thick, beat with wire whisk until frothy. Then fold in stiffly beaten egg whites and whipped cream. Line a 6½ cup mold with orange sections (canned mandarin ones work nicely in a pinch), turn in charlotte mixture and chill until set. Unmold to serve.

A charming charlotte from grandmother's era that has lost none of its appeal over the passing years. We suggest you save this one for ladies, though. Most men don't like it.

Mrs. William E. Shinn, Jr.

SCHAUM TORTE

2 cups egg whites (14 to 16 eggs)
2 tablespoons apple cider vinegar
1 teaspoon salt

2 tablespoons vanilla
3 cups sugar

Pour first 4 ingredients into mixing bowl. Beat until stiff while gradually adding the sugar. Pour into ungreased 10" torte pan and put in 400 degree preheated oven for 5 minutes. Turn off oven but do not open door! Leave overnight without peeking. Delicious topped with fresh strawberries or other fresh fruit or with whipped cream or ice cream.

When you make hollandaise, mayonnaise, or anything else that uses only the yolk, pour your whites into a jar and keep in the freezer (keep a running count on freezer tape attached to the jar). When you have 14 to 16 whites, make schaum torte, slice and serve with fresh fruit . . . and live happily ever after.

Mrs. Billy W. Payne

TOFFEE MERINGUE

6 egg whites
Pinch salt
1 teaspoon or less of vinegar
1½ cups sugar

1 pint whipping cream
6 Heath bars, finely chopped or
ground

Line 2 9" cake pans with heavy paper, lightly greased with butter. Beat egg whites, salt, and vinegar. Gradually add sugar and continue to beat until stiff. Pour in pans and bake at 250° for 1 hour or longer until set. Remove paper immediately and cool. Whip the cream and add the finely chopped Heath bars. Mix together. Put some mixture between the two meringues and use the rest for icing top and sides. Sprinkle top with some of chopped Heath bars. Chill several hours or overnight.

Make the meringues several days ahead and store in tins. In the morning, whip up this modern filling miracle. Tomorrow night serve dinner and dessert. And compliments to the fresh-as-a-daisy chef.

Mrs. J. P. Smartt, Jr.

GATEAU GANACHE

6 egg whites, at room temperature
1½ cups sugar
6 ounces ground pecans (grind in Mouli grater)
1½ teaspoons white wine vinegar
½ teaspoon vanilla
3 ounces semi-sweet chocolate (chocolate chips do well)
1 cup whipping cream

Place egg whites in large mixing bowl and let stand an hour or so at room temperature. Prepare two 8" cake pans: cut 2 rounds wax paper to fit bottom of pan; grease and lightly flour pans; cover bottom with paper; and grease and lightly flour paper.

Beat egg whites until stiff. Add sugar and nuts all at once, and fold in gently with metal spoon. Add vinegar and vanilla and spoon lightly into prepared pans. Put in 375° oven and bake 35 to 40 minutes or until crusty to the touch. Run a knife around edges, cover with wire racks, and quickly invert, turning out meringues. Peel off paper at once. (This can be done 2 or 3 days ahead of time, if meringues are kept in tightly closed tins.)

On serving day: melt chocolate in double boiler. While chocolate is cooling, whip cream until very stiff. Place half the cream in separate bowl and stir in half the melted chocolate. Place one meringue on serving plate and cover with this mixture. Top with second meringue. Cover this one with rest of whipped cream. With spatula, dip into remaining chocolate and make swirls on top for a marbled effect.

Grate a little bitter or semi-sweet chocolate over the top. Refrigerate until ready to serve. This does not keep well overnight.

A truly divine dessert and really not complicated to make, even though it looks it. So pretty that it should be taken to the table to be admired before serving — if you can keep from pinching.

Mrs. William E. Shinn, Jr.

FRUIT PIZZA

1 package refrigerated sugar
  cookie dough
½ teaspoon vanilla
1 8-ounce package cream cheese
1/3 cup sugar
1 tablespoon water

½ cup plus peach preserves
Fruit: orange sections, green grape
  halves, strawberry halves, ba-
  nanna slices, fresh blueberries,
  peaches

Cut dough into ⅛-inch slices. Line 14-inch pizza pan or cookie sheet with slices overlapping slightly. Bake at 375° for 12 minutes. Cool. Blend softened cream cheese, sugar and vanilla. Spread over cookie crust. Arrange fruit over cream cheese layer, beginning with bananas. Glaze with preserves mixed with water. Bake 375° for 12 minutes. Chill before serving. Serves 10 to 12.

An unusually pretty dessert to serve when grapes, strawberries, and blueberries are plentiful.

Mrs. Frederick Sittason, Jr.

RASPBERRY FONDUE FOR FRUIT

2 tablespoons sugar
2 10-ounce packages frozen raspberries, thawed and drained
1 8-ounce package cream cheese,
  softened

1 cup strawberries
Honeydew melon balls
1 cup pineapple strips, fresh or
  canned
1 cup fresh pear wedges, dipped
  in lemon juice

One hour before serving, blend raspberries with sugar. In medium bowl of mixer, at medium speed, beat cream cheese until smooth. Gradually add raspberry pulp to mixture. Refrigerate. Arrange remaining fruit on tray around deep bowl containing fondue.

A really fun dessert for guests that keep them busy instead of you.

Mrs. Charles B. Howell

GREEN GRAPES IN BROWN SUGAR

1 pound fresh seedless grapes
¼ cup dark brown sugar

1 cup sour cream

Mix sour cream and brown sugar together well. Stir in grapes and thoroughly chill. Serve in sherbet glasses.

A really simple yet delicious concoction that can be used as salad or dessert as your whim directs.

Mrs. Bruce Flake

GRAN'S AMBROSIA

2 dozen large California navel
  oranges
1 28-ounce can crushed pineapple,
  optional
¾ cup Angel Flake coconut

½ cup maraschino cherries
1 ounce cherry juice (or enough
  to add slight color)
¾ cup sugar, vary according to
  sweetness of oranges

Peel oranges. Section, being very careful to remove all membrane. Cut sections into small pieces. Add other ingredients and cover. Refrigerate overnight before serving.

A note to the ambitious: grate your own fresh coconut for really delicious ambrosia.

Mrs. James Hurst

BANANAS FOSTER

4 nice large bananas, cut in 4
  pieces each
½ cup brown sugar
8 pats butter

Dash cinnamon
2 tablespoons banana liqueur
Rum as desired (about 4 ounces)

Cook bananas in electric skillet in sugar and butter until tender, medium heat. Sprinkle with cinnamon. Pour banana liqueur over and add rum. Ignite and serve with rich French ice cream.

Straight from the chef at Brennan's in New Orleans, a dish that will add a spark of life to even the deadest dinner table conversation. It tastes wonderful, too!

Mrs. John E. Wilks, Jr.

BAKED APRICOTS

2 17-ounce cans peeled apricots,
  drained
1 box light brown sugar

1 large box Ritz crackers, crumbled
Butter

Arrange a layer of apricot halves in a greased, 8"x8" baking dish. Cover with brown sugar, then a layer of crumbled crackers, and dot with pats of butter. Repeat layers. Bake slowly in a 300° oven approximately 1 hour. The top should be thick and crusty. Serves 10 to 12.

It's unfair that anything this delicious could be so easy to do. But for goodness sake, take advantage of the injustice!

Mrs. Ralph Huff

247

APRICOT PARFAIT

1 3-ounce box lemon flavored gelatin	1 cup boiling water
1 3-ounce box orange flavored gelatin	3 cups apricot nectar
	1 pint vanilla ice cream

Mix gelatin with boiling water until dissolved. Add apricot nectar. Add ice cream and stir until ice cream melts. Let stand until mixture becomes slightly thickened. Stir well and pour into parfait glasses or sherbet dishes. Refrigerate until ready to serve. Makes approximately 10 servings of ½ cup each.

Serve in tall frosted parfait glasses with whipped cream and a sprig of mint. Children love it and so do grown-ups.

Mrs. L. Denton Cole

CHERRY PARFAIT

2 cups fresh Bing cherries, or canned sweet cherries	2 tablespoons lemon juice
1½ tablespoons cornstarch	¼ teaspoon almond flavoring
½ cup sugar	Few drops red food coloring
1 cup orange juice	1 quart vanilla ice cream
	Whipped cream

Halve and pit cherries. Mix cornstarch and sugar until well blended. Stir in orange juice. Cook and stir until thickened and clear. Stir in cherries, lemon juice, almond flavoring and food coloring. Cool. Alternate cherry sauce with scoops of ice cream in chilled parfait glasses, with a dollop of whipped cream on top. Makes 6 to 8 servings.

Mrs. Charles W. Belt

PEACH PARFAIT

1 3-ounce package lemon flavored gelatin	1 to 2 cups fresh peaches, sliced and drained
1¼ cups hot water	Whipped cream
1 pint vanilla ice cream	

Dissolve gelatin in hot water. Add ice cream by spoonfuls. Stir until melted. Chill until thickened. Stir in fruit. Pour into parfait glasses or into baked pie crust and refrigerate.

When you tire of plain sliced peaches — if that is possible — we suggest mixing up these peach parfaits or making a peach pie with the same mixture.

Mrs. Robert C. McAnnally

MEXICALLI ICE CREAM DESSERT

4 ripe bananas	½ teaspoon cinnamon
¼ cup Kahlua liqueur (coffee liqueur)	8 scoops chocolate chip ice cream
Juice and grated peel of 1 lemon	¾ cup Kahlua
¼ cup brown sugar	½ cup freshly toasted grated coconut

Peel bananas and slice on diagonal. Marinate in ¼ cup Kahlua and lemon juice for 30 minutes or longer. Use shallow oven-proof pan. Just before ready to serve, sprinkle with brown sugar, cinnamon and grated lemon peel. Broil for 2 minutes or until light brown and bubbly. Meanwhile, warm ¾ cup of Kahlua in saucepan. To serve, put one scoop ice cream in 8 separate dishes. Spoon some of the broiled bananas and sauce over (about ½ banana per person), add 1½ tablespoons warmed liqueur over each serving and top with toasted coconut. Serves 8.

From Colorado, a strange conglomeration of ingredients, which together produce the most amazing dessert — delicious and elegant.

Mrs. Dale A. Crites
Lakewood, Colorado

ICE CREAM DESSERT

1 quart vanilla ice cream	4 ounces Kahlua liqueur
4 ounces vodka	

Mix all ingredients until smooth in blender. Put in freezer and chill thoroughly. Serve in champagne glasses or parfait glasses. Serves 8.

Mrs. Norman W. Harris, Jr.

ICE CREAM A LA ARGENTINA

1 gallon vanilla ice cream	1 12-ounce jar apricot jam
1 6-ounce can frozen lemonade	

Stir all together and freeze. Serves 20.

Mrs. Benjamin C. Stevens

HOT FUDGE TOPPING

¾ cup cocoa	1½ cups evaporated milk
3 cups sugar	½ cup butter
Pinch salt	1 teaspoon vanilla

Mix cocoa, sugar, salt, milk and butter. Boil 7 minutes and add vanilla.

Mrs. William Sexton

249

HEAVENLY HOT FUDGE

½ cup butter
4 squares unsweetened chocolate
3 cups sugar

¼ teaspoon salt
1 13-ounce can evaporated milk
1 teaspoon vanilla

Melt butter and chocolate over very low heat. Stir in sugar about ¾ cup at a time being sure it is blended before making another addition. Mixture will become very thick and dry. Add salt and stir in milk gradually. Continue to cook 7 to 8 minutes to blend and dissolve sugar. Remove from heat and add vanilla. Serve hot or cold over ice cream or cake.

This keeps well in the refrigerator.

Mrs. Jim L. Thompson, Jr.
Mrs. John R. Taylor

CARAMEL SAUCE

1 cup sugar
1 tablespoon flour
½ teaspoon salt

¼ cup butter or margarine
1½ cups milk
1 teaspoon vanilla

In skillet over medium heat combine first four ingredients and caramelize, stirring constantly. Add milk and cook until smooth and thick. Stir in vanilla.

Mrs. Elmer S. Loyd, Sr.

WHISKEY SAUCE

1 cup flour
2 cups sugar
Water

1 egg
Nutmeg, to taste
Whiskey, to taste

In top of double boiler mix flour and 1 cup sugar. Stir in small amount of cold water. Add enough boiling water to make consistency of thick cream. Boil gently for several minutes, stirring constantly. Meanwhile, beat remaining sugar with the egg until very light. Add 2 or 3 tablespoons of hot mixture to egg mixture and stir. Then pour all into top of double boiler Continue to cook until thickened. Add nutmeg and whiskey. Serve over rice pudding, baked apples, etc.

Mrs. Benjamin C. Stevens

LEMON SAUCE

½ cup sugar
1 tablespoon cornstarch
1 cup boiling water

1 tablespoon lemon rind
2 tablespoons butter
2 tablespoons lemon juice

Combine sugar and cornstarch. Stir in water and lemon rind and cook over moderate heat until thick and clear. Remove from heat and add butter and lemon juice. Serve slightly warm.

Mrs. William Sexton

ICE CREAM

FREEZER ICE CREAM

1 quart milk
2 cups sugar
2 heaping tablespoons flour
3 egg yolks, slightly beaten
3 egg whites, beaten

2 tablespoons sugar
1 quart milk
1 tablespoon vanilla
Sweetened fruit

Mix sugar and flour until smooth. Add milk and slightly beaten egg yolks. Cook over medium heat, stirring constantly, until of thick custard consistency. Cool and add vanilla. Beat the egg whites until almost stiff. Add the 2 tablespoons of sugar, continuing to beat. Fold egg white mixture into custard. Add sweetened fruit if you prefer, and add the additional quart of milk as needed to fill freezer 2/3 full.

A good, basic vanilla that is especially well suited to the addition of chocolate chips, peaches, or strawberries. Maybe even instant coffee?

Mrs. Charles W. Belt

LOW CHOLESTEROL ICE CREAM

½ gallon 2% skimmed milk
1 13-ounce can evaporated skim
milk

1 1/3 cups sugar
Vanilla to taste — 1 tablespoon or
more

If you must watch your weight and/or his, yet can't go a summer without getting out the freezer, this is especially for you. It tastes very much like snow ice cream.

Mrs. John R. Guice

MYRT'S BANANA ICE CREAM

5 eggs
2 13-ounce cans evaporated milk
2 cups sugar
3 cups milk

3 cups mashed bananas
1 tablespoon vanilla
1 teaspoon almond extract

Beat eggs in large bowl of electric mixer at medium speed. Mix in evaporated milk, sugar, whole milk, bananas, vanilla and almond extract until sugar dissolves. Pour into freezer. Yields approximately 1 gallon.

We suspect that banana runs a close second to peach in the home-made ice cream popularity poll — in Cotton Country, at any rate. This version is excellent.

Mrs. John R. Guice

251

CREAMY CUSTARD ICE CREAM

2 cups milk
3 egg yolks
1 cup sugar

¼ teaspoon salt
2 cups whipping cream
4 teaspoons vanilla flavoring

Scald milk in double boiler. Beat eggs, sugar and salt. Pour milk over mixture, stir, and return to double boiler. Cook until mixture coats the spoon. Cool completely. Add cream and vanilla flavoring. Freeze in ice cream freezer. Makes two quarts.

This is the smoothest, creamiest, richest of all the ice creams we've tried. A truly special French vanilla.

Mrs. Dalton Guthrie

BOILED CUSTARD ICE CREAM

2 tablespoons flour
1½ cups sugar
6 eggs
½ gallon milk

½ pint whipping cream
2 teaspoons vanilla
Dash of salt

Mix flour and sugar. Add eggs and mix. Scald milk and pour into flour, sugar and egg mixture very gradually to keep from cooking your eggs. Stir while adding milk. Cook over medium heat until mixture coats spoon. Add whipping cream, vanilla, and salt. Cool. Pour into gallon freezer. Makes 1 gallon.

Wonderful, old fashioned, frozen boiled custard — the very best of all ice cream to boiled custard lovers.

Mrs. James E. Brown

CUSTARD ICE CREAM

2 quarts milk
2 tablespoons cornstarch
9 eggs, beaten

2 cups sugar
1 tablespoon vanilla
1 pint heavy cream, whipped

Heat milk to boiling point in large boiler, but do not boil. Combine sugar, cornstarch and eggs together. Add this mixture slowly to hot milk. Stir constantly. Cook about 15 minutes on medium high. Stir constantly. Take from heat and place lid on mixture. Cool several hours. (Can be placed in refrigerator to hurry cooling). When cool add vanilla and whipped cream. Place in electric or hand-crank ice cream freezer and follow directions. Makes 4 to 5 quarts.

A nine egg vanilla custard, which has to be delicious alone or with fresh berries or peaches on top.

Mrs. Robert H. Hosey

CARAMEL ICE CREAM

6 eggs, slightly beaten
1 cup sugar
Pinch of salt
1 quart half and half (or whole milk, if you must)

2 cups sugar
1 quart heavy cream, half-whipped
2 teaspoons vanilla

Add sugar, salt, and half and half to beaten eggs in top of double boiler and cook over boiling water until custard has thickened.

While custard is cooking, caramalize 2 cups sugar in a heavy pan or skillet until it is a good brown. When custard is thick, add the caramalized sugar while it is very hot. (Be careful — it will splatter.) Strain and cool.

Add vanilla and half whipped cream. Freeze in electric freezer. Serve topped with toasted slivered almonds.

An ice cream marvel to make only when you feel extravagant, this "burnt sugar cream" is the richest, smoothest ice cream imaginable. A dessert for a lovely luncheon or elegant dinner — definitely not a "let's make ice cream in the back yard" type.

Mrs. William E. Shinn, Jr.

LEMON ICE CREAM

2 cups sugar
3 lemons

3 pints half and half or whole milk
1 pint cream

Pour juice of two lemons over sugar and let stand 2 hours. Add milk. Slice remaining lemon very thinly and add to mixture. Add whipped cream. Freeze in freezer.

Delicately flavored with fresh lemon juice and whole lemon slices — rich and smooth with lots of cream.

Mrs. C. Wilson Taylor, Jr.

LOTUS CREAM

3 quarts sweet milk, fresh
1 quart sugar

1 cup fresh lemon juice
1 lemon

Put lemon juice over sugar and let stand awhile. Have freezer cold, put in the sugar and juice, turn until thoroughly cold. Then pour in the milk and turn pretty fast for a while so as to mix well. Slice 1 lemon and put in mixture. This is delicious and makes 1 gallon of cream.

Handed down for generations, and written just as handed down, this lotus cream is u lemon flavored ice made with whole milk and no cream.

Mrs. Gilbert J. Key
Birmingham, Alabama

253

PEACH ICE CREAM

3 cups good, ripe peaches
(chopped in blender)
1 pint half and half
2 quarts milk

1 can sweetened condensed milk
2 cups sugar
2 or 3 drops red coloring

Mix all ingredients and chill in freezer can, then freeze in freezer.

Again the Southern Peach stars — in summer's favorite ice cream. This recipe is inexpensive and very simple, since there is nothing to cook or cool. Just put it all in the freezer and grind away (or plug in if you're lucky.)

Mrs. Dan M. Crane

SIX-THREE'S ICE CREAM

Juice of 3 lemons
Juice of 3 oranges or ¾ cup
orange juice
3 bananas, mashed

3 cartons (½ pint, each) whipping
cream
3 cups milk
3 cups sugar

Mix sugar with juices and bananas. Add whipping cream and milk. Freeze in either an electric or manual freezer. Makes 1 gallon.

Easy to remember, easy to make, easy to eat. Very hard to keep.

Mrs. John A. Woller

FRUIT MEDLEY ICE CREAM

4 bananas, crushed
3 lemons (juice)
3 oranges (juice)
1 20-ounce can crushed pineapple
1 small jar maraschino cherries,
drained and chopped

2 cups sugar
Pinch of salt
1 tablespoon vanilla
1 13-ounce can Pet milk
1 pint half and half cream or more
if needed to fill freezer

Combine all ingredients. Freeze in ice cream freezer.

A marvelous and refreshing ice cream: the lovely stuff sweet dreams are made of.

Mrs. William A. Sims

QUICK FREEZER ORANGE SHERBET

It's hard to imagine anything this easy and inexpensive — yet so tasty and refreshing.

1 can sweetened condensed milk
1 20-ounce can crushed pineapple
(optional)

7 carbonated orange drinks

Place in ice cream freezer and freeze until hard.

Mrs. John E. Wilks, Jr.

254

FRUIT SHERBET

1 ¼ cups sugar
1 cup fruit (orange juice,
  mashed peaches, or strawberries)
2 tablespoons lemon juice

Dash of salt
1 13-ounce can Pet milk
1 egg white

Combine sugar, fruit, lemon juice and salt. Stir until sugar is dissolved. Add milk, stirring constantly. Put in tray and freeze until mushy. Turn mixture into bowl and add unbeaten egg white. Beat rapidly until mixture is fluffy. Return to tray and freeze until firm.

A creamy sherbet recipe that doesn't require an ice cream freezer and that is extremely versatile — you decide what flavor appeals today and whip it up.

Mrs. Ralph Huff

DYANN'S UNCOOKED VANILLA ICE CREAM

6 eggs, separated
2 cups sugar
1 can sweetened condensed milk

1 teaspoon salt
2 tablespoons vanilla (or to taste)
½ gallon whole milk

Separate eggs and beat whites until stiff. Add slightly beaten egg yolks to the egg whites. Add remaining ingredients to the egg mixture. Blend and freeze in electric or manual freezer.

A very sweet, uncooked vanilla ice cream that brings smiles of nostalgia and sighs of "just like Grandmother used to make" — especially from husbands.

Mrs. George W. Hansberry

CAKES

APPLE SAUCE CAKE

1 cup butter or margarine
3 cups sugar
2 eggs
1 teaspoon soda
2 cups freshly cooked apple sauce
  (takes about 4 or 5 large cooking apples)

3 cups flour
½ teaspoon salt
1 teaspoon ground cloves
2 teaspoons baking powder
2 teaspoons cinnamon

Cream butter and sugar together; add the eggs, beat well. Mix the soda with the apple sauce (will bubble up) then add to creamed mixture. Add other ingredients which have been sifted together.

Grease and flour pan, bake for 1 hour and 15 minutes in 350° oven. Can be baked in tube pan, bundt pan, or in 2 loaf pans.

This recipe may be halved successfully. The cake freezes well and stays moist for many days.

Mrs. Walter Brand, Jr.
Des Moines, Washington

255

FRESH APPLE CAKE WITH CARAMEL FROSTING

1½ cups salad oil
2 cups sugar
2 large eggs
1 teaspoon salt
1 teaspoon soda
2 teaspoons baking powder
1 teaspoon vanilla
2½ cups flour
1 cup chopped pecans
3 cups chopped raw apples

Prepare raw apples and set aside. Measure salad oil into large mixing bowl. Add sugar and eggs. Beat until creamy on low speed with electric mixer. Sift flour and measure. Sift again and add salt, soda and baking powder. Add a small amount of the flour mixture at a time to the creamed mixture. Beat well after each addition. When all flour has been added, or when batter becomes very stiff, remove electric mixer. Fold in chopped pecans and chopped apples. Spread evenly into a 9" x 13" pan (or two 9" pans) lined with wax paper.

Bake in 350° oven for 55 or 60 minutes. Turn onto cake rack, remove wax paper, cool and frost. Use Mrs. Harris' caramel frosting in this section.

The apples should be tart and crisp for this prize winning recipe. Everyone will like your apple cake, but for a house full of men, it's a must!

Mrs. R. W. Orr, Jr.

BANANA NUT CAKE

Cake:
2½ cups sifted cake flour
1 2/3 cups sugar
1¼ teaspoons baking powder
1¼ teaspoons soda
1 teaspoon salt
2/3 cup Crisco
1/3 cup buttermilk
1¼ cups mashed bananas
1/3 cup buttermilk
2 large unbeaten eggs
2/3 cup chopped nuts
Frosting:
1 box plus 2 cups sifted confectioners' sugar
¾ cup Crisco
Scant ½ cup evaporated milk
Dash salt
1 teaspoon maple flavoring

Sift together first five ingredients. Add next three ingredients and beat vigorously for two minutes. Add next two ingredients and repeat beating for two minutes. Fold in chopped nuts and bake in greased and floured pans for 30 or 35 minutes at 350°. Makes three 8" layers or two 9" layers.

Frosting:

Mix together all ingredients and beat vigorously for 20 minutes. Spread on cooled layers.

The maple flavored frosting compliments the banana cake beautifully.

Mrs. Billy W. Payne

CARROT CAKE

2 cups flour
2 teaspoons soda
1 teaspoon salt
2 cups sugar
2 teaspoons cinnamon

1½ cups Wesson oil (or Crisco oil)
4 beaten eggs
3 cups finely grated raw carrots

Sift together dry ingredients and add oil, eggs, and carrots. Mix well. Bake in three 8" layers at 350° for 25 to 30 minutes. Make sure pans are greased and floured. Can be baked in 13" x 9" pan at 350° about 40 minutes or until firm in center. This will make 60 cup cakes. Bake 350° about 20 minutes.

Icing:

1 package confectioners' sugar
1 8-ounce package cream cheese
1 cup chopped pecans

½ cup margarine
1 3½-ounce can coconut
2 teaspoons vanilla

Cream softened margarine and sugar. Add softened cream cheese. Beat until smooth. Add vanilla, nuts and coconut.

Don't shy away from this wonderfully moist cake when you see "3 cups finely grated raw carrots". Turn on the blender and get that chore done in a jiffy. The rest of the mixing is a snap. You'll be glad you did!

Mrs. Lloyd Nix

SAUERKRAUT CAKE

2/3 cups butter
1½ cups sugar
3 eggs, slightly beaten
1 teaspoon vanilla
2¼ cups flour
½ cup cocoa

¼ teaspoon salt
1 teaspoon baking powder
1 teaspoon soda
1 cup water
2/3 cup sauerkraut

Cream butter and sugar. Beat in eggs. Sift dry ingredients and add alternately with water. Rinse, drain, chop and stir in the sauerkraut. Bake in two 8 inch greased and floured pans or one 9" x 13" pan until center springs back. Bake at 350° about 30 minutes. Frost with one of the icings in this section.

They'll all declare this chocolate cake is full of coconut. Just smile sweetly and don't say a word! And think of the money you've saved.

Mrs. John E. Wilks, Jr.

QUEEN'S CHOCOLATE CAKE

4 ounces (2/3 cup) chocolate chips
2 tablespoons dark rum
1 stick unsalted butter (not margarine) softened
2/3 cup sugar
3 eggs, separated

1/3 cup ground almonds
¼ teaspoon almond extract
¾ cup sifted cake flour
¼ teaspoon cream of tartar
Pinch salt
2 tablespoons sugar

Melt the chocolate chips in the rum over hot water until it is liquid and smooth. Cool.

Cream butter and sugar. Beat in egg yolks. Add tepid chocolate to butter, sugar, and egg mixture. Add the ground almonds (these can be purchased or you can easily grind whole blanched almonds in the blender) and the almond extract. Add sifted flour and mix well. The batter should be quite soft.

Beat egg whites. When frothy, add scant ¼ teaspoon cream of tartar and pinch of salt. Then beat in the two tablespoons sugar. Beat until soft peaks form.

Fold beaten egg whites into batter. Pour batter into one buttered and floured 8" round cake pan.

Bake for 25 minutes at 350°. Test with toothpick. Outside should be perfectly set, center should be slightly gooey.

Cool in pan 10 minutes, then unmold onto rack and cool two hours. Use the following glaze.

Glaze:

2/3 cup (4 ounces) chocolate chips
2 tablespoons dark rum

6 tablespoons softened unsalted butter

Soften chocolate in rum over hot water. Add butter and mix well until blended. Stir over ice water until thick enough to use as glaze. Glaze cake on the rack over wax paper, since the glaze will drip over the side. Then transfer to plate and decorate with whole blanched almonds. Serves 6 to 8.

This is a tiny one layer 8" cake, quite expensive and a lot of trouble. But just taste it! It's well named.

Mrs. William E. Shinn, Jr.

WELLESLEY FUDGE CAKE

2 cups sugar
1 cup butter or shortening
2 teaspoons baking powder
¼ teaspoon salt

2 cups cake flour
1 1/3 cups milk
2 eggs
1½ squares bitter chocolate

Cream sugar and butter until fluffy. Combine dry ingredients and add to mixture alternately with milk. Stir in eggs. Add melted chocolate. Bake in three 8" layers 25 minutes at 350°.

Filling:

Toast 1 cup chopped pecans in 4 tablespoons butter (stir constantly). Add pecans to 3 cups sifted confectioners' sugar and 6 tablespoons cream. Add 2 teaspoons vanilla and spread between layers.

Icing:

Combine 2 cups sugar, 2 tablespoons white Karo syrup, 1½ tablespoons cocoa, ¼ teaspoon salt, 1 cup evaporated milk. Cook to soft ball stage. Add 2 tablespoons of butter and beat. Spread thin and fast.

A delicately flavored chocolate cake with a buttery toasted pecan filling and a light chocolate frosting. Beautiful and good!

Mrs. Robert C. McAnnally

LARRY'S BIRTHDAY CAKE

(Devil's Food Cake)

2 cups sugar	1 (rounded) teaspoon soda
1 cup butter or margarine	¼ teaspoon salt
5 eggs	3 squares chocolate (melted)
2½ cups flour	1 teaspoon vanilla
1 cup buttermilk	

Cream butter and sugar, add eggs, one at a time, beating after each addition. Sift dry ingredients together and add alternately with buttermilk. Add chocolate and vanilla. Bake at 350° for 30 to 35 minutes. Makes two 9" layers.

Icing:

3 cups sugar	Pinch salt
3 squares chocolate (melted)	¼ teaspoon cream of tartar
1½ small cans evaporated milk— about 9 ounces	1 teaspoon vanilla
	Lump of butter (2 tablespoons)

Mix cream of tartar and salt with sugar. Add milk and stir constantly until it comes to a boil. This mixture is thick—be careful not to burn. Add chocolate and continue cooking until soft ball stage. Add vanilla and butter. Let cool. Beat and spread on two layer cake.

Larry is a chocolate lover of very discriminating taste. Once you try his rich dark cake with its very chocolatey cooked icing, it will be your cake too. You don't have to wait for a birthday either!

Mrs. Walter Penney

WHITE CHOCOLATE CAKE

½ cup boiling water
4 ounces white chocolate (candy)
1 cup butter
2 cups sugar
4 egg yolks, unbeaten
1 teaspoon vanilla

2½ cups sifted Swans Down Cake
  Flour
½ teaspoon salt
1 teaspoon baking soda
1 cup buttermilk
4 egg whites, stiffly beaten

Melt chocolate in boiling water. Cool. Cream butter and sugar until fluffy. Add egg yolks, one at a time, beating well after each. Add melted chocolate and vanilla; mix well. Sift together flour, salt and soda. Add alternately with buttermilk to chocolate mixture; beat well or until smooth. Fold in whites. Pour into three 8 or 9 inch layer pans which have been lined, greased and floured. Bake at 350° for 30 to 40 minutes.

Icing:

2 cups white sugar
1 cup margarine

1 teaspoon vanilla
Dash salt
1 small can evaporated milk

Combine all ingredients and let stand for one hour, stirring occasionally. Cook until soft ball stage. Beat until creamy and spread on cake. Don't use too much frosting between layers so you can have enough for outside of cake.

White chocolate might be hard to find. Dime stores sometime sell it — so do candy shops.

Mrs. Jim L. Thompson, Jr.

CHOCOLATE COOKIE SHEET CAKE

2 cups flour
2 cups sugar
½ teaspoon salt
1 teaspoon cinnamon
1 cup margarine
1 cup water

3 tablespoons cocoa
2 eggs
1 teaspoon soda
½ cup buttermilk
1 teaspoon vanilla

Sift flour, measure, and resift with sugar, salt and cinnamon. Bring to boil the margarine, water and cocoa. Pour over the flour and sugar mixture. Mix eggs, soda, buttermilk and vanilla together. Add to above mixture. Bake in a greased and floured 15½ x 10½ x 1 inch pan for 20 minutes at 350°. May use 9 x 13 inch pan. Cook about 40 minutes.

Icing:

½ cup margarine
3 tablespoons cocoa
6 tablespoons milk

1 box confectioners' sugar
½ cup chopped pecans
1 teaspoon vanilla

Start cooking icing the last five minutes cake is baking. Mix margarine, cocoa and milk in saucepan over low heat. Remove and add sugar, nuts and vanilla. Frost cake while hot. Makes 36 squares.

The cinnamon makes the difference!

Mrs. Lloyd Nix

FUDGE CAKE

1 cup butter
4 squares Baker's Chocolate
2 cups sugar
4 eggs
1 cup flour (generous)

¼ teaspoon soda
¼ teaspoon salt
2 cups chopped pecans
1 teaspoon vanilla

Melt butter and chocolate together. Add sugar and beat in eggs. Sift flour, salt, and soda, and add to mixture. Add nuts and vanilla. Bake in a greased and lined pan (13" x 9") in a slow oven (275°) for 30 to 45 minutes.

Very good served hot with ice cream. As long as you've gone that far, might as well add a few more calories and top it all with hot fudge sauce!

Mrs. Judson E. Davis

COCA-COLA CAKE

2 cups sugar
2 cups flour
1 cup butter
3 tablespoons cocoa
1 cup Coca-Cola
1 teaspoon baking soda

½ cup buttermilk
2 eggs, beaten
1 teaspoon vanilla
1½ cups miniature marshmallows
   (optional)

Sift sugar and flour together. Boil butter, cocoa, and Coca-Cola. Pour over flour and sugar. Dissolve soda in buttermilk and pour in with the above ingredients. Then add eggs, vanilla and marshmallows. Pour into greased 13" x 9" pan and bake 45 minutes in 350° oven.

Icing:

½ cup butter
3 tablespoons cocoa
6 tablespoons Coca-Cola

1 box confectioners' sugar
1 teaspoon vanilla
1 cup broken pecans

Bring to boil the butter, cocoa, and Coca-Cola. Add the sugar, vanilla and pecans. Pour over cake in the pan while icing is hot.

A favorite of man, woman, and child. Very moist and easy to make. The Troups are Decatur's Coca-Cola people. Obviously they feel compelled to put Coke in everything. Seriously, this is a good chocolate cake.

Mrs. Frank Troup

MAYONNAISE CAKE

3 cups unsifted flour
1½ cups sugar
1/3 cup cocoa
2¼ teaspoons baking soda

1½ cups Hellman's real Mayonnaise
1½ cups water
1½ teaspoons vanilla

Grease two 9" layer pans, or one 9 x 13 x 2 inch pan. Sift together dry ingredients into large bowl. Stir in mayonnaise, then gradually stir in water and vanilla until smooth and blended. Pour into prepared pans. Bake in a 350° oven about 30 minutes, or until cake springs back when touched. Cool. Remove from pans and ice.

A fool proof chocolate cake you don't have to beat. With Betty Crocker's Sour Cream White Icing on the top, nobody will know that baking is not your thing.

Mrs. Judson E. Davis

MERINGUE CRADLE CAKE

Meringue:
4 egg whites
1 cup sugar

1 cup chopped pecans
1 1-ounce square of chocolate grated

Beat egg whites to soft-peak stage, then gradually add sugar and beat until stiff peaks form. Fold in 1 cup chopped pecans and grated chocolate. Spread meringue evenly over bottom and halfway up sides of greased tube pan that has been lined with waxed paper.

½ cup butter
1 cup sugar
4 egg yolks, well beaten
¾ cup milk

1 teaspoon vanilla flavoring
2 cups sifted flour
3 teaspoons baking powder
1 teaspoon salt

Cream butter and sugar, add egg yolks and vanilla. Add dry ingredients alternately with milk to creamed mixture beginning and ending with dry ingredients. Spoon into meringue lined pan. Bake in 325° oven about 65 to 75 minutes. Cool 20 minutes before turning out.

Mrs. John R. Guice

DATE AND APPLE SAUCE CAKE

½ cup butter or margarine
1 cup light brown sugar
2 eggs
2 cups flour
½ teaspoon cinnamon
½ teaspoon nutmeg
¼ teaspoon cloves

1 cup chopped dates
1 cup seedless white raisins
1 cup chopped nuts
2 teaspoons soda
1½ cups applesauce
1 teaspoon vanilla

Cream butter, add brown sugar and beat until light and fluffy. Add eggs one at a time, beating well after each addition. Sift together flour and spices. Sprinkle one half of this flour mixture over the dates, raisins, and nuts. Stir until coated. Add soda to apple sauce and then add to the butter mixture alternately with the flour. Add vanilla. Stir in the dates, raisins, and nuts. Spoon into a greased and floured 8¾" tube pan. Bake at 325° for 1 hour, or until cake starts to pull away from side of pan. This is a moist spicy cake that freezes well.

Buttermilk Frosting:

3 cups sugar
1 to 2 tablespoons light corn
  syrup

1½ cups buttermilk
1½ teaspoons soda

Dissolve soda in buttermilk, add sugar and corn syrup. Cook in a large pan, stirring often, to soft ball stage. Cool and beat until smooth and creamy.

Lucy Caddell's daughter-in-law — who is a marvelous cook and an accomplished cake-baker herself — says of this rich, moist cake, "It's my very favorite thing!"

Mrs. John Caddell

DATE CAKE AND TOPPING

1½ cups sugar
1 cup shortening
1½ cups flour
1 teaspoon soda
1 teaspoon baking powder
½ teaspoon cinnamon
½ teaspoon cloves

½ teaspoon allspice
1 cup sour milk
2 eggs
½ cup raisins
½ cup nuts
½ cup chopped dates
1 teaspoon vanilla

Cream sugar and shortening. Sift dry ingredients together and add alternately with the milk. Add eggs and vanilla. Fold in raisins, nuts, and dates. Mix only enough to blend. Bake for 35 to 40 minutes at 350° in a greased and floured 13 x 9 x 2 pan.

Topping:

1½ cups sugar
½ cup chopped dates

1 cup heavy cream
1 tablespoon butter
1 teaspoon vanilla

Mix sugar, dates and cream. Cook until it coats the spoon. Add the butter and vanilla and beat until thick enough to spread. Cover cake.

Double delicious with dates in both the cake and its topping. Double trouble for dieters. Especially good served warm.

Mrs. Robert C. McAnnally

ORANGE DATE CAKE

1 cup butter or margarine
2 cups sugar
Pinch salt
4 cups flour
4 eggs

1 1/3 cups buttermilk
½ teaspoon soda
2 tablespoons grated orange rind
1 pound chopped dates
1 cup chopped pecans
½ cup coconut

Cream butter and sugar. Add pinch of salt. Add flour alternately with eggs. Continue beating. Add buttermilk in which the soda has been dissolved. Fold in orange rind, dates, pecans and coconut. Bake 1 hour and 10 minutes in a greased and floured tube pan at 325°. Remove from pan and while still warm, melt the following ingredients for glaze. Spoon over cake until it is all absorbed.

1 cup orange juice
2 cups sugar

3 tablespoons grated orange rind

Mrs. C. P. Beddow

DATE-NUT CAKE

½ pound dates
1 teaspoon soda
¼ cup boiling water
2 tablespoons butter
1 cup sugar

1 egg
1¼ cups sifted flour
¾ cup milk
½ cup chopped nuts

Cut up dates. Add soda to dates. Pour boiling water over dates and let stand until cool. Cream butter and sugar well; add beaten egg. Add date mixture, stirring to blend. Add the flour alternately with milk. Stir in chopped nuts. Pour into 8 x 8 x 2 greased pan. Bake at 350° for 35 minutes. Cool.

A small one layer date cake to cut in squares and serve with ice cream. Lemon perhaps.

Mrs. William H. Nabors

DRUNKEN CAKE

5 eggs, separated
1 cup sugar
2 tablespoons lemon juice
2 tablespoons water

1 cup sifted cake flour
¼ teaspoon salt
¼ teaspoon cream of tartar

Beat egg yolks until thick. Gradually beat in ½ cup of the sugar. Continue beating, gradually adding lemon juice and water. Beat until mixture is light in color and very thick. Gently stir in flour. Beat egg whites with salt and cream of tartar until soft peaks form. Gradually beat in ½ cup of the sugar, beating until whites are stiff but not dry. Fold into egg yolk mixture. Turn into ungreased 9" tube pan or bundt pan. Bake at 350° for 35 to 45 minutes or until cake springs back when lightly touched. Invert on rack or Coke bottle and cool thoroughly in the pan. To remove from pan, give cake several sharp cracks on counter. It will fall out.

Topping:

1½ cups sugar
2/3 cup Malaga wine
(sherry or sweet Madeira can
be substituted)

Dash cinnamon
Heavy cream, whipped

In heavy skillet, cook sugar until caramelized. Remove from heat. Very slowly stir in wine mixed with cinnamon. Continue stirring until caramel is dissolved. Slowly pour over cake and let stand until most of syrup is absorbed. Serve with whipped cream.

A very light airy sponge cake sauced with pungent wine flavored caramel. Children don't like it, men may not, but your bridge group will adore it (it makes them feel so wicked!). Be sure to serve with whipped cream.

Mrs. William E. Shinn, Jr.

FRENCH CHRISTMAS CAKE

1 cup butter (not margarine)
2 cups sugar
6 eggs
1 box vanilla wafers (12 ounce)
finely crushed in blender

1 7-ounce can coconut
1½ cups broken pecans
½ cup milk

Cream butter and sugar. Beat until smooth. Add eggs one at a time, beating well after each addition. Then add vanilla wafer crumbs and milk, alternately, a little at a time, beating well after each addition. Stir in pecans and coconut. Pour into greased and floured 9" tube or bundt pan. Bake at 350° for 1½ hours. Let cake cool completely before removing from pan. It breaks very easily if removed while still warm.

Again the blender comes to your aid — this time to crush the vanilla wafers (though if you are blenderless, a plastic bag and a rolling pin work nicely). Once that's done, the cake is very easy to put together and it will be a favorite addition to your cake repertoire. One word of caution. Check cake after an hour, particularly if you are using a dark teflon lined pan. It may not take the full 1½ hours.

Mrs. William E. Shinn, Jr.

HOLIDAY FRUIT CAKE

3 cups sifted flour
3 teaspoons baking powder
¼ teaspoon salt
1 cup butter

2 cups sugar
5 eggs
1 cup cold water
2 teaspoons vanilla

Sift the flour, baking powder and salt together three times. Cream butter with sugar; add eggs, one at a time, beating after each addition. Add dry ingredients alternately with water. Stir in vanilla. Make two 8" layers out of half of the batter. Grease and flour the pans. Bake at 350° for 25 to 30 minutes.

TO THE REMAINING HALF OF BATTER, ADD:

2 cups finely cut dates
1½ cups chopped pecans
½ cup chopped walnuts

1 small bottle maraschino cherries
(drained and cut in halves)
4 large slices pineapple
(drained and cut small)

Pour fruit-filled batter in two 8" layer cake pans that have been greased and floured. Bake at 350° for 30 minutes.

Filling:

2 cups sugar
1 cup water
2 cans Angel Flake coconut

Grated rind and juice of 3 lemons
1 beaten egg
2 tablespoons cornstarch
1 cup cold water

Boil together 3 minutes the sugar and 1 cup water. Add coconut, grated rind and juice of lemons. In another saucepan, mix the beaten egg, cornstarch and 1 cup cold water. Cook over low heat until thick, stirring all the while. Add coconut mixture. Let cool and spread between layers and on top of cake — alternating a fruity layer and a plain layer of cake.

A glamorous candidate for the culinary sweepstakes is Mrs. Brewer's Holiday Fruit Cake. Not at all the traditional fruit cake — and much more interesting.

Mrs. Albert P. Brewer
Pike Road, Alabama

FRUIT CAKE

2 cups butter
3 cups sugar
6 eggs
6 cups flour
1 teaspoon salt
3 teaspoons baking powder
1 tablespoon mixed spices

1 cup wine — light sherry
2 quarts shelled pecans, broken
1½ pounds white raisins
1½ pounds candied pineapple,
cut in pieces
1½ pounds candied cherries,
cut in pieces

Flour fruit with part of 6 cups of flour. Cream butter and sugar. Add eggs one at a time, beating after each addition. Add sifted dry ingredients alternately with wine. Fold in pecans, raisins and fruit. Pour into three loaf pans lined with brown paper and greaseu slightly. Bake 250° for 3½ hours. Pour additional sherry over cake while hot. Wrap in sherry soaked cloth, and store in tin.

Mrs. William A. Sims

JAPANESE FRUIT CAKE

1 cup butter	1 scant cup milk
2 cups sugar	1 teaspoon vanilla
4 eggs	1 teaspoon cinnamon
3¼ cups cake flour	1 teaspoon allspice
2 teaspoons baking powder	½ teaspoon cloves

Cream butter and sugar. Add eggs one at a time, beating after each addition. Sift together flour and baking powder, and add alternately with milk. Add vanilla. Divide the batter into three parts. To one part add the cinnamon, allspice, and cloves. Bake in three layers at 350° to 375°. Use the spice layer as the middle layer, and put together with the following filling.

Filling:

Juice from 3 lemons	1½ cups boiling water
Grated rind from 1 lemon	3 tablespoons flour
1 good sized coconut, grated	1 cup raisins
3 cups sugar	1 cup chopped pecans

Put all together in a sauce pan and cook, stirring constantly until mixture drops in lumps from spoon. Cool and spread between layers and on top and sides. The juice of one orange may be substituted for one of the lemons. A milder flavor results.

Whether or not this cake really came from Japan we don't know, but then that's really beside the point. There is no fruit in the cake itself, but the lemon filling between the layers — two yellow and one spice — is full of coconut and pecans and good eating.

Mrs. John D. Davis, Jr.

HEATH BAR CAKE

1 cup brown sugar	1 egg
½ cup white sugar	1 cup buttermilk
½ cup butter or margarine	1 teaspoon baking soda
2 cups flour	6 Heath Bars

Mix first four ingredients like you would mix a pie crust. Take out ½ cup and save. Add the egg, buttermilk and baking soda to rest of mixture. Put in a greased and floured 9" x 13" pan. Sprinkle the remaining sugar-flour-margarine mixture combined with broken Heath bars over top of batter. Bake in a 350° oven for 30 minutes.

A yankee recipe from Wisconsin that even we Southerners have to admit is simply delicious!

Mrs. Joe D. Burns

ITALIAN CREAM CAKE

½ cup margarine
½ cup vegetable shortening
2 cups sugar
5 egg yolks
2 cups flour
1 teaspoon soda
1 cup buttermilk
1 teaspoon vanilla
1 7-ounce can Angel Flake Coconut
1 cup chopped nuts
5 egg whites (stiffly beaten)

Cream shortening and margarine, add sugar and beat until mixture is smooth. Add egg yolks and beat well. Combine flour and soda and add to creamed mixture, alternating with buttermilk. Stir in vanilla, coconut, nuts. Fold in egg whites. Pour batter into 3 greased and floured 9" cake pans. Bake at 350° for 25 minutes. Cool. Frost with the following frosting.

Cream Frosting:

1 8-ounce package cream cheese
¼ cup margarine
1 box confectioners' sugar
1 teaspoon vanilla
½ cup chopped nuts

Beat cheese and margarine until smooth. Add sugar and mix well. Add vanilla and beat until smooth. Spread between layers. Sprinkle nuts between layers. Spread frosting on sides and top.

Great for entertaining! Most cakes are best the day they're made. This one is more moist the next day.

Mrs. Lynn C. Fowler

SMOKY MOUNTAIN JAM CAKE

¾ cup butter or margarine
1 cup sugar
½ teaspoon vanilla
3 eggs
1½ cups sifted self-rising flour
¼ teaspoon soda
½ teaspoon cinnamon
½ teaspoon cloves
½ teaspoon allspice
¼ cup buttermilk
½ cup strawberry preserves
½ cup blackberries or blueberries (drained)
1 cup plum jelly

Preheat oven to 325°. Grease thoroughly, and lightly dust with flour two 8" square pans. Cream butter and sugar. Add vanilla, and then eggs one at a time. Sift together (two times) flour, soda, cinnamon, cloves and allspice. Add flour and milk alternately to creamed mixture, making three additions of flour and two of buttermilk. Fold in preserves and berries. Pour into pans and bake 45 to 50 minutes. Cool in pans. Spread jelly between layers and let age one or two days before frosting with caramel icing. Use one of the caramel icings in this section.

If you use plain flour, add ¼ teaspoon salt to flour and increase soda to ½ teaspoon.

Mrs. Tom White

MILKY WAY CAKE

4 10c Milky Way candy bars	½ teaspoon soda
1 cup margarine (2 sticks)	1¼ cups buttermilk
2 cups sugar	2½ cups cake flour
4 eggs, separated	2 cups chopped pecans

Melt candy and 1 stick margarine over boiling water. Cream sugar and other stick margarine. Add candy mixture to this and stir. Add egg yolks one at a time, beating well after each. Dissolve soda in buttermilk, then add flour and buttermilk alternately, ending with flour. Add nuts. Fold in stiffly beaten egg whites. Bake in three greased and floured 9" layer pans at 350° for 30 minutes.

Frosting:

1 cup evaporated milk	6 ounces semi-sweet chocolate bits
½ cup margarine	1 cup marshmallow cream (small
2½ cups sugar	jar)

Cook milk, margarine, and sugar until soft ball forms in cold water. Add the chocolate bits and the marshmallow cream. Stir until smooth and frost cake.

This delicate and beautiful cake is one cake everybody will love. Cook for tonight's company and just hope there'll be some left for tomorrow. The children will be furious if there's not!

Mrs. Arnold Rankin

LANE CAKE

1 cup butter	1/8 teaspoon salt
2 cups sugar	1 teaspoon vanilla
3 cups sifted flour	8 egg whites (beaten stiff)
1 cup milk	2 teaspoons baking powder

Cream butter, add sugar gradually and cream until fluffy. Add sifted dry ingredients alternately with milk. Add vanilla. Fold in beaten egg whites. Pour into two 9" pans or three 8" layer pans. Bake at 350° for about 25 minutes.

Lane Cake Filling:

8 egg yolks	1 cup raisins (cut in thirds with
1 cup pecans (chopped fine)	scissors)
1 cup sugar	½ cup blackberry wine
½ cup butter	1 cup fresh grated coconut
1 teaspoon vanilla	

Beat egg yolks. Add sugar and butter. Cook in double boiler until it coats wooden spoon. Remove from heat and add wine, raisins, coconut, and pecans. (Do not use canned coconut.) Spread filling between layers and on top of cake.

Mrs. George McCrary

LANE CAKE FROSTING (DIVINITY)

2½ cups granulated sugar
1/8 teaspoon salt
1/3 cup dark corn syrup

2/3 cup water
2 egg whites
1 teaspoon vanilla extract

In a saucepan, combine sugar, salt, corn syrup, water. Cook over low heat, stirring until sugar disolves. Bring to boil uncovered without stirring. In small electric mixer bowl with mixer at high speed, beat egg whites until foamy; add three tablespoons syrup mixture, beating until stiff but not dry. Boil rest of syrup to 240° on candy thermometer or until it spins a thread from spoon. Pour syrup slowly over egg whites, beating until frosting begins to lose gloss and hold shape. Add vanilla. A drop or two of hot water may be added if it becomes too thick. Spread on sides of cake. This icing does not form a crust.

Mrs. James Odom

LEMON CAKE

1 cup butter or margarine
2 cups sugar
4 cups sifted flour
4 teaspoons baking powder

1 cup water or milk
6 egg whites
1 teaspoon vanilla

Cream butter and sugar. Sift flour and baking powder two or three times. Add flour and baking powder alternately with water or milk to creamed butter and sugar. Beat until all is well-blended and smooth. Then fold in stiffly beaten egg whites and vanilla. Bake in three 8 or 9" greased and floured pans in moderate oven (350°) about 25 minutes.

Lemon Filling:

6 egg yolks
1½ cups sugar
2 tablespoons flour (rounded)
Juice of 3 or 4 lemons
    (about ¾ cup)

Juice of 1 or 2 oranges
    (about 1 cup)
¾ cup water
2 tablespoons butter
1 teaspoon lemon extract

Beat egg yolks. Add sugar and flour and beat until light and fluffy. Add lemon and orange juice. Then add water and butter. Cook in double boiler on very low heat. Stir constantly. Cook until thick enough to spread on cake. Let cool and add extract before spreading between layers. Use white icing to cover top and sides of cake.

Mrs. Barrett Shelton, Jr.

LEMON CHEESE CAKE

1 cup butter
2 cups sugar
3 cups sifted flour
2 teaspoons baking powder

½ teaspoon soda
1 cup milk
6 egg whites (beaten)
1 teaspoon vanilla

Cream butter and sugar. Sift together flour, baking powder, and soda. Add flour alternately with the milk. Beat egg whites until stiff, then fold into batter. Add vanilla. Bake in three 8 or 9" greased and floured pans in a 325° oven for approximately 25 minutes. Cool and put together with the following filling.

Filling:

8 egg yolks
½ cup butter

1 cup sugar
Juice and rind of two lemons

Cook the above in a double boiler until thick. Spread between layers. Use a white frosting for the top and sides. You might use the seven minute frosting in this section. This cake takes extra time to make, but is good for special occasions. It would also make a great coconut cake; just put grated coconut over top and sides.

Mrs. Joe W. Walker

PINEAPPLE MERINGUE CAKE

½ cup shortening
½ cup sugar
4 egg yolks
1 cup cake flour sifted

2 teaspoons baking powder
1/8 teaspoon salt
1 teaspoon vanilla
5 tablespoons milk

Cream shortening and sugar together — add egg yolks and mix thoroughly. Add flour, which has been sifted with baking powder and salt, alternately with the vanilla and milk. Pour into two 8" round layer cake pans which have been well greased and floured. Then add:

4 egg whites
1 cup sugar

1 teaspoon vanilla
¾ cup chopped nuts

Beat egg whites stiff, then add a light sifting of sugar, continue beating and adding until all sugar has been used. Add vanilla and spread meringue on each layer. Sprinkle with the nuts. Bake at 350° 30 to 35 minutes. Allow to cool, then remove from pans and spread with the following filling. Spread filling on sides.

Pineapple filling:

1 cup drained crushed pineapple
1½ cups heavy cream (whipped)

1½ teaspoons confectioners' sugar
¼ teaspoon vanilla

Combine all ingredients. Place one layer meringue side down on cake plate and spread with filling. Place second layer on top of cake with meringue side up. Refrigerate.

Each layer is really two — one cake and one meringue. There are many in Decatur and environs who insist this is the best cake they've ever tasted. We've never heard anyone argue the point — and that must mean something. Must be refrigerated.

Mrs. Tom Caddell

271

PINEAPPLE—NUT SPICE CAKE

2½ cups sifted self-rising flour
2 cups sugar
1½ cups Crisco oil
4 egg yolks
1 small (8½-ounce) can crushed
  pineapple and juice
1½ teaspoons nutmeg

2 tablespoons hot water
2 teaspoons cinnamon
1 teaspoon butter extract
1 teaspoon coconut extract
1 teaspoon vanilla
1 cup chopped nuts
4 egg whites beaten

Combine all ingredients except nuts and egg whites. Beat well, and then add nuts. Fold in egg whites. Pour into greased and floured tube pan. Place in cold oven. Set oven for 325° and bake 1 hour and 15 minutes. Let cool 15 minutes before removing from pan.

This easy to make cake which must have Polynesian inspiration if not origins, has been very successful at the annual Junior Service League Bakesale. We know of at least one customer who looks for it every year.

Mrs. Whit King, Jr.

UPSIDE-DOWN CAKE

4 slices canned pineapple
3 tablespoons butter or margarine
6 tablespoons brown sugar
Cake batter:
¼ cup sugar
¼ cup butter or margarine

1 egg, separated
1 cup sifted cake flour
1½ teaspoons baking powder
Pinch salt
½ cup pineapple juice
½ teaspoon vanilla

Cut pineapple in wedges. Melt the butter in a 9" iron frying pan. Add the sugar and cook until blended using a low heat. Remove from heat, and arrange pineapple in the sugar. To prepare the batter: Cream the butter, add the sugar; blend until fluffy, and add the egg yolk. Sift the flour, baking powder, and salt together; add alternately with the pineapple juice and vanilla. Beat the egg white until stiff and fold into the batter. Pour this batter over the pineapple-sugar mixture. Bake in a preheated 350° oven for 25 minutes. Turn out carefully on a serving dish, the pineapple side up. Serve plain or with whipped cream. Serves six.

You may use other fruits as a substitute for the pineapple if you wish.

Didn't everybody's grandmother make pineapple upside-down cake? Don't you remember how good it was just out of the oven simply covered with the cream she had skimmed off the top of the bottle and whipped.

It's so easy to do and bake right along with the rest of your dinner. Your children — and grandchildren — will remember it too!

Mrs. George Hansberry

OATMEAL CAKE

1 cup oatmeal (uncooked)	2 eggs
1¼ cups boiling water	1½ cups flour
½ cup butter	1 teaspoon soda
1 cup brown sugar (packed)	1 teaspoon cinnamon
1 cup white sugar	½ teaspoon salt

Pour boiling water over oatmeal and let stand 20 minutes. Cream white and brown sugar with butter. Add eggs one at a time. Add oats, mix and beat well. Stir in flour which has been sifted with other dry ingredients. Pour into greased 9 x 13 x 2 inch pan. Bake at 350° for 40 minutes.

Topping:

½ cup brown sugar	¼ cup evaporated milk
¼ cup butter (soft)	1 cup coconut (can of Angel
1 cup chopped nuts	Flake)
	¼ teaspoon vanilla

Mix all the ingredients together and spread on hot cake. Return to oven and broil about 10 minutes. Cut into squares.

A moist, bland cake that all children and their daddies will love — even those who vow they'll never touch oatmeal. Just keep the name and ingredients under your hat and fill them up with protein.

Mrs. A. L. Rowe

NUT CAKE (BOURBON PECAN CAKE)

4 cups flour, sifted	2 cups sugar
1 teaspoon nutmeg	1½ cups butter
1 teaspoon cinnamon	6 whole eggs
½ teaspoon cloves	½ cup molasses mixed with 1 tea-
1 box seedless raisins	spoon soda
6 cups chopped pecans	½ cup bourbon

Preheat oven to 275°. Grease one 10" tube and one loaf pan. Line bottom of pans with wax paper. Roll raisins and nut meats in ½ cup of the flour. Sift together remaining flour and spices. Cream sugar and butter until fluffy. Add the eggs and beat well. Add flour and spice mixture alternately with molasses and bourbon, beating only until mixed after each addition. By hand, fold in the raisins and pecans. Pour into prepared pans. Bake slowly for 2 hours or until toothpick inserted in cakes comes out dry. Bake the loaf cake in less time (approximately 1½ hours). After cakes have cooled, wrap well in saran, then foil. They keep for several weeks and taste better with a little age.

A traditional Thanksgiving and Christmas dessert in many locales. Start a new tradition at your house this year.

Mrs. Herbert Street

PLUM-GOOD CAKE

1 cup Crisco oil
2 cups sugar
3 eggs
2 cups self-rising flour
1 teaspoon cinnamon

1 teaspoon cloves
1 large can purple plums
  (remove pits and chop)
1 cup chopped pecans
Grated rind of an orange

Cream oil and sugar, beat in eggs. Add flour sifted with dry ingredients. Fold in plums, nuts and orange rind. Bake in a greased and floured tube or bundt pan in a 350° oven for 50 minutes.

Icing:

Mix juice of 1 orange, plus some rind (amount desired), and 1½ cups confectioners' sugar. Pour over cake while hot.

The men will adore you when you bake this exceptionally tasty plum colored cake that stays moist as long as there is any. For lazy day baking, substitute two small baby food jars of plums with tapioca for the can of plums.

Mrs. John E. Wilks, Jr.

POUND CAKE

1 cup real butter
1 2/3 cups sugar
5 eggs

2 cups sifted flour
1 teaspoon vanilla
¼ teaspoon almond extract
¼ teaspoon mace

Cream softened butter and sugar in mixer. Add the 5 eggs all at once, and beat just until smooth and creamy. Don't over beat. Gradually add sifted flour and mace. Blend until creamy again and add vanilla and almond extracts. Place in a greased and floured 8½ x 4½ x 2½ loaf pan. Bake 1 hour and 20 minutes in a 325° oven.

Blue ribbon pound cake. Leave out mace for a more delicate flavor.

Mrs. John R. Cook

RUTH FITZPATRICK'S POUND CAKE

½ cup margarine (not butter)
½ cup Crisco
2 cups sugar
¼ teaspoon salt

6 medium eggs (not large)
2 cups flour
1 teaspoon almond extract or
  your own favorite flavoring

In electric mixer, blend softened margarine, Crisco, and sugar until frothy and light. Continue to beat and add eggs one at a time. Still beating, gradually add flour, salt and flavoring. Pour into a well greased and floured 10 inch tube pan. Bake 1 hour in a pre-heated 350° oven (test with straw at 55 minutes). Let stand on wire rack to cool 10 minutes before removing from pan. Sprinkle with confectioners' sugar, if you desire.

Delicious sliced thin, toasted and topped with vanilla ice cream and chocolate sauce.

Mrs. Fletcher Eddens

BROWN SUGAR POUND CAKE

1 cup butter	½ teaspoon baking powder
½ cup shortening	3½ cups flour
1 box, plus 1 cup light brown sugar	1 cup milk
5 eggs	1¼ teaspoons vanilla

Cream butter, shortening and brown sugar. Add eggs. Sift baking powder and flour; add alternately with milk to creamed mixture. Add vanilla. Pour into well greased tube pan lined with wax paper. Bake in a 325° oven for 1 hour and 30 minutes.

Topping:

½ cup butter	1 box confectioners' sugar
1 cup chopped pecans	Milk
	1 teaspoon vanilla

Combine ¼ cup of butter and pecans. Cook until brown. Remove from heat and add remaining ingredients, adding enough milk to spread. Spread over cake.

A particularly good pound cake made with brown sugar and with a rich butter pecan topping.

Mrs. Ralph Huff

BUTTERMILK POUND CAKE

1½ cups Crisco	1 tablespoon lemon flavoring
2½ cups sugar	3½ cups flour
4 eggs	½ teaspoon salt
1 cup buttermilk	
½ teaspoon soda (dissolved in 1 tablespoon water)	

Cream Crisco and sugar. Add one egg at a time, beating well after each addition. Add milk, soda and flavoring. Add flour and salt last. Beat until fluffy. Bake in a greased and floured tube pan in a 300° oven for 1½ hours.

Glaze:
Juice and rind of 2 lemons
Juice of 1 orange
1½ cups sugar

Dissolve, but do not boil. Let cake stand 10 minutes after taking from oven. Then spoon glaze over top and sides of cake.

Mrs. Ralph Huff

CHOCOLATE POUND CAKE

1 cup butter	½ teaspoon baking powder
½ cup shortening	5 tablespoons cocoa
3 cups sugar	½ teaspoon salt
5 eggs	1 cup milk
3 cups flour	2 teaspoons vanilla

Cream butter and shortening. Add sugar gradually. Add eggs one at a time, beating after each addition. Sift together flour, baking powder, salt and cocoa and add to butter mixture alternately with milk. Add vanilla. Bake 1½ hours at 325° in a greased and floured 10 inch tube pan.

This is a favorite cake with all. Moist; keeps well.

Mrs. S. Britt Owens

COCONUT POUND CAKE

1 cup margarine	1 cup milk
¾ cup Crisco	1 teaspoon vanilla
3 cups sugar	1 teaspoon butter flavoring
5 eggs	1 teaspoon almond flavoring
3 cups flour	1 7-ounce can Angel Flake coconut

Cream margarine, Crisco, and sugar. Add eggs. Then add flour alternately with milk. Add vanilla, butter flavoring, and almond flavoring. Fold in coconut. Bake in a greased and floured 10 inch tube pan for about 1½ hours in a 300° oven.

Mrs. S. Britt Owens

RUM CAKE

1 cup Crisco	½ teaspoon soda
2 cups sugar	½ teaspoon baking powder
4 eggs	½ teaspoon salt
1 cup buttermilk	1 teaspoon vanilla
3 cups flour	2 teaspoons rum extract

Cream together Crisco and sugar. Add eggs one at a time, beating after each addition. Add soda, baking powder and salt to flour. Sift. Add flour alternately with milk to creamed mixture. Add vanilla and rum extract. Bake in a well greased and floured 10 inch tube or bundt pan. Bake for 1 hour in a 350° oven. Let stand 10 minutes before removing from pan. While cake is still warm put the following sauce on.

Heat over medium heat until the sugar is melted. Pour over cake.

Sauce:

¼ cup rum	½ cup sugar
½ cup butter	½ teaspoon vanilla

Marvelous with good orange sherbert — especially if you can get the sherbert with bits of peel scattered through, from your local ice cream or specialty shop. Since the cake freezes well, keep one and some sherbert in your freezer for an easy company dessert.

Mrs. W. H. Tankersley

APRICOT BRANDY CAKE

3 cups sugar
1 cup butter or margarine
6 eggs
3 cups flour
¼ teaspoon baking soda
½ teaspoon salt
1 cup sour cream

1 teaspoon rum flavoring
1 teaspoon orange extract
¼ teaspoon almond extract
½ teaspoon lemon extract
1 teaspoon vanilla
½ cup Apricot Brandy

Grease and flour 10 inch tube pan. Preheat oven to 325°. Cream butter and sugar. Add eggs, one at a time beating thoroughly after each addition. Sift together flour, baking soda and salt. Combine sour cream, flavorings and brandy. Add flour and sour cream mixture alternately to the sugar mixture. Mix just until blended. Pour into prepared tube pan. Bake about 70 minutes.

A sour cream pound cake of sorts with the most unusual flavor — a combination of several flavorings and Apricot brandy. Peach brandy could be used.

Mrs. Arnold Rankin

PRUNE CAKE

1½ cups sugar
1 cup oil
3 eggs
2 cups flour
1 teaspoon soda
1 teaspoon cinnamon
1 teaspoon nutmeg

1 teaspoon allspice
½ teaspoon salt
1 cup buttermilk
1 cup chopped cooked prunes
1 cup chopped pecans
1 teaspoon vanilla

Blend the sugar and oil. Add eggs. Add dry ingredients alternately with the milk. Add nuts, prunes and vanilla. Pour into greased 9 x 13 x 2 pan and bake in 350° oven for 40 minutes. Frost while hot.

Frosting:

½ cup sugar
1 teaspoon corn syrup
½ teaspoon soda

½ cup buttermilk
1 teaspoon vanilla
¼ cup butter

Mix all ingredients together and boil until it forms a soft ball. Do not beat. Pour over hot cake.

Here, a grand recipe for the traditional heavy prune cake topped with buttermilk frosting — good warm or cold. It keeps for days and gets better every day. Try it for breakfast. For variation use raisins instead of prunes.

Mrs. Dales A. Crites
Lakewood, Colorado

MONTEVALLO PRUNE CAKE AND ICING

1 cup butter or margarine
1 cup sugar
3 eggs, separated
½ teaspoon cinnamon
½ teaspoon cloves
1 teaspoon soda
2 cups flour

1 teaspoon baking powder
½ teaspoon salt
½ cup buttermilk
1 cup chopped prunes (cooked
  tender)
½ cup chopped pecans

Cream butter and sugar. Add egg yolks. Then add the sifted dry ingredients alternately with the buttermilk, beginning and ending with flour. Fold in beaten egg whites, then prunes and pecans. Bake in two 8" pans at 325° about 25 minutes. After it has cooked 20 minutes, watch to see that it doesn't over-cook. Remove when it pulls away from the sides of the pans slightly, and toothpick comes out clean when inserted.

Icing:

1 tablespoon grated orange rind
4 tablespoons orange juice
1 tablespoon lemon juice
1 teaspoon grated lemon rind

3 tablespoons butter or margarine
1 egg yolk (unbeaten)
¼ teaspoon salt
3 cups confectioners' sugar

Combine the grated rinds and the juice of both orange and lemon. Let stand while you mix the butter, egg yolk and salt. Add sugar alternately with juice mixture until smooth. Spread between layers and on top and side of cake.

Not at all what we usually think of as prune cake. The Montevallo version is a tender, light layer cake iced with citrus flavored icing. We can't think of enough nice things to say about it.

Mrs. Ed Phillips

WHITE LAYER CAKE
(Using Buttermilk)

1 cup shortening (half Crisco—
  half margarine or butter)
2 cups sugar
3 cups sifted cake flour
2 rounded teaspoons baking
  powder

1 cup buttermilk
1/8 teaspoon soda
5 egg whites
Pinch of salt
1 teaspoon vanilla or mixed
  fruit flavors

Pre-heat oven to 350°. Have ingredients at room temperature. Cream shortening and 1¾ cups sugar. Sift flour and baking powder together two or three times. Add flour and baking powder alternately with buttermilk. (Soda should be stirred into buttermilk before adding).

278

Beat until well blended and smooth. Add pinch of salt to egg whites and beat until almost stiff. Sprinkle in remaining ¼ cup of sugar and continue to beat until stiff. Fold gently into batter; add vanilla and blend. Bake in three 8" or two 9" greased and floured layer pans. Bake at 350° 25 to 30 minutes.

Mrs. William A. Sims

BLACK TIE CHOCOLATE CAKE

1 dark chocolate or fudge cake mix
4 eggs
½ cup Crisco oil
1 small package instant chocolate pudding mix

¾ cup plus 2 tablespoons water
1 small package semi-sweet chocolate morsels
¼ cup rum

Preheat oven to 350°. Prepare 10 inch tube cake pan by oiling lightly and lining bottom with wax paper. Empty chocolate morsels into small, deep bowl and pour the rum over them. Let soak, stirring occasionally, while you mix the cake batter. Mix all other ingredients in large bowl and beat for four minutes on medium speed. Blend in rum and chocolate mixture on low speed. Pour into pan and bake 60 minutes.

Serve with homemade vanilla ice cream or chantilly cream. For a butterscotch variation, use yellow cake mix, butterscotch pudding, butterscotch morsels and follow the same method.

Mrs. Herbert Street

CHOCOLATE ANGEL CAKE

Use any angel cake recipe (a mix is good). Add 1 tablespoon instant coffee and ¼ cup regular cocoa to flour mixture. Add one extra tablespoon water to egg whites.

Frosting:

6 ounces semi-sweet chocolate bits
½ pound or 16 marshmallows

½ cup milk
1 cup whipping cream (whipped)

Mix chocolate, marshmallows and milk. Place over medium heat in top of double boiler. Stir until blended. Chill. Fold in the whipped cream. Cut the cake in three layers across; frost between layers and then entire cake.

A light and elegant dessert that is easy to make. It's even better if you double the frosting recipe.

Mrs. George Hansberry

279

CHOCOLATE CRUNCH CAKE

1 package devil's food cake mix   ½ cup chopped pecans
1 6-ounce package chocolate chips   ¼ cup melted butter or margarine
1 cup graham cracker crumbs

Prepare cake mix according to package directions. Pour into two well greased and floured 9" round cake pans. Mix the other ingredients — chocolate chips, crumbs, nuts and butter together and sprinkle over cake batter. Bake at 350° for 30-35 minutes. Cool in pan for 15 minutes, remove and cool on rack, crunch side up. Ice between layers and top with 1 cup cream whipped with 4 tablespoons sugar. Or you may leave cake plain, and simply cut in wedges and serve with vanilla ice cream.

Mrs. William E. Shinn, Jr.

QUICK AND EASY STRAWBERRY CAKE

1 box Betty Crocker White Cake   1 cup frozen sliced
  mix   strawberries
1 3-ounce package strawberry   4 eggs
  gelatin   2/3 cup Wesson oil

Let strawberries thaw and then mash. Mix gelatin with cake mix, and add strawberries and juice from berries. Add eggs and oil. Pour into three greased and floured 8 inch layer pans. Bake at 350° for 25 minutes.

Icing:

1 box confectioners' sugar   ½ cup margarine
½ cup strawberries

Let margarine soften, and then add sugar and strawberries. Frost cake.

Put together a few convenience items — a mix, strawberry gelatin and frozen strawberries — and discover a moist, rich cake you'll make again and again. The same recipe makes pretty little cupcakes too.

Mrs. Lloyd Nix

REFRIGERATOR COCONUT CAKE

1 box Duncan Hines Yellow   3 tablespoons Wesson oil
  Cake mix

Mix according to directions, add Wesson oil and bake in three 8" pans. Cool and use the following icing.

Icing:

2 packages frozen coconut (6 or   1 carton sour cream
  9 ounces) thawed   1 teaspoon vanilla
1 cup sugar   ½ teaspoon salt

Mix thoroughly and ice cake. Keep in refrigerator.

There is probably no cake that is as delicious or popular as a fresh coconut cake. There is no cake that is more trouble to make. This is a very quick, very simple coconut cake, so close to the real thing that you may never go through the ordeal of cracking the old nut again!

Mrs. Walter M. Penney

SHERRY CAKE

1 box yellow cake mix
1 box instant Jello vanilla pudding

¾ cup Wesson oil
¼ cup plain sherry
5 eggs

Beat first four ingredients in electric mixer on medium speed for three minutes. Add eggs one at a time, beating after each. Pour into greased 10 inch tube pan. Bake at 350° on middle shelf for 40 minutes. Add ½ of the topping to cake while hot. Then let cool 15 minutes. Turn cake on to plate and spoon on remaining topping.

Topping:
¾ cup confectioners' sugar
Mix well, do not cook.

½ cup sherry

Perfect for a galloping gourmet — or even a tired mother.

Mrs. John A. Caddell

STRAWBERRY CAKE

½ cup bourbon
1 stick cinnamon
1 box Pillsbury Yellow cake mix
1 jar Smuckers strawberry jelly

1½ cartons whipping cream (whipped)
2 cartons (16 ounce cartons) strawberries sliced

Soak for one week or more the whiskey and cinnamon.
Bake yellow cake as directed. Bake in two round cake pans. Cut each of these layers with a strong thread, so that you have four layers. Spread a thin layer of jelly over each, and then spread with frozen sliced strawberries and half of the whipped cream. Chill over night. Next day ice cake with remaining whipped cream to which the cinnamon-bourbon mixture has been added to taste.

"Fabulous" was the word we heard most often when this cake was served. Can you imagine anything any more beautiful? Unlike most mix cakes, this is not a spur of the moment dessert, since you must soak the bourbon and cinnamon stick for at least a week. You could make it on a day's notice though, if you are prudent enough to keep some bourbon and cinnamon soaking at all times.

Mrs. William Eyster

CHEESE CAKE

Crust: Mix the following ingredients and put in the bottom of a spring form pan which has been greased and floured:

6 tablespoons margarine	1 egg
1 cup flour	1 scant teaspoon baking powder
½ cup sugar	½ teaspoon vanilla

Filling:

3 8-ounce packages cream cheese	1 teaspoon vanilla
4 eggs	1 ounce lemon juice
1 cup sugar	

Beat together cream cheese, eggs, sugar, vanilla and lemon juice. Pour into crust. Bake for 1 hour at 325°. Remove, cool and spread 1 can blueberry pie filling on top if desired and refrigerate.

Cranberry Topping (optional, may be used in place of blueberry pie filling):

2 cups fresh or frozen whole cranberries	1 cup sugar
¾ cup water	1½ teaspoons unflavored gelatin
	2 tablespoons water

In a saucepan combine the cranberries, water and sugar. Cook mixture 5 minutes or until skins pop on cranberries, stirring occasionally. Meanwhile, soften the gelatin in water, then stir it into the hot cranberries until dissolved. Refrigerate until it just begins to thicken. Pour over cooled cheesecake and refrigerate.

Cookie crust adds to flavor of this superb cheesecake. Optional topping of cranberries makes a pretty Christmas dessert.

Mrs. Jim L. Thompson, Jr.

PETITE ORANGE CUPCAKES

Cupcakes:

½ cup shortening	¼ teaspoon salt
1 cup sugar	2/3 cup buttermilk
2 eggs, beaten	2 cups flour
	1 teaspoon soda

Cream shortening and sugar. Add eggs one at a time and beat after each addition. Add sifted dry ingredients, alternating with buttermilk. Fill greased petite cupcake pans (do not line) with about 1 teaspoon batter. Bake at 375° about 12 minutes. Makes about 60.

Sauce:

Juice of 3 oranges	1 cup sugar
Grated rind of one orange	

Combine and heat only until sugar is dissolved. When cupcakes are removed from oven, immediately pour 1 teaspoon sauce on each cake. Allow to cool in pan.

Mrs. John R. Guice

CHOCOLATE REFRIGERATOR CUPCAKES

½ cup margarine
1½ blocks bitter chocolate
1 cup sugar
2/3 cup flour, unsifted

1 teaspoon vanilla
2 eggs, well beaten
1 cup nuts, cut

Melt 1½ blocks chocolate and margarine together in double boiler. Mix other cupcake ingredients and add chocolate-margarine mixture. Put into party-size paper cups in muffin tins, half full. Cook 12 minutes at 350°. Caution: they may not look done; but do not over-cook!

Frosting:
2 tablespoons margarine
1 block bitter chocolate

¾ box confectioners' sugar
Cold coffee

While cupcakes bake, melt margarine and chocolate. Gradually add confectioners' sugar and enough cold coffee to make mixture smooth. Thickly ice cupcakes while still hot. Refrigerate.

Mrs. John R. Taylor

CARAMEL ICING

3 cups granulated sugar
1 tablespoon flour

1 cup milk
¾ cup margarine

In deep vessel put 2½ cups sugar and one tablespoon flour. Mix well and add 1 cup milk. In iron skillet put ½ cup white sugar. Start both at same time on high. When milk and sugar mixture comes to a boil add melted and slightly browned ½ cup of sugar from skillet. (It will boil up so be careful.) Stir until all of browned sugar is mixed in well. Turn down to medium heat and put candy thermometer in. Cook until it registers slightly below soft ball. Remove from heat. Add margarine and stir until mixed in well. Can be put in cold water while stirring in margarine. After margarine is in, either continue beating in cold water or let rest until cool and then beat with mixer. Usually it changes color slightly, loses shine and is getting firm when ready to put on cake. It may take quite a while after it has been well beaten to get firm enough. If it gets too hard or grainy it has been cooked too long.

Real caramel icing — burnt sugar and lots of butter. Two or three tender yellow layers put together and covered with this delight is heaven.

Mrs. Gil Crane

CARAMEL ICING (MOCK)

½ cup butter
1 cup brown sugar

¼ cup milk
1 box confectioners' sugar

Cook butter and sugar together until well blended. Add ¼ cup milk and one box of confectioners' sugar. Mix and add just enough milk to spread.

Mrs. Robert Harris

FUDGE ICING (COOKED)

2 cups sugar
¼ teaspoon salt
½ cup milk
¼ cup white Karo

2 1-ounce squares unsweetened chocolate
½ cup shortening or margarine

Stir ingredients together. Cook over low heat until chocolate and margarine melt. Bring to a rapid boil (one you cannot stir down). Boil exactly one minute. Set aside to cool. Beat until mixture loses its gloss If too stiff, add a few drops of cream. If too thin, add sifted confectioners' sugar.

Guaranteed not to fail — ever — and without a candy thermometer to boot! You'll never use an uncooked icing again.

Mrs. Norman Self

WHITE ICING

2½ cups sugar
½ cup water
5 tablespoons white Karo syrup

Pinch salt
2 egg whites
1 teaspoon vanilla flavoring

Cook sugar, water, syrup and salt on high heat, stirring for the first three minutes. After the first three minutes, cook without stirring until syrup will spin an 8-10" thread (242° with candy thermometer). In mixer beat the egg whites until stiff. Slowly add the syrup while beating on high speed. Add vanilla flavoring and continue beating until of spreading consistency. Will frost a three layer cake.

This may also be used for divinity candy, adding pecans and dropping by spoonfuls on wax paper.

Mrs. William A. Sims

Brown Sugar Frosting

Use 1¼ cups brown sugar and 1¼ cups white sugar in the above recipe. This frosting is particularly good when chopped nut meats or toasted coconut shreds are sprinkled over it.

SEVEN MINUTE FROSTING

2 egg whites
1½ cups sugar
Pinch salt
½ cup water

2 teaspoons light corn syrup
1 teaspoon vanilla

Place egg whites, salt, sugar, corn syrup, and water in the top of a double boiler and mix well.

Beat mixture with rotary beater for about 7 minutes until it holds in peaks. Remove from the boiling water, add flavoring, and beat until the frosting is cool and will stand in firm peaks. This takes about another 6 minutes.

This frosting is very creamy, fluffy, and swirls easily. Use it for frosting fresh coconut cakes or Devil's Food.

Orange Frosting

Use the above recipe replacing the water with frozen concentrated orange juice and the vanilla with the grated rind of ½ lemon.

Mrs. George W. Hansberry

LEMON CHEESE FILLING

6 egg yolks	Grated rind of three lemons
1½ cups sugar	6 tablespoons lemon juice
3½ tablespoons flour	1/3 cup butter

Beat egg yolks. Mix sugar and flour. Add to egg yolks. Add other ingredients. Cook in double boiler until it coats a wooden spoon.

Mrs. George McCrary

PIES

PASTRY

2/3 cup Crisco or Snowdrift	1 teaspoon salt
2 cups plain flour	¼ cup cold water

Sift flour and salt. Cut shortening into flour until like coarse corn meal. Make four or five holes in flour and pour in water. Mix very quickly with fork. Let dough chill thirty minutes in refrigerator before rolling out. Yield: two 9-inch pie crusts. Bake as recipe directs.

Pastry tips:

1. Always try to refrigerate dough at least ½ hour before rolling out.
2. A pastry cloth and a stockinet-covered rolling pin makes handling dough easier. On lightly floured surface, place ball of pastry and gently flatten.
3. Then roll lightly from **center** out to edges in all directions, forming a circle about 1½ inches wider than inverted 8" or 9" pie plate.
4. Be sure to lift rolling pin near edge of circle, to keep edge from splitting or getting thin. If edge splits, pinch cracks together. If pastry sticks, loosen gently with spatula; then lift and lightly flour surface again.
5. Roll pastry around rolling pin. Lift onto ungreased pie plate and gently unroll. If the pastry needs centering more, shake the pie plate so the pastry will slide over. Do **not** pull or stretch. Use bent right index finger to fit pastry gently into plate. (Be sure there are no cracks or holes for juices to seep through.) Trim pastry 1-inch beyond edge of plate. Fold overhang under: turn pastry up to make stand-up rim. Firmly place right index finger on inside of pastry rim; with left thumb and index finger, pinch pastry at that point. Repeat every ¼-inch.

Mrs. Lindsay A. Allen

TWO-CRUST PASTRY

2 cups flour
1 teaspoon salt

2/3 cup Snowdrift
1/3 cup milk

Sift flour and salt. Cut in shortening. Then add milk. Mix well with fork. Chill before rolling out. Yield: two 9-inch pie crusts.

Baked pie shell: With 4-tined fork, prick close and deep on bottom side. Bake at 450°, 12 to 15 minutes or until golden. Peek after 5 minutes: if bubbles appear prick again. Cool before filling.

CANADIAN PASTRY

5 cups flour
1 teaspoon salt
2 teaspoons confectioners' sugar
1 teaspoon baking powder

Mix these ingredients together and cut in 1 pound lard
Beat 1 egg in a cup: add 2 teaspoons vinegar then fill cup with cold water.

Blend all the above together lightly; then gather up into a ball and roll. Makes dozens of tart shells or 6 or more pie crusts. The use of **pure** lard is the secret to this recipe. Other shortenings will **not** do.

Mrs. George L. McCrary, Jr.

INDIVIDUAL MERINGUE CRUSTS

4 egg whites (room temperature)
¼ teaspoon cream of tartar

¼ teaspoon salt
1 cup granulated sugar

1. In large bowl of electric mixer, let egg whites warm to room temperature: 1 hour.

2. At high speed, beat egg whites with cream of tartar and salt just until very soft peaks form when beaters are slowly raised.

3. Gradually beat in sugar, 2 tablespoons at a time, beating well after each addition. Continue beating until very stiff peaks form. Meringue should be shiny and moist. Preheat oven to 275 degrees.

4. On heavy brown wrapping paper, placed on large cookie sheets, spoon heaping tablespoons of meringue to form 8 mounds, 3 inches apart. With back of spoon, shape the center of each mound into shell. Bake 60 minutes or until light brown and crisp. Turn off heat and open oven door. Let cool. To store meringues: Wrap cooled meringues in waxed paper. Store in cool dry place.

Meringues have a myriad of uses. Serve with vanilla ice cream topped with sweetened fresh strawberries or peaches. Fill with chocolate filling or lemon cheese filling and top with whipped cream. For a special fillip, sprinkle toasted pecans or almonds over whipped cream. The variations are endless — peach ice cream with frozen raspberries spooned over —

any fresh or frozen berry with a soft lemon custard poured over. Let your imagination go, and you'll want to have meringues handy at all times. To add crunch and flavor to the meringues, fold in (don't beat in) ¾ cup to 1 cup broken pecans to meringue before baking.

Mrs. Lindsay A. Allen

FROZEN CHEESECAKE PIE

3 packages (3 ounces) cream
   cheese softened
1 cup sugar
3 eggs separated
½ pint heavy cream, chilled
   and whipped

1 teaspoon vanilla
Pinch of salt
About 1¼ cups graham cracker
   crumbs. Reserve two tablespoons
   of crumbs for top of pie.

Soften cheese to room temperature and cream it well. Add sugar and mix thoroughly. Beat egg yolks and add to sugar and cheese. Stir into this mixture the **whipped** cream, vanilla, and salt. Beat egg whites until stiff and fold into mixture. Line bottom of ice trays, pie pan, or cake tin with crumbs. Spoon the mixture into tray or pan. Cover top with a few crumbs. Freeze at least 4 hours. This may be made at least two days before and not lose its flavor.

A rich frozen version of cheesecake. Serve it as is or with any fruit topping you wish. To vary the flavor, a small can of drained, crushed pineapple may be added to the pie mixture before freezing.

Mrs. R. W. Orr, Jr.

CHOCOLATE ICE CREAM PIE

CRUST

½ cup margarine
¼ cup packed brown sugar
1 cup sifted flour
½ cup chopped pecans

FILLING

1 pint vanilla ice cream
1 cup milk
1 package instant chocolate
   pudding

Crust: Mix margarine and sugar. Add flour and nuts. Spread thinly on cookie sheet. Cook for 10 to 15 minutes at 400°, stirring occasionally. Remove from oven and immediately break with fork into crumbs. Set aside ¾ cup of crumbs for topping. Press remainder of crumbs into a greased 9" or 10" pie plate.

Filling: Break up ice cream with electric mixer. Add milk and pudding. Mix until blended. Pour into crust and top with the ¾ cup crumbs set aside. Refrigerate till firm. This is as good or better the day after it is made.

An easy chocolate pie, made with ice cream, in a wonderfully crunchy pecan filled crust (which, happily, you don't have to roll out). Children beg for more. Polite guests would like to.

Mrs. C. W. Belt

COCONUT ICE CREAM PIE

1 pint vanilla ice cream
1 cup whole milk
1 package coconut Jello instant
    pudding mix

Baked pie shell
½ pint heavy cream, sweetened
    and whipped
Toasted coconut

Soften ice cream with milk. Add pudding mix and blend well. Pour into baked pie shell. Chill in refrigerator. Before serving spread cream that has been whipped and sweetened on top and sprinkle generously with toasted coconut. Keep in freezer!

A good "made the day ahead" pie.

Mrs. James R. Fite

CHOCOLATE BLENDER PIE

1 cup sugar
3 tablespoons cocoa
2 tablespoons corn starch
¼ cup of butter or margarine
1 cup milk
Pinch of salt
3 egg yolks

1 teaspoon vanilla
MERINGUE
3 egg whites
1 tablespoon cold water
Pinch of salt
3 tablespoons sugar

Put half of milk in blender. Put rest of ingredients **except** vanilla in blender; add the other half cup of milk. Blend well. While blending let a heavy skillet warm over medium heat. Pour into skillet and start stirring constantly. Let come to a boil. Take from heat, add vanilla and pour into 8" or 9" cooked pie shell.

Meringue: Before beating whites add salt and 1 tablespoon **cold** water. Start beating. Add sugar gradually. Beat until stiff. Spread on cooled pie. Brown at 375°, 10 to 12 minutes. **Chill before serving.**

An old fashioned chocolate meringue pie made by a new-fangled method. Blender mixing the ingredients assures a smooth filling with not a single lump. We guarantee a marvelous taste.

Mrs. David E. Bowers

CHOCOLATE PIE

1½ cups sugar
3 tablespoons cocoa
3 tablespoons flour
1½ cups milk
3 egg yolks
4 tablespoons butter
1 teaspoon vanilla

1 unbaked pie shell
MERINGUE
3 egg whites
6 tablespoons sugar
½ teaspoon vanilla
¼ teaspoon cream of tartar

288

Sift together sugar, cocoa and flour, removing all lumps. Beat egg yolks into milk until smooth. Add enough milk to dry ingredients to make a thick paste, stirring until mixture is smooth and free of all lumps. Add remaining milk and cook over medium high heat until mixture comes to a rolling boil. Remove from heat and add butter and vanilla and stir until butter melts. Pour into an **unbaked** pie shell and bake at 350° until pie shell is browned. (Pie custard cooks further during oven baking.) While pie is cooking, make meringue as follows: Beat egg whites until foamy, continue beating and slowly add sugar, 2 tablespoons at a time. Add cream of tartar and vanilla and beat egg whites until they stand in peaks, but not until dry. Place on top of pie and brown.

Another excellent recipe for the all time pie favorite. The chocolate filling and crust bake together.

Mrs. L. Denton Cole

PEANUT BUTTER PIE

1 baked 9" pastry shell
1/3 cup peanut butter

¾ cup sifted confectioners' sugar

Blend peanut butter with confectioners' sugar until mealy. Sprinkle mixture over baked pie shell.

1/3 cup all-purpose flour
½ cup sugar
⅛ teaspoon salt
2 cups milk, scalded

3 egg yolks, slightly beaten
2 tablespoons butter or margarine
1 teaspoon vanilla

Combine flour, ½ cup sugar and salt in the top of a double boiler. Stir in scalded milk. Cook over boiling water, stirring constantly, until thickened. Stir a small amount of cooked filling into the egg yolks. Combine with remaining hot mixture and cook several minutes longer. Add butter or margarine, and vanilla. Pour into pie shell. Top with meringue.

Meringue:

3 egg whites
¼ teaspoon cream of tartar

½ cup sugar
1 teaspoon cornstarch

Beat egg whites until stiff, add cream of tartar. Gradually add sugar mixed with cornstarch. Beat until stiff and shiny. Pile on pie and bake. Cool pie before serving.

One of Cotton Country's most popular pies — with young and old alike — is peanut butter pie. Made with ingredients every mother has on hand, this is an exceptionally good version with a beautiful meringue.

Mrs. John E. Wilks, Jr.

MARY LEE'S LEMON PIE OR TARTS

1 cup sugar
2 heaping tablespoons corn starch
Pinch of salt
1¼ cups warm water
Juice of one lemon

1 grated lemon rind
3 eggs, separated
2 tablespoons butter
1 8-inch baked pie shell or
 tart shells

Mix sugar, corn starch and salt together well. Add water, a little at a time. Then add lemon juice and rind. When mixture is well mixed cook in top of a double boiler over boiling water, stirring until mixture thickens. Add a little of the hot mixture to the egg yolks that have been well beaten, then gradually stir yolks into hot mixture. Cook about 10 minutes longer, stirring constantly. Add butter. Cool. Pour into 8 inch baked pie shell or tart shells. Beat egg whites until stiff, gradually beating ¼ cup sugar into them. Spread meringue over pie and bake in a slow oven, 250 degrees, until delicately browned.

An old favorite.

Mrs. Lindsey Allen

SOUTHERN PIE

½ cup butter
1 cup sugar
2 eggs, separated

1 tablespoon vinegar
1 cup chopped nuts
1 cup chopped dates or raisins

Cream butter and sugar. Add egg yolks, vinegar, nuts, and dates. Fold in stiffly beaten egg whites. Bake in an unbaked pie crust for 45 minutes in 350° oven.

This was a famous pie on the menu of a small hotel dining room in the South for over 30 years. The hotel was acclaimed for its excellent food.

Mrs. Charles B. Howell

PECAN PIE

Cotton Country is also pecan country, and pecan pie is probably served more often in this area than any other pie. There is no easier pie to make — nor is there a richer, more fattening one.

1 cup of broken pecans
3 eggs
½ cup of butter or margarine
¼ cup white sugar

1 cup brown sugar
1 cup dark Karo syrup
1 teaspoon vanilla
Pinch of salt

Break up 1 cup of pecans and sprinkle on bottom of unbaked pie crust. Melt butter. Mix eggs, butter, sugars, syrup, vanilla and salt together well. Then pour into pie shell. Bake at 325° for 1 hour, until almost set.

Mrs. Charles Eyster, Jr.

GOLDEN PECAN PIE

1 cup Golden Eagle syrup
½ cup sugar
3 tablespoons butter

3 eggs, beaten
1 teaspoon vanilla
1 cup pecan pieces

Mix syrup, sugar, and butter. Cook over medium heat until it strings from a spoon. Have eggs beaten until light (low speed.) Pour the syrup mixture over the eggs slowly. Beat well on low speed. Add vanilla while beating. Pour into pie shell. Sprinkle pecan pieces over top. Bake at 350° until pie crust is done, 30 to 45 minutes. Eggs must be beaten on the lowest speed so they won't fluff. When they fluff it makes the pie brown too fast on top.

A bit more specialized is this version made with Golden Eagle Syrup (no substitutes, please!) You'll make a perfect pie.

Mrs. David E. Bowers

CARAMEL PECAN PIE

1 envelope gelatin
½ pound (28) caramels
¾ cup milk
Dash salt

1 cup whipping cream
½ cup pecans
1 teaspoon vanilla
Prepared graham cracker crust

Soften gelatin in ¼ cup cold water. Melt caramels in milk over simmering water. Add the softened gelatin and salt. Stir to dissolve. Chill until slightly set. Fold in whipped cream, broken pecans and vanilla. Pour filling into crust and trim top with pecan halves. Chill 2 or 3 hours or until firm.

Surprisingly easy — rich with toffee flavor. This would be absolutely delicious with toasted pecans.

Mrs. John Hamilton

PECAN PIE WITH MERINGUE

1 cup sugar
3 egg yolks
1 teaspoon vanilla
½ cup margarine

½ cup evaporated milk
1 9" pie shell, unbaked
1 cup pecan halves
Meringue

Combine sugar, egg yolks, vanilla, margarine and evaporated milk. Mix well and pour into pie shell. Bake at 350° until pie puffs in the middle. Then arrange pecan halves on top. Turn oven to 300° and bake until pie is firm. Allow pie to cool. Top with meringue and brown delicately. Good and different!

Perhaps not quite so rich is this pecan pie with — surprise — meringue on top.

Mrs. M. E. Edwards

CHOCOLATE-PECAN PIE

2/3 cup evaporated milk
2 tablespoons butter
1 package (6 ounce) semi-sweet
  chocolate bits
1 cup sugar
2 eggs

2 tablespoons flour
¼ teaspoon salt
1 cup pecans
2 teaspoons vanilla
1 pie shell, unbaked

Mix milk, butter, and chocolate in double boiler. Heat until chocolate melts. Stir in remaining ingredients, adding vanilla last. Pour into pie shell and bake 35 minutes at 375°.

Chocolate pecan pie that is "easier than pie" to make. Substitute butterscotch bits for the chocolate ones for another tasty treat.

Mrs. Lynn C. Fowler

MRS. RAY KELLY'S COCONUT CREAM PIE

2 cups milk, scalded
3 large egg yolks, well beaten
Sift together:
4 rounded tablespoons flour
Pinch of salt
½ cup sugar

2 tablespoons butter or margarine
1 teaspoon vanilla
1 can flaked coconut
  (Reserve ¼ cup for meringue)
1 9" baked pie shell

Scald milk, using double boiler being careful not to get milk too hot. Pour a small amount of scalded milk into well beaten egg yolks. Then add this milk and egg mixture to the scalded milk. Add dry ingredients. Stir well. Cook until thickened. Remove from heat and add vanilla, butter and coconut. Cool, then pour into baked pie shell.

Meringue: Use 3 to 4 egg whites. Beat egg whites until frothy then add 2 tablespoons sugar to each egg white used. Add a pinch of salt. Beat until stiff. Cover pie, top with reserved coconut, and bake at 425° for 5 minutes. Turn off oven and let cool in oven for 15 minutes with door closed, watching closely. Refrigerate.

There are those who think there is no other pie.

Mrs. Lindsay A. Allen

MRS. GODWIN'S COCONUT PIE

1 6-ounce package frozen coconut
1 1/3 cups milk
1 cup sugar
3 whole eggs

1 tablespoon flour
1 teaspoon vanilla
¼ cup butter, melted

Beat eggs and sugar. Add other ingredients. Pour into unbaked pie crust. Bake at 325° about one hour. Good and easy.

Mrs. George Godwin, Jr.

KENTUCKY COCONUT PIE

1 9" pie shell	½ teaspoon vanilla
2 eggs, beaten	½ teaspoon butter flavoring
1¼ cups sugar	½ cup of milk
1½ tablespoons flour	3½-ounce can flaked coconut
¼ cup melted margarine	

Mix sugar and flour together. Add mixture to beaten eggs. Add the remaining ingredients to the sugar, flour, egg mixture, and mix well. Bake pie shell about 10 minutes at 450°. Put filling in shell, reduce heat to 325°. Cook about 35-40 minutes.

Mrs. Russell Lynne

CHESS PIE

5 egg yolks	2 tablespoons flour
1 cup milk	1 teaspoon vanilla extract
2 cups sugar	2 unbaked pie shells
½ cup butter or margarine	(Tart shells may be used)
2 tablespoons plain corn meal	

Cream butter and sugar. Blend egg yolks and milk. Add all ingredients to butter and sugar mixture. Blend well. Put in two 8-inch uncooked pie crusts. Cook at 375 degrees for 15 minutes, then turn down to 325° and cook about an hour.

Chess pie is one of the oldest of all pies, and we suspect it is the granddaddy of our regional pecan pie.

This old fashioned, delicious version uses egg yolks only. You might freeze the whites for later use in making meringues or divinity. (Egg whites freeze beautifully. Pour into small jar or other container, label as to number of whites and store in freezer. Don't thaw in hot water, though, or they'll cook.)

Mrs. Randolph Pickell

OLD FASHIONED CHESS PIE

1½ cups sugar	3 eggs, beaten
½ cup margarine	5 tablespoons sweet milk
1 tablespoon plain corn meal	1 teaspoon vanilla
1 teaspoon vinegar	Unbaked 9-inch pie shell

Cream butter and sugar. Mix all other ingredients well. Add to first mixture. Pour into pie shell. Bake at 400° in preheated oven for 10 minutes, then turn oven back to 325°. Cook 25 minutes or until set. (To test, insert knife. It comes out clean when done.)

Smooth, easy to make chess pie with whole eggs and milk.

Mrs. Joe D. Burns

LEMON CHESS PIE

2 cups sugar
1 tablespoon flour
1 tablespoon corn meal
4 eggs, lightly beaten
¼ cup melted butter

1 to 4 tablespoons grated lemon
   rind
¼ cup evaporated milk
¼ cup lemon juice
½ teaspoon salt
9" pie shell

Combine sugar, flour, corn meal; toss lightly. Add remaining ingredients in order given. Beat with mixer until smooth. Pour into pie shell. Bake at 375° for 15 minutes. Lower temperature to 300°. Bake 35 to 45 minutes.

Lemon-flavored chess pie, again very rich and a "no-no" for dieters. This one has grated lemon rind in it and a good hearty lemon taste.

Mrs. S. Britt Owens

SPEEDY LEMON CHESS PIE

More delicately lemon flavored, this is marvelous topped with unsweetened whipped cream. Sprinkle with grated lemon rind.

Cream together:
¼ cup margarine
1½ cup sugar
4 eggs, added one at a time

Add:
Juice of 2 lemons (6-8 tablespoons)
1 tablespoon plain corn meal

Pour into one 9" unbaked pie shell. Bake in 300 degree oven for 60 minutes.

Mrs. Robert Hosey

BUTTERMILK PIE

½ cup margarine
1½ cups sugar
3 eggs
½ cup buttermilk

2 tablespoons flour
2 tablespoons vanilla
8" unbaked pie shell

Melt margarine, add sugar and flour; beat. Add eggs, one at a time, buttermilk, vanilla; beat and pour into unbaked pie shell. Bake in 325-350° oven 45 minutes.

The next time you need to feed an army or head for a covered dish supper, double this recipe and fill three 8" bought pie shells. Quick and simple.

Mrs. Jon Moores

EGG CUSTARD PIE

¼ cup butter or margarine
1 cup sugar
Pinch salt
5 eggs

2 cups milk
1 teaspoon vanilla
Nutmeg, if desired

Cream butter, sugar and salt. Beat eggs into mixture and add milk and vanilla. Pour into a 9" partially baked pie shell. Sprinkle with nutmeg. Bake 350° for 25 minutes or until filling is firm. (Be sure to have eggs and milk at room temperature.)

Rich, and delicious.

Mrs. John E. Wilks, Jr.

CANADIAN BUTTER TARTS

1 cup brown sugar, packed firmly
1 egg
3 tablespoons melted butter

1 teaspoon vanilla
2 tablespoons sweetened
  condensed milk
Dash of salt

Mix well, until frothy. Fill unbaked tart shells 2/3 full and bake at 350° about 25 minutes or until done. Yield: 6 tarts. Chopped nuts may be added if desired.

Sometimes known as brown sugar tarts, these bring back pleasant memories of days gone by. Brown sugar tarts a la mode were always a special treat — and still are!

Mrs. George McCrary, Jr.

JAPANESE FRUIT PIE

2 unbaked pie shells
  Mix together:
2 cups sugar
1 cup margarine, melted
1 cup coconut
1 cup pecans

2 teaspoons vanilla
  Add:
4 beaten eggs
Topping: ½ pint heavy cream,
  whipped

After mixing the ingredients together place in 2 pastry shells and bake in 300° oven for 50-55 minutes. Top with heavy cream, whipped.

This pie should be outlawed — but we won't. We just beg you to serve very small pieces, with unsweetened whipped cream.

Mrs. Robert Hosey

SOUR CREAM PIE

3 egg yolks
½ pint sour cream
1 tablespoon flour
1 cup sugar
⅛ teaspoon cinnamon

⅛ teaspoon allspice
½ cup raisins
½ cup pecans
Pinch salt
Cooked pie shell

Combine all ingredients and cook until thick. Put into cooked pie pastry. **Meringue:** Use the 3 egg whites beaten with 3 tablespoons sugar and pinch of salt for top of pie. Brown in oven.

Mrs. John C. Bragg

MYSTERY APPLE PIE (no butter)

1 10" unbaked pie crust
11 cups pared Winesap apples
    (about 9 medium sized apples)
2 cups sugar
4 tablespoons flour

1 teaspoon salt
1/3 cup of half and half cream
¼ cup milk
¼ teaspoon cinnamon

Place apples in **deep** 10 inch pie plate or souffle dish on unbaked crust. Thoroughly combine sugar, flour, salt; add cream, milk; beat. Cover apples with mixture. Sprinkle with cinnamon. Bake at 375 degrees for 1½ to 2 hours or until apples are soft. (Cover pie loosely with foil and cover oven rack with foil to catch drippings.)

Serve with wedges of Cheddar cheese or scoops of vanilla ice cream. A real man pleaser!

Mrs. John R. Taylor

DUTCH APPLE PIE

A beautiful pie that is as good as it is pretty. If you are in a hurry, stop now. This one takes time — to cut and arrange the apple slices. Particularly suited to those of you who are perfectionists at heart.

Rich pie crust
5 pounds tart apples
1 cup sugar
2 tablespoons cornstarch

1 tablespoon flour
1 cup milk or thin cream
Butter
Cinnamon

Line 10" pie tin with rich pie crust. Core, pare, and cut apples in ¼ inch wedges, and lay them in crust, overlapping flowerlike. Mix sugar, cornstarch and flour, sift over apples. Pour milk or cream over apples, dot with butter, sprinkle with cinnamon. Bake at 400° for 15 minutes, then 350° for 35 minutes. Best when served warm.

Mrs. John D. Sherrill

PEACH PIE

3 cups sliced fresh peaches
1 cup sugar
2 eggs
¼ teaspoon salt
Butter

½ of 10-ounce package pie crust
   mix or ½ recipe pastry
1½ cups milk

Slice peaches and put in oblong pan. Dot with butter. Beat eggs until light and fluffy, add sugar, milk and beat well. Pour over peaches. Make pie crust as directed. Roll thin. Cut strips and top peaches in lattice fashion. Bake in 350 degree oven till golden brown — about 30 minutes.

In our part of the country, in midsummer, when fresh peaches are so plentiful, what could be better?

Mrs. W. Blanton McBride

MY MOTHER'S PEACH CUSTARD PIE

2 tablespoons flour
1 cup sugar
2 eggs
3 tablespoons lemon juice

½ teaspoon vanilla
3 or 4 tablespoons butter
3 or 4 fresh peaches
1 9" pie crust, unbaked

Make pie crust according to your favorite recipe and arrange in a 9" pie plate. Peel peaches and cut each in half. Place halves cut-side up in unbaked crust. Mix all remaining ingredients and pour over peaches. Bake 1 hour at 350°.

An unusual pie: fresh peach halves, custard, and pie crust all baked together.

Mrs. John R. Taylor

FRESH PEACH PIE

For peach devotees, who prefer their fruit au natural, but want a dressier dessert than a peach with the fuzz still on, this pie is the perfect answer.

3 tablespoons cornstarch
4 tablespoons peach flavored
   gelatin

1 cup water
1 cup sugar
1 baked pie crust

Bring all the above to a rolling boil. Set aside to cool. Cut up about 3 large peaches. Add a few drops lemon juice and a little sugar. Add to cooled gelatin mixture. Pour into baked pie crust. Cover with Dream Whip or whipped cream. Refrigerate. This is like the fresh strawberry pie.

Mrs. John E. Wilks, Jr.

STRAWBERRY PIE

Fresh strawberries
1 baked 8" or 9" pie crust
1 cup sugar
1 cup water
3 tablespoons corn starch

Pinch of salt
4 tablespoons strawberry flavored
  gelatin
1 pint heavy cream, whipped

Mix sugar, water, cornstarch and salt and cook until thick — about 5 minutes. Remove from heat and add 4 tablespoons strawberry gelatin. Put as many berries as you like in pie crust and pour mixture over berries in pie. Top with whipped cream.

We flatly state that there is no prettier nor more delicious pie!

Mrs. Robert H. Harris

BLUEBERRY-BANANA PIE

2 envelopes Dream Whip
1 8-ounce package cream cheese
Juice of 1 lemon
1 cup sugar

2 large bananas
1 can blueberry pie filling
2 9" baked pie shells

Beat 2 envelopes of Dream Whip, according to directions on package. Cream together cream cheese, juice of lemon, and 1 cup sugar. Mix creamed mixture with Dream Whip. In baked pie shells put layer of bananas, then mixture of Dream Whip, cream cheese, lemon juice, and sugar. Top with blueberry pie filling. Refrigerate until served. Yield: 12 servings.

Mrs. William S. Coles

BLUEBERRY CREAM CHEESE PIE

Filling:
3 ounce package cream cheese
  (room temperature)
1¼ cups powdered sugar
1 package Dream Whip
Crust:
1¼ cups graham cracker crumbs
¼ cup margarine, melted

½ cup pecans, finely chopped
¼ cup granulated sugar
Topping:
½ can blueberries
1 tablespoon granulated sugar
1 tablespoon cornstarch
1 teaspoon fresh lemon juice
Pinch of salt

Crust: Combine graham cracker crumbs, pecans, and ¼ cup granulated sugar. To this, add the melted margarine. Mix well, press into 8" or 9" pie plate, and bake in 325° oven until golden brown or until nuts look well toasted, about 10 to 15 minutes. Set aside to cool. (This crust may be made in advance and refrigerated.)

Filling: Mix Dream Whip according to directions on package and set aside. Mix cream cheese and powdered sugar until well blended and fluffy. To this mixture add the prepared Dream Whip and blend until smooth. Pour into cooled pie crust and refrigerate.

Topping: Drain juice from berries, saving both juice and berries. Blend cornstarch with a small amount of the juice, gradually adding the balance and 1 tablespoon granulated sugar. Heat slowly until thick, stirring constantly. Add lemon juice, pinch of salt, and blueberries. Allow to cool thoroughly, stirring along, before pouring over pie filling. Refrigerate.

It is just as easy to make two pies at one time by doubling the recipe, using a full can of blueberries and an 8 ounce package cream cheese.

If you wish the pie to look prettier, push up a little ridge of the cream cheese filling around the edge of the pastry leaving the pie at a slightly lower level the balance of the way. Then pour the blueberry topping into the lower portion, leaving the white rim just inside the pastry edge.

Mrs. James E. Brown

BOURBON COUNTY MINCE PIE

1 9" frozen unbaked pie shell
1 28 ounce jar prepared
  mincemeat
½ cup broken walnuts

½ cup broken pecans
¼ cup Bourbon
1 tablespoon orange juice
1 tablespoon lemon juice

Preheat oven to 400°. In a large bowl mix mincemeat, nuts, Bourbon and juices. Spread evenly in pie shell. Bake 30 minutes. To serve: Heat 2 tablespoons Bourbon in a ladle, flame and pour over center of pie. Serve flaming. Serves 6.

A gastronomical and conversational delight!

Mrs. Frank Troup

PUMPKIN PIE

3 large 9" pie shells
    or
4 small pie shells
6 eggs
2½ cups sugar
3½ cups pumpkin (canned)

1 teaspoon salt
3 teaspoons cinnamon
2 teaspoons ginger
1 teaspoon allspice
¼ teaspoon ground cloves
3½ cups milk

Mix all ingredients in blender or mixer, adding milk last. Pour into unbaked pie shells. Bake at 325° for one hour.

Grandmother had to wait until "the frost was on the pumpkin," so this was saved for Thanksgiving or Christmas fare. Grandmother also had to go to a great deal of trouble to make pumpkin pie. With readily available canned pumpkin, and this simple blender method, however, you can serve it any time you please, and with a minimum of effort. Still, pumpkin pie does seem most appropriate for the winter months.

Mrs. Fred Sittason, Jr.

SWEET POTATO PIE

1 unbaked 9" pie crust
2 pounds sweet potatoes or
  equivalent in canned potatoes
½ cup butter
1 teaspoon cinnamon
¼ teaspoon ground cloves
½ teaspoon ginger

¼ teaspoon salt
¼ cup brown sugar
¼ cup white sugar
3 eggs, separated
¼ cup lemon juice
½ cup milk
3 tablespoons brandy or sherry

Preheat oven to 450°.

Cook sweet potatoes, peel and mash or put through ricer. Add spices, butter, sugars, and salt. Beat until light and smooth. Beat egg yolks until light and add to above mixture. Stir in lemon juice, milk, and sherry. Mix well. Beat egg whites until stiff and gently fold in. Pour into unbaked pie shell and bake 10 minutes. Reduce heat to 350° and bake 25 to 35 minutes longer or until pie is puffed up and firm. **This is very rich!**

Like the little girl who had a little curl, when sweet potato pie is good, it's very, very good, but . . . . This is an excellent recipe, but a great deal depends upon the quality of the potatoes. If you have doubts about that, do use the canned potatoes. Sweet potato pie is a Southerner's version of the more universal pumpkin pie.

Mrs. Michael D. Scroggins

KEY LIME PIE

Baked pie shell
4 eggs, separated
1 can sweetened condensed milk

1/3 cup fresh lime juice
Few drops green coloring
½ pint heavy cream, whipped

Beat 4 yolks and 1 white until thick. Add milk and beat until very well mixed. Add juice and rind. Beat until thick. Fold in 3 egg whites (stiffly beaten.) Add green coloring to desired color. Pour into baked shell. Bake at 325° 10-15 minutes. After it cools, refrigerate. When ready to serve place sweetened whipped cream on top. **Very rich.**

There once was a lime from Key West

Who was used to take rust from a vest,

Then he flavored a pie

With meringue so so high

And a daiquiri laid him to rest.

Mrs. Robert Hosey

MAUDE BARTEE'S LEMON PIE

1 14 or 15-ounce can sweetened
condensed milk
1 small can frozen lemonade

1 small size Cool Whip
1 prepared graham cracker
crust

Put milk and lemonade in mixer and beat well. Then fold in Cool Whip. Pour in graham cracker crust and refrigerate for at least 4 hours.

A busy day wonder!

Mrs. W. F. Dozier

LEMON ANGEL PIE

Crust:
4 egg whites
¼ teaspoon cream of tartar
1 cup sugar
Filling:
½ cup sugar

4 egg yolks
¼ cup lemon juice
1 tablespoon grated lemon rind
1 cup heavy cream, whipped
¼ cup water

Crust: Beat egg whites until foamy. Add cream of tartar. Beat until stiff and add one cup sugar gradually. Beat until glossy. Line bottom and sides of greased 9" pie pan with this meringue. Bake in a very slow oven, preheated to 275°, for 1 hour. Turn oven off; leave meringue shell in oven 1 hour to cool with door open.

Filling: Beat egg yolks until thick and light. Add sugar, lemon juice, lemon rind, and water. Cook over hot water, stirring constantly until thick. Cool. Spread half the whipped cream in meringue shell, add lemon filling and top with remaining whipped cream. Chill 24 hours.

Airy, meringue crust with delicate lemon filling.

Mrs. William A. Sims

OLD FASHIONED BUTTERMILK CUSTARD PIE

3 eggs
⅛ teaspoon soda
1 cup buttermilk

1 tablespoon flour
1 cup sugar
1 teaspoon lemon flavoring

Separate eggs and beat yolks until lemon colored. Add milk mixed with soda to eggs. Mix flour with sugar and add to the first mixture. Add the flavoring. Pour into top of double boiler and cook until it thickens, stirring constantly. Pour into pastry lined pie pan and bake until custard is set, 350°, and top is slightly brown. (About 30 minutes). Top with meringue made by beating the egg whites with 3 tablespoons sugar until stiff. Return to oven to brown.

Mrs. Otis E. Kirby

BLACK BOTTOM PIE

Crust:
1 box "Famous Chocolate Wafers" crushed
½ cup of margarine, melted
Filling:
2 cups milk scalded
1 cup sugar
4 teaspoons cornstarch
4 eggs, separated

1½ squares or 1½ ounces unsweetened block chocolate, melted
1 teaspoon vanilla
1 tablespoon plain gelatin
¼ cup cold water
¼ teaspoon cream of tartar
2 tablespoons rum flavoring

Crust: Mix melted margarine and crushed cookies well. Press into 9" pie pan and bake at 300° for 10 minutes.

Filling: Soak gelatin in ¼ cup cold water. Scald milk. Combine beaten egg yolks, ½ cup sugar and cornstarch. Gradually stir in the milk, and cook over hot water until custard coats the spoon. Take out 1 cup of the hot custard and add melted chocolate. Stir until well blended, add vanilla and cool. Pour this mixture into cooled pie crust. Add soaked gelatin to remaining hot custard. Stir until gelatin is dissolved. Cool until slightly thick. Beat egg whites until stiff, gradually add the remaining ½ cup sugar and cream of tartar. Fold gelatin mixture into the egg white mixture, add rum and pour over chocolate layer. Chill and top with sweetened whipped cream. Curls of chocolate on top make this pie more attractive.

Mrs. William A. Sims

CHERRY CREAM PIE

Cream filling:
¼ cup sugar
5 tablespoons flour
½ teaspoon salt
2 cups milk
3 egg yolks, slightly beaten
2 tablespoons vanilla

Cherry glaze:
2 1 pound cans sour pitted cherries
1¼ cups cherry juice
1 cup sugar
1/3 cup cornstarch
Baked pie shell

Combine sugar, flour, and salt in top of double boiler; add the milk and egg yolks, mixing well. Cook over rapidly boiling water for ten minutes, stirring constantly. Remove from heat, add vanilla. Cool slightly and then pour into pre-baked pie shell.

Cherry glaze: Drain juice from cherries and heat to boiling point. Combine sugar and corn starch, add enough cold water to make a smooth paste. Pour this into boiling cherry juice. Continue cooking until mixture boils for 3 minutes and is smooth and thick. Add cherries. Allow to cool slightly then pour over cream mixture. Chill. May top with whipped cream.

Mrs. David B. Cauthen

JUBILEE CHEESE PIE

1 unbaked pie shell (at least 2" deep)
Filling:
3 tablespoons Minute Tapioca
1 cup sugar

2 cans tart pie cherries (use liquid from one can only; drain the other)
2 tablespoons butter, melted
¼ teaspoon salt

Let above mixture stand for 15 minutes, or while pastry is being made.

Topping:
4½ ounces cream cheese
2 eggs

½ cup sugar
½ teaspoon vanilla
Whipping cream and nutmeg

Mix together the cherry filling and let stand for 15 minutes before pouring into unbaked pie shell. Bake shell and filling for 15 minutes in 450 degree oven. While this is baking, make the topping by combining cream cheese, eggs, sugar and vanilla. Beat until smooth and creamy. The blender is good for this. At the end of 15 minutes, remove pie from oven and carefully spoon cream cheese mixture over cherry filling. Return to oven, reduce heat to 350° and bake pie for 30 minutes. Remove from oven and cool to room temperature. When pie is cool or ready to serve, beat whipping cream with a little sugar, to taste, and spread over top of pie. Refrigerate. Sprinkle with nutmeg and serve.

A beautiful and rich cheesecake-plus-cherry pie that is unusual in that the cheese portion is atop the cherry filling. It is surprisingly easy to put together and that news is music to the cook's ears.

Mrs. Denton Cole

CHEESE CAKE PIE

2 cups graham cracker crumbs
½ cup sugar
½ cup butter
2 8-ounce packages cream cheese, softened
2 eggs

2/3 cup sugar
1 teaspoon vanilla
1 cup sour cream
2 tablespoons sugar
1 teaspoon vanilla

Combine cracker crumbs, sugar and butter for crust and press into spring form pan. Cream the cream cheese until smooth, blend in eggs, sugar, and 1 teaspoon vanilla. Pour into crust and bake 20 minutes at 375°. Remove from oven, let stand 15 minutes. Meanwhile, combine sour cream with 2 tablespoons sugar and 1 teaspoon vanilla. Spread over baked filling. Bake 10 minutes at 425°. Cool. Chill overnight or freeze. This should serve 10 to 12 people as it is very rich.

Mrs. Joseph B. Ellis, Jr.

ANGEL CHEESE CAKE PIE

Crust:

1¼ cups sifted flour
½ cup flake coconut
¼ cup firmly packed light
　brown sugar
½ cup butter or margarine
Creamy Cheese Filling:
1/3 cup plus 2 tablespoons sugar
1 envelope (1 tablespoon)
　unflavored gelatin

¼ teaspoon salt
½ cup milk
1 egg
1½ cups cream cheese or
　12 ounces
1 tablespoon lemon juice
1 teaspoon vanilla
1 cup heavy cream, whipped

Combine flour, coconut, brown sugar, and cut in the butter. Put into pie tin and bake 10 or 12 minutes at 400° until golden brown, stirring from time to time to prevent it from scorching. Spread out in pan, reserving ¼ cup of crumbs for topping.

Combine 1/3 cup sugar, gelatin, and salt in saucepan. Blend in egg yolk and milk. Cook, stirring constantly until mixture thickens and comes to a boil. Remove from heat and beat in cheese, lemon juice and vanilla. Beat until creamy. Chill until thick but not too firm. Beat egg whites stiff and add remaining 2 tablespoons sugar. Fold into chilled cheese mixture. Whip cream and fold in. Spoon into pan and sprinkle with reserved crumbs. Chill 4 to 6 hours before serving. May be topped with strawberries or peaches.

A light, unbaked cheesecake of German origin which has converted many a cheesecake hater. Everybody likes it.

Mrs. Norman L. Self

COFFEE PIE

Pastry shell:
½ package (10 ounce size) pie
　crust mix
¼ cup brown sugar, firmly packed
¾ cup finely chopped walnuts or
　pecans
1 square unsweetened chocolate,
　grated
1 teaspoon vanilla
1 tablespoon water

Filling:
½ cup soft butter or margarine
¾ cup granulated sugar
1 square, melted and cooled,
　unsweetened chocolate
2 teaspoons instant coffee
2 eggs
Coffee topping:
2 cups heavy cream
2 tablespoons instant coffee
½ cup confectioners' sugar
Chocolate curls, if desired

Preheat oven to 375°. Make pastry shell. In medium bowl combine pie crust mix with brown sugar, walnuts, and grated chocolate.

Add 1 tablespoon water and the vanilla. Using fork, mix until well blended. Turn into 9" **well greased** pie plate; press firmly against bottom and sides of pie plate. Bake for 15 minutes. Cool on wire rack.

Filling: Make while crust is baking. In small bowl, using portable electric mixer at medium speed, beat butter until creamy. Gradually add granulated sugar, beating until light. Blend in melted chocolate and 2 teaspoons instant coffee. Add 1 egg, beat 5 minutes. Add remaining egg; beat 5 minutes longer. Turn filling into baked pie shell. Refrigerate, covered, overnight.

Topping: Make next day. In large bowl combine cream with 2 tablespoons instant coffee and the confectioners' sugar. Refrigerate, covered, for 1 hour. With electric mixer beat cream mixture until stiff. Decorate pie with topping. Garnish pie with chocolate curls. Refrigerate pie at least 2 hours before serving.

Brimming with calories from its own chocolate and nut-filled crust to its chocolate curl top knot, our coffee pie is irresistible to even the most strong willed. It is time consuming to make, but is a really elegant dessert and is good for entertaining for it should be made a day ahead. Go easy on the main course.

Mrs. A. J. Coleman

BRANDY ALEXANDER PIE

½ cup cold water
1 envelope unflavored gelatin
2/3 cup sugar
⅛ teaspoon salt
3 eggs, separated

¼ cup cognac
¼ cup creme de cacao
2 cups heavy cream, whipped
Graham cracker crumb crust

Pour ½ cup cold water over one envelope unflavored gelatin, add 1/3 cup sugar, ⅛ teaspoon salt and 3 egg yolks. Stir to blend. Heat over low heat while stirring until gelatin is dissolved and mixture thickens. Do not boil. Remove from heat and stir in ¼ cup cognac and ¼ cup creme de cacao. Chill until mixture starts to mound slightly. Beat 3 egg whites until stiff. Gradually beat in 1/3 cup sugar, fold into gelatin mixture. Fold in one cup whipped cream, turn into a 9" graham cracker crust. Chill several hours. Top with one cup whipped cream and garnish with chocolate curls. Watch in preparation; do not let gelatin mixture get too firm before folding in egg whites. You can substitute other brandy for cognac.

This pie is great!

Mrs. Robert G. McNelly

GRASSHOPPER PIE

2 tablespoons butter
14 crushed chocolate cookies
  (Nabisco Famous Chocolate
  Wafer is best)
24 marshmallows
½ cup milk

4 tablespoons green creme de
  menthe
2 tablespoons white creme
  de cacao
1 cup heavy cream, whipped

Melt butter and stir it into the crushed cookies. Press into an eight inch pie tin and use for crust. Melt marshmallows in milk, stir in green creme de menthe and white creme de cacao, fold in whipped cream and pour all into pie crust, freeze, serve frozen. Serves 6 to 8.

Mrs. T. S. Simms

ANGEL FOOD PIE

4 egg whites
½ cup sugar
1 teaspoon vanilla
Baked pie shell
1 cup heavy cream, whipped

¼ cup sugar
½ teaspoon vanilla
1 cup ground nut meats or
  crushed peppermint stick candy

Beat 4 egg whites until almost stiff; add ½ cup sugar and 1 teaspoon vanilla. Beat until stiff. Pour into baked and cooled pie shell. Place in 300 degree oven; bake until whites are slightly brown — about 30 minutes. Remove from oven and cool. Whip 1 cup heavy cream; add ¼ cup sugar and ½ teaspoon vanilla. Spread evenly over cooled pie. Sprinkle with either ground nut meats or crushed peppermint.

An airy meringue filling, refreshing peppermint topping — a pretty pie that is light enough to eat after even the heaviest meal. It does not keep well, so make it the day you wish to serve it.

Mrs. Oscar A. Pickett, Jr.
Pensacola, Florida

PARTY CHOCOLATE PIE

Pie shell:
3 egg whites
1 cup sugar

Pinch of salt
1 tablespoon vinegar
Vanilla

Beat egg whites stiff while adding sugar for 20 minutes. Then add salt, vinegar and vanilla. Shape with spoon to fit pie pan. Bake for 40 minutes at 200° in greased 9" pie pan.

2 packages German Chocolate
  (Bakers Sweet)
6 tablespoons water
1½ teaspoons Bourbon

Vanilla to taste
½ pint heavy cream, whipped
¾ cup toasted pecans

Put all but pecans and whipped cream in double boiler. Melt. Cool; then fold in the whipped cream and a pinch of salt. Crush the pecans and sprinkle over the top of pie. Chill at least two hours.

Delicious and easy to make.

This wins top honors as one of the most delicious, one of the most beautiful and one of the very easiest of all pies! Better served the day it is made, for the meringue crust breaks down if stored in refrigerator too long — though that's rarely a problem, since there's never a crumb left.

Mrs. John C. Bragg

EGG WHITE PIE

Crust:
3 egg whites
1 cup sugar
1 teaspoon baking powder
1 teaspoon vanilla
Dash of salt
1 cup broken pecan meats

1 cup (24) soda cracker crumbs
Filling:
1 pint heavy cream, whipped
3 tablespoons sugar
1 teaspoon vanilla
1 can sliced peaches, drained
   and cut

Beat egg whites until stiff. Gradually add sugar, baking powder, vanilla and salt. Beat until very stiff and glossy. Fold in pecans and cracker crumbs. Place in 9" or 10" pie pan and shape to fit pan. Bake at 300° for 40 minutes. Cool completely. Just before serving prepare filling and pour into baked pie shell. Any kind of fresh or canned fruit may be substituted in filling.

A fantasticly delicious crust; a beautiful pie. Adapt the filling to suit your taste — any fresh or canned fruit may be used. If there's any left when your company leaves — and we doubt that there will be — eat it while you are washing the dishes for it doesn't keep well. After a hard night in the refrigerator egg white pie looks terrible!

Mrs. Otis E. Kirby, Jr.

KISS PIE

1 scant cup dates, cut up
3 egg whites
1 teaspoon almond flavoring
1 cup sugar

1 cup pecans
1 teaspoon baking powder
8 single soda crackers, rolled fine

Beat egg whites and sugar. Add baking powder, dates, nuts, and cracker crumbs. Pour into 9-inch pie pan. Bake 25 minutes at 325° Top with whipped cream or Cool Whip.

Also known as Macaroon pie, this scrumptious pie has the delicate flavor and texture of almond macaroons, but with the happy addition of dates and nuts. It slices poorly so you might scoop it out.

Mrs. George Wallace, Sr.

RITZ CRACKER PIE

3 large egg whites
1¼ cups sugar
35 Ritz crackers, crushed

1 teaspoon vanilla
½ teaspoon almond flavoring
1½ cups chopped pecans

Beat egg whites, and add 1¼ cups sugar gradually. Add remaining ingredients and mix well. Pour into pie pan greased with margarine or 8" cake pan and bake at 350° for about 40 minutes. Serve each portion with whipped cream topping and a cherry.

A variation of kiss pie, this one is made with Ritz crackers and is very quick and easy.

Mrs. Whit King, Jr.

BROWNIE MINT PIE

14 chocolate-mint wafers
3 egg whites
Dash salt
¾ cup sugar

½ teaspoon vanilla
½ cup chopped nuts
1 cup heavy cream
3 teaspoons sugar

Chill cookies. Break cookies and roll to crumbs between wax paper. Beat egg whites and salt together until soft peaks form. Gradually beat in sugar; add vanilla. Fold in crumbs and nuts. Spread evenly in buttered 9" pie pan or plate. Bake in slow oven 325° for 35 minutes. Cool thoroughly. Cover with whipped cream sweetened with three teaspoons sugar.

A marvelous something to do with all those Girl Scout cookies!

Mrs. William A. Sims

Cookies and Candy

COOKIES

Don't wait for the holidays — enjoy Ice Box, Cut-Outs and Shaped Cookies the year 'round.

TEA CAKES

½ cup shortening
½ cup sugar
2 egg yolks
2 cups flour

½ teaspoon soda
Pinch of salt
1/3 cup buttermilk

Cream shortening and sugar. Add egg yolks. Sift flour with soda and salt. Add flour mixture alternately with buttermilk. Roll out on floured board. Cut out and place on a lightly greased cookie sheet. Sprinkle with sugar and fresh grated nutmeg. Bake 8 to 10 minutes at 400°. Makes 2 dozen cookies.

Grandmother's tea cakes were usually not very sweet. She sometimes used orange or lemon rind grated for flavoring. Years ago, people used the same recipe for many things, from stack cake to filled cookies.

Mrs. David B. Cauthen

CHINESE ALMOND COOKIES

2½ cups sifted flour
¾ cup sugar
¼ teaspoon salt
1 teaspoon baking powder
¾ cup shortening
1 egg

2 tablespoons water
1 teaspoon almond extract
1/3 cup blanched almonds
Topping:
1 egg yolk
1 tablespoon water

Sift dry ingredients together. Then cut in shortening with two knives or pastry blender until mixture looks like fine meal. Add the unbeaten egg, water and extract, and stir until mixture comes away from sides of bowl easily. Knead until smooth. Chill one hour. Pinch off balls the size of a walnut — about 1 inch, and flatten with palm of hand about ¼ inch thick. Press an almond in the center of each cookie. Brush with mixture of egg yolk beaten with one tablespoon of water. Bake in 350° oven, 20-25 minutes. Makes 2½ dozen cookies.

A special cookie with milk or hot tea — a good ending for that Chinese dinner.

Mrs. Randolph Pickell

CHERRY COOKIES

1 cup margarine	½ teaspoon salt
1 cup sugar	1 teaspoon baking powder
3 eggs	1 3-ounce package cherry gelatin
3 cups flour	

Cream margarine and sugar. Add eggs. Add sifted dry ingredients and gelatin. Chill. A perfect dough for the cookie press. Dough can be formed into balls or made into rolls and sliced. Bake at 350° for 6-10 minutes. Makes about 4 dozen 3 inch cookies.

Good for school parties.

Mrs. John R. Guice

AUNT ANNE'S ICE BOX COOKIES

1 cup butter	½ teaspoon soda
1 cup brown sugar	½ teaspoon baking powder
1 cup white sugar	2 cups flour
1 egg	1 cup nuts, chopped
1 teaspoon vanilla, optional	

Cream butter and sugars. Add egg and flavoring and mix until well blended. Add sifted dry ingredients and nuts and mix together with hands. Shape into rolls, wrap in waxed paper and refrigerate until ready to bake. Slice thin and bake on greased cookie sheet 8-10 minutes at 350°. Watch closely. Makes about 6½ dozen rich cookies. Freezes well.

For an "I don't know what to do now" day, slice the cookies frozen or refrigerated. Place on greased cookie sheet. Put colored sugars, cut raisins, cinnamon and sugar, etc., in muffin tins and let all the children decorate a pan of cookies. Have broom handy!

Mrs. Billy W. Payne

BUTTERSCOTCH ICE BOX COOKIES

2 cups brown sugar	1 teaspoon soda
1 cup shortening	4 cups flour
2 eggs, well beaten	1 teaspoon vanilla
1 teaspoon baking powder	1 cup nuts

Cream sugar and shortening. Combine with eggs. Mix in as much flour as possible, then knead in the rest. Make into 2 round loaves or rolls and let stand in refrigerator overnight. Slice thin. Bake at 375°, 8-10 minutes. Self-rising flour may be used, but omit soda and baking powder. Makes approximately 12 dozen cookies. Freezes well.

Makes more cookies, not as rich as most icebox cookies, but just as crisp.

Mrs. George W. Hansberry

GINGERBREAD BOYS

1 cup margarine
1 cup sugar
1 egg
1 cup mild flavored molasses
2 tablespoons vinegar
5 cups flour

1½ teaspoons soda
½ teaspoon salt
1 teaspoon ginger
½ teaspoon cinnamon
½ teaspoon ground cloves

Cream shortening with sugar. Add egg, molasses and vinegar. Beat well. Sift together dry ingredients and stir into molasses mixture. Chill about 3 hours. Roll out dough on floured surface. (Pastry cloth works better than board due to sticky dough.) Roll out to ⅛ inch thickness and cut with floured gingerbread cutter. Place 1 inch apart on greased cookie sheet. Use red hots for eyes and buttons. Bake in moderate oven, 375°, 5 to 6 minutes or until slightly brown at edges. Remove to rack and cool. Finish decorating with confectioners' icing: To 2 cups of confectioners' sugar add enough light cream or milk to make mixture that will go through decorator tube easily. Yields 4 to 5 dozen "boys".

Remember that rolling, cutting out and decorating cookies can be child's play. Include them in the fun!

Mrs. William A. Sims

SPECIAL DECORATIVE ICING

3½ cups sifted confectioners'
   sugar

3 egg whites (medium large)
1 tablespoon lemon juice

Beat egg whites until stiff. Add sugar gradually, a tablespoon at a time, until half of the sugar is used. Add lemon juice gradually, then slowly add remaining sugar. Beat until stiff enough to spread or use decorator. Keep the icing covered with a damp cloth while decorating. The icing will harden. Coloring may be added depending on the color desired.

When decorating a large number of cookies, this icing is very easy to manage in the decorator and to spread on the cookies. A special time saver, as well as a bonus for tired hands.

Miss Helen Johnson

MOLASSES SUGAR COOKIES

¾ cup shortening (or good
   brand of margarine)
1 cup sugar
¼ cup molasses
1 egg
2 cups flour, sifted

2 teaspoons baking soda
½ teaspoon cloves
½ teaspoon ginger
1 teaspoon cinnamon
½ teaspoon salt

312

Melt shortening in a 3 or 4 quart saucepan over low heat. Remove from heat and let cool. Add sugar, molasses and egg; beat well. Sift together flour, soda, cloves, ginger, cinnamon and salt. Add to first mixture. Mix well and chill in refrigerator for at least an hour. Form in one inch balls, roll in granulated sugar and place on greased cookie sheet. Bake at 350° for 10 to 15 minutes. Makes 4 dozen cookies.

A favorite family cookie.

Mrs. Joe D. Burns

MEXICAN CRINKLES

¾ cup soft shortening
1 cup sugar
1 egg
¼ cup light corn syrup
2 1-ounce squares chocolate, melted

1¾ cups sifted flour
2 teaspoons baking soda
¼ teaspoon salt
1 teaspoon cinnamon
¼ cup sugar (for coating)

Cream together shortening, sugar and eggs. Stir in syrup and chocolate. Sift flour, soda, salt and cinnamon into creamed mixture. Stir to make stiff dough, shape in 1 inch balls and roll in sugar. Place balls on ungreased sheet, 3 inches apart. Bake in moderate oven, 350°, for 15 minutes. Let stand a few minutes before removing from pan. Makes 4 dozen cookies.

Good to freeze. Freeze after rolling in sugar. Before baking, place on cookie sheet, defrost 30 minutes, then bake as directed. Quite different.

Mrs. John Manning

STRAWBERRY FILLED COOKIE

2 cups sifted flour
3 egg yolks
2/3 cup butter
1 cup sugar

½ teaspoon salt
Ground blanched almonds
Strawberry preserves
Confectioners' sugar

Combine all ingredients except ground blanched almonds, strawberry preserves and confectioners' sugar. Knead until smooth then chill for ½ hour. Form into smooth 1 inch balls and arrange on a greased cookie sheet. Brush with slightly beaten egg white and sprinkle with ground almonds. With the handle of a wooden spoon or dowel, press a deep hole in center of each cookie. Chill again for ½ hour. Bake at 350° for 20 minutes or until lightly browned. Remove from pan, fill holes with strawberry preserves and dust with powdered sugar. Makes 3 dozen cookies.

An unusual delicacy.

Mrs. Daren H. Easter

313

PIN WHEEL COOKIES

1 (3-ounce) package cream
  cheese, soft
½ cup butter
1 cup flour

½ cup chopped dates
½ cup chopped pecans
½ cup white Karo syrup
½ cup sugar

Cream butter and cheese; add flour. (If dough is sticky, work in a little more flour). Roll out and cut with round, fluted edge cookie cutter. Simmer dates, nuts, sugar, Karo and a little water (about a teaspoon), stirring constantly until slightly thickened. On bottom pastry, spread about 1 tablespoon of cooked filling. Place top pastry on, pinching outer edges together so filling will not run out. Prick top pastry. Bake about 20 minutes at 350°. Makes about 2 dozen cookies.

Delicious and pretty!

Mrs. William H. Lovin

SUGAR COOKIES

1½ cups sifted confectioners'
  sugar
1 cup butter or margarine
1 egg
1 teaspoon vanilla

½ teaspoon almond flavoring
2½ cups flour
1 teaspoon soda
1 teaspoon cream of tartar

Cream sugar and butter. Mix in egg and flavorings. Blend dry ingredients and stir into creamed mixture. Refrigerate 2 or 3 hours. Heat oven to 375°. Divide dough in half and roll out on lightly floured board to ¼ inch thickness. Cut into shapes. Sprinkle with plain or colored sugar. Place on lightly greased baking sheet. Bake 7 to 8 minutes or until golden brown. Makes 5 dozen 2 to 2½ inch cookies.

Excellent for a tasty, decorated cookie. For bright colors and snappy flavor, use pure lemon juice, confectioners' sugar, and food coloring as icing.

Mrs. Lindsay A. Allen

COFFEE CRISPIES

1/3 cup heavy cream
2/3 cup butter
½ teaspoon salt
¼ cup warm water
1 envelope active dry yeast
1 egg, separated
¼ teaspoon vanilla

2¼ cups sifted flour
⅛ teaspoon nutmeg
¾ cup sugar
2 teaspoons cinnamon
2 tablespoons finely chopped
  walnuts or pecans

Scald cream, add butter and salt and cool to lukewarm. Stir yeast into water to dissolve; stir in egg yolk, lukewarm cream mixture and vanilla; add to sifted flour and nutmeg. Mix well. Cover closely and refrigerate 4 hours or overnight.

314

Sprinkle board with mixed sugar and cinnamon, continuing to do so through whole rolling process to prevent sticking. With floured rolling pin, roll out chilled dough to make a 20 by 8 inch rectangle. Sprinkle dough lightly with sugar mixture. Fold short sides over to make 3 layers. Give dough quarter turn and repeat rolling, sprinkling, folding and turning 2 more times. Roll to 20 by 8 inches. Brush with lightly beaten egg white; sprinkle with remaining sugar mixture and nuts. Cut into ½ inch strips; place 1 inch apart on greased baking sheet. Bake at 375° for 15 minutes or until browned. Strips spread and become flaky. Remove with wide spatula to wire rack. Serve warm. Makes 2½ dozen.

Worth all the effort! May be made ahead, wrapped in foil and rewarmed in low oven before serving.

Mrs. Billy W. Payne

CANADIAN OATMEAL COOKIES

3 cups oatmeal
3 cups flour
1½ cups clear bacon drippings
1½ cups brown sugar

1 teaspoon salt
1 teaspoon soda dissolved in
½ cup boiling water

Mix together oatmeal, flour, bacon drippings and brown sugar with salt. Add water and soda last. Roll out and cut and bake on lightly greased pan, about 12 minutes at 350°. Makes 7 dozen.

This recipe requires a great deal of flour in the rolling process. Roll rather thin and use a floured cookie cutter. Surprisingly easy and good!

Mrs. George McCrary, Jr.

PUFFS

½ cup butter
½ cup margarine
3 tablespoons confectioners' sugar
¼ teaspoon salt

1½ teaspoons almond flavoring
2 cups flour
1 cup chopped pecans

Cream butter, margarine and confectioners' sugar. Add salt, flavoring and flour and mix. Add pecans. Roll in small balls. Bake on ungreased cookie sheet in 325° oven for 20 minutes. Roll in additional confectioners' sugar. Roll again when cold. Makes 3 dozen.

Rich and crunchy for coffee time. For a special surprise, this recipe may be changed by substituting ½ cup finely chopped almonds for the 1 cup chopped pecans. Then, when forming small balls of dough, hide a candied cherry in the center.

Mrs. Paul E. Hargrove

APRICOT DAINTIES

1 cup butter
2 cups unsifted flour
1½ cups sour cream
1 cup apricot preserves
1 tablespoon lemon juice

1½ cups chopped nuts
1 cup chopped coconut
¼ cup maraschino cherries,
  chopped

Cut butter into flour until particles are size of small peas. Add sour cream and stir until dough clings together. Cover dough, chill 6 hours. May be refrigerated 4 days. Combine preserves and lemon juice. Mix nuts, coconut and cherries. Chop any large pieces of fruit in preserves. Roll dough into four 14 x 12 inch rectangles. Spread each with ¼ of apricot mixture. Sprinkle with ¼ of nut mixture. Roll as for jelly roll, starting with 14 inch side. Seal edges. Place on ungreased baking sheet. Bake in preheated oven at 350° for 30 to 40 minutes. Cut into 1 inch slices. Serve warm or cold, sprinkled with confectioners' sugar. Yield: 56 slices.

Guard them while they cool . . . you may find an empty rack if you don't!

Mrs. Tom White

COCONUT CRISPS

½ cup margarine or butter
½ cup brown sugar
½ cup white sugar
1 egg
1 teaspoon vanilla
1¼ cup sifted flour

½ teaspoon baking powder
½ teaspoon soda
½ teaspoon salt
2 cups corn flakes
1 3½-ounce can flaked coconut
½-1 cup pecans

Cream the margarine or butter, add sugars, egg and vanilla, creaming until light and fluffy. Sift together dry ingredients, stir into creamed mixture. Stir in corn flakes, coconut, and pecans. Shape into small balls (¾ inch in diameter). Bake on ungreased cookie sheet at 350° for 10 minutes or until lightly browned. Cool slightly and remove from sheet. Makes 5 dozen.

Happiness is a jar full of these cookies.

Mrs. William G. Stone, Jr.

PEANUT BUTTER COOKIES

½ cup soft shortening
½ cup peanut butter
½ cup sugar
½ cup brown sugar, packed
1 egg

½ teaspoon vanilla
1½ cups sifted flour
½ teaspoon salt
2 teaspoons baking powder

Cream shortening and peanut butter. Add sugars and beat until light and fluffy. Add egg, vanilla and dry ingredients. Mix until smooth. Form level tablespoons of dough into balls. Place 2 inches apart on ungreased cookie sheet. Press crosswise with fork. Bake at 350° for 10 to 15 minutes. Makes 3 dozen.

A childhood favorite.

Mrs. Lloyd Nix

FROSTED ANGELS

1 loaf Angel Food Cake
  (Approximately 10x4x2)
3 tablespoons butter
1/3 cup milk
1 pound confectioners' sugar

1 teaspoon vanilla
2 3½-ounce cans flaked coconut
  or
2 cups finely chopped nuts

Cut Angel Food Cake in one inch slices. Cut each slice lengthwise to make bars. Cut bars to form approximately 1 x 1¼ inch bite size pieces. Heat butter and milk; stir in confectioners' sugar. Add vanilla. Dip cake squares in icing and roll in coconut or nuts. Place on rack to dry. Makes about 60 pieces.

Perfect for company.

Mrs. Ralph Huff

SPRITZ COOKIES

¾ cup shortening
  (half butter)
½ cup sugar
1 egg yolk

½ teaspoon vanilla
2 cups flour
¼ teaspoon salt

Cream shortening, gradually add sugar and continue beating until light. Add egg yolk, vanilla and combined dry ingredients. Mix to a smooth dough. Force through cookie press onto an ungreased cookie sheet. A cold cookie sheet helps keep the cookies on the sheet when the press is lifted. Chill the dough if it seems too sticky to use in the cookie press. Bake at 400° for 7 to 9 minutes until firm, but not browned. Makes about 4 dozen cookies.

Have fun with the cookie press! By changing shape, color and flavor, these rich cookies could be party rosettes or Christmas wreaths with colored sugars.

Mrs. William A. Sims

317

Steel your nerves, get out your plastic bowls and let your children try these fast and easy delights.

HONEY BALLS

1 cup honey
1 cup peanut butter
2 cups dry milk solids

1 cup cornflakes or whole
  wheat flakes crushed

Cream honey and peanut butter. Gradually add dry milk, mixing well. Shape into small balls; greased hands help. Roll in crushed flakes. Can be chilled if a firmer cookie is desired. Yields: Approximately 60 small balls.

Good to use with young children in a school or church setting where a stove is not available. The nibbles that are "snitched" will give them energy to finish the morning.

Mrs. C. P. Beddow

UNBAKED CARAMEL COOKIES

¾ cup margarine
1 small can evaporated milk
2 cups sugar

1 3⅝ or 4 ounce package instant
  butterscotch pudding mix
3½ cups quick cooking oats

Bring margarine, milk and sugar to a rolling boil, stirring frequently. Remove from heat and add one package pudding mix. Add quick cooking oats. Mix together thoroughly. Cool about 10 minutes. Drop by teaspoon on wax paper lined tray. Makes about 3 dozen cookies.

Another one for sticky little fingers which will be devoured immediately.

Mrs. Ralph Huff

CHOCOLATE PEANUT BUTTER COOKIES

2 cups sugar
½ cup margarine

½ cup milk
4 tablespoons Instant Cocoa Mix

Boil above ingredients for 1 minute. Start counting when mixture reaches a full rolling boil. Remove from heat and add:
3 scant cups quick cooking oatmeal
½ cup crunchy peanut butter

Beat well until blended. Spoon onto wax paper. Cool. Makes about 3 dozen cookies.

Teenagers enjoy substituting ingredients such as ¼ cup nuts and smooth peanut butter in place of the crunchy peanut butter.

Mrs. C. P. Beddow

CHOCOLATE COOKIES

1 can Eagle Brand Sweetened
Condensed Milk
1 6-ounce package chocolate
bits

Pinch salt
2½ cups graham cracker crumbs
1 cup nuts

Dissolve chocolate chips in milk in top of double boiler. Remove pan from heat. Add salt. Mix in crumbs and nuts. Drop by spoonfuls on cookie sheet. Bake at 325° for 8 minutes. Do not over cook. Cookies will be soft in the oven.

Very little help needed from mother . . . for cooking or eating.

Mrs. W. Blanton McBride

GRENDIANS

2½ cups graham cracker crumbs,
(about 14 double). No honey
grahams
2 teaspoons baking powder

1 can Eagle Brand Sweetened
Condensed Milk
1 6-ounce package chocolate
chips
1 cup nuts, optional

Mix all ingredients together. Spread in a greased 7 x 11 inch pan. Press in pan. Bake at 350° for 15 to 20 minutes until a medium brown color. When cool, cut into 36 bars.

This is a teenager's special version of the "Seven Layer Cookie" or "Hello Dolly".

Mrs. Fred Trimble

SEVEN LAYER COOKIES

6 tablespoons butter
1 cup graham cracker crumbs
1 cup coconut
6 ounces chocolate chips

6 ounces butterscotch chips
1 can Eagle Brand Sweetened
Condensed Milk
½ cup chopped nuts

Melt butter in an 8 x 8 inch pan. Sprinkle graham cracker crumbs over butter. Spread all the following ingredients over the butter-crumb mixture, making layers starting with coconut, chocolate chips, butterscotch chips and spreading sweetened condensed milk over all these layers. Spread nuts over condensed milk as the top layer. Bake at 350° for 30 minutes until a golden brown. Set aside and cool before cutting into small squares. Makes 2 dozen 1½ inch cookies.

Children enjoy doing this, but save some for your company.

Mrs. John D. Sherrill

319

CHOCOLATE-LEMONADE PARTY COOKIES

8½-ounce box Famous Chocolate
  Wafers
½ cup frozen canned lemonade,
  undiluted and thawed
½ cup butter or margarine

1 cup (heaping) finely chopped
  nuts
1 can coconut
1 pound box confectioners' sugar

Melt butter . . . cool a little. Crush chocolate wafers fine and mix with butter, lemonade, 2¾ cups confectioners' sugar and nuts. Roll into small balls. Then roll in remaining confectioners' sugar. Refrigerate. Makes approximately 5½ dozen cookies.

A "Cotton Country Cooking" original . . . tangy and rich.

Mrs. Jolly McKenzie

Bar Cookies come in every shape; from dainty teas to the hearty snacks.

CHESS PIE COOKIE

1 cup flour
½ cup soft butter

3 tablespoons granulated sugar

Mix above ingredients. Put in bottom of 8 x 8 inch pan. Bake at 350° for 15 to 20 minutes.

1 cup brown sugar
½ cup granulated sugar
1 tablespoon flour

3 eggs
3 tablespoons melted butter
½ teaspoon vanilla

Mix brown sugar, ½ cup granulated sugar and flour. Add to beaten eggs. Add melted butter and vanilla. Mix well. Pour over baked pastry. Bake at 350° for 25 to 30 minutes. Yields 2 dozen 1½ inch squares.

A "Cotton Country Cooking" original party favorite.

Mrs. C. P. Beddow

CHEESECAKE COOKIES

1/3 cup butter or margarine
1/3 cup brown sugar

1 cup flour
½ cup nuts

Cream butter and brown sugar in a bowl. Add flour and nuts mixing to make a crumb mixture. Save 1 cup for topping. Press remainder in 8" or 9" square pan. Bake 350° for 12 to 15 minutes (until light brown).

8 ounce package softened
  cream cheese
¼ cup sugar

1 egg
2 tablespoons milk
1 tablespoon lemon juice

320

Blend sugar and cheese until smooth. Add egg, milk and lemon juice. Beat well. Spread over crust and sprinkle with crumbs. Bake 350° about 20 to 25 minutes. Cool and cut in squares.

Bite size pieces of cheese cake — with a cookie crust; yummy delicious!

Mrs. John E. Wilks, Jr.

BUTTERSCOTCH BROWNIES

½ cup butter or margarine
2 cups brown sugar
2 eggs
2 cups flour, sifted

2 teaspoons baking powder
1 teaspoon vanilla
1½ cups chopped pecans
Pinch salt

Place sugar and butter over low heat until melted. Remove and cool slightly. Add eggs and beat well. Add other ingredients and pour into lightly greased pan, 7 x 11 inches. Bake in 350° oven, about 30 minutes. Makes about 3 dozen 2 x 1 inch bars.

Ideal for those who can't eat chocolate or who like an easy-to-make, delicately flavored cookie. Take a panful on your next picnic.

Mrs. J. P. Smartt, Jr.

QUICK DELICIOUS BROWNIES

½ cup butter
1 cup sugar
4 tablespoons cocoa
2 eggs
1 cup flour

½ teaspoon baking powder
Pinch salt
½ teaspoon vanilla
½ cup nuts, if desired

Melt butter in medium sauce pan. Add sugar and cocoa. Mix thoroughly. Remove pan from heat, then add remaining ingredients, spread batter in a greased and floured 9 x 9 pan. Bake at 350° for 25 to 30 minutes. Makes 2 dozen 1½ inch squares.

Childhood favorite that never makes it to the cookie jar.

Mrs. William H. Nabors

MARGE HAUSER'S ICING

1½ cups sugar
1/3 cup butter

½ cup cream
1 teaspoon peppermint flavoring

Boil first three ingredients to soft ball stage. Add peppermint flavoring and beat until thick and creamy. Green food coloring can be added, if desired. Spread on top of brownies.

Chocolate Layer:

Melt 3 squares of semi-sweet chocolate. Spread melted chocolate over icing on brownies. Cut brownies into small pieces.

Mrs. John R. Guice

BROWNIES

½ cup margarine
2 squares unsweetened baking
  chocolate
2 eggs
1¼ cups sugar

½ cup plus
  2 tablespoons flour
⅛ teaspoon salt
½ to 1 cup nuts
1 teaspoon vanilla

Melt margarine and chocolate. Beat eggs and sugar together. Add margarine and chocolate to egg mixture. Pour this mixture over dry ingredients, which have been sifted together. Add vanilla and stir in nuts. Bake 25 minutes at 350° in well greased pan, 8x8x2. Yields 2 dozen 1½ inch squares.

A good basic brownie made with baking chocolate. For party fare, add Marge Hauser's Icing.

Mrs. Fred Sittason, Jr.

DELICIOUS COCOA BROWNIES

1 cup butter
2 cups sugar
4 eggs
1¼ cups flour

2 tablespoons cocoa
1 teaspoon vanilla
1 cup nuts

Cream butter, sugar and eggs until light. Gradually add flour and cocoa. Add vanilla and nuts. Bake in 13x9x2 inch sheet pan for 45 minutes at 325°. Makes approximately 35 bars, 2 x 1 inch.

A lighter, cake-type brownie; good with fudge icing. See Icing Section.

Mrs. Robert C. McAnnally

RASPBERRY BARS

1 cup flour
1 teaspoon baking powder
½ cup butter
¼ teaspoon salt
2 tablespoons milk
Approximately 6 ounces
  raspberry preserves

2 cups shredded coconut
1/3 cup sugar
1 egg, beaten
1 tablespoon butter
1 teaspoon vanilla

Sift flour, baking powder and salt into bowl. Cut in butter and add milk. Press crumbly mixture into buttered 8x8 inch pan. Spread with raspberry preserves almost to edge. Mix coconut, sugar, egg, melted butter and vanilla thoroughly. Press into cake. Bake until lightly browned at 325° for 25 minutes. Cut into about 25 squares, 1½ inches, when cool.

Missing Ingredients: A big pot of coffee and good friends.

Mrs. John R. Guice

MAMA MOWERY'S SCOTCH SHORT BREAD

1 cup butter
1 cup margarine
1 cup pure lard
1 box confectioners' sugar

1 egg
⅛ teaspoon soda
9 cups flour

Cream butter, margarine and lard. Add sugar and beat until fluffy. Add egg and beat well. Add 4 cups flour sifted with soda. Add remaining flour and mix with hands. Press into a 12 x 16 inch pan, until about ½ inch thick. Prick with fork and bake at 300° until light brown, about 50 minutes. Cut into squares while warm. Cool in pan. May also be cut with cookie cutter, reducing baking time accordingly. Makes approximately 6 dozen 1½ inch square cookies.

Flavor improves with age. May be stored in tins for many weeks. Old Scottish recipe given our family by a lady who baked it in the "old country".

Mrs. Charles B. Howell

CARAMEL FUDGE SQUARES

1 cup butter or margarine
1 pound box brown sugar
½ cup white sugar
4 eggs
2 cups flour

½ teaspoon baking powder
1 to 2 cups (total) any or all:
    nuts, raisins, chopped dates,
    chocolate chips, coconut

Melt butter and sugars in 2 quart pan until mushy. When cool add eggs, one at a time, stirring well. Add flour and baking powder, stir until smooth. Add nuts, etc. Pour into greased 9x11 or 9x13 inch pan and bake at 350° for about 30 minutes. While cake is still warm, sprinkle with confectioners' sugar. Cut into squares. Makes 3 dozen. Store in air tight container.

Adjust to family taste and ingredients on hand.

Mrs. Randolph Pickell

CINNAMON LOGS

1 cup butter or margarine
1 cup sugar
2 cups flour

2 teaspoons cinnamon
1 egg, separated
1 cup ground pecans

Cream butter and sugar. Sift flour and cinnamon together and add to butter-sugar mixture. Add egg yolk. Mix well and spread mixture on greased cookie sheet, 15x10 inches. Brush top with beaten egg white. Sprinkle nuts on top. Bake in 350° oven until slightly brown, about 15 minutes. Remove from oven and cut into bars. Makes 4 dozen 1 x 3 inch logs.

Spicy and "short", easy to make.

Mrs. William A. Sims

323

SWEDISH COOKIES

½ cup softened butter
1½ cups brown sugar
1 cup flour
½ teaspoon baking powder
1 cup (4 ounce can) coconut

2 eggs
¼ teaspoon salt
1 teaspoon vanilla
2 tablespoons flour
1 cup chopped nuts

Cream butter, ½ cup of brown sugar and 1 cup flour until crumbly. Press into greased 9x9x2 inch pan. Bake at 350° for 20 minutes, until slightly brown. Beat eggs, add vanilla, 1 cup brown sugar, 2 tablespoons flour, salt and baking powder. Add coconut and nuts. Pour over baked mixture. Return to oven and bake 30 minutes. Cool 5 minutes and cut. Makes approximately 2 dozen 1½ inch squares.

Unusually rich cookie.

Mrs. John A. Woller

LUSCIOUS CHERRY BARS

2 cups flour
1 cup butter

½ cup confectioners' sugar

Mix together and press in bottom of 9 x 14 inch greased pan. Bake at 350° for 12 to 15 minutes, or until a pale brown color.

1½ cups brown sugar
2 eggs
¼ cup flour
½ teaspoon baking powder
½ teaspoon salt

1 cup finely chopped walnuts or almonds
½ cup maraschino cherries, drained and finely chopped. (Reserve juice)

Mix brown sugar and eggs until fluffy. Add dry ingredients to egg mixture. Stir in remaining ingredients. Spread over baked crust. Bake 20 to 25 minutes at 350°. Frost with cherry icing when cool. Makes 4 dozen cookies.

Cherry Icing:
2 cups confectioners' sugar
¼ cup cherry juice
3 tablespoons butter

½ teaspoon vanilla or almond extract

Blend until smooth, spreadable consistency.

Colorful . . . a must for a Christmas tray.

Mrs. C. P. Beddow

DREAM BARS

1 pound candied cherries
1 pound candied pineapple
1 pound dates
2 fresh coconuts grated or 5 cups canned coconut

2 cans Eagle Brand Sweetened Condensed Milk
6 cups pecans

324

Mix all ingredients after chopping fruit and nuts. Grease long thick pan. Line with brown paper. Grease again. A 12 x 16 inch pan can be used for half the recipe. Cook at 250° for 3 hours. Cut in small squares. Makes approximately 12 dozen 1½-inch squares.

A good Christmas cookie — rich!

Mrs. John R. Taylor

GRAHAM CRACKER BARS

34 2½-inch square graham
  crackers
1 cup butter or margarine
  melted
1 cup sugar
½ cup milk

1 egg, beaten well
1 1/3 cups flaked or fresh grated
  coconut
1 cup chopped pecans
1 cup graham cracker crumbs

Line 9x12 inch pan (approximate size) with half the crackers. Combine in saucepan the beaten egg, sugar, melted butter and milk. Cook, stirring constantly until mixture boils. Remove and add coconut, nuts and crumbs. Spread over crackers in pan. Immediately place remaining crackers on top. Frost with topping and refrigerate for 24 hours. Cut in bars. Makes 70 party size cookies.

Frosting:

Combine and beat until creamy ½ cup butter, 4 tablespoons cream, 2 cups sifted confectioners' sugar and 1 teaspoon vanilla.

For skinny friends only; or fat, weak and willing.

Mrs. John E. Wilks, Jr.

ANN ANDERSON'S TOFFEE COOKIES

1 cup butter
1 cup brown sugar, packed
2 cups flour
1 teaspoon vanilla

1 egg yolk
Pinch salt
1 cup chopped nuts
6 plain Hershey bars

Have butter at room temperature. Mix all ingredients except pecans and Hershey bars together and spread on well greased cookie sheet, 10 x 15 inch. Bake at 350°, 15 minutes.

Remove from oven and while hot place 6 plain Hershey Bars (broken up) on top. Let melt and spread with back of spoon. Slip back in oven for a minute if it gets hard. Sprinkle with plenty of chopped pecans on top while warm. Cut in 4 dozen 1 x 3 inch bars.

Cut in small squares for a festive occasion.

PEPPERMINT CANDY COOKIES

1 cup butter
½ cup confectioners' sugar
1 teaspoon vanilla

2½ cups flour
½ cup chopped pecans

Cream butter with sugar. Add vanilla, creaming well. Slowly add flour. After mixture is smooth, add chopped pecans. Chill dough while making peppermint fudge filling and peppermint candy sugar mixture.

Peppermint Fudge Filling:

½ cup (¼ pound) crushed
  pink peppermint stick candy
½ cup confectioners' sugar
1 ounce (2 tablespoons) cream
  cheese

1 teaspoon milk
1 drop red food coloring

Combine candy and confectioners' sugar. Blend together with cream cheese. Add gradually 1 teaspoon milk until smooth and creamy.

Peppermint Candy — Sugar Mix:
½ cup confectioners' sugar

3 tablespoons crushed peppermint candy

Shape chilled dough into balls using a rounded teaspoon. Make a hole in the center of each cookie to fill after baking. Place on ungreased baking sheets. Bake at 350° for 12 to 15 minutes until set. Roll in peppermint candy sugar mixture. Fill hole in the center of each cookie with ¼ teaspoon peppermint fudge filling. Makes about 4 dozen 2 inch cookies.

Pretty and just right to fill any sweet tooth!

Mrs. John E. Wilks, Jr.

Drop Cookies are ageless, and so are their fans. Collected here are recipes from the past, recipes from the now . . . all for your future.

AUNT MARY'S APPLE SAUCE COOKIES

½ cup vegetable shortening
1 cup sugar
1 egg
1 cup apple sauce
2 cups flour
½ teaspoon salt
1 teaspoon soda

½ teaspoon cinnamon
¼ teaspoon nutmeg
⅛ teaspoon cloves
¼ teaspoon mace
1 cup chopped nuts
1 cup raisins or dates

Cream shortening and sugar. Add egg and blend well. Add apple sauce. Sift flour, salt, soda and spices and slowly mix into other ingredients. Add nuts and raisins, mixing well. Drop by teaspoon onto greased cookie sheet. Bake at 375° for 10 minutes. Yields: 6 dozen small cookies.

Old-fashioned "milk and cookie" type . . .

Mrs. John R. Guice

DROP COOKIES

1½ cups sugar
½ cup shortening
½ cup butter
3 eggs
½ cup buttermilk
1 teaspoon soda

3 cups flour
1 teaspoon cinnamon
½ teaspoon cloves
1 teaspoon baking powder
1 cup chopped nuts
1 cup raisins

Cream sugar, butter and shortening. Add eggs one at a time. Put soda into the ½ cup buttermilk. Mix spices and baking powder with flour and add with the buttermilk to creamed mixture. Stir nuts and raisins into batter. Drop by teaspoon onto greased cookie sheet. Bake at 350° for 8-10 minutes. Makes about 6 dozen cookies.

Just like mother used to make! Store soft cookies by themselves in an airtight container. A slice of orange or apple helps keep them moist.

Mrs. Leo Wright

RICE KRINKLE COOKIES

1½ cups sifted flour
½ teaspoon soda
½ teaspoon salt
1 cup butter or margarine
½ cup brown sugar

½ cup sugar
1 egg, slightly beaten
1 teaspoon vanilla
2½ cups Frosted Rice Krinkles
1 cup chopped pecans

Sift flour, soda and salt. Cream butter. Gradually add sugars, creaming well after each addition. Blend in egg and vanilla. Beat in flour mixture. Stir in cereal and nuts. Drop by teaspoon onto ungreased baking sheets. Bake at 350° for 10 minutes. Makes about 7½ dozen cookies.

The only objection to these is that they go so fast!

Mrs. Allen Hamilton

ANN'S FRUIT CAKE COOKIES

1 box raisins, white preferred
½ cup bourbon
¼ cup butter
½ cup brown sugar (light),
    firmly packed
2 eggs
1½ cups flour

1½ teaspoon soda
3 teaspoons cinnamon
½ teaspoon nutmeg
½ teaspoon ground cloves
2 cups chopped pecans
½ cup diced citron
1 pound candied cherries

Soak raisins in bourbon at least 1 hour, until plump . . . overnight is best. Cream butter and gradually beat in sugar. Add eggs one at a time, beating after each. Sift flour with soda and spices, add to butter mixture. Add raisins, nuts and fruit. Drop by spoonfuls on buttered cookie sheet. Bake in slow oven, 325°, about 15 minutes. Store in tins. Makes 120.

A real "can't fail". A cheese cloth moistened with wine will keep the cookies fresh and they will ripen just as fruitcake.

Mrs. John F. McLaughlin

327

BARBARA'S CHRISTMAS COOKIES

1 pound candied cherries	5 eggs
1 pound candied pineapple	2½ cups flour, sifted
½ cup liquid (a sweet wine or juice)	½ cup flour for fruit
1 cup butter or margarine	½ teaspoon cinnamon
(butter preferred)	½ teaspoon cloves
1 cup sugar	2 cups pecans
2 tablespoons white Karo syrup	

Pour liquid over fruit and let stand overnight. Cream butter and sugar, add syrup and eggs, adding one egg at a time. Add flour. Mix fruit with ½ cup flour. Add fruit to batter. Let stand in refrigerator overnight or until chilled. Grease cookie sheet and drop by teaspoon, not too large. Bake 325° for 10-12 minutes. Do not over bake. Keep unbaked portion cool. Makes around 15 dozen small cookies.

Enough for the entire Christmas Holidays . . . a very sweet fruit cake cookie.

Mrs. John R. Guice

OATMEAL MACAROONS

1 cup margarine	½ teaspoon salt
1 cup brown sugar	½ teaspoon cinnamon
1 cup granulated sugar	3 cups uncooked oats
2 eggs, unbeaten	1 can (3½ ounce) Angel Flake
1 teaspoon vanilla	coconut
1¼ cups sifted flour	1 cup finely chopped nuts
1 teaspoon soda	

Beat together margarine, sugars, eggs and vanilla. Sift flour, soda, salt and cinnamon together. Add to first mixture and mix thoroughly. Fold in oats, coconut and nuts. Drop by teaspoon onto greased baking sheets. Bake in 350° oven for 12 to 15 minutes. Cool a minute before removing from sheet. Approximately 4 dozen.

Children's delight!

Mrs. Dan M. Crane

MRS. GRANT'S CORN FLAKE COOKIES

2 egg whites	1 cup nuts
1 teaspoon baking powder	1 cup coconut
1 cup sugar	As many corn flakes as egg whites
1 teaspoon vanilla	will hold, approximately 1 cup

Add baking powder to egg whites and beat until stiff. Add sugar gradually and continue beating. Add vanilla, nuts and coconut, then add corn flakes. Drop cookies onto a greased cookie sheet. Bake at 350° until browned . . . about 8-10 minutes. Remove cookies from pan while warm to avoid breakage. Yields about 3 dozen.

Store meringue-type cookies in a container that is airtight. A few minutes in a moderate oven may restore crispness.

Mrs. George Godwin, Jr.

TAY'S PARTY COOKIES

1 egg white, beaten stiff
1 cup brown sugar
1 tablespoon flour

⅛ teaspoon salt
1 cup pecans, chopped

Beat egg white until stiff. Slowly add brown sugar. Continue beating until holds very stiff peak. Stir in one level tablespoon flour, salt and pecans. Drop by small spoonfuls far apart onto greased cookie sheet. Bake at 325° for 10 minutes or until light brown. Makes about 4 dozen small cookies.

Mrs. R. D. Williams

SURPRISE MERINGUES

2 egg whites
⅛ teaspoon salt
⅛ teaspoon cream of tartar
1 teaspoon vanilla

¾ cup sugar
1 package semi-sweet chips,
  6 ounces
½ cup chopped nuts (large pieces)

Beat egg whites, salt, cream of tartar and vanilla until it peaks. Add sugar, beat until stiff. Fold in chocolate chips and pecans. Cover cookie sheet with brown paper (half of a grocery bag is ideal). Drop by rounded teaspoon onto sheet. Bake at 300° for 25 minutes. Makes 60-70 cookies. Let cool on cookie sheet for a few minutes and lift off gently.

Sinfully delicious!

Mrs. David E. Bowers

LACY OATMEAL WAFERS

½ cup butter
1 cup sugar
1¼ cups oatmeal (uncooked)

1 egg
1 teaspoon vanilla

Stir butter and sugar over low heat. When melted add oatmeal. Cool and add beaten egg and vanilla. Cover cookie sheet with aluminum foil, shiny side up. Use a level teaspoon to drop cookie dough. Leave room between cookies for spreading. Bake at 350° for 10 to 15 minutes. Watch cookies. They should be a light golden brown. Remove pan from oven. When cookies are cool enough to touch, peel aluminum foil off back of cookie. These are very thin and will come off easily at the correct temperature. Yields about 3½ dozen cookies.

Mrs. Thomas Caddell

HAZEL-ALMOND MACAROONS

5 egg whites
¼ teaspoon salt
2 cups confectioners' sugar
1½ teaspoons lemon juice

1½ cups pecans, ground
1 cup blanched almonds, ground
Maraschino cherries

Beat the egg whites with the salt until firm, but not dry. Gradually add the confectioners' sugar and lemon juice. Beat for 15 minutes. Remove ¾ cup of the mixture and reserve for icing. Into remaining mixture add the pecans and almonds. Drop by teaspoon onto a baking sheet covered with greased brown paper. Top each with a bit of reserved frosting and add a maraschino cherry half into frosting. Bake in 325° oven for about 40 minutes or until done. (Set, but not brown.) This recipe makes about 6 dozen.

A beautiful Christmas or party cookie.

Mrs. C. W. Belt

SESAME SEED LACE COOKIES

¾ cup butter or margarine
2 cups brown sugar
1 egg, beaten
1 teaspoon vanilla

½ cup sesame seeds
1 cup flour
¼ teaspoon salt

Cream together butter and brown sugar until light and fluffy. Add egg, vanilla and sesame seeds and beat well. Add flour and salt and blend well. Drop by level half teaspoons onto greased baking sheet, about 3 inches apart. Bake in moderate oven, 350°, 4-5 minutes. Cool cookies about 2 minutes before removing from baking sheet. If difficult to remove, reheat slightly. Carefully remove with spatula. Makes about 100 cookies.

An unusual cookie ... crisp and light.

Mrs. Otis E. Kirby, Jr.

CANDY

SUGAR APRICOTS

1 package small dried apricots
1½ cups sugar

2/3 cup water
Pecan halves

Mix water and sugar over low heat stirring for one minute. Add apricots and cook until a golden glaze (about 5 minutes). Drain small number at a time. Place pecan half in center of apricot and roll in sugar. Cool on wax paper.

Mrs. Tommy S. Simms

MARGE'S SWEDISH NUTS

4 or 5 cups walnuts or pecans
1 cup sugar
2 egg whites, beaten stiff

Dash salt
½ cup butter melted in jelly roll
   pan (15½ x 10½ x 10)

Add salt and sugar to beaten egg whites. Beat to a stiff meringue. Fold in nuts and coat well. Spread nut mixture in butter in pan. Bake 325° about 30 minutes or until nuts are coated with delicate brown covering and no butter remains in pan. Stir every 10 minutes. If kept long, store in refrigerator. May be freshened by heating a few minutes in oven.

Mrs. John R. Guice

CANDY COATED PECAN HALVES

1 cup brown sugar
½ cup sugar
½ cup sour cream

1 teaspoon vanilla
Dash cinnamon
2½ cups pecans

Combine the two sugars and sour cream and cook to soft-ball (234°). Add vanilla and cinnamon and beat until it begins to thicken. Add nut meats. Stir until well coated. Turn out on well buttered cookie sheet. Separate into pieces. Makes 2 dozen.

Mrs. Bob McNelly uses 2½ cups walnuts rather than pecans.

A sweetmeat of distinction.

Mrs. Bill Sexton

SUGARED PECANS WITH ORANGE

3 cups sugar
1 tablespoon flour
1 cup milk
Juice and peel of 1 large orange
  (cut peel into tiny pieces)

2 tablespoons butter
3 or 4 cups whole pecan halves

Mix sugar and flour well. Add milk. Cook to soft-ball stage (234°). Add orange juice and peel. Cook to soft-ball stage again. Add butter just before pouring. Put pecans into large pan, allowing room for creaming. Pour syrup over nuts and stir gently until covered. Spread on wax paper. Separate pecans which stick together. Beware of overcooking.

A delightful combination of flavors — crunchy and delicious!

Mrs. W. Blanton McBride

BOURBON BALLS

1 cup chopped pecans	½ cup butter
¾ cup good bourbon	½ pound semisweet chocolate
2 pounds confectioners' sugar	½ of 4-ounce bar paraffin

Soak pecans in bourbon overnight in airtight container. Combine 1 pound of confectioners' sugar with bourbon drained from pecans. Cream thoroughly one pound confectioners' sugar with butter which has been softened. Combine the two mixtures. Blend, add pecans. Chill for short time and make into small balls. Dip in melted chocolate and paraffin cooled to 80° by candy thermometer. A spoon works better for me when dipping ball in chocolate. Some use a toothpick. Place on wax paper until set.

A perfectly innocent way for teetotalers to have a nip! Drive carefully after eating.

Mrs. William A. Sims

RUM (OR BOURBON) BALLS

3 cups rolled vanilla wafers	1½ tablespoons cocoa
1 cup confectioners' sugar	2 tablespoons white Karo
1½ cups finely chopped pecans	½ cup rum (or bourbon)

Mix thoroughly and form into small balls, about the size of a walnut. Roll in confectioners' sugar. Store in air-tight container and chill until ready to serve.

Make these early for Christmas as they freeze well.

Mrs. Sam H. Malone, Jr.

RICE KRISPIE BALLS

1 egg, beaten	1 teaspoon vanilla
½ cup margarine	1 cup pecans
1 cup sugar	2 cups Rice Krispies
1 8-ounce package dates, cut up	1 3½-ounce can coconut

Mix all ingredients except pecans, Rice Krispies, and coconut in sauce pan. Bring to boil and simmer 10 minutes, stirring constantly. Add pecans and Rice Krispies. Form into balls and roll in coconut. Makes about 60 small balls. Mrs. Whit King rolls hers in confectioners' sugar rather than coconut, while Mrs. Robert Tweedy uses ¾ cup margarine rather than ½ cup and leaves out the egg. She also uses walnuts rather than pecans.

"Snap, Crackle and Pop" won't recognize their product, but will be more than pleased when they taste these easy and excellent candies. So will you!

Mrs. Leslie Doss

DATE NUT ROLL

1 cup chopped nuts
30 regular marshmallows, cut up
1 package dates, chopped
45 regular graham crackers,
    crushed

1 large can sweetened condensed
    milk

Mix all ingredients in large mixing bowl. Form into 3 or 4 rolls, about 1 inch in diameter. Wrap in wax paper or Saran wrap. Refrigerate until ready to use. Slice as preferred.

A very rich candy that is very easy to make with no pots and pans involved. 'Tis nice to know it can be made up to 2 weeks ahead of time if kept tightly wrapped, or even longer if frozen.

          Mrs. Otis E. Kirby, Jr.

DIVINITY CANDY

3 cups sugar
1 cup white Karo
½ cup plus 1 tablespoon hot water

2 egg whites
Pinch of salt
1 teaspoon vanilla

Boil Karo, sugar and water until it forms a nice long thread. Beat egg whites until stiff and add syrup slowly to egg whites. Continue to beat until candy is thick. Add vanilla and salt. Drop on waxed paper, 2 teaspoons at a time. You can always steam your candy over boiling water if it doesn't harden.

Marguerite Stone's divinity is almost an institution in Decatur. She can make a batch at the drop of a hat, and does for any sick or lonely friend or to add to anybody's occasion.

To dress these candies up, top with a toasted pecan or cherry, or add a cup of chopped toasted pecans to the candy before you drop it.

One of our testers suggests another variation particularly suited to a child's taste: spread the candy in a jellyroll pan lined with wax paper. When the candy is lukewarm, spread a layer of peanut butter over the divinity, roll it up jellyroll fashion. When cold, slice into pinwheels.

          Mrs. Frank Stone

VINEGAR CANDY

2 cups sugar
½ cup vinegar
¼ cup water

2 tablespoons butter
Pinch of salt

Combine all ingredients and stir until dissolved. Cook until the hard-ball stage is reached. Remove from heat and pour into a greased pan. When cold, hit with a knife so that it will crack into pieces.

An old fashioned child pleaser.

          Mrs. Charles B. Howell

WHITE PRALINES

1½ cup white sugar
½ cup milk
1 teaspoon butter

2 cups pecans
1 teaspoon vanilla

Cook the sugar and milk over medium high heat until the soft boil stage. Remove from heat and add butter, vanilla and pecans. Beat slightly and spoon onto wax paper.

A plateful of pralines never fails to provoke an argument concerning pronunciation — is it praw-leen or pra-leen? As these melt in your mouth, the whole question becomes academic and you'll wonder why you wasted so much time talking.

Mrs. George W. Hansberry

PRALINES

2 cups white sugar
1 cup brown sugar
½ cup white Karo
1 6-ounce can Pet milk

2 cups nuts
½ cup butter
1 teaspoon vanilla

Combine first four ingredients. Cook to a soft-ball. (234°). Remove from heat and add nuts, butter and vanilla. Beat by hand and drop by spoon onto wax paper.

A creamy brown sugar flavored praline.

Mrs. Allen Hamilton

CARAMEL CANDY

4 cups sugar
3 tablespoons white Karo
2/3 cup milk

½ cup margarine
1 teaspoon vanilla
1 cup pecans

Put 3½ cups sugar in pan with milk and Karo. Let come to a boil. Melt the remaining ½ cup sugar in small skillet until it becomes a thin, brown syrup. Gradually add the syrup to the other mixture. Boil slowly until it forms a soft ball in cold water. Take off stove, add margarine and vanilla. Beat in electric mixer until it gets hard enough to drop. Add nuts last. Toasted nuts are better.

An original recipe for what we think is the best caramel fudge we've tasted. Heed Mrs. Lynne's suggestion that toasted pecans are better than untoasted. They can make the difference between good candy and superb candy — with this recipe and any other calling for pecans.

Mrs. Russell Lynne

CREAMY CARAMEL CANDY

2½ cups sugar
1½ cups milk
½ cup butter

5-ounce package marshmallows
1 teaspoon vanilla
2 cups nuts, any variety

Melt 1 cup of the sugar in skillet until thin and brown. Pour this into the remaining sugar and milk and cook until soft-ball stage, 234°. Put in butter and marshmallows. Take from stove and add vanilla and nuts. Drop a spoonful at a time on dish.

Marvelous flavor, creamy texture.

Mrs. Gilbert J. Key

WALNUT CHRISTMAS TOFFEE

1 cup margarine
1 cup sugar
1 tablespoon white Karo
3 tablespoons water

1½ cups chopped walnuts
1 6-ounce package semi-sweet
chocolate morsels, melted

Butter a 9 inch square pan. Melt butter in a 2 quart sauce-pan. Stir in sugar gradually. Add syrup and water. Cook over moderate heat stirring occasionally to 290° on candy thermometer or until a little mixture in cold water becomes brittle. Add one cup of nuts and cook 3 minutes more, stirring constantly. Pour into pan. When cold, remove from pan. Melt chocolate over hot water. Coat one side of toffee with chocolate, sprinkle with remaining chopped walnuts. Allow to set for a minute or so. Flip over on wax paper and repeat. Break into bite-size pieces. Makes about 1¾ pounds.

Make this buttery, crunchy toffee by the bucketsfull for Christmas giving. Your thin friends will love you. Your heavier friends may never forgive!

Mrs. Lindsay A. Allen

PEANUT BRITTLE

1 cup sugar
½ cup white Karo
½ cup water
2 cups raw peanuts

1 square inch paraffin
1 tablespoon butter
1 teaspoon vanilla
1 teaspoon soda

Mix first five ingredients and cook until hard-crack stage (290°) or until peanuts stop popping. Add butter, vanilla and soda. Stir and pour into shallow pan and cool.

An unusually good peanut brittle that has educated at least one young man. The originator of this recipe sold her peanut brittle and sent her son through college with the proceeds.

Mrs. Leslie Doss

335

NEVER-FAIL PEANUT BRITTLE

2 cups sugar
2 cups raw peanuts
¾ cup white Karo

¼ cup water
Pinch of salt
4 teaspoons soda

Combine sugar, peanuts, syrup, water and salt. Use candy thermometer and cook until thermometer registers hard-crack (290°). Remove from heat, add soda, beat vigorously. Spread on heavily buttered tray. As soon as it begins to harden, remove from tray and break into pieces. Do not allow candy to stay on tray too long or it will stick and be difficult to handle.

An airy brittle — wonderfully crunchy!

Mrs. Dalton Guthrie

PEANUT SOUR CREAM CANDY

2 cups sugar
⅛ teaspoon salt
1 cup sour cream
½ teaspoon vanilla

⅛ teaspoon cinnamon
3 drops almond extract
1 cup peanuts, salted or toasted

Mix sugar, salt, and cream. Boil gently, without stirring, to the firm ball stage, 238°. Cool to lukewarm, add flavorings and beat until creamy. Fold in peanuts and pour into a shallow buttered pan. When cool, cut into squares. Makes about 48 pieces.

Don't pale at the combination of flavorings. Remember what they say about variety! The cinnamon and almond flavorings combine to give this creamy fudge an intriguing taste — the peanuts add the crunch.

Mrs. Tom White

PEANUT BUTTER FUDGE

2 cups sugar
1 6-ounce can evaporated milk
2 ounces water
2 heaping tablespoons peanut
   butter

2 tablespoons margarine
1 teaspoon vanilla

Cook sugar, milk and water over medium-high heat until it reaches the soft-ball stage (234°). Remove from heat and add peanut butter, margarine and vanilla. Return to heat and cook two minutes. Beat until good consistency and pour into buttered pan.

Hats off to George Washington Carver for his contribution to our cookbook. Wouldn't he be pleased to see just how far his lowly peanut has come? He'd be delighted with this fudge.

Mrs. John E. Wilks, Jr.

CREAMY PEANUT BUTTER FUDGE

1 6-ounce can evaporated milk
1 pound box confectioners' sugar
4 tablespoons peanut butter
2 tablespoons marshmallow cream
1 teaspoon vanilla
½ cup pecans, optional

Combine milk and confectioners' sugar over low heat, stirring constantly until it forms a soft ball in cold water or let it boil 4 or 5 minutes after it starts a good boil. Remove from heat and add peanut butter, marshmallow cream and vanilla. Stir until smooth and pour into buttered dish.

Another version of peanut butter fudge — a bit creamier than the first. So simple a 10 year old can make it.

Mrs. John S. Key

BIRTIE'S CHOCOLATE FUDGE

3 6-ounce packages chocolate
   morsels
1 can sweetened condensed milk
1 jar marshmallow cream
1 to 2 cups pecan halves

Mix milk and cream. Add melted chocolate morsels and mix. Add nuts. Drop on waxed paper with spoon. Let sit overnight or until dry and firm. Gently remove from wax paper and turn over to dry on bottom.

Another quick fudge with no cooking to do — velvety smooth with marshmallow cream.

Mrs. George Godwin

QUICK FUDGE

½ cup cocoa
1 pound box confectioners' sugar
6 tablespoons butter
¼ cup milk
Pinch of salt
1 cup nuts
1 tablespoon vanilla

Put all ingredients in double boiler except nuts and vanilla. Cook over low heat until everything is melted. Add nuts and vanilla. Pour into lightly greased 9 x 13 pan. Cool. Cut in squares.

Don't hesitate when you're asked to be candy chairman for the Halloween carnival or church bazaar. With this recipe up your sleeve, you can produce fudge as if by magic.

Mrs. Charles Eyster, Jr.
Mrs. Rex Rankin

CHOCOLATE FUDGE

2 cups sugar
2 squares unsweetened chocolate,
  chipped in thin pieces
2/3 cup light cream
2 tablespoons white Karo

2 tablespoons butter
Pinch of salt
1 teaspoon vanilla
1 cup or more broken pecans

Place sugar, chocolate, cream, Karo, butter and salt over moderate heat, stirring constantly until sugar is dissolved. Place cover over mixture until it boils. Let candy boil without stirring until it forms a soft ball in cold water. Add vanilla. Plunge saucepan into cold water. When quite cool, beat with spoon or rotary beater until candy is almost ready to set. The candy will lose its shine when ready to pour. Add nuts and turn into greased pan. Cut into squares when lightly firm.

To many, homemade candy means old fashioned chocolate fudge, and is there anything better? Grandmother made it the hard way testing it in cold water until the soft-ball stage was reached. You can use her method, too, if you must; but for a paltry sum you can buy a candy thermometer. It will take the guesswork out of candy making, and insure success every time your sweet tooth signals you to action.

Mrs. C. Wilson Taylor

HEAVENLY HASH

2 (½ pound) Hershey bars
1 sack large marshmallows

4 cups chopped pecans
5 tablespoons Wesson oil

Melt chocolate on low heat in a double boiler. Add oil and pecans, stirring constantly. When chocolate has melted and oil and nuts have been mixed, pour half of the mixture in a 9 x 9 pan. Place marshmallows side-by-side as closely as you can get them until the layer of chocolate is covered. Pour the remaining chocolate over the marshmallows, spreading evenly. Refrigerate until hard. Cut and serve. Makes about 16 pieces.

Heavenly Hash is well named, for it is indeed divine! It does do devilish things with one's figure, however.

Mrs. David C. Harris

CHOCOLATE COVERED STRAWBERRIES

½ cup butter
1 pound box confectioners' sugar
1 tablespoon milk
1½ pints fresh strawberries,
  medium size, ripe

1-ounce paraffin (¼ of 4-ounce
  block)
6 ounces semi-sweet chocolate

Cream butter. Slowly add sugar. Mix well. Add milk and continue to beat. Roll out part of the butter-sugar dough on wax paper or on a slick, cold surface. The dough will be about ⅛ inch thick. Cut in squares the size to cover a berry. Place a berry in the center and gently bring the dough around the strawberry, covering it completely. If the pastry breaks, gently press it together. This must be done very carefully to avoid mashing the berry.

Take a toothpick and dip the dough-covered strawberry into the chocolate mixture which has melted with the paraffin over hot water. Cover the candy well with the chocolate mixture. Keep the chocolate mixture on low heat for a few minutes to keep the water hot for best dipping. (It is easier to dip using double the amount of above chocolate.)

Take the dipped strawberry out of the pan and place it on a cookie sheet covered with wax paper. Remove the toothpick, dip it into the chocolate, and add a drop of chocolate to the berry where the toothpick has left a hole.

The chocolate should be about 83° for dipping. Stir the chocolate after dipping a few berries.

A rare candy treat — a real delicacy. These chocolate covered strawberries will not keep and must be eaten the day they are made — though we can't imagine that this would ever be a problem.

Mrs. John R. Guice

CHOCOLATE COVERED MARSHMALLOWS

75 marshmallows (1 large package plus a few more)
3 6-ounce packages chocolate morsels

1 can sweetened condensed milk
1 jar marshmallow cream
1 cup nuts, finely chopped

Melt chocolate chips, sweetened condensed milk, and marshmallow cream in a heavy pan. Using two forks, roll marshmallows in chocolate. Then roll in chopped nuts. Place on wax paper and cool overnight.

Surprisingly good, these chocolate covered sweets will keep for ages in an airtight tin. They are so simple to make that you might let the children do them during their Thanksgiving holidays to be hidden away until Christmas. One word of caution though: if you plan to have 75 candies at Christmas time, either double the recipe or you do the hiding.

Mrs. Claude Carter

Omaha, Nebraska

339

CHOCOLATE BELLS

½ cup chopped dates or raisins	1 cup peanut butter
½ cup nuts	1 tablespoon butter, melted
1 cup confectioners' sugar	1 tablespoon vanilla

Mix together and refrigerate overnight.

Dipping Chocolate:

½ cup chocolate chips
1 tablespoon butter
½ block paraffin

Melt in double boiler. Shape refrigerated mixture into bells and dip in chocolate mixture. Place on waxed paper.

An uncooked candy, these rich, chocolate covered goodies are great anytime, but when shaped into bells are naturals for a Christmas tray.

Mrs. John E. Wilks, Jr.

CHOCOLATE COATED COCONUT BALLS

2 boxes confectioners' sugar	1 to 2 cups pecans, as desired
1 can sweetened condensed milk	2 6-ounce packages semi-sweet
½ cup butter	chocolate morsels
1 3½-ounce can flaked coconut	1 block paraffin (4-ounces)
Pinch of salt	

Melt butter slowly, add milk. Stir in sugar and salt. Add coconut and pecans. Chill until easily handled. Roll into balls. Insert toothpick and refrigerate until firm. Melt chocolate and paraffin together in double boiler. Remove from heat and dip each ball in chocolate and place on waxed paper.

"Peter Paul" won't have anything on you.

Mrs. John R. Guice

PARTY MINTS

2½ cups confectioners' sugar	½ teaspoon peppermint extract
1 egg white	or your favorite flavoring
2 tablespoon soft butter	Food coloring to make pastel color

Combine all ingredients in mixer and blend well. Add more confectioners' sugar if needed to get desired consistancey. Make rosettes with pastry tube on wax paper and let stand overnight to form a crust. Pack in tins with wax paper between layers. May be frozen several months.

Mrs. John E. Wilks, Jr.

Pickles and Preserves

TIPS ON PICKLING

Preparation: Choose only flawless tender vegetables and firm ripe fruit. For best results with all recipes, fruits and vegetables should be straight from the garden. Canning process should be underway from the vine in 24 hours. Thoroughly wash all vegetables, but do not bruise. Be careful to remove all blossoms from vegetables, especially cucumbers. Stay with the cooking process being careful to avoid overcooking. Fruits and vegetables vary in size and a shorter period of cooking may be indicated.

Ingredients: Salt should be pure granulated, with no noncaking material or iodine added. Lime should be slack or builder's lime. Red cider vinegar is used in recipes for its good flavor, but it will discolor light pickles. Distilled white vinegar is used for pickling when a clear or light color is desired. For brining use a clean crock, unchipped enamel lined utensil or glass container. For heating pickling liquids use utensils of glass, unchipped enamelware or stainless steel, as other metals react to the acids and salts. Use fresh spices to give the best flavor. Spices are best tied in a cloth bag and removed from the solution before canning. Pickling spices may darken pickles in the jar after a long period of time.

Canning: The sterile canning jars must be kept warm in the oven or in hot water until filled. After filling jar and leaving head room of ½ inch at the top, wipe the jar mouth with a clean, damp cloth to remove any spilled pickling solution. Be sure that pickles are covered with liquid. When using a two piece metal lid be sure the lids are hot. Use tongs to remove lids from the boiling water. Shake off excess water and place on jar top. Tighten cap following manufacturer's directions. Best results come from sealing one or a very few at a time.

Water bath: As an extra precaution for a firm seal, removing air from jar and destroying mold and bacteria, a hot water bath is used. After lids are adjusted, place filled jars on a rack in a deep vessel and immerse in boiling water if food is hot; if not hot, start in warm water. Cover two inches over tops of jars. Start counting processing time as soon as filled jars are placed in the canner in actively boiling water. This prevents a loss of crispness and flavor. Ten to fifteen minutes is an average time.

ARTICHOKE RELISH

3 quarts artichokes (Jerusalem roots), slivered
3 pounds cabbage
1½ pounds onions
6 bell peppers
Sauce:
1 tablespoon black pepper
3 tablespoons whole white mustard seed
2 tablespoons turmeric
1½ pounds light brown sugar
1½ pounds white sugar
1 cup flour
1 9-ounce jar prepared mustard
2 quarts vinegar

Cut vegetables, except artichokes, in small pieces as for relish. Soak overnight in a brine made of 1 gallon water to one cup salt.

Make paste of spices, mustard, flour, sugar and vinegar. Boil until thick, stirring constantly. Drain vegetables. Put on towels to dry. Add these drained vegetables to sauce and cook 20 to 25 minutes, stirring constantly. Just before taking off stove, add slivered artichokes. Blender can be used on chop speed to sliver. Seal in sterile jars. Makes about 5 or 6 quarts.

Makes a marvelous spread to put on bread and use with cold cuts.

Mrs. Paul H. Blackwell

MISS KITTY'S CHILI SAUCE

50 ripe tomatoes
25 onions
12 green peppers
1 bunch celery, finely chopped
½ gallon vinegar
2 long hot peppers

1 tablespoon each of allspice, cloves, cinnamon and mace
2 tablespoons salt
3 cups sugar
1 tablespoon flour
2 teaspoons vinegar

Grind tomatoes, onion and green peppers. Crush spices and put with hot peppers in a cloth bag and cook with mixture. Add all ingredients except sugar, flour and vinegar, and boil for 2 to 2½ hours, stirring constantly. Add sugar. Make a smooth paste of the flour and vinegar. Add paste to the sauce to thicken a few minutes before end of cooking time. Pour into hot, sterile jars. Makes approximately 15 pints.

This will make a hamburger fit for a king!!

Mrs. Charles H. Eyster, Jr.

TOMATO SAUCE

1 peck ripe tomatoes (¼ bushel)
2 large onions
2 cups of vinegar
1 tablespoon salt
1 teaspoon cinnamon

½ teaspoon cloves
½ teaspoon red pepper (powdered)
3 cups sugar

Peel and quarter tomatoes, chop onions finely. Cook first seven ingredients on low until very thick. Stir occasionally. It will take most of the day . . . about 8 hours. Add sugar and simmer about three more hours. Seal in sterile jars. Yields about 4½ pints.

You'll be glad you devoted a summer's day to this! It's so good on dried beans, vegetables and hamburgers.

Mrs. David B. Cauthen

EUNICE'S CORN RELISH

½ cup granulated sugar
2 tablespoons salt
1 tablespoon turmeric
1 tablespoon celery seed
3 teaspoons mustard seed
1 cup cider vinegar
4 cups whole kernel canned
corn, with liquid
2 cups fresh tomatoes,
peeled and chopped
2½ cups chopped onion

2 cups cucumbers, peeled and
chopped
1½ cups chopped bell pepper
1 cup chopped celery
1 clove garlic, crushed
2 medium dried red
peppers
2½ tablespoons cornstarch
½ cup water
½ cup chopped pimento

In Dutch oven, mix first five ingredients. Stir in vinegar and add next eight ingredients. Mix together until well blended. Bring to a full boil, reduce heat to simmer and cook for 35-40 minutes, stirring occasionally. Blend cornstarch in water and stir into relish mixture. Simmer 5 minutes longer, stirring occasionally, and remove from heat. Gently stir in chopped pimento. Pack and seal, one pint at a time, in hot sterilized jars. Before placing lid on jar, carefully wipe the top and threads of jar with clean cloth to remove any food particles, since one tiny seed or speck of food is enough to prevent proper seal.

Makes 5 pints.

Bright colors make Eunice's relish attractive to see; a masterful combination of spices and vegetables makes it appealing to the taste.

Mrs. Billy W. Payne

CHUTNEY FROM INDIA

10 cups peeled chopped apples
3 lemons, sliced and cut
4 cups chopped onions
1 pound seedless raisins
4½ cups dark brown sugar
1 pint water
1 quart cider vinegar

2 tablespoons salt
1 teaspoon cayenne pepper
2 large green peppers, chopped
5 tablespoons shaved ginger root
3 ounces mustard seed
1 pound chopped crystalized
ginger

Cook all ingredients, except crystalized ginger, for 1½ to 2 hours. Add the crystalized ginger the last ½ hour of cooking. Makes 12 to 15 half pint jars.

Tenny Ferrell, a Decatur resident, acquired this authentic, rich and spicy chutney recipe during her travels. The cherished and guarded recipe received such acclaim that she made and sold this specialty, keeping the particular blend secret until her death.

A native of India, now a Decatur resident, who tasted the chutney recently, said, "It makes me homesick."

Mrs. Thomas Caddell

MILD APPLE CHUTNEY

1 cup water
3 tablespoons vinegar
5 tablespoons sugar
½ teaspoon salt
¼ teaspoon allspice
1¼ teaspoons dry mustard

1 whole shaved ginger root
6 tart apples, pared and chopped
1 green pepper, chopped
½ cup seedless raisins
2 teaspoons Worcestershire

Mix the water, vinegar, sugar, salt, allspice, dry mustard, and ginger root. Boil for 5 minutes. Add apples, green pepper, raisins and Worcestershire. Simmer for 45 minutes. Chill. Seal in sterile jars. Makes 1½ pints.

Serve as a condiment for curry.

Mrs. James D. Moore

CHOW CHOW

1 quart green tomatoes
2 sweet green peppers
2 sweet red peppers
2 large onions
1 small head cabbage
½ cup salt

3 cups vinegar
2½ cups brown sugar
1 teaspoon dry mustard
1 teaspoon turmeric
2 tablespoons celery seed

Grind all vegetables, add salt and let stand overnight. The next morning drain all liquid off. Add all other ingredients and bring to a boil. Reduce to a simmer and cook for one hour, stirring occasionally. Put in jars and store in dark place for three weeks before using. Makes 7 half pint jars.

Mrs. Shelton McGaughey

ELIZABETH'S CABBAGE RELISH

1 pint chopped sweet green
  peppers
1 pint chopped sweet red
  peppers
1 quart chopped cabbage
1 pint chopped onions

5 tablespoons salt
4 tablespoons mustard seed
2 tablespoons celery seed
2 hot peppers
½ cup sugar
1 quart vinegar

Mix vegetables together; cover with the salt and let stand overnight in a crock or enameled pan. Boil vinegar, water, sugar and spices for 5 minutes. Drain vegetables, then add to the boiled syrup mixture and bring to a boil. Pack in clean, hot, pint jars. Put on caps, screwing the band tight. Process in water bath, simmering for 15 minutes. Yields about 7 pints.

If you use a few vegetables at a time, the chop speed on the blender will save time.

A colorful relish with a good, good crunch. Mix with salad dressing to add zip to a sandwich or salad.

Mrs. John R. Guice

345

MRS. BARNETT'S MUSTARD PICKLES

1 quart green tomatoes	6 red bell peppers
1 quart celery	6 green bell peppers
1 quart onions	1 quart vinegar
1 quart dill pickles	

Chop all the above vegetables and mix together. Simmer chopped vegetables with 1 quart vinegar for 20 minutes.

Sauce:

2 tablespoons turmeric	1 cup flour
1 tablespoon celery seed	3 cups sugar
1 tablespoon white mustard seed	1 12-ounce jar prepared mustard
2 teaspoons salt	1 quart vinegar

Mix the spices, salt, flour and sugar together. Add mustard, mixing well. Slowly add vinegar to make a paste. Add rest of vinegar combining well. Pour this sauce into the vegetable mixture and cook for 10 minutes. Stir carefully and taste. If sweeter sauce is desired, add more sugar. Pour into hot sterile jars and seal. Makes about 15 pints.

The addition of the dill pickles makes this an unusual treat for roasts, seafoods and cold cuts.

Mrs. James B. Odom

WATERMELON PICKLES

10 pounds prepared rind	40 drops oil of cinnamon
12 pounds sugar	40 drops oil of cloves
1 quart white vinegar	Green food coloring

Prepare the watermelon rind by cutting off all green and red, then cut into long narrow pieces. Cover rind with cold water and allow it to stand in refrigerator 24 hours. Wash and drain. Cover with cold water and slowly bring to a boil. Simmer 5 minutes. Drain. Wash in cold water and let stand in colander until cool. Dry on towel. Place in enamel or pottery container. Mix sugar, vinegar, oils and coloring and pour over rind. Stir as frequently as possible during next 24 hours. Then bring to a hard boil and cook for 10 minutes. If you do not use food coloring, leave a little bit of the red on the watermelon strips. This makes a pretty pickle.

Pour mixture into a large crock with a cover and stir each day for 5 days. Place in sterilized jars and seal. Yields 12 pints.

If you're a compulsive lets-not-waste-anything buff, gather up the rind after a watermelon feast and have a little pickling spree.

Mrs. William G. Stone, Jr.

MILLION DOLLAR PICKLES

4 quarts sliced cucumbers	4 cups sugar
8 to 10 small onions	½ teaspoon celery seed
2 small green peppers	1 teaspoon turmeric powder
2 small red peppers	2 tablespoons white mustard seed
½ cup salt	1 teaspoon mixed pickling spices
½ quart cider vinegar	

Slice cucumbers, onions, and peppers. Put in large crock. Sprinkle salt over them and cover with water. Soak overnight. Drain. Combine vinegar, sugar, celery seed, turmeric powder, mustard seed and spices in large kettle; bring to boil. Put drained cucumbers in syrup and cook 20 minutes or until tender. Do not overcook or pickles will become mushy. Pack in hot sterilized jars. Seal. Yields 6 pints.

A fast and never fail recipe — good for the beginner pickler and the experienced.

Mrs. John R. Taylor

SWEET CUCUMBER PICKLES

1st Day:

7 pounds cucumbers, washed and sliced	1 cup lime
	Water to cover

Soak cucumbers in lime water being sure all are submerged.

2nd Day:

4 pounds sugar	1 tablespoon salt
1 quart vinegar	
1 tablespoon pickling spices tied in cloth	

Rinse cucumbers thoroughly, twice, in cold water. Drain and soak in mixture of sugar, vinegar, pickling spices and salt.

3rd Day:

Simmer cucumbers and the above solution for 20 minutes after it starts to boil. Don't cook fast. Put in jars and seal with a hot water bath. Yields approximately 9 pints.

You'll want to make a big batch of these delectable, sweet, very crisp pickles.

Mrs. James D. Moore

MOTHER WALKER'S 14-DAY SWEET PICKLES

2 gallons cucumbers
2 cups salt, dissolved in
  1 gallon boiling water
1 gallon boiling water

1 gallon boiling water with
  1 tablespoon powdered alum
  added
1 gallon boiling water

Wash cucumbers and slice lengthwise. Place in a stone jar. (Cucumbers must be sliced regardless of size.) Pour salt and boiling water solution over cucumbers while hot. Weight down the cucumbers below the liquid and cover the jar. Allow to stand one week. On the 8th day, drain. Pour 1 gallon plain boiling water over the cucumbers and let them stand 24 hours. On the 9th day, drain and pour 1 gallon boiling water over them to which has been added 1 tablespoon powdered alum. Let stand 24 more hours. On the 10th day, drain again and pour another plain gallon of boiling water over the cucumbers. Allow to stand 24 hours and drain off all liquid.

Pickling mixture:

5 pints boiling vinegar
6 cups sugar

½ ounce celery seed
1 ounce cinnamon sticks

Pour this over pickles. Allow to stand 24 hours. Drain off liquid and heat for three successive mornings, adding 1 cup extra sugar each morning and pour back over pickles. Do not add all sugar at one time. With third and last heating, pack pickles into sterile jars. Cover with hot liquid and seal. Makes about 14 pints.

Crisp and full of flavor.

Mrs. William A. Walker

PARTY PICKLE STICKS

1 gallon cucumber sticks
  (use extra large mature
  cucumbers)
1 gallon water
1 cup household lime
Syrup:
2 quarts white vinegar
1 teaspoon salt

1 teaspoon celery seed
1 teaspoon cloves
2 teaspoons pickling spice
1 teaspoon red or green cake
  coloring
4½ pounds sugar (2 cups equal
  1 pound)

This recipe takes 3 days.

1st day: Peel and cut cucumbers into 3 inch sticks, about ¼ inch thick, being careful to remove all seed pockets (very important). Mix lime and water in glass container . . . no metal. Pour over cucumber sticks; let stand in refrigerator 24 hours.

2nd day: Remove, drain and wash in cold water until water is clear. Cover with clear water and let stand 24 hours in refrigerater. Drain.

3rd day: Make syrup with vinegar, sugar and spices, tied in a cloth. Bring to a rolling boil and pour over cucumber sticks. Let stand 24 hours. Conclude by bringing to a boil and simmering 40 minutes. Take out spices. Fill ½ pint jars with pickle sticks and cover with hot syrup and seal. Makes 16 jars-½ pint size.

Crunchy little pickle sticks. You'll not be able to resist.

Mrs. Joe D. Burns

SWEET DILL PICKLES

2 quart jars whole dill pickles
2 cups cider vinegar
4 cups sugar
Whole cloves, about 20

4 sticks cinnamon broken into
   lengths of 1 inch
½ teaspoon ground cloves
½ teaspoon cinnamon

Slice pickles about ¼ inch in size and drain. Combine all ingredients, except pickles, and boil until juice thickens. Put pickles in jar with knife inserted. Pour syrup over pickles. Remove knife and seal. Pickles will be ready in about a week.

Wave your wand (it's not quite that easy, but almost) and change bought dill pickles to homemade sweet ones that have an especially intriguing taste.

Mrs. Robert M. Miller

GARLIC DILL PICKLES

20 large cucumbers
1 or 2 hot peppers

1 tablespoon dill seed
2 cloves garlic

Wash cucumbers and rinse in hot water. Slice cucumbers lengthwise and place in quart jars. Put the above ingredients in each jar. Then add the following boiling liquid:

1 cup cider vinegar
1 cup plain salt

1 gallon water
1 teaspoon alum

Seal jars. This makes about 10 quart jars.

Mrs. S. Britt Owens

REFRIGERATOR PICKLES

4 quart jars of cucumbers,
   sliced thin
4 cups sugar
4 cups cider vinegar

½ cup plain salt
1 1/3 teaspoons turmeric
1 1/3 teaspoons celery salt
1½ teaspoons dry mustard

Slice cucumbers and put in quart jars. Heat vinegar, sugar, salt, and spices until sugar is dissolved. Pour over cucumbers to cover. Keep in refrigerator.

Unbelievably crisp and delicious, and the easiest pickle possible, since there's no canning involved. Just slice, mix, pour and eat!

Mrs. Charles L. Murphree

PICKLED OKRA

Use small okra, no longer than 3 inches, leaving ½ inch of stem on pod for easy handling. Wash fresh raw okra and place in sterile jars, standing vertically. In each pint jar place:

1 teaspoon dill seed
1 pod red pepper
3 garlic cloves (this makes a
    hot pickle, may be cut to 1
    garlic clove)

Boil and pour over okra:
2 quarts white vinegar
2 quarts water
1 cup dairy salt

Seal jars and leave for 6 weeks. This is enough brine to make 10 to 12 pints.

Green beans may be pickled in this same manner. Carefully wash and string tender green beans straight from garden. Pack in pint jars and proceed as above.

Mouthwatering little pickles that are hot enough to make your eyes water too!

Mrs. Inge Hill
Montgomery, Alabama

SHARON'S SQUASH PICKLES

8 cups sliced, small tender
    yellow squash
2 cups sliced onions
3 bell peppers, sliced in
    lengthwise strips
Salt

3 cups sugar
2 cups white vinegar
2 teaspoons mustard seed
2 teaspoons celery seed

Place onions, squash and peppers in mixing bowl and sprinkle with salt; gently combine. Let stand one hour and drain. Heat other ingredients and pour over squash. Bring to a boil. Place in hot sterile jars and seal. Serve cold. Makes 4 to 5 pints.

Different, pretty, and quite delicious.

Mrs. James B. Odom

PICKLED PEACHES

7 pounds peeled peaches
3 pounds sugar
1½ pints vinegar

½ box stick cinnamon
½ box whole cloves

Make syrup by boiling sugar, vinegar and spices together. Add peaches and cook until just tender and syrup is clear. Place carefully in hot sterile jars. Seal. Store in cool area and wait a few weeks before using. Yields about 5 quarts.

Good pickled peaches are simply no longer available at the grocery. If you like them as much as we do — and what else can you serve with cold baked ham and potato salad? — You'll just have to do your own!

Mrs. Shelton McGaughey

CRISP GREEN TOMATOES

7 pounds green tomatoes
2 gallons water
3 cups lime

Slice tomatoes. Mix water and lime and pour over tomatoes. Soak all of this for 24 hours. Drain all the liquid off and soak in fresh water for 4 hours, changing water every hour.

Sauce:
5 pounds sugar
3 pints vinegar
1 teaspoon ginger
1 teaspoon whole cloves
1 teaspoon allspice
1 teaspoon celery seed
1 teaspoon mace
1 stick cinnamon

Bring all of the ingredients to a boil. Pour this sauce over tomatoes and let stand overnight. After standing overnight, bring ingredients to a boil slowly and let simmer for 1 hour. Seal in hot, sterile jars. Yields 9 pints.

The best reason we know of for not caring when frost threatens before your tomatoes are all ripe; and special enough for you to buy some green ones even if you don't grow your own.

Mrs. Shelton McGaughey

PICKLED BEETS

1 1-pound can sliced beets, drained
1 small onion, sliced thinly
¾ cup apple cider vinegar
¼ cup water
1 tablespoon brown sugar
½ teaspoon carraway seed
½ teaspoon cinnamon
¼ teaspoon cloves
¼ teaspoon salt

In a ¾ to 1 quart glass dish, layer beets and onions which have been separated into rings. Stir remaining ingredients together in an enamel saucepan and heat to full rolling boil. Pour over beets and onion rings, immediately. Cover, and refrigerate overnight.

If onions are omitted, beets will pickle in 6 hours.

For a zippy variation of this recipe, substitute ½ teaspoon celery seed and ¼ teaspoon dry mustard for cinnamon and clove.

Almost a must with a vegetable dinner, especially if turnip greens are on the menu.

Mrs. Billy W. Payne

351

FRANCES GUYTON'S CAULIFLOWER PICKLES

2 medium cauliflowers
2 cups tiny white onions
¾ cup salt
Ice cubes
8 cups white vinegar

1¼ cups sugar
2 teaspoons turmeric
2 teaspoons mustard seed
1 tablespoon celery seed
1 hot red pepper

Divide cauliflowers in 1 or 2 inch pieces (about 8 cups). Scald and peel onions, add salt to vegetables; mix with ice cubes, cover with additional ice cubes and let stand 3 hours. Drain. Combine remaining ingredients in large kettle and bring to a boil, stirring to dissolve sugar. Add vegetables and cook about 10 minutes, or until tender but not soft. Pack in hot sterilized jars. Reheat vinegar to boiling and pour over vegetables. Seal jars. Makes 5 pints.

Mrs. Allen Hamilton

PICKLED EGGS

12 hard boiled eggs (for
    appetizers use small eggs
    or quail eggs)
3 cups cider vinegar
2 tablespoons sugar

1 teaspoon celery seed
2 tablespoons salt
6 peppercorns
2 cloves

Combine vinegar, sugar, celery seed, salt, peppercorns and cloves. Simmer 10 minutes. Strain spices out of liquid.

In a quart jar add peeled eggs and:

1 sliced onion, in rings
3 cloves

Sprig of dill weed
1 garlic clove, if desired

Pour liquid over eggs. If more liquid is needed, finish with vinegar. Cover and refrigerate. Let set at least 3 days before using. Will keep, refrigerated, about a month.

Save any of the pickling solution from canning or use juice left from "store bought" pickles to make a quick solution for pickling eggs.

We know several husbands who like to have a jar of these eggs in the refrigerator all the time. Why not add your man to that group?

Mrs. O. B. Evans

PICKLED LEMONS

6 lemons
3 tablespoons salt
2 cloves garlic, mashed
1 teaspoon paprika

3 tablespoons crushed dried hot
    red pepper; less if desired
¼ teaspoon peppercorns
1 cup salad oil

352

Select thin skinned lemons. Wash lemons, cut in quarters lengthwise and remove obvious seeds. Roll lemon wedges in salt, using a little more salt, if necessary. Pack in two pint jars, cover and let stand at room temperature for four days. Heat remaining ingredients in saucepan until first few light bubbles appear. Pour over lemons and let stand at room temperature 4 or 5 days longer. Store in refrigerator when process is completed. Makes 2 pints.

Hot and tart . . . this pepper specked relish is especially good served as an accompaniment with seafood or pork.

Mrs. Billy W. Payne

MAGIC GRAPE JUICE

1 cup firm, ripe grapes   Boiling water
½ cup sugar

Wash grapes. Place in sterile quart jar with ½ cup sugar. Fill jar to ½ inch of top with boiling water. Seal and process in a water bath for 30 minutes. Put in a dark cool place for a few weeks. After a rich color has formed and the juice is ready, pour off juice and discard grapes. Serve ice cold over ice with a sliver of lemon.

Mrs. John R. Guice

PORT WINE JELLY WITH SNOW TOPPING

3 cups sugar   ½ bottle liquid fruit pectin
2 cups port wine   Snow topping for jelly

Measure sugar and wine into top of double boiler; mix well. Place over rapidly boiling water and stir until sugar is dissolved, about 3 minutes. Remove from heat. Stir in fruit pectin at once and mix well. Skim off foam, if necessary. Pour quickly into glasses. Cover at once with snow topping.

Snow Topping:

2 bars paraffin

Melt paraffin over boiling water. Pour a thin layer over hot jelly, using about 1 tablespoon melted paraffin for each jelly glass. Cool remaining paraffin until it becomes cloudy and starts to solidify. Quickly whip with rotary beater until foamy and starts to harden. If paraffin becomes too hard, re-melt and start again. Place snow toppings over thin layer of paraffin.

Most any kind of wine can be used — Sherry, Burgundy, Sauterne, etc. A nice Christmas rememberance when put in a stemmed wine glass with velvet ribbon tied at base.

Mrs. Harold Pilgrim, Jr.

353

GRAPE, BLACKBERRY, SCUPPERNONG, OR MUSCADINE
JELLY

Wash the fruit and put in pan. Put just enough water in the fruit so that you can see the water. (I use 3 or 4 cups of water with 6 quarts of scuppernongs.) Cook the fruit down, boiling to start it, and then continue on low heat. The fruit should cook 45 minutes or a little longer, until the seeds and hulls are cooked apart. Pour juice and all into a cheese cloth bag and let it drip several hours. Add a cup of sugar to every cup of juice. Boil, fast at first, then slower. Test with a silver tablespoon. Jelly is ready when three drops run together and drop off. It takes about 30 minutes. Skim the foamy part off. Pour into jelly glasses. Let cool. When cool seal with paraffin.

Mrs. William B. Eyster

HOT PEPPER JELLY

2/3 cup green hot peppers
1 bell pepper
1½ cups vinegar
6 cups sugar

1 bottle Certo
1 teaspoon food coloring,
    red, green or any other
    color.

Chop peppers and put in blender with vinegar. Add sugar and mix well. Bring mixture to a rolling boil. Strain. Return to stove and again bring to a rolling boil. Remove from heat and at once add Certo and food coloring. Pour into 6 half pint jars and seal.

Pepper jelly is a necessity in many area households. Spooned over a block of cream cheese and served with Ritz crackers (and a cheese knife) it is one of the most delicious appetizers you'll ever taste — and the easiest. It is also excellent served with roast beef.

Mrs. Frank T. Richardson, Jr.

PRESERVED ORANGES

6 oranges
2 cups sugar
½ teaspoon cinnamon
¼ teaspoon whole cloves

Juice of ½ lemon
¾ cup light corn syrup
2 cups water

Select thin skinned oranges, without blemish. Cut oranges in eighths, lengthwise, and remove obvious seed and any center membrance that might be unattractive. In saucepan, cover orange sections with water, bring to a boil, reduce heat and simmer for 20 minutes, covered. If peels are not tender, simmer a few minutes longer. Remove from heat and allow to cool in water. Drain. Arrange sections in 2½ quart casserole. Mix sugar and cinnamon together in saucepan and add remaining ingredients. Boil 5 minutes. Pour syrup mixture over oranges, cover, and bake for 1 hour at 350°. Pack in hot jars and seal. If immediate use is desired, allow to cool and refrigerate. Unsealed refrigerated preserved oranges will keep three months.

A pretty and mildly spiced fruit that is a pleasing accompaniment for ham, lamb and some poultry dishes. The oranges may also be used as dessert: Place sections in sherbet glasses, top with sprig of mint and maraschino cherry. Cover sherbet glasses and refrigerate 2 hours before serving; this allows a hint of mint flavor to permeate orange sections. Refreshing!

Mrs. Billy W. Payne

MRS. MAURER'S FREEZER STRAWBERRY JAM

1¾ cups crushed ripe strawberries   2 tablespoons lemon juice
4 cups sugar   ½ bottle Certo Fruit Pectin

Place crushed strawberies into a large bowl. Add sugar and mix well. Combine lemon juice and Certo and stir into strawberries. Continue stirring 3 minutes. Pour quickly into jars. Cover at once with tight lids. Allow to stand at room temperature for 24 hours. Then store in freezer. For use within 3 weeks, may be stored in refrigerator. Yields about 5 medium jars.

Mrs. Maurer, kindergarten teacher of renown, lets her students make this jam. If the little ones can do it, we bet you can too.

Mrs. Charles B. Howell

STRAWBERRY OR PEACH PRESERVES

4 cups fresh strawberries or peaches
4 cups sugar

Bring to a boil 2 cups sugar and 4 cups strawberries. Cook 10 minutes. Add the 2 additional cups sugar. Boil slowly until it reaches preserve consistency, about 15 minutes. Skim. Let stand overnight in pyrex dish. Spoon into jars and seal.

If peach variation is used, cut peaches in about 8 pieces.

For Ginger Peach Preserves, proceed as above, except add about 1 teaspoon ground ginger to peach preserve mixture.

Mrs. John Taylor

BLACKBERRY JAM

Sort berries twice. Use only the best fruit, with stems removed. Using proportions of ¾ cups sugar to 1 cup berries, cook until very thick, about 2½ hours for 8 cups berries. Pour into jars and seal.

Eight cups berries equals 4 cups jam.

Mrs. Elmer S. Loyd, Jr.

FIG-STRAWBERRY PRESERVES

3 cups peeled mashed figs   3 cups sugar
2 3-ounce packages strawberry
flavored gelatin

Thoroughly mix figs, gelatin and sugar in a large sauce pan. Bring to a boil over medium heat and continue boiling for 3 minutes, stirring occasionally. Pour quickly into glasses. Cover at once with ⅛ inch hot paraffin. Makes 6 medium glasses.

Amazing! If you are lucky enough to have a fig tree in your yard, run, don't walk, to pick some and stir this up.

Mrs. Ralph Huff

AUNT GEORGIA'S FIG PRESERVES

2 pounds figs   Stick cinnamon
1½ pounds sugar   Few slices of lemon
¾ cup cold water

Soak figs in water with one tablespoon soda about 20 minutes. Rinse and drain. Boil sugar, water, cinnamon and lemon slices until mixture forms a thin syrup. Add figs, cook for 20 minutes. Remove figs and let syrup cook for 10 more minutes. Add figs and cook 5 more minutes. If syrup is not thick, cook longer (figs and syrup together). Avoid overcooking.

Cook one batch at a time.

Mrs. Charles H. Eyster, Jr.

APRICOT JAM

½ pound dried apricots   1 8-ounce can crushed pineapple
1 whole orange (grind all   3 cups sugar
except seeds)

Soak apricots overnight in water to cover. Cook apricots in this soaking water until tender. Mash thoroughly, add orange and pineapple and bring to a boil. Stir in sugar and continue cooking, stirring constantly until thick. Put into 4 sterile half pint jars and seal.

Make this excellent preserve any time, since there is no season for dried apricots.

Mrs. William A. Sims

Southern Hospitality

Modeled after George Washington's Inaugural site in New York, the Old State Bank Building is one of Decatur's earliest landmarks. Constructed in 1832, it survived the Civil War and served as a hospital and garrison for both Federal and Confederate troops.

(Photo Courtesy of The Decatur Daily)

INTRODUCTION

In 1820, President James Monroe ordered that a site be set aside near a great river and named for the War of 1812 hero, Commodore Stephen Decatur. Thus, Rhodes Ferry, nestled peacefully in a lush, green valley next to the mighty Tennessee River, became Decatur, Alabama.

The burning and looting of the Civil War left its mark and by 1865 only two houses and the old bank building were left standing. Reconstruction was painful, and Decatur was hit hard by a yellow fever epidemic and then the depression of 1929. A real era of prosperity did not begin until after the Tennessee Valley Authority was created and moved into the area.

Cotton was the big money crop in Decatur's early days and still ranks high in agricultural importance. During the last twenty years this quiet cotton town has changed its appearance and has become a city expanding to meet the needs of modern industry which has located on this river site. One thing remains unchanged, however, and that is Decatur's love of good food and its ability to produce it. Taking advantage of the gardens which thrive in the fertile Tennessee Valley soil, most of our food is simple but distinctive and always with that inimitable Southern flair!

View of Decatur's Keller Memorial Bridge

This picture was taken of Mrs. Greene and Romey in the kitchen of the Lyons (Hotel) just before the Dining Room closed in 1966.

SOUTHERN HOSPITALITY

Ask anyone who ever stopped at the dining room of the once famous Lyons Hotel on Bank Street, and he will verify that here was Southern cooking and Southern hospitality at its best.

"The Lyons" and Mary (Mrs. J. C.) Greene are synonymous. When she took over the management of the dining room, the crowds were unbelievable. There'd be a civic club meeting in the big room back of the kitchen, a posh luncheon for 60 in the private room to the side of the main dining room, the regular public lunch being served in the main dining room . . . all at one time. In those days there was no buffet line, though many times would-be diners had to sit in the hotel lobby until a table could be vacated and cleared.

People for miles around had their palates tickled by the best food to be found at a public restaurant anywhere. There was nothing in the way of food that couldn't be obtained and it was always superb. One of the highlights of each meal was the passing of the dessert tray at the end of the main course. We can't tell you about all the foods that were served, so we're giving you a number of Mrs. Greene's favorite dessert recipes. Mrs. Greene says that she always used real butter and cream — never any substitutes! Her dessert tray was a delight to behold and to sample.

* * * * *

LYONS' DESSERT TRAY

QUEEN OF TRIFLES	BUTTERSCOTCH PIE	PUMPKIN PIE
CHOCOLATE PIE	ANGEL PIE	QUEEN ELIZABETH
	CHESS PIE	

* * *

QUEEN OF TRIFLES

4 egg whites
1 cup sugar
1 quart whipping cream
1 cup broken pecans
3 tablespoons crushed pineapple
1 teaspoon vanilla
1 small jar red maraschino cherries, cut in small pieces

1½ dozen almond macaroons, crumbled (use stale macaroons, two to three weeks old; the fresh ones are too moist and sticky.)

Beat the egg whites, adding half of the sugar and continue beating until the mixture will stand in peaks. Whip the cream separately, adding the other half of the sugar. Fold the whipped cream and egg whites together by hand and add the remaining ingredients. Put in a gallon container and keep in the freezer.

CHOCOLATE PIE

1 cup sugar
3 tablespoons cocoa
2 tablespoons cornstarch
Pinch salt (about ⅛ teaspoon)

½ cup butter or margarine
1 cup milk
3 egg yolks, beaten
1 tablespoon vanilla

Mix all dry ingredients, adding enough milk to make a smooth, stiff paste. Add the rest of the milk and the butter and cook over direct heat until this is of a thick consistency. Remove from heat and add small amount to egg yolks. Return to heat, stirring constantly until very thick. Pour while hot into baked pie shell. Have meringue ready to go on at once.

Meringue:

3 egg whites
⅛ teaspoon salt
1 tablespoon cold water

3 tablespoons sugar
Few drops lemon juice, (about
½ teaspoon)

Beat egg whites, adding salt and water. When whites are whipped slightly, add sugar, 1 tablespoon at a time, whipping after each addition. Add lemon juice, a little at a time, at the time sugar is added. Whip until thick and glossy, spread over hot filling and bake about 15 minutes at 300° to 350°, depending on oven.

BUTTERSCOTCH PIE

1 cup dark brown sugar,
  firmly packed
2 tablespoons cornstarch
⅛ teaspoon salt
¼ cup real butter (do not
  substitute)

1 cup milk
3 egg yolks
1 tablespoon vanilla

Mix all dry ingredients, adding enough milk to make a smooth paste. Add butter and milk, cook over direct heat, stirring constantly until of thick consistency. Remove from heat and add small amount of hot mixture to egg yolks. Stir into remaining hot mixture and return to heat, stirring constantly until very thick. Add vanilla and pour at once into a baked pie shell. Use same meringue recipe as for Chocolate Pie.

ANGEL PIE

4 tablespoons cornstarch
¾ cup sugar
1½ cups boiling water
3/8 teaspoon salt
3 egg whites

3 tablespoons sugar
2 teaspoons vanilla
½ cup heavy cream
Peppermint candy

Mix cornstarch and sugar together, then pour in boiling water. Cook over direct heat, stirring constantly, until thick and clear. Add salt to egg whites and beat until stiff, adding sugar, a little at a time, and vanilla. This is easier to do in an electric mixer, but do not use a blender. Pour the cooked mixture slowly into the egg whites, beating slowly. "Don't mix too long," says Mrs. Greene; "you won't think it is beaten enough. It shouldn't be too stiff." Chill this mixture, then pour into a previously baked pie shell and cover with the whipped cream. Just before serving, sprinkle with finely crushed peppermint candy. "King Leo Candy is best," says Mrs. Greene.

PUMPKIN PIE

1 29-ounce can pumpkin
2 cups sugar
4 eggs
1 teaspoon salt

1 tablespoon vanilla
½ cup real butter (melted)
2/3 cup cream (half & half)
½ cup milk

Mix all ingredients together and pour in 2 - 9" uncooked pie shells Bake at 350° until filling doesn't wiggle. About 45 minutes.

CHESS PIE

1½ cups sugar
½ cup real butter
3 eggs
1 tablespoon cornmeal

1 teaspoon vinegar
5 tablespoons cream
1½ teaspoons vanilla

Cream butter and sugar. Add other ingredients, mix well and pour into an uncooked pie shell. Cook at 350° until it doesn't wiggle.

QUEEN ELIZABETH CAKE

1 cup dates, cut
1 cup boiling water
1 teaspoon soda
¼ cup butter
1 cup sugar
1 large egg

1 teaspoon vanilla
1 1/3 cups flour
1 teaspoon baking powder
1/3 teaspoon salt
½ cup chopped nuts

Cut dates and pour boiling water over them. Add soda and let cool. Cream butter and sugar and add egg and vanilla. To the creamed mixture add the date mixture, then the flour mixture (dry ingredients), alternating until all is added. Add nuts. Bake in a 13"x9" pan for 30 minutes.

Topping:
5 tablespoons dark brown sugar   Pecans
¼ cup butter   Coconut
5 tablespoons cream

Combine and cook for 2 or 3 minutes and pour over top of cake. Sprinkle chopped pecans and coconut on top. Cut in squares and serve.

Louis Bell Woods, better known as "Romey", was chef at the Lyons Hotel for 26 years until its closing. He is now the chef at The Decatur Inn. In addition to his daily duties there, Romey can be prevailed upon to do special meats and other dishes to be taken out. He is an expert on meat and game, and as Mrs. Greene says, "Romey was born to cook." He is a tradition in Decatur.

One of the things Romey does best is a standing rib roast. What could be more distinctive, yet simpler to serve, at a dinner party for twenty.

ROMEY'S DINNER PARTY FOR 20

*Standing Rib Roast of Beef

*Stuffed Potato

Broccoli with *Hollandaise Sauce

Tossed Green Salad with Italian Dressing, Page 83

Rolls and Butter

Brandy Alexander Pie, Page 305

Coffee

*   *   *   *   *

ROMEY'S STANDING RIB

At your favorite butcher's select a choice rib roast. Request that it be "oven prepared" so there won't be much trimming to do. An 18 pound roast should be adequate for 20 people.

On the top side of the standing rib, slice layer of fat next to meat line and fold back. Season well with salt and white pepper and replace. Season on both sides and ends with salt and white pepper. Use garlic powder lightly. Sprinkle with Accent and tie with string. Cook fat side down for 1 hour at 350°. Turn roast over with fat side up and sprinkle salt and pepper again lightly over top. Reduce oven to 300°. Cut up an onion, add it to juice from the roast and·baste the roast with this seasoned juice every 30 minutes. For a rare roast (18 pounds), the total cooking time at 300° (after it has been turned) is approximately 1½ hours.

Plan to have the roast ready at least 20 minutes before time to start carving. The meat will slice much more easily. Place the roast on a heated platter, fat side up, to carve.

364

ROMEY'S STUFFED POTATOES

20 medium Idaho potatoes
1 cup butter or margarine
2 tablespoons salt
1 teaspoon red pepper
2 cups sour cream
2 cups grated American
  cheese

3 tablespoons dried chives
½ pound bacon, fried crisp and
  crumbled
1 cup chopped onions, sauteed in
  margarine
Milk

Place the washed but ungreased potatoes in a pan and put another pan on top (not air tight). Bake at least one hour at 450°. Remove from oven and cut off tops, enough to scoop out pulp. Work while the potatoes are hot! (This, says Romey, is the secret of a good stuffed potato.)

In a large bowl, mix potato pulp with remaining ingredients except milk. Add enough milk to reach a medium consistency. Stuff potatoes and cook at 400° about 10 minutes.

ROMEY'S HOLLANDAISE SAUCE (for twenty)

1 egg yolk
½ cup lemon juice
½ cup butter or margarine,
  melted

1 teaspoon salt
1 teaspoon white pepper
½ cup water
1 teaspoon cornstarch

Beat egg yolk until smooth. Add lemon juice, melted butter, salt, and pepper. Mix together in double boiler and cook until thickened. Mix cornstarch in water and add to the thickened sauce (this keeps mixture from curdling).

Another protege of the famed Lyons Dining Room is Russell Priest, renowned throughout North Alabama for his Gourmet Catering Service. A native of Decatur, he began his work as a busboy at the Lyons and then became a full time waiter. Over a period of ten years he had learned enough to become the cook at Monsanto's guest house. There he specialized in making hors d'ouevres and did a variety of gourmet cooking.

While working at the guest house, Russell began a catering service, selling cakes and pies and, in his spare time, serving full meals. He is now at Pineview Hospital in Hartselle managing the menus and kitchen and, in addition, has the Gourmet Catering Service.

When Russell caters a party, he and the hostess plan the menu; then everything else is left to him — even such details as bringing the ice and brewing the coffee! Since most entertaining in Decatur now is done rather informally at home, the small dinner party is one of Russell's most frequent engagements.

DINNER PARTY FOR TEN

*Shrimp Crabmeat Galore

*Hominy Grits Supreme

*Baked Tomato

Peas and Mushrooms

Tossed Salad with Assorted Dressings

Rolls and Butter

*Grasshopper Pie

Coffee

SHRIMP CRABMEAT GALORE

1 cup finely chopped bell pepper
2 cups finely chopped celery
3 tablespoons finely chopped fresh onion
1½ cups crabmeat
4 to 5 cups boiled shrimp, cut into 2 or 3 pieces
½ teaspoon pepper
1½ tablespoons Worcestershire
¼ teaspoon Tabasco
2 teaspoons Accent or monosodium glutamate
1¼ to 1½ cups mayonnaise
1 to 2 cups buttered cracker crumbs

Mix all ingredients listed except mayonnaise and cracker crumbs. Then add mayonnaise and mix well. Pour into casserole and top with buttered cracker crumbs. Bake at 350° until hot, bubbly and brown.

HOMINY GRITS SUPREME (for 10)

4 cups cooked grits
8 tablespoons butter
6 cups grated Cheddar cheese
1 cup milk
8 eggs, well beaten

$\frac{3}{4}$ teaspoon Tabasco
2 teaspoons Accent or monosodium
  glutamate
Salt, to taste ($\frac{1}{2}$ teaspoon or less)
$\frac{1}{4}$ teaspoon powdered garlic

Mix hot grits, butter and cheese until cheese is melted. Add remaining ingredients. Pour into 2 quart casserole and sprinkle with additional cheese and paprika. Bake at 375° for 45 minutes until set.

BAKED TOMATO

Tomato, small size
$\frac{1}{2}$ teaspoon Worcestershire
Salt and pepper, to taste
$\frac{1}{4}$ teaspoon dry mustard

$\frac{1}{2}$ teaspoon finely chopped onion
$\frac{1}{2}$ teaspoon butter
Buttered bread crumbs
Dried parsley

An hour or two before serving, make a curved slice in top of tomato. Sprinkle ingredients which have been mixed together on top of tomato. Bake for 30 minutes at 325°. For 1.

GRASSHOPPER PIE

30 large marshmallows
$\frac{1}{2}$ cup light cream (half & half)
2 drops green food coloring

$\frac{1}{2}$ teaspoon peppermint extract
1 cup heavy cream, whipped

In double boiler mix marshmallows and cream until marshmallows are melted. Add food coloring and let mixture cool. Then add extract and fold in whipped cream. Pour into shell and chill until set.

Shell:

18 to 20 Hydrox cookies, crushed   2 teaspoons butter, melted

Mix and press into 9" pie pan. Bake 5 minutes at 350°. Cool and add filling.

Many a Decatur hostess takes advantage of the warm Southern climate which is with us so much of the year, and does her entertaining out of doors. A popular and less formal version of the cocktail supper is the Patio Party. Russell Priest gives us an excellent menu.

PATIO PARTY

*Beef Tenderloin, cooked in Wine
with
Miniature French Bread, thinly sliced
Sweet 'n Sour Pork Ribs
*Marinated Shrimp
Relish Tray with Dip for Vegetables, Page 16
Marinated Artichokes
Potato Chips with *Red Devil Dip

* * * * *

BEEF TENDERLOIN, COOKED IN WINE

3 beef tenderloins, about 2 or 3 pounds each
½ cup Worcestershire sauce
1½ cups Burgundy or cooking wine
3 tablespoons lemon juice
½ teaspoon Adolf's seasoned tenderizer
2 teaspoons Accent
2 teaspoons dry mustard
¼ teaspoon powdered garlic
5 tablespoons melted butter

Trim tenderloins; place in pan. In order listed, add ingredients over meat. Broil 5-8 minutes and turn, basting often. Let broil 5-6 minutes longer. Cool and slice thin. Serve with miniature French bread.

MARINATED SHRIMP

Cooked shrimp
½ cup wine vinegar
¼ cup salad oil (never olive oil)
1 teaspoon salt
2 cloves garlic, crushed
Dash Tabasco
2 tablespoons chopped dill pickle
2 tablespoons chopped parsley

Fill a 1 quart jar with cooked shrimp (5 pounds of shrimp will fill 4 quart jars, unless shrimp are large.) Use 2½-gallon pickle jars for 5 to 7 pounds of shrimp.) Add remaining ingredients. Shake jar well and store on side in refrigerator, turning often. Marinate at least 2 or 3 days (these will keep for a week). Drain and serve with toothpicks.

RED DEVIL DIP

1 cup sour cream
1 8-ounce package cream cheese, softened
1 16-ounce carton cottage cheese
2 4½-ounce cans deviled ham
1 tablespoon chopped onion
1/3 cup catsup
2 teaspoons Worcestershire
¼ teaspoon Tabasco
Salt, to taste

368

*Russell Priest assists Mrs. Barrett Shelton, Jr. with last minute prepara-
tions before guests arrive on the patio of her Sherman Street home.*

(Photo by Lonnie McDaniel)

When the crowd is larger and the occasion a special one, the cocktail supper is often the form of entertaining chosen. This seems to be the simplest way for guests to mingle and dine without the formality of the seated dinner.

John Harris, now operator of the Lyons Dining Room at The Decatur Inn, has expertly planned and supervised many such occasions at Decatur's Country Clubs. Here is his menu with selected recipes for a cocktail supper for 50.

COCKTAIL SUPPER FOR FIFTY

*Spinach Konspore with Triscuits

Dip with Vegetables

Roast Beef Au Jus in Chafing Dish with Biscuits

*Seafood Newburg in Chafing Dish with Miniature Pastries

Miniature Tarts

with

Lemon and Chocolate Filling

* * * * *

SPINACH KONSPORE

John Harris says this is a popular request. This recipe was given to him by Mrs. Rex Rankin.

10 packages frozen, chopped spinach	30 cloves garlic
10 cans crabmeat	1½ cups sliced scallions
¾ cups cooking oil	20 ounces Parmesan cheese
	Salt and pepper, to taste

Cook spinach for 10 minutes. Drain in colander until dry. Drain crabmeat and add to spinach in colander. Pour oil in pan and saute garlic and scallions. Add spinach and crabmeat to pan. Add cheese and cook mixture for 7 minutes. Salt and pepper to taste. Serve in chafing dish.

This freezes well. Reheat in a double boiler.

SEAFOOD NEWBURG (for 50)

½ cup margarine	2 cups diced shrimp
7½ tablespoons flour	1 cup diced lobster
2½ cups chicken stock	1 cup cooked scallops, chopped
2½ cups light cream	3 tablespoons sherry
Salt and pepper, to taste	4 egg yolks

Make 5 cups rich, medium-thin white sauce from first four ingredients. Add the remaining ingredients and heat to just below boiling point for 5 minutes. Serve in miniature pastries.

Rachel Chandler adds some final touches while demonstrating the art of cake decorating to one of her classes.

(Photo Courtesy of The Decatur Daily)

When Decatur entertains for the ladies with a coffee or tea, and everyone is raving about the lovely delicacies, you can be certain that Rachel Chandler had something to do with the food! She is a delight to work with and has made entertaining so easy and successful for many a hostess.

Rachel came to Decatur in 1950 with her husband, the late R. E. Chandler, who was an avid historian and the originator of a film called "The Decatur Story" which was shown to many civic clubs and organizations. Rachel's fame in food began to build when she served as hostess at the First Presbyterian Church and began taking care of the food at weddings. She also does catering: rolls, birthday cakes, casseroles, sandwiches of all kinds, pastries of all kinds — you name it, she has it. If you are in a sudden jam, she usually has something frozen that can be thawed quickly.

In addition to her catering, Rachel teaches classes at the Aquadome, Decatur's indoor swimming and recreation center. There, homemakers young and old may learn from her such skills as cake decorating, making party food, and sewing.

Whether entertaining a bride-to-be or introducing a friend or newcomer to Decatur, the coffee is a traditional form of Southern hospitality. Guests may be invited for the same hour or for different times of the day, depending on the size of the crowd.

Martha Jane McWhorter recently introduced her two daughters-in-law with lovely coffees in her home on Sherman Street. Behind the dining room door to the kitchen was Rachel Chandler calmly supervising every detail!

MORNING COFFEE

*Miniature Ham Rolls

*Chicken Salad in Toast Cups

*Fresh Fruit Platter

Cheese Straws, Page 14

*Miniature Open-Faced Sandwiches

*Assortment of Cookies

Coffee or Tea

*   *   *   *   *

HAM ROLLS

Rachel suggests buying a Hormel party ham, which may be sliced beforehand and frozen. Miniature homemade rolls can also be made ahead and frozen. Both should be taken out the night before they are used. Plan to serve each guest 2 rolls.

CHICKEN SALAD IN TOAST CUPS

Toast Cups

Toast cups do not absorb the moisture of the chicken salad as pastry shells do. To make, slice the crust off a piece of bread and cut the bread into two-inch squares. Press the squares gently into miniature muffin tins and brush each one with butter. Toast at 350° until the tips are brown. These can be made ahead and frozen. Here again, plan for two per guest.

Chicken Salad

Purchase a 5 or 6-pound hen (this will yield about 1½ quarts of cut-up chicken, which will fill 80 to 100 toast cups). Place the hen in a covered roaster with 1½ cups water. Salt the hen but use no pepper. Cook at 300° for five hours to assure thorough cooking (Rachel says this is the key to good chicken salad). When the hen is done and has cooled slightly, take the skin off and cut up the warm chicken with scissors. You may do this ahead and freeze the cut chicken, but do **not** freeze the chicken salad.

1½ quarts chicken, finely diced	Juice of 1 lemon
2 cups finely chopped celery	Mayonnaise, to desired consistency
4 medium sized sweet pickles, grated	Salt, to taste

Mix all ingredients and fill toast cups, using iced tea spoon, several hours before serving.

OPEN-FACED SANDWICHES

Open-faced sandwiches are good for color on a table. Using her small 1½" biscuit cutter for two rounds and 2" cookie cutter for two more rounds, Rachel gets four rounds from one slice of bread. The rounds may be cut the night before if wrapped tightly, but the sandwiches should be made the next morning.

CUCUMBER SANDWICHES

Have cream cheese at room temperature. Add a little milk to soften until spreadable. Salt to taste. Spread the rounds with softened cream cheese. Do not peel but score a cucumber with a fork, slightly penetrating the green, thus producing a scalloped effect. Slice cucumber very thin and place one slice on each round. On top place a thinly sliced carrot round. May top with a rosette of cream cheese. Sprinkle with paprika.

CHERRY TOMATO SANDWICHES

Spread miniature bread rounds with mayonnaise. Add a very thin slice of unpeeled cherry tomato. Top with a sliver of bell pepper. Sprinkle with salt just before serving.

FRESH FRUIT PLATTER

It is always better to use fruits in season, but canned ones may be substituted or added for more variety. A likely combination: drained pineapple chunks, individual whole seedless green grapes, melon balls, whole strawberries, and a few bananas sliced in rounds. You may prepare all except the bananas the night before, but store separately. Wait until the last minute to slice the bananas. Place fruit in a shallow dish and garnish with a few sprigs of mint. Use sour cream which has been sprinkled with granulated brown sugar as a dip for the fruit. Serve with toothpicks.

ASSORTMENT OF COOKIES
Orange Balls

1 box vanilla wafers (medium size)
½ cup frozen, undiluted orange juice, thawed
¾ cup sifted confectioners' sugar
¾ cup Angel Flake coconut
½ cup finely chopped pecans
¼ cup white Karo

Mix all ingredients and shape into 1" balls. Store in covered container in refrigerator or freezer. When ready to use, sprinkle with confectioners' sugar. (These are not baked). Yields 4 dozen.

Fruit Cake Cookies

1 pound chopped candied pine-apple
1 pound chopped candied cherries
6 cups pecans, chopped
2 boxes dates, chopped
½ pound white raisins
3 cups flour, sifted
4 eggs, separated
3 teaspoons soda
3 tablespoons milk
1 teaspoon cinnamon
1 teaspoon nutmeg
½ cup whiskey or brandy
1 cup brown sugar
½ cup margarine

Dredge fruit in 1 cup of the flour and set aside. Slightly beat egg yolks. Dissolve soda in milk. Sift remaining flour with cinnamon and nutmeg. Cream butter and sugar. Add slightly beaten egg yolks and milk mixture. Mix well. Add flour alternately with whiskey. Fold in stiffly beaten egg whites. Add fruit. Drop by teaspoonfuls onto lightly greased baking sheet. Bake at 300° for 20 to 25 minutes. Yields 14 dozen. If stored in airtight container, these stay fresh 2 weeks. They also freeze beautifully.

Sand Tarts

¾ cup real butter
4 tablespoons sugar
2 tablespoons ice water
2 teaspoons vanilla
1 cup chopped nuts
2¼ cups flour, sifted (or enough to make stiff dough)

Cream butter and sugar. Add all other ingredients. Shape dough into small balls or crescents. Bake on greased cookie sheet, 12 minutes at 400°. Sprinkle with confectioners' sugar just before serving. These may be frozen.

Pictured at a coffee honoring Mrs. Robert McWhorter, Jr. is Mrs. Robert McWhorter, the honoree, and Mrs. Roger Barton McWhorter.

(Photo Courtesy of The Decatur Daily)

THE BRIDGE FOURSOME

Another popular way of "getting the ladies together" is the bridge foursome. Often planned on the spur of the moment, it is less formal than the bridge luncheon, and the food is usually simpler.

For many years the home of Mrs. Frank Darrow Peebles (Eula) has been the scene of numerous gala occasions. Eula's entertaining is a perfect example of Southern Hospitality. Everyone from five to ninety has always wanted to be included in her parties. Today her gatherings are much smaller. There may be six for lunch or supper or her regular bridge foursome.

THE BRIDGE FOURSOME

*Cup Sandwiches

*Marinated Carrots

Buttermilk Pie, Page 294

Coffee

CUP SANDWICHES

1 cup grated sharp Cheddar cheese
1 small bottle stuffed olives, chopped
1 cup canned tomatoes, drained and chopped
1 cup mayonnaise (bought)
1 teaspoon grated onion
2 slices bread, finely chopped
Salt and pepper, to taste
Dash of Worcestershire

Mix all together. If not to be used immediately, store in refrigerator. Spread between buttered bread slices. They're better if toasted.

MARINATED CARROTS

2 pounds carrots, cut into bite-sized pieces
1 teaspoon salt
1 teaspoon sugar
1 teaspoon horseradish
1 teaspoon prepared mustard
1 teaspoon Worcestershire
1 teaspoon Tabasco
1 teaspoon salt
¾ cup oil
¾ cup vinegar
1 can condensed tomato soup
Large onion, thinly sliced

Cook carrots with salt and sugar until tender. Drain and cool. Make a sauce in blender from remaining ingredients except onions. Pour sauce over carrots. Line bowl with sliced onion; add carrots and sauce; cover and let stand 12 hours or longer. Drain and serve.

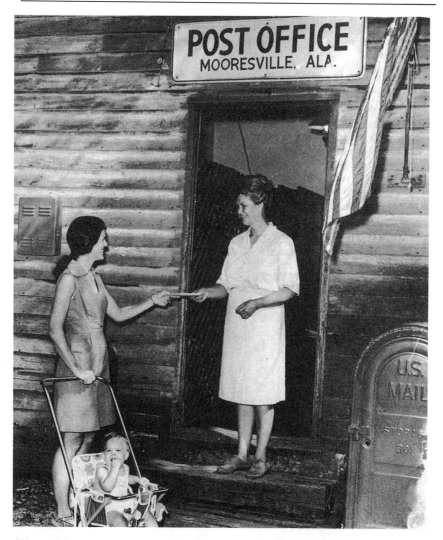

The original Post Office is still in use today. Seen receiving her morning mail from Postmistress, Mrs. Ray Pepper, is Mooresville resident Mrs. A. Julian Harris and daughter Katherine.

(Photo by Lonnie McDaniel)

BRUNCH IN MOORESVILLE

Everybody wants to come to Mooresville. The Travel Editors call it "Williamsburg Unrestored." The tiny south Limestone County town, incorporated in 1818 before Alabama was a state, is the oldest incor-

porated town in Alabama. Although much of the moonlight and mag-
nolias and mammy days has gone, it still remains a serene town, much
unchanged.

Parties for the most part are informal with service plates and finger
bowls remaining on pantry shelves.

One of Fannie and Frank Richardson's favorite parties is a brunch
with guests invited for mid-morning. Most of the food is done the day
before with a typical menu being sausage biscuits, cheese grits, or cheese
sauce over hominy (be sure to add Tabasco to both), tiny sweet rolls,
doughnuts, canned whole spiced apples, to which is added cinnamon,
sugar, butter, etc. and eggs. A small crowd is served scrambled eggs;
to a large crowd its Creole Eggs (page 93) because they will hold
longer.

Hot foods are served in chafing dishes or in oven-to-table dishes
over candle warmers. (Hot trays are also handy for this purpose.) While
Frank takes care of the guests' thirst, Fannie does the last minute kitch-
en things.

In warm weather the buffet is set on the screened porch of the
country house; otherwise, it is set in the living-kitchen where a coal fire-
place is lighted. Nests of tables pull out for additional spaces in the living room, gallery or den.

Belle Mina Hall

(Photo by Lonnie McDaniel)

PLANTATION PARTY AT BELLE MINA

Belle Mina Hall, built in 1826 by Alabama's second governor, Thomas Bibb, is now owned by Mr. and Mrs. Thomas A. Bowles. It is THE place everyone wants to take visitors and is as pretty as anything in the Virginia countryside.

Parties at Belle Mina Hall range from formal seated dinners in Lucille's beautiful dining room to outside gatherings. The enchanting Plantation Party was given for visiting friends from Europe. Guests

379

gathered in the backyard where flickering torches cast their glow, and a strolling minstrel moved among them with his "Greensleeves" and "Scarlet Ribbons." The large old carriage house, transformed into fairyland with boughs of every flowering fruit tree imaginable, housed the bar and the pre-supper relishes . . . one tray with carrot curls, celery, olives, cauliflower and pickles; another with pickled shrimp.

Supper was served buffet style with guests seated in groups around the large back patio and fountain. The menu:

Mock Chicken Legs, Page 132

Sliced Country Ham With Mustard Sauce

Creole Eggs, Page 93

Potato Salad, Page 75

Cornmeal Biscuits, Page 215

Miniature Strawberry Cupcakes, Page 280

After dinner, a small band in the open carriage house provided music for dancing until the striking clock brought every Cinderella and her Prince back to earth.

COURTLAND'S CORN PARTY

Courtland is a beautiful old village about 18 miles west of Decatur; and here, for generations, have been held the "Corn Parties" when that luscious, field-grown corn-on-the-cob is just right.

The parties have been going on for many years. For a very long time they were at Marjorie and Bob Tweedy's; but today Dama and Dave Martin are the hosts each summer and everybody from the Tennessee Valley hopes to wangle an invitation.

Along with the manna-from-heaven, boiled corn on the cob, comes fried chicken, *Courtland stew, country ham, combination salad, hot biscuits and a variety of home-baked desserts.

Prior to the main meal, cheese straws and home-grown, toasted pecans are served. Nothing "store-bought" is ever served at Courtland's Corn Parties.

COURTLAND CHICKEN STEW

1 large hen
2 large onions, cut fine
4 1-pound cans tomatoes
8 large potatoes
1 tablespoon salt
1/3 teaspoon black pepper

¼ teaspoon red pepper
2 tablespoons vinegar
½ pound butter (if hen is not fat)
1 can tomato paste
2 17-ounce cans Pride of Illinois white corn

Boil hen in small amount of salted water. When done remove chicken from bones and cut up same as for chicken salad. (Do not use skin). Return chicken to stock. (Do this one day and make stew the next. Can be done in one day.)

Put potatoes into stock whole and when done, remove and mash. Return to stock. Add remaining ingredients, except corn, at the same time as the whole potatoes. Add the corn after the stew is nearly done. Cooking time is about 5 hours.

Stew may need more salt, pepper and butter to taste.

Mrs. Robert Tweedy

LEGENDARY COURTLAND LUNCHEON

Courtland has always been famous for its hospitality and natural-born Southern cooks; Jessie Gilchrist Lane exemplified these qualities. At Wayside, the gracious family home, she introduced the delicious egg croquettes from Nashville's Mrs. Penn Crockett.

With these croquettes she served country ham, stuffed fresh tomatoes, (or when out of season, tomato aspic) a green vegetable, (often cold asparagus), hot rolls, and lemon meringue pie. Today, ham biscuits may take the place of the country ham and hot rolls.

EGG CROQUETTES

4 hard-boiled eggs
6 tablespoons butter
6 tablespoons flour
1½ teaspoon salt
⅛ teaspoon red pepper
1 teaspoon Worcestershire

2 cups milk
1 tablespoon sherry
2 loaves stale bread
3 eggs, slightly beaten
2 tablespoons milk

This serves nine or makes nine croquettes. Peel and chop hard-boiled eggs. Make very thick cream sauce of butter, flour, salt, pepper, Worcestershire, and 2 cups milk. Sauce this thick is hard to handle and must be beaten until smooth. Add boiled eggs and sherry to hot sauce. Let cool and refrigerate until thoroughly chilled. This may be done the day before.

Peel crust from bread (unsliced bread is better — either French or the kind you buy frozen and bake at home). Grate into shaggy crumbs. Mold egg-sauce mixture into kitchen tablespoon size. Roll croquettes into the bread crumbs. Dip into 3 eggs slightly beaten with 2 tablespoons milk, then roll into bread crumbs again. Croquettes are soft and must be handled gingerly, but there will be no damage if done quickly.

If you have a deep fat fryer with a thermostat, fine; otherwise, have Crisco hot — should be 350° to 370°. Drop in one or two at a time and cook until just less than golden brown. Drain and set aside. They can stand for several hours. Before serving, run into a 250° oven until hot throughout. Top with "Tartar Sauce."

Tartar Sauce:

½ cup grated onion
1 cup sweet pickle, chopped
1 cup dill pickle, chopped
⅛ teaspoon red pepper

Dash garlic juice or garlic powder
2 cups mayonnaise (needn't be homemade)

Mrs. Crockett used chopped sweet pickles, but it is easier to buy sweet pickles already minced or chopped. Ann Lane (Mrs. Roger) McWhorter and Lu (Mrs. W. D.) Gilchrist say use lots of pickle or it will come out "blah."

Put the grated onion and minced pickle in a cheese cloth bag and squeeze gently, discarding juice. Mix all ingredients together.

If serving plates, put a dollop onto croquettes; if serving buffet, put tartar sauce in separate dish. These croquettes are rich and delicious and worth the little extra trouble. This recipe has never before been published anywhere.

BARGE PARTY

Decatur Yacht Club members like entertaining on their big "barge" which offers seating space inside as well as around the sides and on top.

Occasionally they have steaks with the trimmings; most of the time, though, either Gibson's or Woodall's caters with their delicious barbecued pork, beef, or chicken, homemade slaw, potato chips or potato salad and homemade pies, served if you wish in plastic boxes with everything including eating utensils and napkins. Don't forget the hot sauce for pork and the white sauce for chicken, available from the barbecue establishments.

Nowhere in the world can you find barbecue like that in Decatur, Alabama. It is a "must" for any visitor.

HOUSEBOAT PARTY

Houseboating on the Tennessee River and on Smith Lake in Cullman County is a growing form of recreation.

Dr. Sid Nethery of Belle Mina was one of the earlier advocates of the comforts and roominess of houseboats. Mary and Tom Bingham, Joe and Ruby Worthey, Tula and Carl Spanyer, Frank and Fannie Richardson have joined the many others in the Decatur Harbor.

Among the foods for entertaining are steaks for small crowds, babecue for a large crowd (when guests can sit on the top and outside decks), and, of course, tetrazzini or spaghetti which can be made at home and frozen.

However, for spending several days when just the owner, or perhaps one other couple is along, these boat owners have found that four can be served beautifully with such shelf-stored items as canned Louisiana Creoled Shrimp (with an extra can of shrimp added); noodles almondine with an extra can of boned chicken and packaged potato pancakes requiring only 2 eggs and 2 cups water added. Already-made omelettes that do require refrigeration but not freezing will keep at least a week. Bacon can be cooked done and refrigerated ,then put in a warm oven to come out crisp at the meal needed. All sorts of spaghetti and macaroni mixes in boxes can be shelf-stored. When mixed with additional cheese or ground chuck or round, they make great meals.

When tomatoes are out of season, keep the small, whole Contadino tomatoes on the shelf. Refrigerato before using and they are closer to garden tomatoes than anything you can buy.

The boating enthusiasts have also found that empty coffee cans can be decorated, and crackers, chips and cookies will keep indefinitely on the shelf as long as the plastic tops are kept tightly closed.

Spreading a picnic at Point Mallard Park are left to right John Wilks, III, Karen Wilks, Sheryl Sims, Bill Sims, Jr., Kathy Wilks, Libby Sims and Lisa Sims.

PICNIC AT POINT MALLARD

Picnics are always a popular form of summertime entertainment. Decatur's Point Mallard offers a perfect site, and, in addition, provides numerous activities for total family enjoyment — golfing, bicycling, swimming, and boating. Visitors may thrill to one of the few pools in the world that generates its own waves. The Wave Pool has no equal for fun in the sun!

Food always tastes better near the water, and all that exercise is enough to whet any appetite! There is ample space for picnics at the tables shaded by colorful umbrellas or at several other family-designed eating areas.

PICNIC LUNCH (OR SUPPER)

Fried Chicken, Page 132

Vegetable Spread Sandwiches, Page 56

Deviled Eggs

Barbecued Beans, Page 179

Potato Chips

Cheese Cake Cookies, Page 320

Located on the bank of the Tennessee River, the Stone's cabin is an ideal place for a cookout. On the porch of the cabin Frank Stone assists Ed Price with the steaks.

(Photo by Lonnie McDaniel)

386

SUNDAY SCHOOL PARTIES

There are all sorts of Sunday School parties in Decatur, equipped with all sorts of chefs, but the dean of them all is Ed Price, who does all the cooking for the men's class at First United Methodist. Thanks to Frank Stone, who is a member of that class, the parties are usually held at the Stone's river cabin.

Ed makes his own cakes, his own steak sauce, cooks the steaks and adds a great big green salad. Here are a few of his specialties.

STEAK SAUCE

(When asked to define his "dashes" Ed says a dash equals about 1 teaspoon; for "pinch" use about 1/8 teaspoon or less.)

1/2 cup butter or margarine	1 teaspoon onion flakes (optional)
Couple dashes lemon juice	1 bay leaf
Couple dashes tarragon vinegar	Pinch thyme
Couple dashes soy sauce	Pinch basil
Couple dashes Worcestershire	Pinch oregano or Italian season-
"Palm of the hand" brown sugar	ing
1 6 or 8-ounce can V-8 juice	6 or 8 ounces Burgundy

Simmer all together — except wine — for 30 to 40 minutes. Add wine but do not cook after adding. As steaks are grilling, baste continuously. At time of serving, seasoned salt should be sprinkled on. This sauce may be refrigerated and is enough for 10 to 12 steaks.

ED PRICE'S JIFFY CHOCOLATE CAKE

Mix together: **2 cups sugar** and **2 cups flour**
In another pan, mix the following and let come to a boil:

1 cup butter or margarine	1/2 cup port wine
1/2 cup water	3 1/2 tablespoons cocoa

Pour this mixture over sugar and flour, beat together and then add:

1/2 cup buttermilk	1 teaspoon soda
2 eggs, unbeaten	1 teaspoon vanilla

Mix all together and pour into a 11x17x1 pan and bake 20 minutes at 325°. Top with "Frosting."

FROSTING

1/2 cup butter or margarine	1 teaspoon vanilla (may substitute
3 1/2 tablespoons cocoa	port wine)
6 tablespoons milk	1/2 cup chopped nuts
1 box confectioners' sugar, sifted	

Bring butter, cocoa and milk to a boil. Remove from heat and add sifted sugar, vanilla and nuts. Beat well. Spread over the cake while still hot. Cut in squares and, if you wish, serve with whipped cream or ice cream. No calorie counting here!

Enjoying a holiday open-house at the home of Dr. and Mrs. George Hansberry are Mrs. Robert Tweedy III, Mrs. Hansberry and Mrs William Lovin.

(Photo by Lonnie McDaniel)

CHRISTMAS PARTY

There is something about the Christmas season that makes almost everyone want to entertain. Whether it's inviting the neighbors in for coffee and cookies or having an elegant tea, there is some form of entertaining to suit the occasion for any hostess.

A popular party at Christmas time in Decatur is the Open House — it seems to capture the spirit of the Holiday season. The atmosphere is unusually warm and gay, the food plentiful and very decorative, and the hour flexible enough that guests can easily attend at least one other party the same evening! At the open house one is bound to see almost everyone he knows — and perhaps not see a few of these until the following Christmas.

HOLIDAY OPEN HOUSE

Eye of Round Roast Beef, Page 103   Smoked Turkey

Assorted Breads

Marinated Shrimp, Mushrooms, Artichoke Hearts, Page 23

Crab Mousse, Page 26

Curried Cheese Ball, Page 13

Holiday Cake, Page 266

Toasted Pecans, Page 11

Punch

INDEX

INDEX

INDEX

INDEX

INDEX

400

INDEX

INDEX

404

ACTIVE MEMBERSHIP 1972-1973

Mrs. Lindsay A. Allen
Mrs. C. P. Beddow
Mrs. C. W. Belt
Mrs. David E. Bowers
Mrs. Jimmy E. Brown
Mrs. Joe D. Burns
Mrs. David B. Cauthen
Mrs. L. Denton Cole
Mrs. William S. Coles
Mrs. Dan M. Crane
Mrs. Judson E. Davis, Jr.
Mrs. George M. Douthit
Mrs. E. Bruce Flake
Mrs. Lynn C. Fowler
Mrs. W. D. Gilchrist, Jr.
Mrs. George Godwin, Jr.
Mrs. Roland Guice
Mrs. Dalton M. Guthrie
Mrs. George W. Hansberry
Mrs. Paul E. Hargrove
Mrs. A. Julian Harris
Mrs. David C. Harris
Mrs. Norman W. Harris, Jr.
Mrs. Robert H. Hosey
Mrs. Charles B. Howell
Mrs. Ralph Huff
Mrs. James Hurst
Mrs. Arthur F. Jordan
Mrs. John S. Key
Mrs. Whit King, Jr.
Mrs. Otis E. Kirby, Jr.
Mrs. John Manning

Mrs. Robert C. McAnnally
Mrs. Paul McCain
Mrs. George L. McCrary
Mrs. Jolly McKenzie
Mrs. Robert T. McWhorter, Jr.
Mrs. James D. Moore
Mrs. William H. Nabors
Mrs. Lloyd Nix
Mrs. James B. Odom
Mrs. S. Britt Owens
Mrs. Billy W. Payne
Mrs. Randolph P. Pickell
Mrs. Harold Pilgrim, Jr.
Mrs. Malcolm L. Prewitt, Jr.
Mrs. Arnold Rankin
Mrs. Frank T. Richardson, III
Mrs. Norman L. Self
Mrs. William Sexton
Mrs. William E. Shinn, Jr.
Mrs. William A. Sims
Mrs. T. S. Simms
Mrs. Frederick Sittason, Jr.
Mrs. J. P. Smartt, Jr.
Mrs. Benjamin C. Stevens
Mrs. William G. Stone, Jr.
Mrs. Herbert Street
Mrs. John R. Taylor
Mrs. Jim L. Thompson, Jr.
Mrs. Randall S. Troup
Mrs. John E. Wilks, Jr.
Mrs. John A. Woller

ORIGINAL COOKBOOK COMMITTEE

Mrs. William A. Sims --- Editor

Mrs. John E. Wilks, Jr. -- Editor

Mrs. L. Denton Cole -- President, 1971-72

Mrs. Charles B. Howell --------------------------------------- President, 1972-73

Mrs. Lindsay A. Allen

Mrs. William B. Coles

Mrs. John R. Guice

Mrs. George W. Hansberry

Mrs. A. Julian Harris

Mrs. Ralph Huff

Mrs. James E. Hurst

Mrs. John F. Manning

Mrs. James B. Odom

Mrs. Billy W. Payne

Mrs. William E. Shinn, Jr.

Mrs. James P. Smartt, Jr.

Feature Section — Southern Hospitality — Mrs. Frank T. Richardson, Jr.
Mrs. James P. Smartt, Jr.

Promotion Co-ordinator — Mrs. John R. Taylor

Recipe Commentary — Mrs. Willliam E. Shinn, Jr.

The entire League membership has assisted in compiling this book. Our sincere thanks go to associate members, former members and many friends who have also given their time and expertise so generously.